Changing Hands

Changing Hands

Industry, Evolution, and the Reconfiguration of the Victorian Body

Peter J. Capuano

University of Michigan Press
Ann Arbor

Published in the United States of America by the
University of Michigan Press
Manufactured in the United States of America
♾ Printed on acid-free paper

2018   2017   2016   2015   4   3   2   1

A CIP catalog record for this book is available from the British Library.

Library of Congress Cataloging-in-Publication Data
Capuano, Peter J.
   Changing hands : industry, evolution, and the reconfiguration of the Victorian body / Peter J. Capuano.
      pages   cm
   Includes bibliographical references and index.
   ISBN 978-0-472-05284-4 (pbk. : acid-free paper) — ISBN 978-0-472-07284-2 (hardcover : acid-free paper) — ISBN 978-0-472-12140-3 (ebook)
   1. English fiction—19th century—History and criticism.   2. Human body in literature.   3. Literature and society—Great Britain—History—19th century.   4. Mind and body in literature.   I. Title.
   PR878.B63C37   2015
   823'.8093561—dc23

                                                                                    2015008548

For Kerry Leavitt, a saver of lives,
whose hands dispensed light and hope beyond measure.

But then hands are a complicated organism, a delta in which life from the most distant sources flows together, surging into the great current of action. Hands have stories; they have their own culture . . .

—RAINER MARIA RILKE, *AUGUSTE RODIN* (1902)

Acknowledgments

The intellectual core of this book resides where it first took shape, in the Department of English Language and Literature at the University of Virginia. I am indebted to the Presidential Doctoral Fellowship program there for making extended graduate study a possibility for me. It's the people behind programs, though, that make the difference. I would like to take this opportunity to thank those at Virginia who made contributions, large and small, to this book's development: Steve Arata, Dorothe Bache, Alison Booth, Paul Cantor, the late Greg Colomb, Mark Edmundson, Peter Henry, Robin Field, Paul Fyfe, Clare Kinney, Michael Levenson, Michael Lewis, Ray Malewitz, Jerry McGann, Brad Pasanek, Jill Rappoport, Andy Stauffer, Chip Tucker, Cynthia Wall, and Jennifer Wicke. One person in this group deserves special recognition: my dissertation advisor, Karen Chase, who believed from the very first Dickens Seminar that a project about hands could have legs.

I have also benefited enormously from John Jordan's invitation to become a faculty member at the Dickens Project. To me, that organization represents the very best of what any academic could hope for in a professional life: stellar intellectual fellowship, earnest graduate mentoring, and a heavenly geographic location. A partial list of people who have helped to make Santa Cruz one of my favorite places includes Jim Adams, John Bowen, Jim Buzard, Jill Galvin, Nancy Henry, Priti Joshi, Allen MacDuffie, Carol MacKay, Helena Michie, Daniel Pollack-Pelzner, Catherine Robson, Ellen Rosenman, Sharon Weltman, and Carolyn Williams.

This book would not have been possible without support from its current intellectual home at the University of Nebraska. My former chair, Susan Belasco, supported me in everything from securing money for the Department of English's membership in the Dickens Project to arranging for crucial junior faculty leave time. Conversations with both faculty and students in the Nineteenth-Century Studies program kept me working and thinking through the most challenging issues in the book. A grant from NINES (Networked Infrastructure for Nineteenth-Century Electronic Scholarship) enabled me to attend DHSI (Digital Humanities Summer Institute), where I learned about new digital tools in data analytics that inform my larger argument. Brian O'Grady and Kathy Johnson of Love Library have spent years helping me track down the most obscure archival materials. Special thanks also to Michael Burton for help digitizing my illustrations and images. A timely ENHANCE grant from the Dean's Office in the College of Arts and Sciences provided crucial funding to support last-minute travel, permissions, and indexing. The following people have made my time living and working in Lincoln particularly rewarding: Marco Abel, Stephen Behrendt, Steve Buhler, Joy Castro, Aaron Dominguez, Emily Hammerl, Melissa Homestead, Maureen Honey, Matt Jockers, Wendy Katz, Amelia Montes, Seanna Oakley, Brie Owen, Linda Pratt, Ken Price, Steve Ramsay, Guy Reynolds, the late Gerry Shapiro, Julia Schleck, Will and Heather Thomas, Roland Végsö, Ariana Vigil, Stacey Waite, Kay Walter, and Laura White. At the University of Michigan Press, Aaron McCullough has been an enthusiastic, responsive, and fastidious editor ever since he plucked my book proposal from the pile in 2013.

Several professional organizations have provided me with regular outlets for scholarly dialogue. Those that have proven invaluable for this project's maturation include Interdisciplinary Nineteenth-Century Studies, the Victorian Studies Association of the Western United States, the International Conference on Narrative, the North American Victorian Studies Association, the Victorians Institute, and the Dickens Universe. I am also thankful for the invitation to speak at the 2011 meeting of the Victorian Studies Association of Ontario, a York University conference whose theme of "Manipulation: Victorian Variations on Hands, Handling, and Underhanded Behaviour" was almost too perfect to be true. I am thankful as well to Aviva Briefel and Dan Novak, members of the special "hand panel" at MLA 2013 and providers of more hand-oriented puns and joking email exchanges than any sane person would care to recall. Earlier versions of chapters 2, 3, 4, and 5 were published as articles in journals. A portion of chapter 2 appeared in the online research collective, *BRANCH*, under the title "On Sir Charles Bell's *The Hand*, 1833." An early draft of chapter 3 appeared in *Victorian Studies* as "Networked Manufacture in Charlotte Brontë's *Shirley*," 55, no. 2 (Winter 2013): 231–42. Sections of chapter 4 appeared in *Victorians Institute Journal* as "At the Hands of Becky Sharp: (In)Visible Manipulation and *Vanity Fair*,"

38 (2008): 167–91. A kernel of chapter 5 appeared in *Dickens Quarterly* as "Handling the Perceptual Politics of Identity in *Great Expectations*," 27, no. 3 (September 2010): 185–208. I thank *BRANCH* (Dino Felluga), Indiana University Press, *Victorians Institute Journal*, and Johns Hopkins University Press, respectively, for permission to republish this material in revised and extended form.

Finally, I wish to thank my family for their unwavering support through the many years of my schooling and training. My parents, Kerry and Ken Washburn and John Capuano, have always believed that my dream career could become reality. Melissa Capuano Leone, Casey Washburn, Virgil Cain, Oscar Ramsey, and Bixby Franklin have all grounded me in more ways than they know. My brave and beautiful wife, Jessica, has been there through it all—and for that, there are no adequate words.

Contents

Illustrations

Introduction
The Half-Lives of Hands

This book does not claim that human hands became important only in the nineteenth century; there's a mountain of evidence to prove otherwise.[1] It *does* argue that major changes unique to the nineteenth century made hands newly relevant, and that this new relevance reconfigured the hand's relationship to the body in ways that shaped just about every contour of the Victorian novel. And these ways continue to influence how we live in the world today.

The major changes in the nineteenth century which anchor this study may be grouped into two broadly construed categories: (1) unprecedented developments in mechanized industry, and (2) drastically altered evolutionary paradigms. Regarding the first category, John Wyatt announced a mechanism for textile production "to spin without fingers" in 1753, but it was not until the turn of the nineteenth century that machines began to supersede human hands in economically significant ways (Marx 1990: 493). The development was so swift, in fact, that by 1829 Thomas Carlyle could identify a new "Age of Machinery" where "the shuttle drop[ped] from the fingers of the weaver, and f[ell] into iron fingers that pl[ied] it faster" ("Signs of the Times" 1899: 59). Within the second category, anatomical models of Godly design in the natural world shifted from the human eye in the eighteenth century to the hand in the nineteenth century. This entire notion of anthropomorphic exceptionalism was then jarred, of course, by the almost simultaneous "discovery" of anthropoid apes and Darwinian evolutionary theory.

What happened in the wake of these events is surprising and somewhat counterintuitive. Between the eighteenth and nineteenth centuries there was a sudden but sustained spike in representations of hands in British fiction and in English culture more generally.[2] *Changing Hands* analyzes this strange historical phenomenon and addresses what it has meant for the cultural configuration of the body over time. One of the chief concerns of this study is to locate and to historicize the anxiety about the body that appears when the hand is dislocated, destabilized, or rendered otherwise changed by industrial mechanization and evolutionary theory. In the process of doing this, *Changing Hands* tells a new story about the body from within a particularly volatile period. The Victorians were highly cognizant of the physicality of their hands precisely because unprecedented developments in mechanized industry and new advancements in evolutionary theory made them the first people to experience a radical disruption of this supposedly distinguishing mark of their humanity. This disruption actually becomes the condition of their new visibility. So the project is concerned with an escalated level of interest in the hand as a historically locatable response to questions of particular urgency among Victorians: questions about creation, about labor, about mechanization, about gender, about class and racial categorization.

There is also an additional dimension of this book that is inextricably linked to the processes I have outlined above: if particular historical circumstances made the Victorians preoccupied by the materiality of their hands, no one has taken much notice of it. Sartorial convention ensured that the head and the hand were the only two body parts open for routine inspection in the nineteenth century. Of these two locations, the head has received critical attention almost exclusively—a fact which undoubtedly stems from realism's traditional connection to sightedness. Jonathan Crary's *Techniques of the Observer: On Vision and Modernity in the Nineteenth Century* (1992), Carol Christ and John Jordan's edited collection in *Victorian Literature and the Victorian Visual Imagination* (1995), Katherine Kearns's *Nineteenth-Century Literary Realism: Through the Looking-Glass* (1996), and Kate Flint's *Victorians and the Visual Imagination* (2008) demonstrate the robustness of this connection. More specifically, the legacy of determinative nineteenth-century pseudosciences such as phrenology and physiognomy has inspired a bona fide subfield dealing with the face and the head. Mary Ann O'Farrell's *Telling Complexions* (1997), Lucy Hartley's *Physiognomy and the Meaning of Expression in Nineteenth-Century Culture* (2006), Chris Otter's *The Victorian Eye* (2008), and Sharrona Pearl's *About Faces* (2010) are only some prominent recent examples of the scholarly attention that the head and the face continue to receive.[3]

In the rare cases where the hand has been considered a legitimate subject of literary inquiry—as in Bruce Robbins's *The Servant's Hand* (1986), Patricia Johnson's *Hidden Hands* (2001), or Eleanor Courtemanche's *The*

'Invisible Hand' in British Fiction (2011)—it has been treated only metonymically or metaphorically.[4] Ironically enough, the twentieth- and twenty-first-century tendency to take hands for granted has prevented even Marxist, feminist, and cultural materialist critics from noticing the centrality of an embodied handedness to Victorian life. In my approach to this oversight, I seek not merely to point it out, but also to consider why this blind spot exists in the first place. Indeed, it is a major contention of my overarching argument that the hand wields a figurative influence so pervasive that it is actually hard to recognize. All of us, by virtue of living after the nineteenth century, have inherited the hand as a body part always already changed so much that its alteration has become difficult to notice. The time of manual crisis long past, we inhabit a world where it seems almost natural to take our hands for granted. Their functional presence has dissipated, in Percy Shelley's Romantic formulation, into "the mist of familiarity" (2002: 505). In Jamesonian terms, the logic of late capitalism has produced a present culture that treats its hands so metaphorically that to do so (and to not notice it) "has become a veritable 'second nature'" for both critics and general readers alike (1990: ix). Taking the nineteenth-century novel's fascination with hands seriously, which is to say taking them in some senses literally, brings into relief a crucial moment in the history of embodiment that has remained largely unrecognizable to us. To think critically about the new referential pressures novelists placed on hands means reimagining the familiar outlines of what mattered to the Victorians and why.

This particular appendage has not been eclipsed merely by machinery and evolution, though. My wider contention about how hands change has an important additional implication: the general process of our shifting sense of embodiment has been impacted significantly by the vicissitudes of language. The hand is the basis for more metaphors, familiar phrases, and idiomatic expressions than all of the other parts of the body combined. The effect of this lopsided bodily emphasis causes the words we use to describe our hands—take, grasp, handle, make, maneuver—to become abstract concepts, and we tend to forget their concrete connection to our embodied handedness. When we say that someone has built something "with their bare hands," we hardly ever mean it literally. Philosophers of language refer to this as a dead metaphor—where we kill literal meaning through overuse.[5] But literal meaning is also killed by changes in how particular body parts are used (or unused). Mark Johnson argues in *The Body in the Mind* (1987) that concepts expressed through metaphors have a basis in bodily experience that reinforces their social and linguistic implications. Changing experiences of embodiment, therefore, bubble up into language, thereby affecting the metaphors used in different historical periods—a process which then becomes absorbed into the narratives by which a culture defines itself.

This is consistent with my argument in *Changing Hands*: when the uses and meanings of handedness change in the nineteenth century, so too do the modes of expression used to describe such changes. It is no coincidence that the overwhelming majority of idiomatic expressions, clichés, and metaphors involving hands were born in the nineteenth century but consolidated and killed in the twentieth. I mean "killed" here in the sense that by the twentieth century these expressions had been evacuated of their last remnants of literal meaning. It is precisely their deadness that makes them clichés or metaphors now. Such a phenomenon helps explain literary criticism's almost solely metaphorical treatment of key hand-based concepts such as manufacture, manipulation, manners, and manuscripts, which, as we shall see, were still deeply embodied concepts in the Victorian practical consciousness.

Each of the upcoming chapters will reveal the literal basis of what we now uncritically relegate to the realm of the metaphoric, the metonymic, or the idiomatic. The early chapters on *Frankenstein* (1818/ 1831), factory fiction, and *Shirley* (1849) examine the multitude of cultural influences that affect the familiar notion of the "handmade"; the chapter on *Vanity Fair* (1848) reconsiders what "hand-to-hand combat" means in the Victorian drawing room; the chapters on *Great Expectations* (1860) and *Daniel Deronda* (1876) explore the apparatuses of identification behind "having one's hand" in the outcome of events; the final chapters on *Bleak House* (1853), *Lady Audley's Secret* (1862), and *Dr Jekyll and Mr Hyde* (1886) assess the importance of deciphering "the handwriting on the wall" in detective fiction.

The individual chapters of *Changing Hands* do far more than expose our idiomatic distance from the literal experience of the nineteenth century, though. Chapter 1, for instance, claims a new place in literary history for Mary Shelley's *Frankenstein* by situating the novel at the crossroads of a shifting focus in natural history, theology, and Enlightenment science from the eyes to the hands. Victor Frankenstein's "manufacture" of a separate being at once literalizes and challenges the superiority and productivity of God's hand in connection to man's. I trace how Shelley's channeling of this tension through the contentious and repeated interplay between the hands of Victor and those of his creation anticipates anxieties about God's place in a world transforming from handicraft to industrial manufacture. In so far as the creature's hands are figured as man-made instruments gone murderously wrong, they are premonitory of the dangerous factory equipment that becomes so controversial in nineteenth-century debates about industrialism's merits and failures.

Chapter 2 chronicles the fascinating story of how the hand—both as an instrument of God and an appendage of the machine—figured into the oppositional conceptions of mechanization in the period's industrial philosophy as well as its early factory fiction. It explores how an unlikely convergence of scientific, industrial, and religious discourse coalesced around 1830 to make the human hand the most generative but also the most heavily contested site in the British cultural imaginary. Most readers will be surprised to learn how literal these debates could be. The centerpiece of the chapter is Charles Bell's largely unstudied Bridgewater Treatise on *The Hand* from 1833, which is a rare instance of a text with overlapping interests in both evolutionary thought and industrial expansion. I argue that Bell's deep religious faith, combined with his horrific experiences treating the victims of grisly factory accidents, influenced his decision to choose the hand as the topic for a Bridgewater Treatise. At a time when many were celebrating mechanized production, Bell sought to emphasize the ways in which all mechanical contrivances were based on the model of anatomical "perfection" embodied in the divinely constructed human hand. The second half of this chapter then considers how debates about the hand's status impacted the development of early industrial narratives and more conventional midcentury factory fiction.

Chapter 3 links these industrial developments to gender by considering how Charlotte Brontë's sustained oscillation between manual and mechanized forms of manufacture in *Shirley* (1849) marks the earliest boundaries of what would eventually become the rigidly defined separate spheres of middle-class Victorian life. Brontë's decision to backdate the novel to 1811–12 ensures that its action unfolds at the historical moment when *manufacture* began to accrue paradoxically opposing meanings. I argue that Brontë dramatizes these meanings by creating an inverted network from mill to parlor that unites two of the novel's most disparate constituencies: hardened Luddite weavers and middle-class female needle workers. By the laws of technological development, weavers could no longer use their hands professionally and by the stipulations of a nascent middle-class gender ideology, women could *only* use theirs in profitless domestic needlework. The underemployment of machine-breaking hands and the overemployment of domestic needle-working hands thus show how new modes of production directly influenced new ideological conceptions of gender.

The fourth chapter on *Vanity Fair* (1848) extends my focus on the limited opportunities available to women in the rigidly defined gender and class categories discussed in chapter 3. Unlike *Shirley*'s setting in the isolated Yorkshire countryside, though, *Vanity Fair* chronicles the lives of its characters as they mingle in Europe's most refined cities and, as a result of Thackeray's superb understanding of this milieu, the novel provides an ideal glimpse into the complex and high-stakes rituals that make up gendered social interaction at midcentury. This chapter draws on contemporary etiquette literature, household training guides, and biomedical discourse on female "nature" to demonstrate the hand's physical centrality to the construction of gendered boundaries in the Victorian drawing room. The analysis in chapter 3 focuses most intensely on the manual activity of nineteenth-century fiction's most infamous manipulator, Becky Sharp. Where critics of this heavily sifted novel have considered only the metaphorical implications of Becky's uniquely manipulative temperament, I evaluate her gestural ability to transform routine physical rituals into social leverage—both in Thackeray's prose and in his illustrations. A more literal evaluation of Becky's manners uncovers her remarkable capacity to camouflage social propriety and individual aggression in such a way that it evades direct detection. I argue that so powerful is Becky's controlling hand in *Vanity Fair* that Thackeray was compelled to develop the marionette narrative apparatus for the novel. This formal framing device functions ingeniously because the control encoded in Becky's adept handling of intricate social interactions reflects the generic imperative of the marionette theater to expose and conceal simultaneously.

Chapter 5 follows the dramatic shift in the Victorian mindset from the fragility of barriers between genders (chapters 3 and 4) to the riveting idea of the disintegrating barriers between humans and all other animals. This chapter situates Charles Dickens's obsession with hands in *Great Expectations* (1860–61) in the context of a culture similarly obsessed with the ways in which hands became diagnostic of biological, social, and moral subjectivity. The popularization of the "Development Hypothesis," combined with England's "discovery" of the gorilla in the 1850s, rocked the hand from its privileged status as *the* physiological appendage separating humans from presumably lower animals. These scientific developments, culminating in the publication of Darwin's *Origin of Species* (1859), recast with far more intensity the anxieties that first surfaced in Shelley's portrayal in *Frankenstein* of a human being attempting to usurp the power of God's creative hand. Indeed, the horror for many Victorians in the years immediately following Darwin's work was the possibility that God could have *no* hand at all in the order of the natural world. This chapter therefore shows not only how the rupture of biological order signals a breakdown in the Victorian social order, but also how these categories of disintegration collapse into the representation of a single bodily organ.

Chapter 6 works in conjunction with chapter 5 by exploring how Darwin's publication of *The Descent of Man* (1871) shifted the focus of Victorian evolutionary debate to concerns about man's direct physiological inheritances. Here, I place the scientific, racial, and narrative demands of George Eliot's final novel, *Daniel Deronda* (1876), in conversation with my book's chief premise regarding the hand's centrality in the practical consciousness of the nineteenth century. Eliot, like her contemporary scientific thinkers, understood Jewish identity as at once a matter of physiological racial inheritance and cultural construction. But this understanding, particularly of the physiological element, has been extremely problematic for critics of Eliot's realism. How could it be possible that Daniel Deronda's Jewishness could go unmarked on his body until his biological mother confirms it? My interpretation confronts powerful deconstructionist arguments about the presence of a hidden but circumcised penis that have, since the 1970s, remained the most influential way to explain the apparent disconnect between Eliot's scientifically informed views and her "featureless" descriptions of Deronda. Such explanations only reveal twentieth- and twenty-first-century preoccupations with the body, though, and overlook the Victorian interest in the hand's physicality. The conclusions reached in this chapter demonstrate how the surprising location of Jewish identity in the hand fits the myriad of complex narratological and ideological exigencies involved in the text. Considering the hand from this angle offers us a path through the problematic representation of Jewishness in the nineteenth century, a completely new and alternate version of Eliot's approach to realism, and a decidedly physical dimension to her most sacred concern for human sympathy.

The final two chapters of my study widen the scope of Dickens's and Eliot's focus on the hand by analyzing the extent to which other major Victorian novelists linked their narrative frameworks to the materiality of handedness. In order to test the efficacy of this idea more widely, *Changing Hands* treats a series of novels normally considered quite distant from the evolutionary or industrial realms. Doing so allows these closing chapters to revisit the changing focus from the head to the hands that I trace through the scientific and mechanical rhetoric of the book's opening chapters. Here, though, I argue for the overarching claim of a newly important Victorian hand by evaluating the surprising differences between eighteenth-century epistolary fiction and nineteenth-century suspense narratives. One might expect, given the centrality of letters to networks of eighteenth-century communication, combined with the decidedly epistolary nature of its fiction, that novelists of this earlier period would look for opportunities to align their plots with various components of their characters' penmanship. Likewise, one might expect that Victorian novelists, writing in an age when the hand was becoming less and less important in their daily lives, would hardly notice their characters' handwriting. This chapter reveals that the opposite is true on both counts, and then brings the weight of the book's whole central thesis to bear on why this counterintuitive notion makes perfect sense. A sampling of eighteenth-century novels reveals very little—despite their emphasis on issues of mistaken identity—about what a given character's handwritten letters actually look like. On the other side of the century, the narrative architecture of Victorian detective novels depends almost absolutely on the material properties of penmanship. Each of these novelists in the latter group lived and composed their fiction in a period when the hand was jolted from its preeminent economic and evolutionary status. The preoccupation with the hand in the nineteenth century, I argue, demonstrates anxieties about the body that appear only when that part of it becomes threatened or changed.

TWENTY-FIRST-CENTURY BODY STUDIES

As recently as fifteen years ago it was not uncommon to encounter treatment of the body as a primarily, if not entirely, linguistic and discursive construction.[6] This became routine for critics following the archaeology of knowledge unearthed by Michel Foucault, which tended to view the body's materiality as secondary to the logical or semiotic structures encoded within it. In the past few years, however, body studies have taken a corporeal turn from conventional poststructuralism toward new forms of materialism. Practitioners in this field predictably have invested less in the abstraction of the Panopticon and more in Foucault's later work on biopower. This shift has taken many productive forms: from cognitive theory, to affect theory, to the foregrounding of bodies in gender, sexuality, and race studies, to colonial history. None of these movements, though, have taken the materiality of the hand into serious consideration.[7]

As I noted earlier in relation to recent book-length studies, the head and the face still receive the lion's share of critical attention. And this is for good reason in many cases: cognitive approaches necessarily involve the brain; affect theorists largely follow Deleuzean guidance to the face, and many involved in race studies highlight the face in its photographic incarnations.[8] I want to be very precise about the kind of claim I am making in this book. My interest in nineteenth-century hands does not mean that the face (and other parts of the body) is unimportant. It is here that the "Half-Lives" portion of my Introduction's title is most germane. If we continue to pay attention only to the face, we are missing at least one half the story of what mattered to the Victorians. Furthermore, as I touch on in my Conclusion, we are missing out on a crucial chapter of how we have arrived at our current relationship with our hands. My focus on how hands have changed, and on what those changes mean for us today, is an attempt to break an impasse embedded in historicist studies which treat works of art only as cultural symptoms of their own moment.[9] One of the most important tasks for the historicist is to consider the ways in which a present situation (the lack of critical study of the Victorian hand) is affected by the contingency of past events and vice versa.

To return to my more specific assertion that we have been missing out on so much of the Victorians' bodily story, it is important to recognize how frequently the face and the hand worked in tandem to produce literary, cultural, and narratological meaning in the nineteenth century. This is another way of articulating my position that it would be inaccurate to say that hands mattered *more* than heads or faces. We need to pay attention to both. It may surprise some readers that, for instance, Victorian novelists often foreground descriptions of characters' hands before they describe their faces. The famous opening description of Dorothea Brooke in *Middlemarch* (1871–72) is just one instance that follows this pattern. The novel's second sentence informs us that Dorothea's "hand and wrist were so finely formed that she could wear sleeves not less bare of style than those in which the Blessed Virgin appeared to Italian painters" (7). Later in the same section entitled "Miss Brooke," Eliot elaborates on the connection between Dorothea's "beautiful hands" and her passionate temperament: "They were not thin hands, or small hands; but powerful, feminine, maternal hands, She seemed to be holding them up in propitiation for her passionate desire to know and to think . . ." (38). To emphasize this point, I want to consider a representative passage from *Dracula* (1897) that reveals how closely—in a literal sense—the face and the hand were paired as meaning makers in the nineteenth century even when the order of their description is reversed. Here, Jonathan Harker's first description of Count Dracula moves directly from the face to the hands:

> I had now an opportunity of observing him, and found him of a very marked physiognomy.
>
> His face was a strong—a very strong—aquiline, with high bridge of the thin nose and peculiarly arched nostrils; with lofty domed forehead, and hair growing scantily round the temples, but profusely elsewhere. His eyebrows were very massive, almost meeting over the nose, and with bushy hair that seemed to curl in its own profusion. The mouth, so far as I could see it under the heavy moustache, was fixed and rather cruel-looking, with peculiarly sharp white teeth; these protruded over the lips, whose remarkable ruddiness showed astonishing vitality in a man of his years. For the rest, his ears were pale and at the tops extremely pointed; the chin was broad and strong, and the cheeks firm though thin. The general effect was one of extraordinary pallor.
>
> Hitherto, I had noticed the backs of his hands as they lay on his knees in the firelight, and they had seemed rather white and fine; but seeing them now close to me, I could not but notice that they were rather coarse—broad, with squat fingers. Strange to say, there were hairs in the centre of the palm. The nails were long and fine, and cut to a sharp point. As the Count leaned over me and his hands touched me, I could not repress a shudder. (24–25)

Since the head and the hands were routinely the only two body parts open for inspection at the time, the fact that Harker describes these two parts is not remarkable. What *is* remarkable is that critics, in the main, have so much to say about heads and yet so little to say about hands despite their narratological proximity to each other. Upcoming chapters will expose how this blind spot has persisted even in the criticism of texts which seem to privilege the description of hands before and above faces.

The methodologies I employ in this study aim to uncover the various meanings that cohere around the material and discursive subject of Victorian hands; meanings that become intelligible only in historically specific and institutionally mediated ways. Their biological, literal, and ideologically constructed subjectivities make up some of the many half-lives that hands lead throughout the century. Doing interpretive justice to each of these different lives, even on a topic so seemingly small as the hand, requires a range of methodological approaches. My project's emphasis on the close reading of particular historical objects (including hands) has been inspired by the work of Catherine Gallagher and Fredric Jameson, and by the more recent materialist conceptions of "Thing Theory" as iterated by Bill Brown and Elaine Freedgood who turn their attention to the *un*metaphorical past of objects ranging from cash registers to calico curtains.[10] Because of this alignment, a significant part of my methodology could be characterized as "symptomatic" in the Jamesonian sense that it attempts to disclose what is embedded in the text's many, and in some cases, buried layers. Even so, readers will find in *Changing Hands* a strong pull toward what Rita Felski has recently described as "neophenomenology"—a desire to build better bridges between interpretational theory and common sense (2009: 31). One of the ways my study does this is by looking carefully *at* rather than through appearances, by respecting rather than rejecting what is in plain view.[11]

In so far as my project is invested in drawing attention to hands that lie hidden in plain sight, I often employ what has become known as "surface" analysis.[12] Analyzing Victorian novels from a surface perspective demonstrates the extent to which the culture was riveted to the materiality of their hands. The strong literal dimension to *Changing Hands* accords with a kind of surface reading that is far more interested in the various handed presences in texts than the absences that have long characterized symptomatic or suspicious reading practices. The surface reading I practice in this book, therefore, always involves a paradoxical rhetoric of depth in the sense that Mary Poovey envisions when she claims that "modern interpretational habits typically track at too high a level of abstraction to give [materiality its] due" (2004: 202).

My commitment to both surface and depth reflects my sense that the two methodologies are not, and should not be, mutually exclusive. Here, I am in agreement with John Kucich and others in thinking that to pit surface reading against deep reading is a mistake that historicists cannot afford to make (2011: 62). The point is not to privilege surface over depth but to emphasize the nuanced interrelation between the two. This is why I consider surface reading and distant reading not only as closely related to each other, but closely related to the deep-reading methodologies that are so foundational to literary studies more generally. Marjorie Perloff calls this "reading differentially"; reading that merges close / subjective and distant / objective practices (*Differentials* 2004: xxv). Both surface and distant practices can and should lead a researcher to specific questions that require deeper interpretive analysis. As I explain in note 2 of the Introduction, the larger argument of this book has been augmented by a distant, computer-assisted analysis of thousands of nineteenth-century novels. This analysis suggests that hands appear in nineteenth-century novels around eight times more frequently than in all genres of eighteenth-century texts. Stephen Best and Sharon Marcus, even in their enthusiasm for this kind of machine intelligence, correctly note that computers are "potent describers" but "weak interpreters" (2009: 17). What my macro-data potently describes is a spike in hand references between centuries—a spike so marked that hands appear in nineteenth-century novels more often than any other body part including faces, heads, and eyes. A word cloud derived from Matt Jockers's research of the most frequently described body parts in more than 3,500 nineteenth-century novels renders this particular form of "macro" data visually (fig. 1).[13]

Even so, however, this data sparks a question about this strange phenomenon—not an answer. Why are hands the most described body part in the nineteenth-century novel? My far closer and deeper analysis of texts ranging from *Frankenstein* to *Dr Jekyll and Mr Hyde* presents an argument about how and why such a surge in representations of the hand matters

Fig. 1. **Hands word cloud. Used by permission from Matthew Jockers.**

for our understanding of the Victorian novel. With access to topic modeling data on thousands of nineteenth-century novels, it should be clear to any reader that I have had to make qualitative decisions about which novels to include in this study. The point I want to stress is that the ones I have selected for treatment in this book are by no means the only texts that illustrate the phenomenon (spike in hand representations) or the argument (changing hand meanings) that I locate here. Since my aim is to identify the new meanings that accrue around hands in this period, I have tried to reinforce this aim by making original claims about canonical texts that have longstanding, entrenched critical histories. The goal, therefore, is to emphasize how under-noticed hands are by subjecting my argument not to a single subgenre of relatively obscure texts, but to a series of the most heavily scrutinized nineteenth-century novels by virtually any categorization. The best way to demonstrate how much we miss by overlooking hands is to offer novel interpretations of the century's most critically discussed fiction.

The issues I cover—in chapters on novels written by very different authors in a broad sampling of fictional subgenres (gothic, industrial, domestic, sensation, etc.)—reveal the ways in which novel writers helped generate new ways for the hand to continue to be important to a culture struggling with unprecedented change. These authors' shared focus on literal handedness despite their widely different styles, subgenres, and time periods suggests their culture's collective reluctance to disengage themselves wholly from a body part so inextricably linked with their identities as human beings.

THE CHANGED LIVES OF HANDS

I also want to be very clear that my analysis of hands in the nineteenth century is by no means a story of tragic humanist loss. Instead, my focus remains fixed on the remarkably varied constellations orbiting the hand's materiality that cause it *not* to be lost in its changing relationship to the era's cultural imaginary, but rather newly found and pressed into altered service in unexpected places. I contend that at the unique moment when the hand was being superseded by machinery and stripped of its status as a supposedly God-given appendage, it also emerged in the Victorian practical consciousness as a primary locus for a new set of fictionalized identities that are quite removed from, but that nonetheless recapitulate, anxiety provoked by new industrial and scientific relations. *Changing Hands* thus considers how the Victorian novel helped generate these new identities for the hand—ones that demonstrate the mutability of the organ as well as the different kinds of work, worth, and purposes to which it was put.

As a result, my choice of the title for this Introduction, "The Half-Lives of Hands," is somewhat inadequate for the very *full* lives hands lead after unprecedented developments in mechanization and science change their relationship to the body. Katherine Rowe has written brilliantly about the agency "dead hands" acquire in periods ranging from the Renaissance to the Modern. Her contribution to the study of actual hands—even if dead, severed, or otherwise amputated—has had an invigorating influence on my work. However, where Rowe's *Dead Hands* (1999) focuses on hands whose lives have been separated from their bodies, I take as my subject nineteenth-century hands that remain very much alive and connected to the bodies they serve. Indeed, a central vector of this study traces the embodied livelihood led by hands in the Victorian novel. Each of my book's four parts analyzes different literal lines of manual interpretation: manufacture in *Frankenstein* and factory fiction; needlework and manipulation in *Shirley* and *Vanity Fair*, respectively; racialized hands in *Great Expectations* and *Daniel Deronda*; penmanship and the narrative dynamics of identity in *Bleak House*, *Lady Audley's Secret*, and *Dr Jekyll and Mr Hyde*. By building my argument around the materiality of hands, I seek to exchange the metaphorical critical model that has relied for so long on the space between signifier and signified with something more literal—something that has become paradoxically difficult to discern because its contextual meaning has been eroded by a lopsided dependence on our own largely metaphorical relationship to handedness.

Since I approach my subject historically, I have tried to demonstrate how hands change even within a time period in which their meaning is fundamentally altered. That is, the reader will undoubtedly come to see how hands change even within *Changing Hands*. The hand is not an ahistorical subject with a monolithic new meaning after the mechanization of industry and the onset of new evolutionary theory. Rather, it takes on a range of changed meanings that may be traced back to the destabilizations it encounters for the first time in the nineteenth century. What this range of new meanings suggests, I think, is that hands really were experienced as essential markers of nineteenth-century humanity to people who lived through this volatile period. It must be noted that there were exceptions to this categorization before and even during the nineteenth century. As I will explain in chapter 1, late seventeenth- and eighteenth-century (Western European) reactions to anthropoid apes emphasized their similarities to the heads and faces of human beings. And in the nineteenth century, Richard Owen and others sought to distinguish between apes and humans by emphasizing the cerebral primacy of man. The points I make in the following chapters take this into consideration and argue, ultimately, that the supersession of manual labor by machines, combined with the "discovery" of gorillas with hands within a single generation, added up to something of a double whammy for an anxiety-addled mid-nineteenth-century culture that was confronting heaving changes in just about every other area of life. These whammies are not isolated historical occurrences, either. I want to show how there is an intimate, perhaps even causal, relationship between industrialization and evolutionary discourse. In broader terms, *Changing Hands* suggests that the transition to mechanized labor was itself so destabilizing to the (especially Protestant) notion of human dignity's validation through work that evolutionary theory develops as it does to account for the debate about human exceptionalism inspired by industrialization. The rise of mechanized production and radically new evolutionary discourses are parallel themes, to be sure. But these twin themes are also causally related to some degree. In other words, this book argues that evolutionary theory (and its reception) develops in the way that it does in England at least in part because of the heightened destabilization of hands in earlier industrial contexts.

The fact that this study begins in a laboratory (Victor Frankenstein's) and concludes in a laboratory (Dr. Jekyll's) is fitting because of my driving interest in the social history of natural philosophy, science, and technology of the nineteenth century. These categories propel each of the book's eight chapters. Since the topic of hands is so understudied, but yet so seemingly small and ubiquitous (of course hands are everywhere), I have felt compelled to demonstrate how and why their preponderance matters to virtually every node of traditionally charted nineteenth-century studies: industrialization, the "Woman Question," evolution, religiosity, race, and even narratology. A thorough reconsideration of the changing practices and meanings located in the Victorian hand provides my book with its unifying structure and logic. The chapters are organized around original interpretations of major literary works set alongside episodes and artifacts ranging from anatomy to etiquette, religion to needlework, race to penmanship—all of which illuminate a Victorian fascination with hands that has been rendered all but invisible to critics of the period.

That said, this book does not give equal treatment to poetry or to the literature from the very end of the nineteenth century—especially in the fields of queer and postcolonial studies. There are reasons for these omissions, which I can only hope to explain, not justify. First, queer theorists such as Eve Kosofsky Sedwick, Jeff Nunokawa, Christopher Craft, and William Cohen have treated the strange manner of touch between Victorians to the homo-erotic impulses of individual characters. Their readings obviously have not exhausted the topic, but that important work will require additional, more comprehensive studies and other researchers. Second, I have chosen to focus on novelists, not poets, because novelists (as opposed to poets) were the first writers to experience the full industrialization of literary production. As N. N. Feltes has shown, it was novelists who stood at the center of the contro-versial debate over the cultural transformations brought about by mechanical production, new techniques of distribution and circulation, and the astonish-ing expansion of reading audiences. The broader point is that art has always expressed what reason (science, philosophy, etc.) cannot articulate, or not in quite the same way. Contrary to everyday life, in which our perception is char-acterized by slow accretions of the habitual, art (in this case the novel) shows things in new and unexpected ways. Viktor Shklovskii gave us a word for this, *ostranenie* ("defamiliarization"), in his 1917 manifesto of Russian formalism entitled "Art as Technique." Since the novel is the nineteenth-century's most popular art form, it makes sense that in it we can locate the culture's response to its changed relationship to its most quintessential body part.

The final explanation for my topic's scope is baldly extrageneric and, therefore, perhaps the least valid: my treatment of literature ends in the 1880s. The meanings related to embodied hands do not suddenly cease to change at the end of century, of course. My Conclusion touches upon what some of these changes mean for the twentieth and twenty-first centuries. For the most part, though, I leave the fin de siècle and early twentieth cen-tury to other, more capable hands (spare me at least one pun!). This leads me straight to one important additional rationale for the book's coverage. My colleague and compatriot in near total hand immersion these past seven years, Aviva Briefel, is completing a wonderful study on just this topic and period. Its current title nicely accounts for much of what this book leaves out: *Amputations: The Colonial Hand at the Fin de Siècle.* My hope is that our two books will offer a fresh and comprehensive treatment of hands through-out a century in which they were so central and yet so under-noticed.

PART I

Maneuvering Through Natural Theology and Industry

CHAPTER I

Shifting from Gaze to Grasp
"Odious Handywork" in *Frankenstein*

The familiar account Mary Shelley gives for the "ghost story" that would eventually become *Frankenstein* (1818) reveals her novel's central concern with scientific ideas emerging from the Enlightenment. In the introduction to the 1831 edition of *Frankenstein*, Shelley describes how she became acquainted with these ideas: "Many and long were the conversations between Lord Byron and [Percy Bysshe] Shelley, to which I was a devout but nearly silent listener" (1831: 8). These conversations about "the nature of the principle of life, and whether there was any probability of its ever being discovered and communicated" arose from the work of continental philosophers whose materialist and mechanized views of physiology jeopardized the traditional notion of God's divine craftsmanship in the natural world (1831: 8). As Mary Shelley had gathered from listening to Byron and Percy, "galvanism had given token" to the possibility that "a corpse could be re-animated" and, further, that "the component parts of a creature might be *manufactured*, brought together, and endued with vital warmth" (1831: 8, emphasis added). These questions about divine authority in the realm of creation did not appear overnight, of course. Early Enlightenment figures in England such as Robert Boyle and Isaac Newton continued to see God as the source behind their most influential scientific discoveries.

By the middle of the eighteenth century in France, however, the scenario was markedly different. Julien Offroy de La Mettrie's bluntly materialistic and atheistic *L'homme-machine* [*Man Machine*] (1748) drew no essential difference between conscious and unconscious behavior, and identified no moral good beyond the perfectibility of the mechanism inside the body (Hankins 1985: 129). On a more sweeping scale, the Comte de Buffon's multivolume *Histoire naturelle* (1780) chronicled a history of the earth that simply ignored Genesis and biblical chronology altogether. The turn toward materialist science only grew more marked when Luigi Galvani began investigating the relationship between electricity and physiological animation in the muscles of frogs during the 1780s and 1790s. This particular strain of materialist experimentation, to which Mary Shelley alludes, reached England by way of Erasmus Darwin's work. Experiments dedicated to the reanimation of life quickly moved from Darwin's "vermicelli" subjects to human beings; Giovanni Aldini, an Italian physicist and nephew of Galvani, came to London in 1803 to test the effects of electricity on human corpses. Aldini's most famous experiment took place in January 1803 when the body of executed convict George Foster was taken from the gallows of Newgate Prison to an audience of doctors and curious onlookers at the Royal College of Surgeons. There, Aldini attached a battery and conducting rods to Foster's body. Electricity then ran through Foster's corpse and, to the amazement of onlookers, the dead body began to quiver and contort as if it had been alive.

Experiments such as Aldini's lent new poignancy to physiological debates in England over the nature of vitality that, in so many words, were debates over the nature of life itself. Questions about the fundamental distinctions between living and dead bodies directly challenged religious heterodoxies and the scientific institutions that had upheld them for centuries. By adumbrating the opposing positions of two prominent professors at London's Royal College of Surgeons, John Abernethy and William Lawrence, Marilyn Butler has effectively linked the physiological issues in *Frankenstein* to the series of celebrated and publicly staged debates from 1814 to 1819 known as "the vitalist row" (1996: 304–5). Abernethy, a full surgeon at St. Bartholomew's Hospital, believed in a conservative or "spiritualized vitalism"—the status quo position which held that life needed not only materialist physiology to exist, but also a "mysterious 'superadded' force" analogous to a divinely embedded soul (1996: 304). Despite the fact that he was apprenticed as a demonstrator for Abernethy's anatomy lectures before becoming a professor of anatomy and surgery at the Royal College of Surgeons, Lawrence could not have held views more oppositional to those of his former mentor. The young Lawrence was fond of the continental physiology practiced by figures such as Xavier Bichat and Johann Blumenbach, whose materialist ideas left no room for religious influence. Materialist thinkers saw little reason to ascribe the animating power inside animals to anything outside the animal. Bichat, for example, had famously defined life as "the sum of the functions by which death is resisted" (qtd. in Ruston 2005: 13).

Therefore, it is no surprise that Lawrence described the state of vitality with an almost verbatim formulation in his 1816 lectures: "Life is the assemblage of all the functions, and the general result of their exercise" (Ruston 2005: 13). The Shelleys' deep interest in scientific discovery, combined with the fact they were living near London in 1816 when the "vitalist row" was unfolding in the public sphere, propelled Marilyn Butler to her pioneering but now generally accepted claim that *Frankenstein* "acts out" the debate between Abernethy and Lawrence (1996: 307).

My point is not to rehash the merits of Butler's path-breaking claim, but rather to expand on it to show how *Frankenstein* literalizes a far bigger question about God's agentic/designing presence in the natural world. As we shall see from a literary and scientifically historical perspective in the subsequent chapters of my study, this central epistemological question, which pits God's creative power against man's "manufacturing" prowess, arguably begins with *Frankenstein* and lingers anxiously in the periphery of nearly every nineteenth-century novel. For the purposes of this chapter, though, it is necessary to take a brief look at a few representative eighteenth-century novels in order to make the case that something indeed different happens or "begins" with *Frankenstein*. In this brief detour I will draw on fictional examples from the beginning, middle, and end of the eighteenth century to demonstrate the generally representative disembodied invocations of the divine "Hand" that appear consistently in the period's novels. My purpose in returning to earlier fiction is to show how the nineteenth-century vitalist controversy itself crystalized a debate about creation and design which had been, especially in eighteenth-century fictional precursors, metaphorically transacted through the body.

Over the course of only two pages in Daniel Defoe's *Robinson Crusoe* (1719), for example, the shipwrecked Crusoe wonders if "the Hand of God" has meted out his punishment, considers whether "the distinguishing Goodness of the Hand" saved his life, wavers back to a belief that "the Hand of God [was] against [him]," then continues to mull over the prospect that "the present Affliction of [his] Circumstances" come from "[God's] Hand" (2008: 76–77). In Samuel Richardson's *Pamela* (1741), the title character believes that the reformed Mr. B has become a "happy Instrument, in the Hands of Providence" and that her eventual marriage to him has been brought about by "the Hands of thy gracious Providence!" (2001: 309, 363). Similarly, in Fanny Burney's *Evelina* (1778), when Evelina stops Mr. Macartney from committing armed robbery (which she perceives to be a suicide attempt),

Macartney proclaims that "the hand of Providence seemed to intervene between me and eternity" (2002: 231). Burney's "intervening" hand of Providence is no doubt inflected by the Scottish economist Adam Smith's formulation of the "invisible hand" at work in market economies from *The Wealth of Nations* (1776). Even for Smith, though, the "invisible hand" has a decidedly providential thrust and, in this sense, his metaphorical invocation of it parallels its use by eighteenth-century novelists.[1]

If God's agency vis-à-vis his "hand" is so often removed from the physical world by way of metaphor or metonymy, one important way it enters the tangible world of the eighteenth century is through the face. What we see time and time again in late seventeenth-century discourse on natural history—almost one hundred years before Lavater's systematic study of physiognomy—are references to God's production of unique human faces. John Ray, in *The Wisdom of God Manifested in the Works of Creation* (1691), for instance, makes an "argument [for] providence from the variety of lineaments in the faces of men, which is such, . . . there are not two faces in the world absolutely alike" (1827: 203). John Evelyn's *Numismata* (1697) likewise applauds the "Wise and Wonderful Providence, which has ordain'd such variety of Looks, and Countenances among Men, whilst the other Parts and Members of our Bodies are in comparison so little different" (335–36). Quoting the Earl of Shaftesbury's 1713 pronouncement that "Every face must be a certain man's," Deidre Lynch has shown how often eighteenth-century culture linked character and countenance (1998: 33). This view of the synonymy between character and countenance, underwritten as it was by God's authority, quickly established the face as the most legible part of the body in eighteenth-century fiction. As Dr. Harrison phrases it in Henry Fielding's *Amelia* (1751), "A good face . . . is a letter of recommendation" (1837: 364).

Since it was the face that mattered most in this period, it should come as no surprise that the most distinguishable feature of any face—the eyes— became extremely important to natural philosophers and novelists alike. As with the face more generally, a major part of the eyes' "truth-revealing" essence comes from the notion that they were thought to be marvelous technical productions of divine craftsmanship.[2] Newton believed that only a divine creator could have known enough about the laws of light and refraction to make the lens and pupil of the eye "so finely shaped and fitted for vision that no artist could mend them" (qtd. in Brooke 1991: 24). John Ray spent fourteen pages of his *Wisdom of God* discussing the divine perfection of the human eye before eventually treating the body's other components.

Partly because of the legacy of this divine endorsement, authors of eighteenth-century fiction constantly figured the eyes as the register of their characters' most unique, essential being. Eliza Haywood's *Love in Excess* (1719–20) repeatedly contrasts the deceptiveness of verbal communication with the more reliable and truth-revealing "language of the eyes" (Gargano 2009: 513). So, too, in the famous ending of Fielding's *Tom Jones* (1749), Tom's "Pledge" of fidelity is rooted in "those Eyes, that Mind which shines through those Eyes" of Sophia Western (1973: 753–54). On the other end of the eighteenth-century desirability spectrum, Mrs. Jewkes's "dead, spiteful, grey, goggling Eye" in *Pamela* (1741) serves as the best index of her "unGodly," menacing role in the text (Richardson 2001: 114).

EYEING VICTOR FRANKENSTEIN'S MANUFACTURE

It is within this deeply established scientific, historical, and fictional context—one that closely associated divinity with ocularity—that Mary Shelley composed *Frankenstein*. Rightly so, many prominent critics have noted how heavily the creature's eyes haunt the novel. Jay Clayton even goes so far as to claim "the eyes themselves [as] the most horrid organs the creature possesses" (2003: 131). In *The Technology of the Novel* Tony Jackson observes that *Frankenstein* "is literally thick with images of eyes and elaborately described acts of seeing" (2009: 70).[3] I don't disagree. My point, though, is that the novel's emphasis on eyes needs to be historicized and interpreted from within the specific scientific debates to which it was responding. We have seen how Enlightenment rationality and scientific advancement in the field of electricity informed the vitalist debates between Abernethy and Lawrence in the years immediately preceding Shelley's composition of the novel. In order to understand more fully Shelley's treatment of eyes (and, later, hands) in *Frankenstein*, it is necessary to consider the more particular circumstances that made eyes such a highly charged subject in the early 1800s. Eyes were so important in the early 1800s because of the legacy of attention that they received in the previous century. Eighteenth-century scholars have shown how the category of "observation" was a "painstaking" endeavor where observers exhibited "meticulous patience" and maintained a "lynx-eyed virtuosity" (Datson 2004: 101, 115, 110).

One such observer was the Anglican priest and natural philosopher William Paley. He published a work of philosophical theology in 1802 by building on the familiar claims of Newton, Ray, and many others that nature provided the best proof of a designing God. This, as we have seen, was hardly a new idea. My interest lies not in the *kind* of argument Paley was making, but in its degree. Paley explicitly recounts his decision to risk his entire argument on the "evidence" provided in the design of the eye. He specifically claims "[to] have made [a] *choice* of the eye as an instance upon which to rest the [entire] argument" (1840: 69) of a key chapter in *Natural Theology* (1802). "I know of no better method of introducing so large a subject," Paley says, "than that of comparing a [human] eye ... with a telescope" (1840: 50). His goal in the comparison of these two ocular instruments is to demonstrate the "superiority of the [divinely fashioned] eye over the [man-made] telescope" (1840: 54). Paley arrives at his sense of the former's superiority mainly by comparing the different ways that the eye and the telescope account for changes in light conditions. He correctly infers that the eye has to adapt to very "different degrees of light" while also adjusting to "the vast diversity of distance at which objects are viewed by the naked eye ... from a few inches to as many miles" (1840: 54). These difficulties do not present themselves to the maker of the telescope who, Paley asserts, "wants all the light he can get" while never having to direct the telescope to objects at close range. An illustration of the way the eye refracts light onto the retina helps Paley emphasize his position (fig. 2).

He marvels at the way the pupil retains its "exact circular shape" while it contracts or dilates itself to the varying conditions of light—and more importantly, that it performs these functions "without any other assistance than that of its own exquisite machinery" (1840: 55). "Let an artist only *try* to

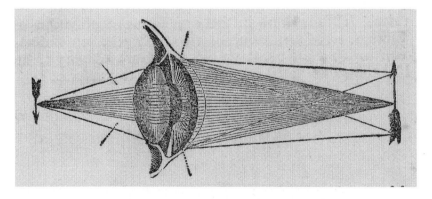

Fig. 2. The human eye. William Paley, *Natural Theology*, 55.

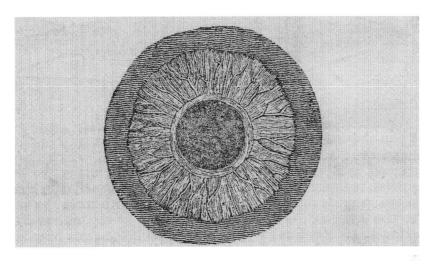

Fig. 3. Human eye. William Paley, *Natural Theology*, 56.

execute the same," Paley avers, "and he will find that his threads and strings must be disposed with great consideration and contrivance, to make a[n exact] circle which shall continually change its diameter yet preserve its form" (1840: 55–56). He adds that "this is done in the eye by an application of fibres, *i.e.*, of strings similar in their position and action to what an artist would and must employ if he had the same piece of workmanship to perform" (1840: 56). Accordingly, Paley supplies an illustrated cross-section of these "fibres" and "strings" at work in fixing the dilation of a human eye (fig. 3).

This illustration emphasizes how the eye focuses on objects at different distances by way of its own internal adjustments whereas the operator of the telescope has to adjust the distances between his glass lenses "with his hand or his screw" (1840: 57). To clinch his bold claim that the eye is "a cure for atheism," Paley maintains that "the most secret laws of optics must have been known to the author of a structure endowed with such a capacity of change" and subsequently concludes that "great and little are nothing" in "the hands of the Creator" (1840: 63, 58, 63). Famously, of course, Victor Frankenstein assumes these very hands as he attempts to replicate this "exquisite machinery" within his own creation.

Percy and Mary Shelley's interest in contemporary science brought them into contact with Paley's immensely popular work, but they were also familiar with the functions (and malfunctions) of the eye through their personal connection to Lawrence.[4] As it turns out, Abernethy's opponent in the vitalist debates was a specialist in ophthalmology, appointed surgeon in 1814 to the London Infirmary for Diseases of the Eye. Percy had experienced repeated bouts of ophthalmia and had consulted William Lawrence about his health as early as 1815. As Nora Crook and Derek Guiton point out, given his interests, expertise, connection with St Bartholomew's Hospital, and closeness to the Shelleys, Lawrence was an ideal doctor for Percy to see in 1817 when he was suffering through a particularly intense bout of ophthalmia (1986: 109). It is also no coincidence that one of England's most controversial materialist and atheistic voices on matters of human physiology specialized in *dis*orders of the eye; his position brought him into direct and sustained contact with imperfect eyes.[5]

The Shelleys' personal relationship to Lawrence should prompt us to reassess Victor Frankenstein's account of how he assembles his creation. Indeed, ophthalmological familiarity informs Frankenstein's investigation of "how the worm inherit[s] the wonders of the eye" (1818: 30). At Ingolstadt, he comes to embody (to a fault) the "painstaking care and exactitude, infinite patience, unflagging perseverance, preternatural sensory acuity, and insatiable appetite for work" that Lorraine Datson and Peter Galison attribute to nineteenth-century objectivity (1992: 83). Moreover, Shelley's descriptions suggest the creature's eye as the specific body part under construction when Frankenstein recalls the "inconceivable difficulty" he encounters while trying to connect "the minuteness of the parts" that form the "intricacies of fibres, muscles, and veins" (1818: 30–31). Frankenstein concedes that his work in this area may "be imperfect" but he forges ahead with the creation nonetheless. As a result, Shelley's account of the creature's "birth" emphasizes the multiple imperfections of the creature's eyes:

> It was already one in the morning; the rain pattered dismally against the panes, and my candle was nearly burnt out, when, by the glimmer of the half-extinguished light, I saw the dull yellow eye of the creature open; it breathed hard, and a convulsive motion agitated its limbs.... His limbs were in proportion, and I had selected his features as beautiful. Beautiful!—Great God! His yellow skin scarcely covered the work of the muscles and arteries beneath; his hair was of a lustrous black, and flowing; his teeth of a pearly whiteness; but these luxuriances only formed a more horrid contrast with his watery eyes, that seemed almost of the same colour as the dun white sockets in which they were set. (1818: 34)

Denise Gigante has traced the yellow, watery, and generally dull descrip-tion of the creature's eyes to Burkean aesthetic theory that designated "*clear-ness*" as the universal standard for beauty (2000: 571). Given the Shelleys' connections to Lawrence, however, I am suggesting that the creature's eyes' "unearthly ugliness" comes from their practical imperfection as well. It is quite apparent that the eyes Victor installs in the creature work poorly in comparison to their ostensibly divinely manufactured counterparts in other human beings.

This is why the first sign of Victor's faulty workmanship appears in the form of the creature's malfunctioning eyes. Indeed, the creature describes his awakening consciousness mainly as a struggle to see *anything*:

> By degrees, I remember, a stronger light pressed upon my nerves, so that I was obliged to shut my eyes. Darkness then came over me, and troubled me; but hardly had I felt this, when, by opening my eyes, as I now suppose, the light poured in upon me again ... dark and opaque bodies had surrounded me, impervious to my touch or sight ... The light became more and more oppressive to me ... I sought a place where I could receive shade ... I knew and could distinguish nothing. (1818: 68)

Here the creature's poorly functioning eyes seem to confirm the enormous gap in "workmanship" that Paley predicted if an "artist only tr[ied] to exe-cute the same" operations as God (1840: 55–56, emphasis original). Shelley draws attention to this gap by constructing early scenes of the novel that depend on Victor's ability to see in widely alternating conditions of light and darkness and, hence, on what Paley identifies as "the exquisite machin-ery" of the God-given eye's automatic dilation. For example, Victor marvels at his ability to see accurately even during a lightning storm near the sum-mit of Mont Blanc:

> [The storm] was echoed from Salêve, the Juras, and the alps of Savoy; vivid flashes of lightning dazzled my eyes, illuminating the lake, making it appear like a vast sheet of fire; then for an instant everything seemed of a pitchy darkness, *until the eye recovered itself from the preceding flash.* ... While I watched the storm ... I perceived in the gloom a figure which stole from behind a clump of trees near me; I stood fixed, gazing intently: I could not be mistaken. A flash of lightning illuminated the object, and

discovered its shape plainly to me; its gigantic stature, and the deformity of its aspect, more hideous than belongs to humanity, instantly informed me that it was the wretch, the filthy dæmon to whom I had given life. (1818: 48, emphasis added)

In contrast to his creation, Victor's discovery of the creature's presence in this scene actually hinges on the capability of his eyes to adjust to rapidly changing conditions of extreme lightness and darkness. The creature's eyesight eventually improves (though we do not learn by what means) as the novel progresses and Victor remains haunted by their clouded appearance and insistent gaze. He claims that "[the creature's] eyes, if eyes they may be called, were fixed on [him]" in the moments after animating his creation in his chambers at Ingolstadt (1818: 35) and later that his dark world is "penetrated by no light but the gleaming of two eyes that glared upon [him]" (1818: 126). This emphasis on the eyes becomes heightened by the creature's repeated assertions of indefatigable watchfulness, reminding Victor that he "shall watch [his] progress with unutterable anxiety" (1818: 100). In this sense, the "yellow, watery, but speculative eyes" of the creature do more than reverse the terms of monstrosity as many critics contend; they also serve as an ironic perversion of the all-seeing eyes of an omnipotent God (1831: 9).

As I mentioned at the start of this chapter, the reason *Frankenstein* is an exemplary novel is because it captures the scientific, historical, and cultural shift in interest from the eyes to the hands within a single narrative. My analysis of Shelley's treatment of hands, along with the topics I explore in my upcoming chapters, will show how the novel effectively predicts the overarching concern for hands in relation to productive manufacture, divine intentionality, and human identity that comes to transfix the nineteenth century's cultural imagination. Although the first (1818) edition of *Frankenstein* appeared during a time of significant debate about mechanized industry, the ghost story origin of the text was considerably removed from this controversy, focusing as it did almost exclusively on the natural philosophical (vitalist) viability of the human production of "life." Shelley makes it quite clear in the 1818 edition that such an endeavor requires not only human labor, but manual labor of a very specific kind. Victor "disturb[s], with profane fingers, the tremendous secrets of the human frame" as he works with his hands for a period of nearly two years to connect the minute "intricacies" of the creature's "fibres, muscles, and veins" (31–32).

MANUAL LABOR AND NATURAL HISTORY

Shelley's focus on the handmade status of the creature makes Victor a manual laborer in the most literal sense of the term, but this does not mean that his handiwork is unproblematic; quite the opposite is true. We might even say that the central problem of *Frankenstein* hinges on the nature of the creature's handmade status in relation to the generally accepted tenets of traditional Anglican religiosity: on both theological and practical levels, Shelley continually pits Victor's creating hand against God's. Victor's fingers are "profane" precisely because they attempt to manufacture life with neither divine authorization nor participation. He boldly confronts one of the most basic dogmas of Anglican religious hierarchy by asserting that "No father could claim the gratitude of his child so completely as I should deserve their's" (1818: 32). Victor goes even further in describing his endeavors within a traditionally religious context as he claims "to animate lifeless clay" into living matter (1818: 32). Shelley does not stop here in contrasting Victor's hands with an Anglican God's, though. When Victor finally achieves the capability "of bestowing animation upon lifeless matter," he relays the discovery to Walton in conspicuously manual rhetoric: "What had been the study and desire of the wisest men since the creation of the world, was now *within my grasp*"; ". . . I found so astonishing a power placed *within my hands*" (1818: 30–31, emphasis added).

Thus Shelley's representation of Victor's overreaching materialism is constantly preoccupied with images, metaphors, and literal formulations concerning the usurpation of divine handiwork. There are traces of religiosity even in Professor Waldman—the novel's most clearly articulated materialist mouthpiece. Waldman's panegyric lecture on the powers of chemistry and empirical science starkly presents the expanded capacities of man's eyes and hands in relation to God's:

> But these [natural] philosophers, whose hands seem only made to dabble in dirt, and their eyes to pour over the microscope or crucible, have performed miracles. They penetrate into the recesses of nature, and show how she works in her hiding places. They ascend into the heavens. (1818: 27–28)

Even though Waldman's speech distills the positions held by materialist thinkers that Mary Shelley knew and read, the rhetoric she uses to characterize these views is never free from what Timothy Morton has appropriately called *Frankenstein*'s "Christianizing language" (1994: 51). Specifically, Waldman's repetition of the pronoun "they" may refer either to the new philosophers themselves or, more literally, to their eyes and hands. In this latter sense, Victor's microscopic vision and dabbling hands "perform miracles" expressly by rivaling a Judeo-Christian God's all-seeing eyes and clay-molding hands. Their "ascent into the heavens" is part of a deeply embedded orientational and metamorphic system by which even secular materialists lived in the first quarter of the nineteenth century (Lakoff and Johnson 1980: 24).

Jonathan Bate has convincingly offered a passage from Humphry Davy's *Discourse, Introductory to a Course of Lectures on Chemistry* (1802) as the template for Waldman's speech. Chemistry, writes Davy, "has bestowed upon [man] powers which may be almost called creative ... and by his experiments to interrogate nature with power, not simply as a scholar ... but rather as a master, active with his own instruments" (qtd. in Bate 2000: 477). In so far as we have seen how closely nature and the divine were aligned scientifically at this time, Davy's formulation of a scholar-turned-master "*with his own instruments*" suggests a scale at least relational—if not superior—to God's. We shall see as well how, time and time again in *Frankenstein*, the most important of Victor's "own instruments" are his hands. He mentions no mechanical tools in the construction of the creature, emphasizing instead "the work of [his] own hands" (1818: 48). Ironically, even the conspicuous absence of a traditional God figure in *Frankenstein* acts as the strongest evidence of such a figure's looming presence both in the novel and in the culture in which Shelley composed it.[6]

The closest we get to an actualized Judeo-Christian God figure in *Frankenstein*, without question, comes via the creature's discovery of Milton's *Paradise Lost*. Shelley goes out of her way to characterize Victor as materialistically atheistic at the start of the novel ("a church-yard was to [him] merely the receptacle of bodies deprived of life"), but the creature's literalist interpretation of *Paradise Lost* ensures that he cannot avoid a direct comparison of his creation to that of a Christian God. The creature reads *Paradise Lost* "as a true history" (1818: 87) and hence he interprets the references to God's hand pouring divine grace on Adam as a literal manipulation of "the dust of the ground" (*PL* 4.364–65; Gen. 2:7). The creature methodically recounts to Victor how Adam "come[s] forth from the hands of God a perfect creature, happy and prosperous" (1818: 87). Just as Milton's work offers the creature a blueprint for man's "perfect" creation by God, his discovery of Victor's laboratory journal allows him to access the entire materialist "history" of his own "accursed origin." Indeed, the journal provides the creature with "the minutest description" of the process that brought him to life, but it is pivotal to note that the discovery is equally horrifying to Victor by this point in the narrative. No longer is Victor proud to be "the creator and source" of life; witnessing the creature come alive causes him to develop "a violent antipathy even to the name of natural philosophy" (1818: 32, 42). Listening to the detailed description of his creation's manufactured "birth" in the laboratory journal forces Victor to relive "that series of disgusting circumstances" but, crucially, without the resistless and frantic impulse that previously blinded and urged him forward (1818: 87).

The scene where the creature recounts his reading of *Paradise Lost* provides a crucial turning point in *Frankenstein* symbolically, thematically, and literally. It is at this narrative juncture that hands (both Victor's and his creature's), because of their unmediated relationship to the physical and theological act of creation, surpass even the watery eye as the most abhorrent body part in the novel. The transition culminates in the final part of the Montanvert section when Victor furiously reacts to seeing his laboratory journal and to hearing its contents narrated back to him by his creation. Victor berates his creature:

> "Why do you call to my remembrance circumstances of which I shudder to reflect, that I have been the miserable origin and author? Cursed be the day, abhorred devil, in which you first saw light! Cursed (although I curse myself) be the hands that formed you! You have made me wretched beyond expression. You have left me no power to consider whether I am just to you, or not. Begone! relieve me from the sight of your detested form." (1818: 67)

Listening to his creator curse his own appendages allows the creature to identify hands as the parts of the body that Victor increasingly detests, primarily because they are the most tangible and "unhallowed" connection between Victor and his bungled creation (1818: 32). The creature clearly senses this, and instead of heeding his creator's directive to "begone," he doubles down, histrionically "plac[ing] his hated hands before [Victor's] eyes." Shelley makes sure that we perceive the effect of this taunting gesture in Victor's account of his reaction: "I flung [the hands] from me with violence" (1818: 67).[7]

If, as I have suggested, there is a transfer of attention from eyes to hands in the novel at this point, such a shift parallels Shelley's earlier treatment of the creature's malfunctioning eye. The creature's hands, like his eyes, seem to work improperly at first. Hands are the instruments by which humans manipulate the world's resources, express feeling, and experience touch. Considering these as the dominant functions of properly working, human(e) hands, it is possible that the first murder victim (Victor's brother William) is the result of the creature's malfunctioning, too powerful hands. A closer look at Shelley's description of the circumstances surrounding William's murder exposes this possibility. The creature tells Victor that he had originally wanted to make a friend of William, hoping that the young child would be "unprejudiced" as a result of living "too short a time to have imbibed a horror of deformity" (1818: 96). Upon hearing himself yet again denounced as a "monster," an "ugly wretch," and an "ogre" by William, though, the creature admits *not* to willful murder but to an attempt merely to stop the epithets: "I grasped his throat to silence him, and in a moment he lay dead at my feet" (1818: 96, 97). The pace and phrasing of this description hardly reads like intentional, malevolent homicide. Instead, William appears to be a victim of Victor's poor handiwork rather than the creature's homicidal volition.

The Montanvert scene discussed above also sheds light on Victor's almost inscrutable aversion to being reminded of his indirect culpability in the murder—no matter what the level of intentionality. That is, "the print of the murderer's finger" on William's neck always reminds Victor of the "infernal machinations" of his own hands (1818: 45, 127). After Montanvert, the creature becomes aware of and then exploits Victor's great fear of "see[ing] those whom [he] most loved die under the grasp of a daemon whom [he] himself had created" (1818: 117). Thus "the print of the murderer's finger ... on [William's] neck," "the black mark of fingers on [Clerval's] neck," and "the murderous mark of the fiend's grasp ... on [Elizabeth's] neck" all serve as deliberate and perverse reminders to Frankenstein of his disastrous *manufacture* of life (1818: 45, 121, 136). Instead of killing Victor's family by tearing them "limb from limb, as the lion rends the antelope"—something the creature assures Victor he is capable of doing—he realizes the extent to which Victor despises the link between their hands and dedicates himself to an exploitation of this particular connection (1818: 91). The linkage is so strong, in fact, that Victor makes numerous declarations of guilt for the creature's murders by way of explicit references to his own hands: "I called myself the murderer of William, of Justine, and of Clerval"; "William, Justine, and

Clerval all had died through my infernal machinations"; "William, Justine, and Henry—they all died by my hands" (1818: 122, 127, 128). There is something not merely figurative about these statements. The specific articulation in terms of "my hands" doesn't necessarily mean only Victor's actual hands, but also the monstrous and malfunctioning hands he has created. Victor's father hears these seemingly wild self-accusations (they seem wild precisely because of their figurativeness) and wonders if his son has gone mad. Paradoxically, though, Victor maintains his sanity for the remainder of the novel only through his constant reflection on and iteration of the fact that the literal "crime" of his own hands (from a Judeo-Christian perspective) connects him to the crimes of his creation. This is one reason why virtually anything having to do with the creature's physical handedness enrages Victor. Think, for instance, of how the creature's "marks in writing on the barks of trees, or cut in stone" instigate Victor's fury on the manhunt he undertakes through the wilds of the arctic (1818: 142).

EARLY ANTHROPOID DISCOVERY
AND FACIAL ANXIETY

I do not use the term "manhunt" insouciantly. Despite the creature's primitive violence toward Victor's family and friends, the novel has a relative dearth of evolutionary anxiety, which in turn ensures that we see the creature as more human than animal. There are cultural and historical reasons for this phenomenon—reasons that curiously do not rely on the Western "discovery" of anthropoid apes. In 1642, the Dutch physician Jakob de Bondt (Jacobus Bontius) posthumously published an account of a Bornean orangutan, and in 1698 Edward Tyson published *Anatomy of a Pygmy*, based on Angolean chimpanzees.[8] Unlike what we will encounter in chapter 5's analysis of anthropoid apes in the immediate aftermath of Darwin's *Origin of Species* (1859), what was so shocking to seventeenth- and eighteenth-century audiences was not the hands of these animals but their human-like faces. Laura Brown's recent study, *Homeless Dogs & Melancholy Apes* (2011), elucidates how natural philosophers ranging from Bondt to Tyson and Linnaeus to Buffon saw the human-like simian face as its most disorienting feature. Bondt was troubled to "contemplate this wonderful Monster/ With a human face, so like human-kind not only/ In groaning, but also in wetting the face with weeping" (qtd. in Brown 2011: 27). Brown also traces how

Bondt's illustrations of "the monster with a human face" influence Linnaeus's 1760 illustrations, and how Bondt's work continues to do so all the way up to St. Hilaire's 1798 characterizations (2011: 33).

Even when the similarities of human and simian hands begin to attract attention at the turn of the nineteenth century, the attention is decidedly unthreatening. For example, in *The Temple of Nature* (1803), Erasmus Darwin posited that man had a very different thumb and sense of touch compared to the monkeys he observed on the banks of the Mediterranean. He critiques those who might maintain the idea that simians "accidentally had learned to use the adductor pollicis, or that strong muscle which constitutes the ball of the thumb," claiming rather definitively that "common monkeys do not" (1804: 68). Perhaps the best evidence that ape-handedness had not yet reached the level of alarm in the early nineteenth-century cultural imagination that it will in the 1850s comes not from natural philosophy but from literature. Thomas Love Peacock's humorous novel *Melincourt* (1817), published barely a year before *Frankenstein*, for example, concerns an intellectual (based in part on Percy Shelley) who adopts an orangutan that manages to secure a baronetcy and a seat in Parliament. We will see in chapter 5 how this satiric levity eventually gives way to a very palpable and poignant anxiety in the 1850s. But in 1818, as Tom Tyler points out in *Ciferae: A Bestiary in Five Fingers*, the simian appendage was widely viewed as "an inadequate, preposterous homologue" to the human hand (2012: 7).

As a result, the specter of violent harm in *Frankenstein*, figured in the act of strangulation, functions throughout the novel not as an evolutionary threat but instead as a symbolic reminder of Victor's original physico-theological overreaching.[9] But I want to suggest that even overreaching—the blanket term so many critics and general readers use to describe Victor's actions—fails, on several levels, to go far enough. When we consider Victor's direct association of the work of his hands with the crimes of his creature's hands, *Frankenstein* seems to be more specifically and more literally a story about *overgrasping* than overreaching.[10] Indeed, Shelley associates the trope of grasping with Victor even before the creature comes to life. We have seen how Victor marvels that the secret of "bestowing animation upon lifeless matter" appears "within [his] grasp" (1818: 30, 31). This manual thematic continues to influence Victor's description of his creature's first moments of life as he reports that "one hand [of the creature] was stretched out, seemingly to detain [him]" (1818: 35). Victor later says that "[he] felt the fingers of the monster already grasping [his] neck" and that his "old fears revive, which were soon to clasp

[him], and cling to [him] forever" (1818: 122, 134). Yet even Victor, the educated and refined middle-class man of science, imagines a revenge consisting of the same barbaric and murderous strangulation. "I possessed a maddening rage," Victor comments, "when I thought of him, and desired and ardently prayed that I might have him within my grasp to wreak a great and signal revenge on his cursed head" (1818: 138). The sustained interplay of both creature's and creator's "grasping" appears frequently enough to suggest that Shelley aims to conflate the two in the reader's mind. Near the end of the story, after the creature has strangled each of his victims to death, Victor feverishly recounts to Walton the manner in which "the devil eluded [his] grasp" and how he "appeared almost within grasp of [his] foe" several times on the ice fields (1831: 206, 211). Here we see how the oft-cited conflation of Victor and his creature occurs primarily by way of their hands' constant grasping.

In a text full of malevolent tension and barbaric tensility, overgrasping seems a more accurate term to characterize Victor's never-quite-specified crime. The "great crime" to which Victor refers in the 1818 edition becomes far more explicit when we consider the information Shelley supplies in the Author's Introduction to the 1831 edition: "Frightful must it be; for supremely frightful would be the effect of any human endeavor to mock the stupendous mechanism of the Creator of the world" (1831: 9). Later on I will treat the various pressures Shelley experienced in the decade and a half leading up to the 1831 edition and the specific textual revisions she makes therein. Here, though, I think it is useful to take Shelley more or less at her word when she claims to have "changed no portion of the story nor introduced any new ideas or circumstances" (1831: 10). Granting Shelley this point helps us evaluate why Victor feels "as if [he] had created [committed?] some great crime" (1831: 112) while embarking on the manufacture of his second creature:

> During my first experiment, a kind of enthusiastic frenzy had blinded me to the horror of my employment; my mind was intently fixed on the sequel of my labour, and my eyes were shut to the horror of my proceedings. But now I went to it in cold blood, and my heart often sickened at the work of my hands. (1831: 113)

Victor is sickened by the work of his hands precisely because he realizes, especially now after hearing about *Paradise Lost* in relation to his laboratory journal, that he is performing a kind of manual labor reserved for "the Creator of the world."

Fig. 4. Grant of Arms of the Royal College of Physicians.

In this respect, Shelley invokes the religiously charged rhetoric of a far older and more deeply established tradition concerning the dissection of human bodies. In the early modern period, the unique relationship between divine and human hands became solidified iconographically and medically. Consider the Grant of Arms of the Royal College of Physicians (fig. 4): The illustration reveals the common image of God's hand emerging from gilded clouds as it grasps the wrist of the human patient below. Katherine Rowe has shown how medical illustrations from the early modern period forward drew on these iconographic conventions by directly asserting God's hand as *the* most important model for anatomical exposition. In fact, early English anatomists dissecting the human hand learned "to trace the action of Creation" by making visible "the trace of God's molding hand in a kind of *imitatio Dei*" (Rowe 1999: 49). The anatomist John Banister put it this way in his *Historie of Man* (1578):

> Thus if we wel perpend the construction, and composition of the partes, and bones of the hand, our senses shall soone conceive the maner of the action, with no lesse admiration, in beholding the handy worke of the incomprehensible Creator. (qtd. in Rowe 1999: 33)[11]

This is exactly the kind of "handy worke" that Victor finds so odious as he attempts to construct his second creature. The repugnance Victor experiences at this later point in the novel could not be more literally connected to the dire repercussions of his previous dabblings "among the unhallowed damps of the grave" (1818: 32)

Although Shelley presents this experience as "heart sickness" rather than religious sin, the sustained interplay of Victor's profane fingers and "the Creator's" flawless hands situates the novel's science within a distinctly Judeo-Christian tradition. On this point, though, I concur with Alan Rauch and J. Paul Hunter that *Frankenstein*'s allusions to traditional Christianity do not necessarily stake out a clear belief system for the text (or for Mary Shelley). Instead, they ensure that the novel is historically positioned in a revered tradition of ideas and questions.[12] My point is that critics claiming to resist "simpler" interpretations of *Frankenstein* as a moral fable of presumption do so at least in part because they fail to recognize how Shelley's treatment of hands excludes the possibility of interpreting the text in purely secularizing terms.[13] The problem is that twentieth- and twenty-first-century critics by and large have clung to a too-metaphorical sense of what "overreaching" means in this novel. That is, they do not take literally enough what overreaching—or, as I have suggested, *overgrasping*—means to a culture at the privileged (and fleeting) Romantic moment just before evolutionary angst and industrialist alarm begin to merge in the first quarter of the nineteenth century.

HANDLING THE 1831 EDITION

Shelley's republication of *Frankenstein* in 1831 remains an extremely controversial subject for critics. I think it is less productive to speculate about Mary

Shelley's own philosophical positions or to dispute which edition is "truer" to her original creative impulse than it is to consider what was happening in England in between the two editions.[14] The beginning of this chapter traced the contours of English culture leading up to the 1818 publication. But what was the scientific, religious, and (eventually) industrial atmosphere like in England during the decade and a half between the 1818 and 1831? To answer this complicated question, we must first answer the easier one regarding what Shelley actually changed between editions.[15] The 1831 version eliminates some of its original context by removing a number of references to contemporary science such as the electrical experiments that Victor's father demonstrates for him. It gives a fuller account of domestic harmony in Victor's family and makes Elizabeth an adopted orphan instead of a cousin. The 1831 edition also mitigates the influence of Godwinian philosophy, particularly in Elizabeth's toned-down critique of the justice system that incriminates Justine. Perhaps most importantly, Mary Shelley added a new "Author's Introduction" meant to address her readership's curiosity about how "a young girl, came to think of and dilate upon so very hideous an idea" (1831: 5).

Since the 1831 republication of Frankenstein was slated to be the ninth in the Standard Novels series, Shelley would have known that Bentley insisted his authors supply new material either in text or as paratextual prefaces so that he could legitimately claim a new copyright. She would have known as well that Bentley's books were priced at less than one-fifth the cost of a new novel and, therefore, they targeted a much larger audience. William St Clair, in The Reading Nation in the Romantic Period, demonstrates how this larger audience was, for the most part, "conservative, indeed reactionary, in its political and religious opinions" (2004: 359). Gauging the ways in which England had become increasingly conservative during these years will require us to take up once again the scientific controversy as it played out with John Abernethy and William Lawrence. This time, however, we will rejoin the vitalist debate in 1818—the year Frankenstein was first anonymously published—and evaluate how it affected the 1831 edition.

A sampling of the reviews in major cultural outlets reveals a distinct backlash against scientific materialism almost immediately after 1818.[16] A review in the Edinburgh Magazine from March 1818 sees the "dark and gloomy views of nature and of man, bordering too closely on impiety" (qtd. in Shelley 2007: 383). From 1818 on, the leading cultural journal, the Anglican and Tory Quarterly Review, began to call for the revival of the long-neglected charge of blasphemy against irreverent writings. After the 1819 publication of his *Lectures on Physiology, Zoology and the Natural History of Man*, William Lawrence—on whose materialist theories *Frankenstein* had drawn "nourishment, energy, [and] importance"—became a juicy target for conservative and religious outrage (Butler 1996: 303). A lengthy July 1819 *Quarterly Review* article by George D'Oyly not only denounced Lawrence's "doctrine of materialism," it went so far as to call for him to relinquish his position in the Royal College of Surgeons for harboring opinions "hostile to religion" (D'Oyly 1820: 30, 34).[17]

Of particular concern to the *Quarterly Review* was Lawrence's capability as an instructor to pervert the religious tenets of the young and inexperienced medical students with teachings that ran counter to "revealed religion," particularly "the Mosaic account of the creation and the history of the world" (D'Oyly 1819: 7, 12). We can discern much about the changing social and political complexion of England (and its reaction to a very early event in the public reception of evolutionary theory) by considering the events after the *Quarterly Review* article. Not only did the Royal College of Surgeons suspend Lawrence's membership, it decided not to reinstate Lawrence until he withdrew his book entirely. Lawrence's fear of losing his appointment as surgeon to the London hospitals eventually came to pass. The governors of the Bridewell and Bethlehem hospitals ruled to suspend Lawrence from his duties as a surgeon in 1819. As a result, Lawrence caved in to public and professional pressure by writing a letter to the governors retracting his "infidel opinions" and promising "to suppress and prevent the circulation of his book" (Anon. 1822: 544).

Because the plot of *Frankenstein* was thought by so many in the public to be closely aligned to Lawrence's style of materialist science, Shelley very well could have altered several key components of the story to make it more palatable to this wider, more conservative audience in 1831. A number of these changes are small but telling. For instance, Shelley adds several new paragraphs that incorporate the Christian idea of heaven (1831: 96–97). This addition is heralded by changes she makes to the lower-case "h" in the word "heaven" to a capitalized "H" in 1831 on at least three separate occasions (1831: 150, 209, 219). She also adds more lengthy descriptions of the prostration and relative peace Victor experiences while travelling through ravines, rivers, and mountainous icescapes. In one particular set of paragraphs added to the 1831 edition, Victor recounts his relief in the rhetoric of religious hierarchy as travels near Chamounix:

> The weight upon my spirit was sensibly lightened as I plunged yet deeper in the ravine of Arve. The immense mountains and precipices that overhung me on every side—the sound of the river raging among the rocks, and dashing of the waterfalls around, spoke of a power mighty as Omnipotence—and I ceased to fear, or to bend before any being less almighty than that which had created and ruled the elements. (1831: 97)

Additions with rhetoric such as this would have compelled religiously conservative readers to interpret Victor's musings as necessarily connected to God and to the "Creator of the [natural] world" that Shelley discusses in her 1831 Author's Introduction (1831: 9).

Butler and others argue that these changes render the 1818 edition "neutered or at best over-freighted with inessential additions" (1996: 304). My contention is that Mary Shelley's 1831 changes, while perhaps inessential, reveal anxieties about the human body that persist for the remainder of the nineteenth century. In particular, Shelley's emphasis on the physicality of the relationship between the hand of God and the hand of man takes center stage in 1831 and, as I will show in my upcoming chapters, stays there for the rest of the century. Only with the 1831 Author's Introduction, for example, do we get any inkling of tension between what is divinely made, what is manmade, and what is machine made.[18] In the 1818 edition, Victor "collect[s] the instruments of *life* around [him], that [he] might infuse a spark of being into the lifeless thing that lay at [his] feet" (34, emphasis added). The 1831 Introduction discusses the possibility of a corpse being "re-animated," "manufactured, brought together, and endued with vital warmth" via "the working of some powerful engine" (8, 9). Though it is clear that Victor's creation is still handmade, Shelley introduces a concept totally absent from the 1818 text: God's creative power in relation to the combination of mechanized and handmade "manufacture." This new relationship emerges in one of the most oft-cited passages from the 1831 Introduction:

> I saw—with shut eyes, but acute mental vision—I saw the pale student of unhallowed arts kneeling beside the thing he had put together. I saw the hideous phantasm of a man stretched out, and then, on the working of some powerful engine, show signs of life, and stir with an uneasy, half-vital motion. Frightful must it be; for supremely frightful would be the effect of any human endeavor to mock the stupendous mechanism of the

Creator of the world. His success would terrify the artist; he would rush away from his odious *handywork*, horror-stricken. (9, emphasis added)

It is important to note that only here does Shelley mention Victor's use of mechanized aid in the manufacture of his creature; for the rest of the revised text, the emphasis is still on the "unhallowed" nature of the scientific experiments themselves.

On one other occasion in the 1831 edition Shelley has Victor refer to the construction of the creature as specifically unsanctioned by God. The final words of a new set of paragraphs added to the 1831 ending to Volume 1 have Victor lamenting the "hapless victims to [his] unhallowed arts" in conjunction with "the work of [his] thrice-accursed hands" (90). This is significant because, by this point in the plot, the creature has murdered only William. Thus, Victor's reference to his "thrice-accursed" hands refer firstly (and primarily) to his original manufacture of the creature, secondly to the murder of William, and thirdly to the execution of Justine. This additional passage is striking also in the sense that it renders Victor and his creature manually indistinguishable; both could have uttered the creature's words on the penultimate page of both editions: "it is true that I am a wretch. I have murdered the lovely and the helpless; I have strangled the innocent as they slept, and grasped to death his throat who never injured me or any living thing" (1818: 155; 1831: 224). In the sense that the creature's hands are man-made instruments gone murderously wrong, *Frankenstein*, by 1831, had quite possibly become the first industrial novel.

CHAPTER 2

The Anatomy of Anglican Industry
Mechanical Philosophy
and Early Factory Fiction

As we saw in Mary Shelley's alterations to *Frankenstein*, England's political and cultural stakeholders had become increasingly conservative by the 1830s. The rededication to religious conservatism was no doubt a response to fear that Continental materialism had gained too strong a foothold in the early part of the century. William Lawrence's public renouncement of his early writings testifies to the fact that the students and radical physicians who attended his classes and read his work were far less influential than the Council of the Royal College of Surgeons, the hospital governors, and the authoritative chancellor himself, Lord Eldon—a dogmatically orthodox conservative who held the post from 1801 to 1827. In officially sanctioned scientific circles it had become virtually mandatory to use anatomy as evidence of God's shaping hand in the creation of the human body and the natural world. What is little known, however, is just how literal this formulation had become by the third decade of the nineteenth century.

This chapter explores how an unlikely convergence of scientific, industrial, and religious discourse coalesced around 1830 to make the human hand the most generative but also the most heavily contested site in the British cultural imaginary. Assessing the threat posed to traditional Anglicanism by nascent evolutionary theory (emanating most intensely from France and Germany) requires a consideration of English responses to such threats. Though there are many that fit this description, I would like to look more closely at one particular response—Sir Charles Bell's Bridgewater Treatise on *The Hand* (1833)—because it remains relatively unexamined and because it provides an early and rare instance of a text which struggles to address both natural philosophy and industrial expansion. If *Frankenstein* represents a key transitional moment when discussions in natural philosophy moved from the eyes to the hands, Bell's Bridgewater Treatise demonstrates how evolutionary discourse on the hand became imbricated with grave new questions about mechanized manufacture.

The Earl of Bridgewater died in February 1829 and bequeathed £8,000 to the president of the Royal Society to publish works of natural theology on the "Power, Wisdom, and Goodness of God as manifested in the Creation" (Bell 1833: vi). The Royal Society selected Charles Bell to compose one in a series of eight publications.[1] Since a central objective of *Changing Hands* is to shift the focus of bodily interpretation from the facial to the manual, Charles Bell provides a case study *par excellence*. He wrote professionally about both the face and the hands and yet he is remembered almost solely for his work on the face. The familiarity of Bell's name (if it is familiar at all) derives from his work on the face. He wrote *Essays on the Anatomy of Expression in Painting* (1806) and published *On Nerves* (1821)—an essay on the paralysis of facial muscles from which the well-known condition of Bell's Palsy was named.

However, this friend and colleague of John Abernethy and member of the conservative guard of the Royal College of Surgeons also authored the Bridgewater Treatise on *The Hand* in June 1833. His treatise on the "mechanism and vital endowments" of the human hand appeared as the fourth of eight in a series that became one of the most widely circulated works on science published in the first half of the nineteenth century—despite its relative obscurity today (1833: vi).[2] Bell's treatise takes up his subject comparatively, exhibiting a detailed anatomical overview of animal appendages descending from the human hand to the "hand-like" extremities of monkeys, the paws of bears and lions, the wings of birds, and the fins of fish. These physical morphologies are unproblematic for Bell because of his belief in the prevailing notion that "man [was] created last of all"—as "the highest and most perfect" creation of a God who had intended it to be ordered in exactly this fashion (1833: 21, 34). The deeply religious Bell was the son of an Episcopal Church of Scotland clergyman and believed without hesitation that the human hand—as opposed to the eye—was "the last and best proof of that principle of adaptation which evinces design in the creation" (38). Bell was so personally and professionally dedicated to the "Design" model that he was chosen to edit and even to illustrate later editions of Paley's *Natural Theology*. Because of this association, Bell's Treatise on *The Hand*, when it

Fig. 5. *The Hand*, by Charles Bell. Cambridge Library Collection, 2009. Used by permission of Cambridge University Press.

has been acknowledged, is treated almost exclusively as a distinct but unremarkable integer in the wider calculus of British philosophical thought built on "purposeful" adaptation in the natural world. The cover of the 2009 Cambridge republication of the text contributes to its traditional placement in the history of natural theology.

However, Bell's 1833 treatise is also a key transitional text linking nineteenth-century ideas about "Creation," industrialization, and representations of the factory in early-industrial British fiction. Just as *Frankenstein* took shape amid earlier debates about religious creation and design, Bell's treatise was composed during the hotly contested "Machinery Question" as it unfurled during the 1820s and 1830s. Whereas chapter 3 of this volume treats the specifically Luddite revolts from the winter of 1811–12, the period examined in this chapter includes the years between 1820 and 1855. I choose these dates in part because labor historians associate this period with the most exponential development and implementation of mechanized production. Raphael Samuel, for example, claims that "the machinery question attract[ed] attention chiefly in the 1820s and 1830s, when Cartwright's loom was throwing thousands out of work, and when the rival merits of an agrarian and an industrial society ('past and present') were being canvassed on all sides" (1977: 9). Likewise, François Crouzet estimates in *The Victorian Economy* that the number of power looms increased by a factor of ten between 1820 and 1833—the year of Bell's treatise on *The Hand* (1982: 199).[3] The rapid development and implementation of all-metal mechanisms made the textile machine simultaneously both a philosophical symbol and a tangible reality. "On every hand," Thomas Carlyle famously commented in his 1829 "Signs of the Times," "the living artisan is driven from his workshop, to make room for a speedier, inanimate one" in which "the shuttle drops from the fingers of the weaver, and falls into iron fingers that ply it faster" (1899: 59). Though the inward sense of mechanization was clearly Carlyle's greatest concern for what he termed "the Age of Machinery," the tangible effects of automatic manufacture were beginning to register in unprecedented, disorienting, and, as we shall see, physically perilous ways. Bell believed that the machinery itself posed a challenge to the "perfect," God-given human hand as the model of all productive activity (1833: 172). It is in this sense that Bell's Bridgewater Treatise registers, and extends, the concerns of Shelley's 1831 *Frankenstein*.

Thus, if we consider this context in conjunction with Bell's experiences during this time as a practicing surgeon who treated victims of industrial accidents at Middlesex Hospital and Leeds Infirmary, his Bridgewater Treatise may be seen not only in an evolutionary context, but also in its larger cultural one: as an important response to the era's struggle with the grim physical realities attendant upon the supersession of hand labor by automatic manufacture.

The proliferation of this new productive power quite obviously had wide-ranging effects. For the first time in history, mechanized textile equipment employed automatic appendages that functioned more productively and more efficiently than the human hand alone. Mechanical contrivances had moved worlds beyond Vaucanson's eighteenth-century automatons to accomplish significant industrial tasks. Mechanized gig-mills, shearing frames, and multi-bobbin power looms outperformed work that had been previously accomplished by skilled craftsmen for centuries. Unlike manual labor, machines began to operate with unparalleled rapidity, regularity, and tirelessness. Therefore, the body part that had been the primary emblem of human exceptionalism in the natural and economic world—the part that had been celebrated as "the instrument of instruments" from Aristotle to Galen, Shakespeare to Bulwer—began to appear physically inadequate in an inconceivably altered way. Peter Gaskell describes this process from the human worker's point of view in his *Manufacturing Population of England*:

> The labourer is indeed a subsidiary to this [machine] power. Already he is condemned, hour after hour, day after day, to watch and minister to [the machine's] operations—to become himself as much a part of its mechanism as its cranks and cog-wheels,—already to feel that he is but a portion of a mighty machine, every improved application of which, every addition to its Briareus-like arms, rapidly lessen his importance. (1833: 183)

Another contemporary presciently noted in the 1830s that the prevalence of automatic machinery was "rendering *hands* artificially *superfluous*" (Place 2003: 171, emphasis original).

The result was not simply one of scale or degree. In fact, newspaper accounts and working-class literature reveal that the increased productivity brought on by machine manufacture was only one unsettling feature of England's rapid progression to mechanized production. The frequent injury, and often death, endured by factory workers as a result of their interactions with automatic machinery quickly became a far more immediate concern for those in closest proximity to the supposedly self-acting mechanisms. As Jamie L. Bronstein has noted in *Caught in the Machinery*, crushed fingers "resulting in the amputation of one or several joints, were common" (2007: 2). So often did the new mill gearing tear off fingers, in fact, that Bronstein reports "factories were filled with workers missing parts of their hands" (96). It is here that my earlier assertion of the 1831 *Frankenstein* as the first industrial novel comes into sharper focus: harm by man-made appendages moves from the organic to the inorganic in the shift from *Frankenstein* to factory narratives.

MANUAL "PERFECTION" AND THE INDUSTRIAL QUESTION

By the late 1820s factory accidents attracted attention all over England. The scenes of grisly dismemberment in *A Memoir of Robert Blincoe* (which ran in *The Lion* from 25 January through 22 February 1828) helped establish and then popularize what became known as "the man-eating-machine" genre in daily newspapers. Thomas Lacqueur has shown how these stories forged a "humanitarian narrative" linking those who suffered and those who read about such suffering (1989: 176). *The Times* published a representative example of this new narrative in its reporting of the death of Daniel Buckley, a mill worker who died in 1830 as a result of gruesome injuries to his hand by a machine used for carding horsehair. The article recounts in graphic detail how Buckley's left hand "was caught and lacerated, and his fingers crushed" by the studded teeth of a cylinder before the machine could be stopped by his co-workers ("Coroner's Inquest" 1830). *The Times* article also reports that Buckley died after spending two full weeks in Middlesex Hospital—the same facility in which Sir Charles Bell, the future author of the Bridgewater Treatise on *The Hand*, was employed as the lead surgeon.

Other accounts of factory life from this period show the extent to which workers were constantly confronted with the specter of losing their hands to machines. The *Narrative of the Experiences and Sufferings of William Dodd, a Factory Cripple* recounts the life of a young boy who enters the factory in 1809 and leaves it with an amputated hand in 1837. Though he does not describe his own maiming, Dodd describes how his sister's right hand became entangled in a carding machine barely ten pages into the narrative:

> Four iron teeth of a wheel, three-quarters of an inch broad, and one-quarter of an inch thick, had been forced through her hand ... and the fifth iron tooth fell upon the thumb, and crushed it into atoms ... This accident might have been prevented, if the wheels above referred to had been boxed off, which they might have been for a couple of shillings; and the very next week after this accident, a man had two fingers taken off his hand, by the very same wheels—and still they are not boxed off! (1841: 285)

P. W. J. Bartrip and S. B. Burman have demonstrated in *The Wounded Soldiers of Industry* how factory workers had few, if any, rights to compensation from their employers after their survival from workplace accidents. This was partly because the rapidly expanding economic activity provided employers with financial incentives to ignore the law (1983: 21). It was simply cheaper for employers to pay nominal fines when there were injuries and to keep the factory equipment running as usual than to stop the machines and fence off the most dangerous parts. As a result, factory production in this unregulated era created large numbers of industrial amputations, particularly of the hands and fingers (Bronstein 2007: 2).

Furthermore, many factories maintained policies that did not allow for their engines to be shut down even during service or maintenance (Cawthon 1997: 49). *The Times* reported on the case of William Lloyd who was oiling the cogs of an operating engine when it drew in his left hand and severed it at the wrist (March 24, 1838). Surgeons consequently trained their students to operate with an awareness of their patients' chances to gain employment after hand injuries. One surgeon at St. George's hospital cautioned his students that "a finger or a thumb, or even the stump of a finger, [would] always be more useful than any artificial appendage, particularly when the accident occurs to a mechanic" (qtd. in Cawthon 1997: 59). Stories abound of workers who attempted to return to their former factory positions only to be turned away because of mangled hands. What's worse, machines existed for those who had survived lower-body injuries because such machines could be operated from a seated position. None, however, could operate without the assistance of hands. Therein lay a particularly cruel historical irony: the hand became simultaneously the most valuable and most vulnerable part of the human body for a factory worker.

Tending to hand injuries in the 1820s compelled Charles Bell to visit surgeons at other hospitals in England's manufacturing towns. One of the colleagues Bell visited was Samuel Smith, his former student and a surgeon at the Leeds General Infirmary, where severe injuries to the arms and hands occurred in disproportionately large numbers. Smith testified to Michael Sadler's Parliamentary Committee on Factories in July 1832 that he had "frequently seen accidents of the most dreadful kind that it is possible to conceive . . . cases in which the arm had been torn off near the shoulder joint . . . the upper extremity chopped into small fragments, from the tip of the finger to above the elbow . . . the most shocking cases of lacerations that it is possible to conceive" (Smith 1832: 503). Bell toured the region's hospitals during that summer and heard similar reports of the gruesome hand injuries sustained by the area's workers. He testified before the same parliamentary committee less than a month later, saying that he "was very much struck with the nature and number of the accidents received [from machinery]" both in his own hospital and in those he visited (Bell 1832: 605).

The experiences of many other medical practitioners reveal similar responses. William Lutener, a Montgomeryshire surgeon, testified that he "had frequently to amputate the hands and fingers of children" who would most likely become paupers for life (1832: 179). The Sadler Committee's report was controversial with factory owners partly because its grim findings were thought to lack firm data. The Factory Act of 1833, though, required official inspectorates to keep lists of injuries with specific headings such as "Time, place and Mode of Maiming," "Distorted," and "Description or Degree of Distortion" (*Instructions* 1833: 34–35). This more formally collected data confirmed that the most common injury requiring hospitalization was the severing or pulverization of the hand by mechanized fly-wheels. In one year during this decade, for instance, severe injuries to the hand, thumb, or fingers accounted for 243 of the 261 patients (over 93 percent) treated at the Leeds Infirmary in cases related to mill accidents (Lee 1964: 89).

Bell's deep religious faith, combined with his experience treating victims of these kinds of factory accidents at Middlesex Hospital, undoubtedly influenced his decision to choose the hand as his topic when he was invited to contribute a volume to the Bridgewater Treatises. For him and, as the 1831 Introduction of *Frankenstein* also makes clear, for many Britons in the nineteenth century, "the perfection" of the human hand directly signified "the presence of the hand of the Creator" (Bell 1833: 223). In two lengthy chapters of the treatise, Bell analyzes how "the Author of nature" constructed the superior sense of touch in the hand and states the chief reason for doing so: "to show that the most perfect proof of power and design" resides in the hand's sensory apparatus (172, 175). Its flawless design reflects Bell's belief in a world quite literally wrought "pure from the Maker's hands" (220). What I want to emphasize in drawing attention to this point is how Bell's experience treating the victims of factory injuries leads to a "bodily" update of Paley's 1802 work on the eye. Once jeopardized, hands become the new threshold for evaluating "Design" in the natural world. Defending the wonders of the Enlightenment and the very early nineteenth-century eye became, in effect, scientifically and religiously outdated with the onset of automatic manufacture. Bell's 1833 treatise thus updates Paley with its focus on the newly important body part.

The Hand taps into the same religiosity that made Victor Frankenstein's attempt at handmade human creation so "supremely frightful" in Shelley's 1831 introduction (9). New with Bell, though, is a different, more timely, inflection of cultural anxiety surrounding the process and perils of industrial mechanization. As recent critics have shown, machines were often described by pro-industrialists as organic and cooperative improvements to the human anatomy.[4] Charles Babbage's Economy of Machinery and Manufactures, for example, is principally interested in the substitution of machinery for human limbs. Published just one year before Bell's The Hand, Babbage's Economy glorifies mechanisms that "exer[t] forces too great for human power" and that "execut[e] operations too delicate for human touch" (1833: 47). Babbage praises the "giant arm" of the engine that works "with almost fairy fingers [to] entwin[e] the meshes of the most delicate fabric" (49, 50). This focus on mechanical prosthetic improvement (and thus the limitations of the human hand) stands in direct opposition to Bell's notion of an appendage designed "pure from the Maker's hands" (1833: 220). Babbage's comments nonetheless show how critics and supporters of the factory system produced alternate and contradictory representations of body-machine relations.

None of this is meant to suggest that Bell was hostile to factory production or even mechanization *per se*; we will encounter more from those on the opposition side to the "Factory Question" later on in the chapter. Nowhere in Bell's treatise, in fact, does he criticize the productive power of automatic manufacture. Instead, he is at pains to demonstrate how *all* mechanical contrivances are themselves based on the model of anatomical perfection embodied in the divinely constructed hand. The subject matter of Bell's introduction is telling in this respect. He does not open his treatise

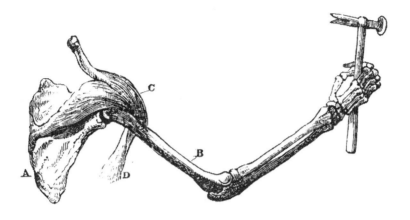

Fig. 6. Charles Bell, *The Hand*, 115.

with a discussion of the perfection of the human hand in comparison to animal appendages as one might reasonably expect in a work of natural philosophy. This highlights why we should read Bell against the strictly evolutionist/"Design" grain. In contrast to traditional works of natural philosophy, Bell opens with an unexpected anecdote about how the perfection of the hand "makes us insensible to its use" (1833: 13) in the increasingly mechanized world of the 1830s:

> A man will make journeys to see an engine stamp a coin or turn a block; yet the organs [hands] through which he has a thousand sources of enjoyment, and which are in themselves more exquisite in design and more curious both in contrivance and in mechanism, do not enter his thoughts. (12)

Indeed, Bell's repeated emphasis on the God-given hand as the model for all "mechanical contrivances" becomes the dominant theme of the treatise (114). In one notable demonstration of this theme, Bell illustrates the skeletal mechanism running from the hand to the shoulder required to make use of a traditional hammer (fig. 6).

According to Bell, the hand's use of the hammer "is, in truth, similar to the operation of the fly wheel, by which the gradual motion of an engine is accumulated to a point of time, and a blow is struck capable of crushing or of stamping a piece of gold or silver" (1833: 116). This reasoning prompts him to ask, "in what respect does the mechanism of the arm differ from the engine with which the printer throws off his sheet?" (116). Here and throughout his treatise, Bell focuses not so much on judging the usefulness of the new productive power offered by automatic machinery. Instead, he emphasizes the ways in which machinery achieves its productive power by utilizing a series of mechanical components originally designed by the Creator in the hand. His era's tendency to overlook what he considers the original perfection—and by extension, God's role in scientific development—often appears as Bell's chief concern regarding the era's unprecedented industrial advancements.

Looking at a meteorological analogy from the latter part of the treatise should help illustrate this point. If "one sees the fire of heaven brought down into a phial," Bell writes, "and materials compounded, to produce an explosion louder than the [original] thunder, and ten times more destructive, the storm will no longer speak an impressive language to him" (1833: 230). In Bell's metaphor, "the fire of heaven brought down in a phial" represents the human co-option of the hand's divine construction in mechanical inventions such as Babbage's, where man-made automatic "hands" work "with almost fairly fingers" to accomplish previously human tasks (Babbage 1833: 50). Extending Bell's meteorological metaphor along these lines, the "materials compounded, to produce an explosion louder than the original thunder, and ten times more destructive" signifies the man made, technical, and therefore more powerful improvements made to God's original design. Lastly in Bell's metaphor, man's development and implementation of this mechanized system makes God's originating manual component "no longer . . . impressive . . . to him."[5] William Dodd emphasizes a similar point as he compares factory machinery with the human body: "[The worker] sees nothing but an endless variety of shafts, drums, straps, and wheels in motion; and though these may, at first, inspire him with a feeling of respect for, and admiration of, [the machinery] . . . this feeling will vanish, when he reflects on their power to destroy or render useless for life *that exalted piece of mechanism formed by and after the image of God!*" (1968: 312, emphasis added).

Of course, for all the mechanical implications of Bell's treatise, given the terms of the Earl of Bridgewater's bequest, the treatise actually does also defend an argument for "Design" from an evolutionary standpoint. Bell performs a sustained comparison of human hands in relation to "lower" animals for large sections of the text. But even this strategy is framed by a critique of his culture's tendency to be drawn more to "what is uncommon and monstrous" than to "what is natural and perfectly adjusted to its office" (1833: 12). Bell maintains that "a vulgar admiration is excited by seeing the spidermonkey pick up a straw, or a piece of wood, with its tail; or the elephant searching the keeper's pocket with his trunk" (13). This chiding is relatively innocuous in Bell's work, though, precisely because the imperative to distinguish humans from animals by way of the hand was not yet as urgent in the 1820s and 1830s as the one to distinguish them from the machines that were injuring and maiming them in the process of mechanical supersession.

The extraordinary sales figures for Bell's treatise before *The Origin of Species* (1859)—and, therefore, before the full-blown debate about evolutionary adaptation—suggest that Bell's view of "manual perfection" was reassuring to a culture whose hands were being outperformed, displaced, and mangled by machines. When *The Hand* was published in June 1833, the first edition was already oversubscribed by 300 copies (Topham 1998: 244). This is impressive, considering that a successful print run at that time would have been around 500 copies. Pickering published 2,000 additional copies in September 1833, 3,000 in April 1834, and 2,500 in October 1834 (Topham 1993: 284). Thus Bell's 1833 treatise marks another distinct historical moment when representations of the hand sat precariously between perfection and superiority in relation to animals on the one side and between imperfection and productive inadequacy in relation to machines on the other. The "Hand" as a factory operative therefore becomes a powerful locus for thinking about relations of human, animal, and mechanism. The "Machinery Question," as those in the nineteenth century experienced it, was ultimately a question about the limits of the human—and the debate about industrialization was the most poignant context for asking that question about human limits until Darwinian evolutionary theory.

Many cultural commentators came to the same conclusion in exactly the same year. In an article entitled "The Factory System" from April 1833, an author for *Blackwood's Edinburgh Magazine* (John Wilson) located human factory operatives in this same liminal space between machines and animals: "Though as a class they are degraded, they are yet human; they feel, though you treat them as such, that they are neither machines nor brutes" (450). The anxiety stemming from the precariousness of the body part so essential to notions of what it meant to be human helped inaugurate an intense cultural fascination with the hand for the remainder of the nineteenth century.

INDUSTRIAL DISCOURSE, EARLY FACTORY FICTION,
AND THE DISCURSIVE STRUGGLE FOR DIVINE CONSENT

Andrew Ure's *Philosophy of Manufactures* (1835) was another important text built on the corporeal schema of pro-industrialist discourse. In many respects, Ure's work reads like a point-by-point response to Bell's treatise by invoking the rhetoric of anthropomorphic and mechanical "perfection" of its own mechanical kind. Ure discusses, for instance, the "present perfection" of the self-acting machine's "automatic organs" and "mechanical fingers" (1861: 368, 32, 15). What made the debate about factory work in contemporary discourse so contentious was the manner in which both sides claimed divine consent. Ure situates the machines themselves (not the "design" upon which they are built) as Providential "*blessings* which physico-mechanical science has bestowed on society" (6–7, emphasis added). According to Ure, "the new [factory] system of labour was designed by Providence" to be "a benefaction, which, wisely administered," would "become the best temporal gift of Providence to the poor"—"a progression of improvement designed by Providence to emancipate [the poor's] animal functions from brute toil, and to leave his intelligent principle leisure to think of its immortal interests!" (14, 370).

At several junctures *Philosophy of Manufactures* operates as propaganda, or at least positive advertising, for the recruitment of factory workers described by Ure as "young persons about to make the choice of profession" (1861: 6). He makes this case for recruitment by directly comparing the difficulty of handicraft work to the relative "ease" of automatic manufacture: "the non-factory weaver, having everything to execute by muscular exertion, finds the labour irksome, makes in consequence several short pauses, separately of little account, but great when added together; earns therefore proportionally low wages, while he loses his health by poor diet and the dampness of his hovel" (7). Where Marx and others saw the factory as a monstrous and dangerous amalgam of the human body and the machines controlling them, Ure presented a view of workers as the intelligent directors of machinery within comfortable—even leisurely—conditions:

old, young, and middle-aged of both sexes, many of them too feeble to get their daily bread by any of the former modes of industry, ear[n] abundant food, raiment, and domestic accommodation, without perspiring at a single pore, screened meanwhile from the summer's sun and the winter's frost, in apartments more airy and salubrious than those of the metropolis in which our legislative and fashionable aristocracies assemble. In those spacious halls the benignant power of steam summons around him his myriads of willing menials, and assigns to each the regulated task, substituting for painful muscular effort on their part, the energies of his own gigantic arm . . . (17–18)

While it was no doubt true that agricultural work was difficult and strenuous, Ure perhaps overstates the salubriousness of the factory when he claims that industrial labor is punctuated by long stretches of leisurely activity: "though [the child worker] attends two mules, he has still six hours of non-exertion. Spinners sometimes dedicate these intervals to the perusal of books" (310–11).

It is not surprising that Ure treats the topic of factory injuries sparingly in *Philosophy of Manufactures*. What is surprising, though, is that when he does broach the subject, he does so by yoking injury to a failure to follow the rules of automatic labor—which he then quite boldly links to God: "Of the amount of the injury resulting from the violation of the rules of automatic labour [the factory operative] can hardly ever be a proper judge; just as mankind at large can never fully estimate the evils consequent upon an infraction of God's moral law" (1861: 279). Commentary in this Providential vein reveals how surprisingly theological pro-industrialist texts could be. Critics of factory expansion sensed blasphemy in these accounts and often met their Providential rhetoric with even stronger deistic and anthropomorphic invocations of their own. A letter from an 1835 delegate meeting of Preston cotton spinners, for example, appealed to the kind of interventionist power of God's hand in the Old Testament by calling on "the arm of Omnipotence, humbly imploring his power and approbation" on their behalf (Place 2003: 170). Providential body rhetoric was not limited to such contexts, either. The speaker of Elizabeth Barrett Browning's well-known poem "The Cry of the Children," from *Blackwood's Magazine* in 1843, for instance, maintains a prayer that God will reach down during the child factory workers' "hour of harm" and "hold [them] within His right hand which is strong" (ll 114, 120).

Representations of factory work such as Ure's had long been contested within established journals. In the previously cited article on "The Factory System" in the April 1833 installment of *Blackwood's*, John Wilson proclaimed the guilt which England was contracting in the kindling eye of Heaven, when nothing but exultations were heard about the perfection of her machinery, the want of her manufactures, and the rapid increase of her wealth and prosperity! (420)

Similar religious objections to the factory system eventually spilled over from journalism to fiction, where they provided the impetus for England's earliest industrial novels. Thus the industrial novel began as a genre that bluntly extended the continuities between nonfictional social discourse and fictional subjects that dramatized the various positions and counter positions of the "Machinery Question."

Charlotte Elizabeth Tonna's *Helen Fleetwood* (1839–40) is probably the best example of fiction responding directly to pro-industrialist positions on the factory system. Tonna's novel is by no means a work of high artistic merit but its uniqueness lies in its employment of official reports and inquiries as the factual basis of its narrative. As Ivanka Kovačević and S. Barbara Kanner have noted, Tonna was the first author to translate the recorded testimony of witnesses in official documents like the Saddler Committee Report, *Hansard's Parliamentary Debates*, reformist pamphlets, and even contemporary police reports into dialogue for her novel (1970: 164). *Helen Fleetwood*, first serialized in *The Christian Lady's Magazine*, is unabashedly propagandist in its dependence on government reports and ultra-Evangelical in its outward religiosity, but it remains one of the very few works of fiction to describe the actual conditions of the *inside* of factories from the perspective of the factory operatives themselves.[6] Tonna designed her fictional work to operate with the swiftness of nonfictional forms of anti-industrialist discourse but with a different target audience in mind. She wanted to expose the grim official reports to a middle-class audience of wives and mothers (who were not likely to have read them otherwise) so that they could in turn influence their voting husbands, fathers, and sons (Kovačević and Kanner 1970: 156).

Helen Fleetwood tells the story of a family coerced by industrial recruiters into moving from the agricultural English coast to the city of "M.," a thinly disguised Manchester, in order to pursue a better life in the textile mills. The family's situation in their agricultural town is far from ideal. The concentration of land ownership to fewer families meant that landless laborers were forced out of tenancies by rising rents in the first decades of the century. This is exactly what is happening to the Green family at the start of the novel, and so a move to the city initially seems logical. True to the government statistics and Blue Book reports, though, the family members who acquire work in the factory in the city of M. appear in constant danger of losing their limbs to machinery accidents. A veteran factory operative admits that "the worst thing are the accidents," warning the newly arrived ("Green") family of the physical perilousness of the factory system: "You must step back, and run forward, and duck, and turn, and move as [the machines] do, or off goes a finger or an arm" (1841: 78–79). One of Tonna's main characters, a young girl named Sarah who is missing a hand from a factory accident, is a living representation of this danger from the moment the Greens arrive in the city. Sarah's crippled presence throughout the text—she often interrupts the narrative to ask others to write letters for her, for instance—serves as a constant reminder of the gruesome physical realities involved in factory labor. This reminder becomes reinforced as the reader meets other similarly maimed children and working adults who bear "the marks of bodily injuries" from their time in the factories—a fact that connects them to earlier nonfiction factory narratives (75, 291).

It is remarkable how well *Helen Fleetwood's* themes and rhetoric align with the "divinely manual" focus that we've been tracing from the 1818 edition of *Frankenstein* through Bell's 1833 Bridgewater Treatise. To put the same point less abstractedly, *Helen Fleetwood* is not only a novel about the maiming of human hands by factory machinery, but one that deliberately sets up this context in relation to blunt anthropomorphic references to a Judeo-Christian God figure. Regularly, for example, in this novel where workers lose their appendages to machinery, Tonna's characters reference "the unseen arm of Omnipotence" (1841: 203), "the hands of Him who is Father to the fatherless" (39), "the hand [of Christ]" who holds even "the weakest lamb" (366), "the arm of the Lord Jesus" (358), "the higher hand" that "over-rul[es] all for good" (26), "He who orders all things . . . at his hand" (23), and on and on. The elaborate two-sentence paragraph with which the narrative opens could hardly be more representative in this regard:

Who that has seen the sun's uprising, when his first bright gleam comes sparkling over the billows on a clear autumnal morning, but has felt a thrill of gladness at his heart—an involuntary, perhaps an unconscious ascription of praise to the Creator, who has so framed him that all his innate perverseness cannot bar the entrance of that thrill? The brisk wind that curls the wave, and flings its light spray abroad, does but multiply mirrors for the imaged ray to flash from; and when the mighty orb has wholly lifted his disk above the swelling outline of the beauti-fully-rounded horizon, and looks down upon the surmounted barrier, sending beam after beam to traverse that watery world, and to gild it with dazzling splendor, who does not accord *the palm of natural magnifi-cence* to that of which no adequate idea can be conveyed to one who has not looked upon it—sunrise at sea? (1, emphasis added)

Tonna establishes an important structural theme by beginning her novel in this way. As Raymond Williams has noted, "the pull of the idea of the country is toward old ways, human ways, natural ways"—and to this list in *Helen Fleetwood*'s case, we may add "Godly" ways (1973: 297). Tonna inaugurates the Creator as the entity that actively "frame[s]" the country-side with a "palm of natural magnificence." This device does double duty for Tonna; it frames not only the opening paragraph, but also the rural agricul-tural coast as beautiful and providential in contrast to the city of M., which is predictably unappealing and devoid of God. She highlights these frames throughout the narrative by combining what Janis McLarren Caldwell calls the "two-text epistemology" of Nature and Scripture in a single character who moves openly and often between the Green family's old pastoral life and its new industrial one (2004: 2). Richard, the seventeen-year-old fam-ily member, stays behind and vows to depend on the strength of his "two hands," but he makes several crucial visits to M. which allow Tonna to jux-tapose an agrarian—and therefore providentially "Natural"—lifestyle with an industrial one wherein "a great many people ... shun and even revile religion" (1841: 156).

Catherine Gallagher first pointed out how this country/city divide becomes deeply problematic for staunch Evangelical authors. Tonna and other religious reformers were torn between the contradictory components of their own propaganda; they wanted both to assert their belief in human free will and a benign Providence, and to illustrate the helplessness of indi-viduals caught in the industrial system. "The moral consequences of indus-trialism aroused Charlotte Elizabeth Tonna's religious indignation against the factory system," Gallagher notes, "but they also made it impossible for her to fit the industrial world into a providential scheme" (1985: 45). Quite obviously, having a benevolent, designing, and all-seeing God who allows the disorientation and maiming of the factory operatives is a significant theo-logical and narratological problem for Tonna.[7] Susan Zlotnick builds on

Gallagher's insights by contending that Tonna accommodates the determining environment of M. with her Evangelical faith in free will and a benign providential order "by establishing M. as a separate, antiprovidential zone" in the novel (1998: 140).

In terms of the argument I have been making, it is even more salient that Tonna portrays this "antiprovidential zone" of the factory as completely man made and, therefore, subject to all manner of antireligious accusation. For instance, the factory in *Helen Fleetwood* is figured as a "blasphemous" place where "deliberate scoffing at God's name and word, infidel jests, [and] atheistical arguments" prevail for both factory owner and worker alike (1841: 347). Tonna's phrasing heralds the split between divine and human manufacture far more explicitly than any of Shelley's 1831 alterations and additions, though. In *Helen Fleetwood*, the entire factory system is resolutely "none of God's making"—from those who constructed it in the accumulation of their wealth "by this [new] species of labor" to those fallen workers who "constantly tr[y] to prove [the Bible] the vilest book ever written" (355, 204, 349). Tonna at times emphasizes the factory's bald irreligiousness with more nuance. In one of these instances of relative subtlety, the extreme physical disorientation new factory workers experience highlights the inversion of a "natural" religious hierarchy:

> Move, move, move, everything moves. The wheels and frames are always going, and the little reels turn round as fast as they ever can; and the pulleys and chains, and great iron-works over-head, are all moving; and the cotton moves so fast that it is hard to piece it quick enough; and there is a great dust, and such a noise of whirr, whirr, whirr, that at first I did not know whether I was not standing on my head (96)

Here, Tonna presents the worker's world as figuratively, but also religiously, turned upside down. The traditional notion of a God situated above watching "blessed country labor" (as in the novel's opening paragraph) becomes supplanted by an iron machine that hangs "over-head" (1841: 75). The "cheerless ... noisy monotony" of factory life represents the "unkindliness of an atmosphere such as God never made" (323).[8] This example is quite clearly a literary volley in the wider cultural debate over which side God takes in the "Machinery Question." It is also important to recognize this debate as an extension of the question in *Frankenstein*, where the limits of human manufacture intersected with divine "Creation."

What constitutes this mechanized atmosphere as one (in Tonna's mind) that "God never made" is not only its spatial orientation with the machine operating overhead of the operative, though. As we have seen throughout the first two chapters, the metaphorical absence of God's hand figured by the literal absence of a human hand also connotes a feeling of deep ontological disorientation for a culture that—from time out of mind—had viewed its hands as essential markers of human identity. We see this from a slightly more secularized position only a few years after *Helen Fleetwood* in a scene from Benjamin Disraeli's *Coningsby* (1844), when the eponymous character enters the factory for the first time and says: "it is the machinery without any interposition of manual power that overwhelms me. It haunts my dreams" (1948: 150). The fact that the lack of manual power in automatic manufacture induces Coningsby's "haunted" dreams recalls Shelley's inverted nightmare scenario where Victor Frankenstein's "odious handywork" mocks "the stupendous mechanism of the Creator of the world" (1831: 9). Not surprisingly, *Helen Fleetwood* ends with Richard working "like a man, not like a wheel and pulley" in a rural country scene (1841: 319). This conflict between the divine made and the man made has, by 1840, moved far beyond the scientific-theological debates that preoccupied *Frankenstein*. But, as we saw with *Frankenstein*, Bell's Bridgewater Treatise, and manufacturing philosophies of every stripe, the human hand emerged in the first part of the nineteenth century as a site of heightened significance for a society living through unprecedented scientific and industrial change.

THE MANUAL PREOCCUPATIONS OF CANONICAL FACTORY FICTION

Though my focus in Part 1 has been on tracing the hand's place in the British cultural imagination from the beginning of the century to one of the first "industrial" novels, it is important to consider the reverberations of this new hand-consciousness in later, more canonical industrial fiction. We can identify a distinctly manual consciousness both within later fiction itself and in the cultural contexts in which these novels exist. No one would characterize Dickens's *David Copperfield* (1849–50) as an industrial novel, for instance, but my sense is that we can glean something precursory of Dickens's later, more explicit positioning against unbridled factory expansion from his first semiautobiographical novel. Dickens, both in his life and in his novels, subscribed wholeheartedly to the Victorian cult of work.[9] David Copperfield repeatedly figures his path to economic self-sufficiency as a clerk, as a parliamentary reporter, and as an author with metaphors of difficult manual labor. "What I had to do," the young Copperfield remarks, "was, to take my woodman's axe in my hand, and clear my own way through the forest of difficulty, by cutting down trees" (1981: 505). This sentimentalized language was not merely a nostalgic flourish for Dickens. The title of his Guild of Literature and Art, as well as his manner of addressing other authors ("my fellow labourers"), reveals an earnest desire to align himself with strenuous labor even as he became a successful author.[10] As we have seen, among the most toilsome and perilous labor at midcentury was factory work. This was not lost on Dickens; he wrote (and lobbied) perseveringly in the late 1840s and 1850s for stricter regulations on the fencing of dangerous factory equipment.

Dickens also owned a copy of Bell's Bridgewater Treatise, which suggests a wider familiarity with the evolutionary, industrial, and religious importance of the hand (*Catalogue* 1935). In fact, his familiarity with Bell's work was so entrenched from a cultural perspective that we find him using distinctly Bridgewateresque rhetoric in an 1844 speech to Birmingham's Polytechnic Institution:

> [I]t surely cannot be allowed that those who labour day by day, surrounded by machinery, shall be permitted to degenerate into machines themselves; but, on the contrary, they should be able to assert their common origin in that Creator from whose wondrous hands they came, and unto whom, responsible and thinking men, they will return. (1960: 61)

If, as I have claimed, Dickens wanted to stress his identification and solidarity with laborers who toiled in this way, we should be able to find evidence of it even in his "unindustrial" fiction. And we do. Consider David Copperfield's description of his rise to professional authorship:

> I wrote a little something, in secret, and sent it to a magazine, and it was published in the magazine. Since then, I have taken heart to write a good many trifling pieces. Now, I am regularly paid for them. Altogether, I am well off; when I tell you my income on the fingers of my left hand, I pass the third finger and take the fourth to the middle joint. (1981: 610)

Here we have a good example of the critical tendency to overlook the embodied hand in the middle of the nineteenth century. Despite what we know of Dickens's personal (and, as we shall see shortly, public) advocacy for machine fencing laws, his general association with manual labor, and his particular identification with industrial metaphors in *David Copperfield* ("keeping all his irons in the fire"), critics nonetheless interpret this passage in solely monetary terms.[11] There is no doubt that Dickens is talking about money in this instance. However, he is framing the money not only in terms of time, but also in terms of a kind of manual labor that has become perilous for so many factory workers. The image of David's truncated fourth finger necessarily (and literally) interpolates the professional author in historically specific debates about the mechanized industry, the changing nature of what it means to "manufacture" work, and, as we'll see in chapter 7, how these questions apply more specifically to the rapid industrial expansion of print technology.

The association I'm making between David's four-and-a-half-fingered hand and Dickens's sympathetic view of the perils of factory work comes into sharper focus if we move ahead a few years to the publication of his unquestionably industrial novel, *Hard Times* (1854). In a chapter of *The Body Economic* entitled "*Hard Times* and the Somaeconomics of the Early Victorians," Catherine Gallagher brilliantly argues that Dickens's repetitive phrases and grammatical constructions in *Hard Times* enact the very monotony of industrial labor he criticizes (2008: 63). She then connects this "mime[d] ... monotony" to the "severe workfulness" that Dickens was experiencing as he labored to write the novel week by week (63, 80). "I am in a dreary state planning and planning the story of Hard Times," Dickens writes in April 1854 (qtd. in Gallagher 2008: 81). He "is 'crushed' at the very outset of the writing (February 1854), 'stunned with the work' as it continues (July 14, 1854), and 'used up' (July 17, 1854) by the end" (80). The picture Gallagher paints of the "pointless efficacy of the narrative, the repetitiveness of the allegories," and "the monotony of motivation" (80) is enough to make us take seriously what *Punch* satirized in an 1847 illustration of the author in the age of industrialization (fig. 7).

This uncannily fits Dickens's description of David's truncated "fourth finger," since the illustration depicts the author's (screened) left hand as the closest one in proximity to the industrial gearing that could catch and mangle it. The illustration also captures Gallagher's sense of the laborious monotony Dickens experienced writing *Hard Times* so effectively that it

Fig. 7. "The New Patent Novel Writer." *Punch* 7 (1847): 268.

should be placed in conjunction with the *only* (prose) view into the factory that this most iconic of industrial novels provides its reader:

> Stephen bent over his loom, quiet, watchful, and steady. A special contrast, as every man was in the forest of looms where Stephen worked, to the crashing, smashing, tearing piece of mechanism at which he labored. Never fear, good people of an anxious turn of mind, that Art will consign Nature to oblivion. Set anywhere, side by side, the work of God and the work of man; and the former, even though it be a troop of Hands of very small account, will gain from the comparison. (2001: 71)[12]

This anxiety—of whether the work of God (and by extension, "Nature") would always trump the work of man—is precisely what fueled the vitalist debates at the turn of the century, the composition and recomposition of *Frankenstein* in 1818 and 1831, the new philosophies of economic expansion, the Bridgewater Treatises, and the earliest industrial fiction. And still, even in 1854, the literal hands of the "Hands" remain on the center of the nine-teenth-century stage despite our largely metaphoric and metonymic recognitions of them.

Dickens famously mixed news making and novel writing as the editor of his weekly *Household Words*—the original home of his serialized *Hard Times* (1854). It was in this venue that he more expressly waded into the contemporary debate over the enforcement of fencing laws. According to Sally Ledger, Dickens was incensed by factory owners' resistance to 1850s legislation which proposed larger fines for unfenced machinery (2010: 212).[13] One article from *Household Words* which reflects Dickens's stance on this issue is entitled "Ground in the Mill" from the April 22, 1854, installment. The piece, written by Henry Morely, could not be more specific in its enumeration of the damage sustained by industrial operatives; Morely calculates that "one thousand two hundred and eighty-seven (or, in bulk, how many bushels of) fingers were lost by factory workers since the 1844 Factory Act had supposedly held mill owners accountable for fencing their machinery" (225). While there are officially no fingers lost in *Hard Times*, Dickens's composition of a very telling episode alluding to the maiming of Rachel's sister's hand made it all the way through the manuscript and into the corrected proofs before it was deleted. Fred Kaplan and Sylvère Monod maintain that Dickens deleted the passage because he seemingly changed his mind about how prominently he wanted to treat the topic of industrial accidents (Dickens 2001: 253).

Since we can do no more than speculate on the reasons Dickens might have had for deleting the material related to the maiming of Rachel's sister's hand, it is ultimately unproductive to attempt to interpret what does not exist. However, this deletion helps explain one of the more puzzling occurrences that *does* exist in the May 6 (No. 215) 1854 installment of *Household Words*—the section of *Hard Times* that appeared only two weeks after Morely's piece about the 1,287 fingers lost to unfenced machinery. A "strange old woman" stops Stephen in the street in the moments before he enters the factory, shakes his hand, and then awkwardly insists on kissing it (2001: 80). She asks how long Stephen has worked in the factory. Twelve years, Stephen responds. Upon hearing this, the woman makes a very unusual request for a stranger in the nineteenth century:

"I must kiss the hand," said she, "that has worked in this fine factory for a dozen year!" And she lifted it, though he would have prevented her, and put [the hand] to her lips. What harmony, besides her age and her simplicity, surrounded her, he did not know, but even in this fantastic action there was something neither out of time nor place: a something which it seemed as if nobody else could have made as serious, or done with such a natural and touching air. (81)

We later learn that the old woman is Bounderby's long lost mother. Her "fantastic action" clearly registers her relief—or, more probably, her disbelief—that a hand could remain intact and undamaged after so many years of working around dangerous machinery in the cotton factory. After what we have seen, this is what is "neither out of time nor place" in 1854. Indeed, there is something fantastic about the fleeting reversal of alienation in having the mother of Josiah Bounderby, quite possibly English fiction's biggest human reductionist, praise the actual flesh-and-blood hand of a "Hand." Bounderby's mother's gesture literalizes the most popular synecdoche for labor and, in doing so, for a moment, she helps make visible the long story of evolutionary, religious, and industrial anxiety that patterns the nineteenth-century hand.

PART II

Manufacturing and Manipulating the Separate Spheres of Gender

CHAPTER 3

Luddism, Needlework, and the Seams of Domesticity in Charlotte Brontë's Shirley

Part II of *Changing Hands* begins by shifting the focus from the religious and physically perilous outgrowths of nineteenth-century manufacture to its historical and economic subsoil. My goal in making this seemingly anachronistic shift is to treat the effects of industrialization in the order in which the nineteenth century experienced them. Obviously, this is no facile task of causation; rather one of nuanced historical correlation. Chapters 1 and 2 revealed just how imbricated questions about handmade and mechanized manufacture were with debates within the interrelated fields of natural history and religion. The chapters in Part II will confront the more secular, social implications of England's exponentially increased use of mechanized production in the 1840s—specifically regarding the separation of gendered spheres. While chapter 4 (on *Vanity Fair*) will analyze this separation from the perspective of the Victorian drawing room, this chapter does so by investigating the time when mechanization and gender were mixed and poured into the concrete that would rigidly set the "separate spheres" of midcentury economic life.

I am aware of the incongruencies of my own metaphorical rhetoric, here. But I use it because it fits the history that unfolds in Charlotte Brontë's *Shirley* (1849, edited by Andrew Hook and Judith Hook, 1985). My invocation of concrete is not unlike what Brontë promises the reader in the second paragraph of the novel: "Something real, cool, and solid lies before you" (39). The story of how Caroline Helstone and Shirley Keeldar move from promising representatives of female autonomy to stultified and homebound wives is indeed "something as unromantic as Monday morning" (39). My point is that *Shirley* is a historical novel precisely because it accurately recounts how this happens in the lived experience of the middle class. To analyze the ineluctability of this fictionalized occurrence is not only to uncover the pre-history of Victorian gender separation; it is, as I go on to suggest, to change the terms by which we understand such separateness.

SURFACE READING *SHIRLEY*'S CONTEXT

It will be helpful to shift now from metaphors of construction to those of cuisine, since Brontë figures food prominently at the outset of *Shirley*. Following the far more commercially successful *Jane Eyre* (1847), Brontë knew her second novel would be unpalatable. After all, this is exactly how the narrator characterizes the book on the first page: "it shall be cold lentils and vinegar without oil; it shall be unleavened bread with bitter herbs, and no roast lamb" (39). The point is that Brontë privileged historical accuracy over fictional entertainment in *Shirley*. We can ascertain this clearly from a letter she wrote to her publishers in response to the novel's tepid critical reception: "You . . . dwell too much on what you regard as the *artistic* treatment of the subject—. Say what you will—gentlemen—say it as ably as you will—Truth is better than Art . . . Ignorant as I am, I dare to hold and maintain that doctrine" ('To W. S. Williams,' 1995: 185). Patrick Brantlinger has noted how the "tough-minded" Brontë recognized the "causal relationship between automation and unemployment" from an economist's perspective (1979: 125). For Brontë, the "Truth" about the utterly separated spheres of middle-class life at midcentury is a gendered consequence of the mechanization of England's industry.

This is why she was so adamant about maintaining historical accuracy in *Shirley*. Brontë pored over the files of the *Leeds Mercury* from the years 1811 through 1814 because she wanted to get her story as factually representative as possible. Her insistence on historical accuracy makes *Shirley* a prime candidate for "surface reading"—an interpretational strategy which seeks to draw meaning from what is visible on the text's surface rather than from what is buried below in symptomatic (suspicious) interpretations.[1] A surface-level inquiry into the modes of *Shirley*'s manufacture reveals an inverted network from the mill to the parlor; that is, the redundancy of human hands caused by mechanization in the mill is concurrent with a surplus of female handiwork in the novel's middle-class homes. This chapter will eventually show how this inverted relationship becomes the most important literal, thematic, and structural dynamic in Brontë's construction of the prehistory of separate Victorian spheres.

For almost fifty years now, criticism of *Shirley* has been preoccupied by subsurfaces. It has hinged on tropes of displacement of one kind or another that supposedly operate as stand-ins for what appears on the surface of the text. The dominant critical reflex has been to interpret the novel's explicit Luddism as implicitly concerned with more contemporary (1849) issues ranging from trade unionism to Chartism, "hungry forties" food shortages to cholera.[2] I would like to propose a different tack, though—one that takes the text at its word, which is to say in this case, at its time. The precise positioning of the novel's setting in 1811–12 matters, and it matters not only because Brontë herself thought of it as an "industrial" novel.[3] Indeed, the longstanding question about how to categorize *Shirley* bears quite heavily on my argument. The majority of critics, since they subscribe in one way or another to interpretations of displacement, have traditionally debated whether the text is a "political novel," a "woman question novel," or a satiric "etiquette novel."[4] This chapter makes a more surface, rehistoricized, and physiologically embodied claim about how Brontë's treatment of new practices of industrial manufacturing connect—via the hand—two of the novel's most disparate constituencies: hardened Luddite machine-breakers and disposed middle-class women.[5]

The inverse relationship in the text between the deficit of male handwork and the surfeit of female handiwork (knitting, crocheting, embroidering, etc.) makes perfect sense if we approach the novel from within its original historical context. Brontë's backdating of *Shirley's* setting to 1811–12 situates the novel's action at the interesting cultural moment when manufacture began to accrue paradoxically opposing meanings.[6] Looking back at the first mechanized power-looms, Andrew Ure noted how the word "manufacture" could, for the first time in history, "signify the reverse of its intrinsic meaning ... denot[ing] every extensive product of art, which is made by machinery, with little or no aid of the human hand" (1861: 1). Brontë's constant oscillation between the intrinsic (handmade) and the new denotative (machine-made) meanings of "manufacture" ensures that the novel never drifts too far from the industrial—even, and especially, in its relentless focus on the tedium and monotony of middle-class domestic handicraft.

Thus where the majority of critics see in *Shirley's* structure the "virtual abandonment of the industrial issue" (Bodenheimer 1988: 42), I see its constant emphasis in the fluctuation back and forth from the mechanized to the domestic. The rapid development and incorporation of teazeling machines and mechanical shears, the type of machinery en route to Robert Moore's

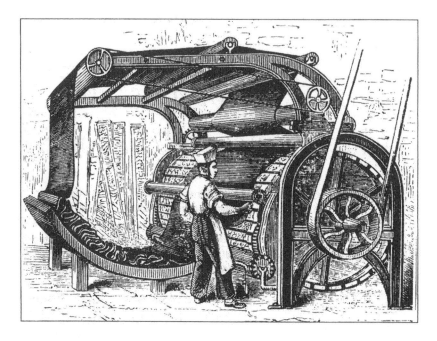

Fig. 8. A gig-mill, from *The Luddite Rebellion* by Brian Bailey (New York: New York University Press, 1998): 34. Reprinted with permission from the History Press.

mill at the outset of the novel (fig. 8), fostered a revolution not only in working methods, but also a complete disruption of a way of life for the hand croppers who had been the highest paid of all woolen workers for centuries (Bailey 1998: 26).[7] By eliminating the labor required to raise the nap of the wool by hand with the spiky bracts of the teasel plant (fig. 9) and to crop it with manual shears (fig. 10), the process of finishing whole cloth was reduced from over a week to less than a single day.

Shirley records this development from both the macro and micro perspectives. Brontë informs the reader from a distant historical position that "certain inventions in machinery were introduced into the staple manufactures of the north, which, greatly reducing the number of hands necessary to be employed, threw thousands out of work, and left them without means of sustaining life" (62). She also shows the effect of these new production methods at a more personal level in the forced unemployment of male workers like Joe Scott and William Farren, both of whom plead with Robert Moore on different occasions to implement his labor-saving machinery

Fig. 9. The head of the teasel plant, *Dipsacus fullonem*, from *The Luddite Rebellion* by Brian Bailey (New York: New York University Press, 1998): 26.

Fig. 10. Hand cropping shears, from *The Luddite Rebellion* by Brian Bailey (New York: New York University Press, 1998): 27.

"more slowly" (157, 178). Later on in this chapter, we will see how Robert Moore's responses regarding the inevitability of mechanical invention match Brontë's rhetoric regarding the ineluctability of the widening chasm between the middle class's separate spheres. For now, though, let us treat one aspect of mechanization at a time.

The relationship that the novel establishes between the loss of manual labor among working men and the surge in handiwork among middle-class women occurs also in the wider cultural discourse of the period. While pro-industrialists like Ure were promoting self-acting machines that manufactured with "mechanical fingers and arms" (1861: 15), middle-class magazines such as Jane Louden's *Ladies' Companion* were celebrating the fact that "never were fingers more actively engaged [in handicraft] than those of the rising female generation" ("The Work Basket" 1849). Scholars of Victorian materialist practices have sought to account for this somewhat odd phenomenon by considering the ways in which handicrafts provided domestic compensation for the loss of manual authenticity in the industrial realm. In *The Victorian Parlour*, for example, Thad Logan notes that "there seems to have been a compensatory emphasis on the amateur practices of ornamental sewing and handcrafts" as industrial capitalism began to dominate production (2001: 164). Talia Schaffer has more recently gone a bit further, claiming that "the craft paradigm" represents "an ideal solution" (2011: 4), "a creative outlet that allowed middle-class women to articulate their relation to the industrial economy in a satisfyingly complex way" (5–6). Such craftwork, by these lights, allowed middle-class women to feel that they were participating in the "exciting work of industrial modernity" (120).

This reasoning certainly suffices for the overwhelming majority of Victorian prose related to domestic craftwork. But it fails to explain why Charlotte Brontë treats handicrafts so differently. In all but the very last chapters of *Shirley*, needlework appears as a bitter, dispiriting, and profoundly depressing activity; one that is representative of a more generalized feminine futility because it so often occurs alongside the stimulating middle-class male enterprise of industrial manufacture. The historians Leonore Davidoff and Catherine Hall call needlework "one of the great silences about [middle-class] women's lives" in the nineteenth century (1987: 387).[8] With *Shirley*, Brontë gives voice to this silence from a historically accurate perspective.

Figuring out why needlework is treated so anomalously in *Shirley* requires us to focus more narrowly and more literally on the historical model that Brontë chooses to employ for her novel. The Luddite rebellions mark the first and most distinct of many radical changes to England's process of industrialization and, as such, they also mark an early stage of what would become, by the time Brontë composed the novel in 1848–49, the rigid and entrenched gendered spheres of middle-class life in Britain. Considered from this vantage point, *Shirley* chronicles the pivotal ways in which new modes of production influenced new modes of relation within the middle-class household.

THE "NEW," DOMESTIC MIDDLE-CLASS WOMAN

One could argue that Thomas Malthus's *Essay on the Principle of Population* (1798) was one of the earliest "scientific" articulations of separate-sphere ideology because it emphasized woman's biological rather than her economic functions. However, as Davidoff and Hall have shown, women's contributions to the mostly agrarian economic system in England were historically robust, to say the least, despite their biology. One of Davidoff and Hall's prime examples of the labor-intensive female contribution to agrarian family life for hundreds of years before the nineteenth century comes in their discussion of cheese making. According to their study, the difficult task of cheese making, "which had taken place on almost every farm" before 1800, was made possible only because "the farmer's wife used her own labour augmented by her daughters, nieces, sisters or living-in dairymaids" (1987: 273). By 1843, however, the Royal Commission on Women and Children in Agriculture made an investigation which led to a pronouncement that "the patience, skill and strength needed to produce cheese made this work unsuitable for women" (274). It is no coincidence that the Royal Commission's finding that cheese making was no longer an acceptable female endeavor followed closely on the heels of parliamentary investigations (of the kind we saw in chapter 2) wherein factory work was exposed as a distinctively lower-class female occupation.[9]

I hesitate to spend too much time discussing midcentury events only because Brontë's point, I think, in backdating *Shirley* to 1811–12 is to provide a historical, social, and economic genealogy by which to explain how the gendered spheres became so rigidly separated later on. The events of her novel demonstrate how middle-class women became economically and spatially separated from the site of work for the first time in history. As we have seen in the dominant agricultural realm, previous views of labor tended to stress an inclusive attitude toward the many working tasks which needed to be completed on a daily basis. This seventeenth- and eighteenth-century conception of work made women as well as men important to the nation's economic industriousness. The relatively sudden implementation of machine technology in the first decade of the nineteenth century (especially in Yorkshire's woolen mills) and the attendant movement of work from weavers' cottages to larger-scale factory settings began to solidify the definition of labor as off-limits to middle-class women (Bythell 1969; Hudson 1986; Berg 1994).

One way to gauge the "newness" of the altered position of women in this changed economy is to consider the rise to prominence of that "best-known ideologue of domesticity," Mrs. Sarah Stickney Ellis (Davidoff and Hall 1987: 182). Ellis's first tract, *The Women of England*, starkly delineates a separation of the man's world ("in the mart, the exchange, or the public assembly") from the woman's ("the fireside comforts" of "the home," 1839: 46–47). Ellis also makes it clear that her delineation of gendered spaces is meant specifically for the rapidly expanding middle class in England: as Ellis put it, for "those who are restricted to the services of from one to four domestics" (21). The number of new editions of this work and Ellis's other more specifically targeted ones (*The Wives of England*, *The Mothers of England*, *The Daughters of England*) testify not only to the middle class's growth, but also to the desire among at least some of its female constituents for a clear articulation of their new position in society. In the opening chapter of *The Daughters of England*, Ellis remarks that "the sphere upon which a young woman enters ... is so entirely new ... that ... we cannot doubt that she will make these, or similar questions, the subject of serious inquiry—'What is my position in society?'" (1842: 9–10). This question, inflected by its severely limited answer, is in effect the one Caroline Helstone asks herself midway through *Shirley*: "As far as I know, I have good health: half a century of existence may lie before me. How am I to occupy it? What am I to do to fill the interval of time which spreads between me and the grave?" (190). Ellis flattens the seriousness of these questions by providing a blanket response: "the first thing of importance [as women] is to be content to be inferior to men—inferior in mental power, in the same proportion that you are inferior in bodily strength" (1842: 11). Even amidst such a stark delineation between genders along these lines, we would do well to recall the work of Karen Chase and Michael Levenson which urges us "to remember that neither [Ellis's] orthodoxy nor her reputation dropped out of the sky" (2000: 67). The very fact that the emerging middle class needed a "monitress" to advocate so publicly (and so often) for the domestic positioning of their women suggests a break or at least a significant divergence from the gendered arrangements that had existed previously.

Brontë wastes no time in *Shirley* dramatizing the definitiveness and antagonism that separate these newly gendered spheres of life in Yorkshire. The opening pages include a dinner at the Gale household, where the local curates and parsons meet to air their usual "clerical quarrels" (44), but also to discuss the delivery of mechanized shearing frames to Robert Moore's mill (44–47). The scene culminates with the clergymen gathering their pistols to meet at Hollow's End Mill in case the machines are met with any trouble. During the dinner there is a particularly hostile interaction between Mr. Malone, the curate of Briarfield, and Mrs. Gale, the middle-class wife who hosts the dinner. Mr. Malone's arrogant and urgent request for more bread prompts the following exchange:

> Mrs. Gale offered the loaf.
> "Cut it, woman," said her guest; and the "woman" cut it accordingly. Had she followed her inclinations, she would have cut the parson also; her Yorkshire soul revolted absolutely from his manner of command. (42)[10]

I agree with Igor Webb that the quotation marks around "woman" indicate that Brontë intends to draw our attention to the falsity of the distinctions Malone makes between the sexes (1981: 143). More specifically, Brontë's alignment of the clergy with Moore's machinery and Mrs. Gale's Yorkshire inclination to "revolt" underscores the relative newness of the distinction between male and female roles in this burgeoning industrial society. We see throughout the text this pattern of distinguishing between the gendered spheres, whether in Reverend Helstone's command for Caroline to "stick to the needle—learn shirt making and gown-making, and pie-crust baking" or Robert Moore's condescending comparison of his injuries to the way Caroline "might scratch [her] finger with a needle in sewing" (122, 350).[11]

As these scenarios indicate, middle-class women like Caroline Helstone increasingly were expected to remain at a literal and symbolic distance from the new world of mechanized production. Doing so, in fact, became the most precise marker of their new middle-class identity. Brontë brilliantly reinforces this point by arranging to have Caroline's first needlework session occur during the same afternoon that Moore's second shipment of labor-saving machinery is delivered to the mill:

The afternoon was devoted to sewing. [Hortense], like most Belgian
ladies, was specially skillful with her needle. She by no means thought it
a waste of time to devote unnumbered hours to fine embroidery, sight-
destroying lacework, marvelous netting and knitting, and, above all, to
the most elaborate stocking-mending. She would give a day to the mend-
ing of two holes in a stocking at any time . . . It was another of Caroline's
troubles to be condemned to learn this foreign style of darning, which
was done stitch by stitch so exactly to imitate the fabric of the stocking
itself . . . All afternoon the two ladies sat and sewed, till the eyes and fingers, and even the spirits of one of them were weary. (107–8)

Brontë follows up this tiresome description of handiwork with a seemingly
innocuous scene in which the family gathers around the hearth to read
Coriolanus. Putting aside for the moment the connection between Robert's
treatment of his mill workers and Coriolanus's treatment of his countrymen,
it is important to note that Hortense uses this moment to continue Caroline's education in the middle-class ideology of separate spheres. "When the
gentleman of a family reads," Hortense declares matter-of-factly, "the ladies
should always sew" (115). This is a particularly striking declaration because of
the way it atomizes the separation of public and private spheres even *within*
the home: the male publicly handles (again, metaphorically and literally) the
object of relevance, while the female busies her hands with work that has
value—if any at all—only within the home.[12] The fact that Hortense falls
asleep while knitting in this scene highlights needlework as merely a way
to pass time and foreshadows its monotonous treatment later in the novel.

Once Caroline sews so much and so often that she can do so without
thinking, her hatred of its tediousness quickly overwhelms her. Charitable
sewing for the missionary and Jew baskets is particularly difficult for Caroline because of the work's utter disconnection from the laws of authentic,
real-world trade. She yearns to help out in the mill, even going so far as
to "wish nature had made her a boy instead of a girl, that she might . . . be
[Robert's] clerk, and sit with him in the counting house" (104). Instead, Caroline must settle for making domestic objects that are "quite useless" to the
middle-class men who are obligated to buy them at "four or five hundred
per cent above cost price, for articles quite useless to them" (134). As Talia
Schaffer accurately concedes, the violations of ordinary business practice
that originate in the missionary baskets "confirmed that women were merely
'playing,' in a separate realm not bound by the laws of trade" (2011: 12).

And yet, contrary to what we see for most of *Shirley*, many middle-class women—brought up in the 1830s and 1840s reading Ellis's work and knowing of no alternative models of femininity—deeply embraced needlework. Berlin wool-work (needlepoint-type embroidery) became extremely popular from 1830 onwards, when copper-plate designs no longer had to be imported from Germany. Elizabeth Stone's *The Art of Needle-work* (1841) reported that more than 14,000 different plate designs became available by 1840 (398). New publications such as *The Ladies' Work-Table Book* sprouted up to meet middle-class woman's desire to participate in the activity this book calls the "monitor to the female heart" and her "constant companion throughout the pilgrimage of life" (1843: xiii, xii).[13] The historical contemporaneity of the relationship between woolen needlework and its mechanization is uncanny; Berlin patterns, to be crocheted or embroidered with wool from the Yorkshire region, arrived in England around 1805. This means that a particularly popular form of middle-class female handicraft developed almost in lock-step with development and implementation of mechanized woolen machinery which rendered working-class male hands superfluous.

In Brontë's fictional world, though, Caroline Helstone desperately wants an occupation beyond that which "only keep[s] one's hands employed" (114). She offers her services as a potential apprentice in the cloth trade only to be left at home to sew with Hortense while Moore goes out to visit Sykes's wool warehouse (100). Her uncle's stern prohibition against employing herself as a governess, combined with Moore's professional and romantic spurning, officially inaugurate her into life as a spinster-in-training. The charitable sewing activities that structure the days of Miss Mann and Miss Ainley are almost too bleak for Caroline to imagine. The circumstances that make her an unmarried middle-class woman require her not only to imagine such a life, though, but to start living it. The narrator reports that Caroline "tried to sew—[but] every stitch she put in was an ennui, the occupation was insufferably tedious" (130). Brontë's description of Caroline's sewing as an "occupation" has unfortunately become all too accurate. Where she once dreamed of " 'an occupation . . . a pleasant way of learning a business, and making [her] way in life,'" she faces the prospect of living with "no earthly employment, but household work and sewing; no earthly pleasure, but an unprofitable visiting" (98–99, 377).

Fixating on this kind of futility prompts Caroline to consider older models of female work where women actively participated in the economic well-being of their families. During one of her most tedious sewing sessions

Caroline recognizes the artificiality of the separation between the public and private spheres. Brontë highlights this artificiality by introducing biblical women who enjoy more professional agency than nineteenth-century women. Caroline recounts chapter 31 of Proverbs[14] nearly word for word as she ponders Solomon's "virtuous woman" who participated in both public and private spheres, who "had something more to do than spin and give out portions: she was a manufacturer—she made fine linen and sold it: she was an agriculturalist—she bought estates and planted vineyards. *That* woman was a manager" (378, emphasis original).

In the character of Shirley Keeldar, owner of the land upon which Moore's mill sits, Brontë updates Caroline's model woman from the distant biblical past to the immediate present of 1812. We learn that Shirley "is lax of her needle" and that "she never sews" because she must tend to the daily operations of her estate (372, 373). In the few times that Shirley does sit down to sew, the narrator tells us that "her thimble is scarcely fitted on, her needle scarce threaded" before she is called away to tend to animals "with her own hand" and to decide "whole agricultural matter[s] on the spot" (372, 373).

The circumstances that allow for a character like Shirley in a Victorian novel, however, are as rare as the real-life Emily Brontë upon whom the fictional Shirley was based. Far more likely is the scenario we see play out in each of the other female lives in the text. Caroline somberly evaluates these conditions in part of a longer meditation on the state of middle-class women:

> This stagnant state of things makes them decline in health: they are never well; and their minds and views shrink to wondrous narrowness. The great wish—the sole aim of every one of them is to be married, but the majority will never marry: they will die as they now live. They scheme, they plot, they dress to ensnare husbands ... Fathers ... are angry with their daughters when they observe their manoeuvres: they order them to stay at home. What do they expect them to do at home? If you ask,—they would answer, sew and cook. They expect them to do this, and this only, contentedly, regularly, uncomplainingly all their lives long, as if they had no germs of faculties for anything else. (377)

This tautological meditation on the hopelessness of the middle-class woman's life leads Caroline to hold men responsible for denying nineteenth-century women the occupational opportunities afforded even to biblical characters:

Men of Yorkshire! do your daughters reach this royal standard [of Solomon's "virtuous woman"]? Can they reach it? Can you help them reach it? Can you give them a field in which their faculties may be exercised and grow? Men of England! look at your poor girls, many of them fading around you, dropping off in consumption or decline; or, what is worse, denigrating to sour old maids,—envious, backbiting, wretched, because life is a desert to them; or, what is worst of all, reduced to strive, by scarce modest coquetry and debasing artifice, to gain that position and situation by marriage, which to celibacy is denied. Fathers! cannot you alter these things? (378)

Brontë's repeated appeal to the "Men of Yorkshire," "Men England," and "Fathers [of England]" is a rather transparent salvo directed at Sarah Stickney Ellis's popular trilogy which addressed *The Women of England* (1839), *The Daughters of England* (1842), and *The Wives of England* (1843).

Eventually, Brontë establishes a thematic relationship between the powerlessness of the hand croppers in an unbridled capitalist economy and the powerlessness of middle-class women in a patriarchal hierarchy. It's no coincidence that this relationship depends on the materiality of hands.[15] In an oddly Lamarckian context that we will encounter again in Part III, the supersession of the cropmen's hands by machines parallels Caroline's and Shirley's sicknesses—both of which are registered principally in the diminishment of the size of their hands. The narrator remarks that "it g[ives] pain to see" the "attenuation" of Caroline's "wasted hand" while Henry Sympson claims that Shirley's death is near because of his observation that "her hands are growing quite thin" (403, 471). Brontë even represents romantic tribulation manually in the text. Here is how she describes Caroline's thoughts when Moore rejects her early on: "You held out your hand for an egg, and fate put into it a scorpion. Show no consternation: close your palm. Never mind: in time, after your hand and arm have swelled and quivered long with torture, the squeezed scorpion will die, and you will have learned the great lesson how to endure without a sob" (128). Similarly, when Shirley must decide between marriage to Robert Moore or Samuel Wynne, Louis Moore reemerges with a ring that we are told used to fit Shirley's forefinger. She tries it on again during her sickness only to find "the ring dropped from [her] wasted little hand" (474–75).

Thus the overemployment of wasting middle-class female hands and the underemployment of Luddite hands both reflect a rapidly changing economic reality that only sharpens the lines delineating the separate spheres for each gender. The technological changes that prove so destructive to the Yorkshire croppers allow lower-class women to perform the work previously accomplished by skilled tradesmen. As a result, middle-class women become further defined by their distance from millwork. So great does this distance become even in 1812 that it takes a partial hallucination on Moore's part to even imagine Caroline on the factory floor amidst the "buxom lasses" who toil there (257). Caroline wishes "fifty times a day" for an occupation to "occupy [her] head and hands" but is met with a new social reality that views, as Reverend Helstone does, "everything but sewing and cooking above women's comprehension" (122, 118). There's an ironic historical similarity in the Luddite Moses Barraclough's desire for the time "when hand-labour were encouraged and respected" and Caroline's desire for work beyond that which "only keeps [her] hands busy" (155, 115).

Brontë solidifies this connection between Luddite men and middle-class women by tracing the suffering caused by mechanization in the industrial sphere to a particular form of suffering in the domestic sphere. Smarting from her rejection by Robert Moore and without the recourse to the kind of productive work from which Shirley benefits, Caroline doubles down on her sewing. The text constantly rehearses the repetitiveness of Caroline's efforts to sew her way through the "solitude, the sadness, the nightmare of her life" (381). Her servant, Fanny, notices that Caroline is "always in the same place, always bent industriously over a piece of work" (191). The narrator remarks that "instead [of finding her] in the blooming garden of an English home," she appears "sitting alone in the alcove,—her task of work on her knee, her fingers assiduously plying the needle, her eyes following and regulating their movements, her brain working restlessly" (380). With these images of Caroline—working unceasingly, in physical discomfort, cramped, bent, and kept indoors—Brontë does what so few works of Victorian fiction do; she symbolically and historically aligns middle-class domestic work with lower-class mill workers and seamstresses.[16] Parliamentary inquiries into the employment and treatment of seamstresses gave shocking reports of women suffering from ailments almost identical to those endured by factory workers: consumption, starvation, neuralgia, and back problems associated with long hours and defective sanitary environments (Ledbetter 2012: 19).

The surface alignment with these classes and professions in *Shirley* fits the historical and topical themes more directly than the displacement models discussed at the start of the chapter (Chartism, hunger, cholera, etc.). Historicist critics generally view the emergence of the seamstress as a product of England's industrialization.[17] T. J. Edelstein (1980) has shown how the overnight success of Thomas Hood's "The Song of the Shirt" (1843) and the ubiquity of Richard Redgrave's attendant paintings codified the subject of the needlewoman in the 1840s cultural imagination. *Shirley's* readers would have been familiar with lines from Hood's poem in connection with Redgrave's work, partly because lines of the poem often accompanied the paintings as they were displayed on the walls of the Royal Academy, British Institution, and Society of British Artists: "A little weeping would ease my heart, / But in their briny bed / My tears must stop, for every drop / hinders needle and thread" (2006: 70–74).

As Elaine Freedgood has noted in her historical assessment of lace work, "the upper-class handworker performs a kind and an amount of work that puts her into a startling occupational proximity to laboring-class women" (2003: 636). Brontë makes good on this surprising proximity, describing Caroline's suffering in strikingly working-class rhetoric at moments when Caroline "closet[s]" herself, "silent and solitary," away from the company of the house (189):

> [Caroline] plied her needle continuously, ceaselessly . . . her head labored to frame projects as diligently as her hands to plait and stich the thin texture of the muslin summer dress . . . Now and then, while thus doubly occupied, a tear would fill her eyes and fall on her busy hands; but this sign of emotion . . . was quickly effaced: the sharp pang past, the dimness cleared from her vision; she would re-thread her needle, re-arrange tuck and trimming, and work on. (244)

Here, Caroline's capacity to labor through tears which fall on the work distinctly echoes Hood's poem. So too does the rhetoric describing Caroline's hands, moving "continuously, ceaselessly" to keep pace with the work, recall Ure's encouragement for workers "to identify themselves with the unvarying regularity of the complex automaton" (1861: 14–15). This is exactly how many middle-class females in *Shirley* view themselves. In the Yorke household, for instance, Jessie Yorke claims that her older sister Rose is an "aut— aut—[automaton] I have forgotten the name, but it means machine in the shape of a human being" (383).

THE GRIP OF THE INEVITABLE

Perhaps the notion of a deeply entrenched historical inevitability is the strongest surface-level connection between male handloom laborers and middle-class handicrafts women in *Shirley*. Robert Moore appeals to the inevitable "progress" of the capitalist enterprise and scientific invention in the rare instances where he engages in dialogue with the Luddite Barraclough: "'What then? Suppose that building was a ruin and I was a corpse, what then?—you lads behind [the machine breaking], would that stop invention or exhaust science?—Not for the fraction of a second of time! Another and better gig-mill would rise on the ruins of this, and perhaps a more enterprising owner come in my place.'" (156). As we have seen, Brontë also registers this sense of inevitability in the words of hand laborers like Joe Scott who plead for more graduated change in methods of production: "'Will n't ye gie us a bit o' time?—Will n't ye consent to mak' your changes rather more slowly?'" (157). Martha Vicinus was one of the first to locate this kind of resignation among the weavers in street ballads and broadsides of the period. In one particular ballad, starkly titled "Hand-Loom v. Power-Loom," Vicinus identifies "capitulation to the inevitable" (1974: 45):

> Come all you cotton-weavers, your looms you may pull down;
> You must get employ'd in factories, in country or in town,
> Four our cotton-masters have found out a wonderful new scheme,
> These calico good now wove by hand they're going to weave by
>   steam. (qtd. in Vicinus 1974: 45)

My point is that the preponderance and degree of suffering experienced by middle-class women in the text suggests a similar level of shock to the females who lived through the earliest and most marked stages of the separation of gendered economic spheres. I have argued that the very need for a trilogy of work delineating the boundaries of middle-class female life like that produced by Sarah Stickney Ellis is indicative of the relative "newness" of gendered spheres. Aside from Caroline's brief meditative eruption challenging "the Men of England," the behavior of *Shirley*'s women tends to embody Ellis's injunction "to suffer, and be still" (1842: 133). Chase and Levenson put it this way: "the clearest aim in [Ellis's] writing project is to persuade women that they ought freely to embrace what they cannot in any case escape: an inferiority, a dependence, a suffering" (2000: 80).

Brontë makes a theater of this kind of inevitability in the domestic interactions of the Yorke household. Upon assessing the dependent state of Caroline's life, Rose Yorke boldly announces her plans to resist her placement on the wrong side of the separate spheres:

> "I will *not* commit [my talent] to your work-table to be smothered in piles of woolen hose. I will *not* prison it in the linen-press to find shrouds among the sheets: and least of all . . . (she got up from the floor)—least of all will I hide it in a tureen of cold potatoes, to be ranged with bread, butter, pastry, and ham on the shelves of the larder." (385)

The interaction with her mother barely a page later, however, reveals Rose's near total capitulation to the "rules" that indoctrinate young women into separation of gendered spheres:

> "Rose, did you bring your sampler with you, as I told you?"
> "Yes, mother."
> "Sit down, and do a line of marking."
> Rose sat down promptly, and wrought according to orders. After a busy pause of ten minutes, her mother asked–
> "Do you think yourself oppressed now? A victim?"
> "No, mother."
> "Yet, as far as I understood your tirade, it was a protest against all womanly and domestic employment."
> "You misunderstood it, mother. I should be sorry not to learn to sew: you do right to teach me, and to make me work."
> "Even to the mending of your brother's stockings and the making of sheets?"
> "Yes." (386)

The brilliance of *Shirley* lies in its inevitable treatment of the transfer of handwork from lower-class male artisans to middle-class female homemakers. In both cases and for both classes, the results are equally inevitable and similarly devastating.

Nevertheless, it would be more precise to say that the results are devastating for most of the novel, or, until Caroline and Shirley embrace their respective marriages—and the needlework that enshrines the feminine sphere within these marriages. It takes 557 pages, the miraculous discovery of her mother, and an agreement to marry Moore, for Caroline to associate needlework and happiness, but we should not ignore the fact that she eventually does so. She tells Moore that he would laugh if he "knew what pleasure [she has] in making dresses and sewing" (557). Perhaps more surprisingly, we learn that Shirley, anticipating her marriage to Louis Moore, is no longer a "Thalestris from the fields, but a quiet domestic character from the fireside" who routinely now plies her needle (473, 477, 510, 581). These dramatic changes—usually discussed in the less specific terms of the dual marriages—have long baffled critics who attempt to find a more feminist message than the one Brontë provides in the ending of *Shirley*.[18] I agree with Bodenheimer that "paternalism is an assumption central to Brontë's imagination of human relations" but I would qualify the interpretation in the case of *Shirley* because I believe that Brontë meant for this to be a truly historical novel (1988: 37). Assuming that this is the case (or, better yet, that I have made this case), what Brontë presents us with in *Shirley*'s "Winding-Up" is neither anti- nor pro-feminist; it is simply the story of how gender relations came to be the way they were as she wrote the novel in 1848–49.[19]

As I conclude, I want to return to a surface-level connection that has remained unsaid in *Shirley* criticism so far. If, as I've tried to demonstrate, a direct manual network exists between the Yorkshire croppers and the middle-class women, then we should be able to identify something analogous to the male Luddite rebellion in the female sphere, something above and beyond Mrs. Gale's repressed desire to revolt with which I began this chapter. We certainly don't see anything like this in Caroline's actions: she pleads for "scope and work" but marries Moore and quiescently returns to the sewing she had so adamantly repudiated (379). Similarly, Rose Yorke, after protesting so adamantly against needlework, obediently sits down to do a line of marking on a sampler and agrees to mend her brother's stockings. Perhaps even more surprisingly, we learn that Shirley yields quite quiescently to Louis Moore's authority. "Only his hand," she says, "shall manage me" (579). The patriarchal reach becomes so inevitable and so pervasive in *Shirley* that it even stretches across Fieldhead's sky, where a "cloud like a man's hand ar[ises] in the west" and "gusts from the same quarter dr[ive] it on and spread it wide" (419).

This is good place to point out *Changing Hands'* central argument about how blinded twentieth- and twenty-first-century critics are to the literal importance of hands in the Victorian period. As I discuss more generally in my Introduction, Bruce Robbins's *The Servant's Hand* (1993 [1986]) comes immediately to mind. His excellent and influential book uses the hand metaphorically in its title, precisely because the book is not about literal hands. I want to be clear that I do not regard this as a shortcoming of Robbins's book; it just takes as its focus a very different topic than mine. The most specific illustration of this point may be found in how Robbins treats hands in *Shirley*. He interprets the insertion of servants into the narrative, not for what their hands physically accomplish, but in terms of how their presence "marks, elicits, and solemnizes words that promise a community in which they might have a larger share" (128). We may trace this same critical interest in the metaphorical implications of handedness in Patricia Johnson's *Hidden Hands: Working-Class Women and Victorian Social-Problem Fiction* (2001). Despite the title of her book and the specific question she poses in her *Shirley* chapter about whether the "theoretical connection between Luddism and feminism" can "be made more than theoretical," Johnson does not analyze women's hands at all. Again, like my point about Robbins, this is not a shortcoming so much as it is an overlooking of the obvious surface connections that I am interested in tracing from a literal and a historical perspective.[20]

There *is* a female rebellion waged against Robert Moore just after the revolt at his mill, though, and it bears historical traces. Rehabilitating at the Yorkes' from a Luddite gunshot wound, Moore is nursed not by Mrs. Yorke or any of the Yorke girls but by a previously unintroduced Mrs. Horsfall. I think this is where Brontë is having some fun with us. Moore falls from his horse when he's shot; moreover, William Horsfall was a real historical figure who owned the Ottiwells Mill at Marsden where proto-Luddic rebellions first occurred in 1803. Brontë's *Mrs.* Horsfall, however, has all the physical characteristics of one of the brutally strong Yorkshire croppers who operated the 50-pound shears that Moore replaced with machines. The narrator describes her as a "giantess" nurse with hands so large that "she could hold half a dozen hands like yours in her one palm" (526, 532). According to the young Martin Yorke who listens from outside the sickroom, Moore "hate[s] the sight of her rough bulk, and dread[s] the contact of her hands" because "she knocks him terribly about in that chamber" for the entire month of November 1811 (526, 532). Her rough bearing, along with her smoking and gin drinking, align Mrs. Horsfall quite directly with the unemployed laborers toward whom Moore acts so callously for most of the novel. The *coup de grâce* is that Mrs. Horsfall starves Moore during his captive rehabilitation at the appropriately named Yorke estate of Briar*mains*. By "eat[ing] most of what goes up on the tray to Mr. Moore," Mrs. Horsfall forces Moore to experience the starvation his unemployed cropmen endured in the months after his shearing frames arrived in Hollow's mill (532).

Key here is how closely Brontë hews to the historical model that she had in mind when she sent for old editions of the *Leeds Mercury* and the *Leeds Intelligencer* during her composition of the text. It's pivotal for *Shirley*'s historicity that Mrs. Horsfall's rebellion, like the Luddite rebellions of 1811 and 1812, is temporary. Moore eventually leaves Mrs. Horsfall's care, marries Caroline, and returns to Briarfield to continue the mechanization of the Hollow—a set of inevitable events that confirms the irreversible loss of agency sustained by textile tradesmen and middle-class women. From her vantage point in 1849, Charlotte Brontë recognized the causal relationship between mechanized manufacture and the hardening of the boundaries in the separate spheres of Victorian social life, yet she offers no moral for the "judicious reader putting on his spectacles to look for" one (599). *Shirley* simply recounts a fictional history of how it came to be this way.

CHAPTER 4

Etiquette and Upper-Handedness in William Thackeray's Vanity Fair

Part of the way through *Shirley*, the eponymous character decides she has a duty to the destitute and unemployed poor of Briarfield, and so designates the spinster Miss Ainsley to administer £300 for the purpose. When Shirley calls a meeting to discuss the implementation of the plan, the curates exhibit their skepticism of the women's ability to execute the delivery of aid. The narrator describes the scene this way:

> Shirley opened the business and showed the plan.
> "I know the hand which drew up that," said Mr Hall, glancing at Miss Ainsley ... Helstone glanced sharply round with an alert, suspicious expression, as if he apprehended that female craft was at work, and that something in petticoats was somehow trying underhand to acquire too much influence, and make itself of too much importance ... At last he muttered:—
> "Well—you are neither my wife nor my daughter, so I'll be led for once; but mind—I know I *am* led: your little female manoeuvres don't blind me." (272–73)

Although it is quite common for critics to trace the relationship between *Vanity Fair* (1848, edited by Peter Shillingsburg 2001) and *Shirley* to Brontë's admiration of Thackeray as "the first social regenerator of the day,"[1] or to Brontë's attempt to adopt a Thackerayan narrative structure,[2] this chapter will do so by way of Brontë's use of the single word "manoeuvre" in situations like the one cited above.

I must first briefly explain my decision to treat these two novels in reverse of their publication dates: Thackeray published *Vanity Fair* in a monthly serial between 1847 and 1848 and Brontë published *Shirley* in a single volume in 1849. The reasons I analyze them opposite their chrono-logical order are both thematic and historical. As I argued in the previ-ous chapter, *Shirley's* substantive connection to England's industrialization helps explain how the separate spheres grew so separate by midcentury. *Vanity Fair* has no industrial component; it chronicles drawing room behavior in the backdrop of the Napoleonic wars. In terms of historical setting, the novels depict roughly similar periods (first quarter of the nine-teenth century) despite their marked thematic and stylistic differences. However, where I argued against historical displacement in *Shirley*, it plays a significant role in my interpretation of *Vanity Fair*. That is to say, part of my aim in this chapter will be to demonstrate how Thackeray's focus on social etiquette responds to a distinctly midcentury concern for increas-ingly blurred class categories—a process which is itself a direct result of Britain's rapid industrialization.

None of this changes the previously unexplored but specifically manual connection I see between *Vanity Fair* and *Shirley*. In fact, analyzing these two texts chronologically in terms of female "maneuverability" can tell us quite a bit about their historical positioning. *Vanity Fair*, by virtually anyone's esti-mation, chronicles Becky Sharp's maneuvering through and manipulation of various social classes and gendered spheres. It is quite clear that Charlotte Brontë has Becky Sharp in mind when she constructs Caroline Helstone's desire for "an interest and an occupation which shall raise [women] above the flirt, the manoeuvrer" (1985: 378–79). In the two novels Brontë com-posed before reading *Vanity Fair* (*Jane Eyre* and *The Professor*), she used the word "maneuver" a total of two times (once in each novel). In *Shirley*, Brontë uses the word (or its variations) ten times. I am of course aware that word frequency means little without context. But the context in both novels is similar. Each time the word appears in *Shirley*, it relates to the separation of gendered spheres. More often than not, as Caroline herself acknowledges, middle-class women maneuver because they are "reduced to strive, by scarce modest coquetry and debasing artifice, to gain [a] position and consider-ation by marriage" (378). Here, Caroline could not more accurately describe the actions of the Becky Sharp character that she read about immediately before composing *Shirley*.

LITERALIZING THE MANIPULATIVE

Our understanding of *Vanity Fair* really should be connected to a careful consideration of how Becky Sharp uses her hands. In keeping with the central point of *Changing Hands*, the twentieth- and twenty-first-century tendency to take hands for granted has prevented critics from seeing how literally hands affected so many crucial aspects of Victorian life. This tendency to overlook what is so close to the surface of a text could hardly be more pronounced than in the case of *Vanity Fair*. As an initial step to proving this, I will point out what is obvious in any survey of *Vanity Fair* criticism from the past 100 years: it is nearly impossible to locate a critic of this novel who does not use the adjective "manipulative" to describe either Becky Sharp herself or Thackeray's ironic narrator. And yet the literal implications of such manipulative behavior on the interpretation of the novel has gone unexplored.

The conventional ways of interpreting *Vanity Fair* not only presuppose but rely on, a Lakoffian metaphoric paradigm of which we are hardly ever conscious (Lakoff and Johnson 1980: 5). I aim to address this topic here in an effort to connect what appears on the surface level in the representation of Becky's hands, both in prose and illustration, to Thackeray's understanding of the separate spheres and, ultimately, to his choice of narrative structure for the novel. Making this kind of argument in such a heavily sifted novel will help solidify one of the largest claims of the first half of *Changing Hands*: namely, that anxieties arising from the industrial milieu surface even in texts like *Vanity Fair* which have no explicitly industrial vector. The constant focus on the embodied hand—even in purely domestic and social settings—recapitulates the importance of this particular body part in the practical consciousness of a culture dealing with the physical and ontological repercussions of its displacement in the industrial realm.

As chapter 3 established, alterations in British social life were closely linked with the country's economic development. The number of those who considered themselves in the ranks of the middle class rose considerably as England continued to industrialize its economy. The rapid proliferation of conduct material from 1830 onwards attests at once to the middle class's desire for behavioral guidance and to the upper class's interest in developing new techniques of etiquette designed to maintain class delineation.[3] The dual threats of gender and class transgression that inhere in Thackeray's portrayal of the socially ambitious Becky thus offer a fictional realization of what many members of the genteel class feared most: those who merely *acted* like they belonged to proper society. Charles William Day, in *Hints on Etiquette and the Usages of Society*, wrote that "etiquette is the barrier which society draws around itself as a protection against offences that 'law' cannot touch; it is a shield against the intrusion of the impertinent, the improper, and the vulgar,—a guard against those persons" who seek to gain access to social circles in which they do not belong (1844: 11). An expanding corps of etiquette writers wanted to do just what Day hoped to defend against, though. New etiquette writers offered the upwardly mobile formal directions on how to socialize with more well-born members of society.[4]

Alexander Walker's popular etiquette guide of 1839 sounded a more serious alarm aimed specifically at woman, whose perpetual search for "safety," in Walker's mind, required her "instinctively to regulate her language and actions more particularly for the purpose of pleasing, and renders her an adept in the art of POLITENESS *" (40). The note corresponding to the asterisk elaborates on this point:

> It is the instinctive faculties of women, as well as the other qualities already described, that fit them better for passing from the lowest level to the highest ranks: this explains to us, why an almost uneducated girl becomes quickly a very charming wife when fortune smiles upon her, and how it is that a female suddenly raised to rank imbibes without effort the sentiments of her new condition, and has rarely the aukwardness [sic] and rude manners that distinguish those men whom chance has placed in a similar position." (1987: 40)

This sufficiently describes the generalized threat Becky Sharp poses to the social order of *Vanity Fair*. As we shall see, it is the politeness of her aggression that becomes the greatest threat to the established social order of the day. Feminist critics have long identified how nineteenth-century authors employ a wide range of tactics to obscure but not obliterate their most subversive impulses. While Thackeray may seem an unlikely advocate for female subversive behavior, his treatment of Becky's hands demonstrate the extent to which he participated in his culture's debate about gendered spheres.[5] We shall see that Becky's subversive gestures have social efficacy because they are both observable and camouflaged. Such indeterminacy allows her to perform subordinate actions while still freely asserting a potent individual agency of the kind envisioned by Vilém Flusser in his work, *Gestures*. According to Flusser's formulation, gesture is "a movement through which a freedom is expressed, a freedom to hide from or reveal to others the one who gesticulates" (2014: 164). This chapter argues that Becky's freely gesticulating hand is so frequently the object of Thackeray's narrative and pictorial attention not merely because the hand had become an especially dense transfer point for a whole system of binary oppositions between the sexes at midcentury,[6] but also because it provided a dynamic location for *Vanity Fair's* unique and overarching concern with the psychic and physical foundations of control in the social sphere.[7]

MANUAL LEVERAGE IN THE VICTORIAN DRAWING ROOM

At the point in the narrative when Napoleon's forces invade Brussels, Thackeray's narrator claims not "to rank among the military novelists" (293). "When the decks are cleared for action," he continues, "we go below and wait meekly" (293). The occasion seems to represent a particularly germane instance of what Peter Shillingsburg labels the "ironic insincerity" of the narrator's voice (2001: 75). But in this case the misdirection is by no means elaborate. Despite the narrator's assertion that "our place is with the non-combatants," we have been embedded by this point for thirty chapters in a fierce battle for inheritance and financial leverage, where the story of war and invasion becomes displaced from the battlefield to the drawing room (293). Becky's status as an aggressive woman of French heritage, while decidedly separate from Napoleonic war, nonetheless emphasizes the threat of such warfare in the English domestic sphere of *Vanity Fair*. For this reason, the narrator's insistence that "we [w]ould only be in the way of the manoeuvres that the gallant fellows are performing" on the battlefield should alert us to pay closer attention to the social maneuvering deployed in the drawing room—containing as it does all the precision and treacherousness of military life in the time of war (293).

One of Becky's first and most precise tactical maneuvers occurs at the outset of the novel when she applies "ever so gentle a pressure" to Jos Sedley's hand on a public stage, in front of the watchful eyes of the host family she hopes to join via marriage (26). The specific "move" to which the narrator refers happens when Becky initiates contact with Jos's hand in the drawing room at the moment he attempts to apologize for serving a spicy Indian dish at a Sedley family dinner:

> "By Gad, Miss Rebecca, I wouldn't hurt you for the world."
> "No," said she, "I *know* you wouldn't," and then she gave him ever so gentle a pressure with her little hand, and drew it back quite frightened and looked just for one instant in his face, and then down at the carpet-rods, and I am not prepared to say that Joe's heart did not thump at this little involuntary, timid, gentle motion of regard on the part of the simple girl. (26)

It is important to acknowledge the more specific context of this scene in order to appreciate the transgressiveness of Becky's seemingly innocuous gesture. She is already holding Jos's hand but decides to apply "ever so gentle a pressure" on a public stage, in front of the watchful eyes of Mr. and Mrs. Sedley. Yet she is trying to win a husband and a life beyond governessing without the aid of a family—the most important criterion in the arrangement of Victorian marriages. Even with family offering "aid," as Caroline Helstone objected, women were "reduced to strive, by scarce modest coquetry and debasing artifice" in order to achieve marriage (Brontë 1985: 378). Sally Shuttleworth sums up this "double-bind" in which women found themselves at midcentury: "[Women are] deemed of social value only if they succeed on the marriage market, but considered worthless if they are *seen* to be trying to achieve that end" (1984: 195, emphasis added). Under these circumstances, Becky has few verbal options and even fewer physical ones with which to display romantic interest.[8]

The boundaries of proper feminine behavior in public were so constrictive that critics have analyzed the development of a rhetorical "code," or "double-discourse," among women who wished to conceal their unacceptable desires beneath acceptable surfaces.[9] Where critics working in this vein tend to focus on verbal coquetry, I contend that Becky's manual tactics constitute a uniquely threatening yet socially sanctioned mode of resistance in their own right.[10] The pressure she applies to Jos's hand at the dinner table, her "gentle motion of regard," for example, is socially acceptable because it is simultaneously aggressive and indecipherable. Its physical pressure partakes of both language *and* body as it supplements the verbal with an ephemeral materiality that belies the gesture's radical assertiveness. Becky's maneuver also stands out because of its contrast with Thackeray's depictions of the

Fig. 11. "Mr. Osborne's welcome to Amelia." *Vanity Fair*, 130.

more stereotypical feminine subordination in other areas of the text. In one such instance (fig. 11), the tyrannical Mr. Osborne glowers at his wife, his daughters, and Amelia as each holds her hands in silent but conspicuous positions of respect and submission. Despite revealing Mr. Osborne's patriarchal dominance, Thackeray also hints at the elder Osborne's mistrust of this dominance; the illustration catches him looking back for reassurance of feminine submission as he exits the room.[11]

When considered within such a tightly surveilled environment, Becky's aggressive behavior at the Sedley dinner table becomes even bolder. The reaction of Thackeray's narrator confirms its boldness, in fact. Immediately following the fleeting and hardly discernible transgression, the narrator launches into a lengthy meditation on the audacity of Becky's maneuver:

> It was an advance and as such perhaps some ladies of indisputable correctness and gentility will condemn the action as immodest—but you see poor Rebecca had all this work to do for herself. If a person is too poor to keep a servant, though ever so elegant, he must sweep his own rooms; if a dear girl has no mamma to settle matters with the young man, she must do it for herself. And oh what a mercy it is that these women do not exercise their own power oftener. We can't resist them if they do. Let them show ever so little inclination and men go down on their knees at once, old or ugly it is all the same. And this I set down as a positive truth. A woman with fair opportunities and without an absolute hump, may marry WHOM SHE LIKES. Only let us be thankful that the darlings are like the beasts of the field, and don't know their own power. They would overcome us entirely if they did. (26–27, emphasis added)

This euphemistic yet protracted evasion of the actual "advance" establishes a tone of mock-epic warfare, which has substantive implications for the rest of the narrative. The narrative persona's voice is notoriously slippery in *Vanity Fair*, but critics traditionally identify this passage as an example of the narrator's straightforward and even overt ploy to affirm a sense of shared supremacy with his male readers.[12] I maintain, however, that even at this early stage in the novel, the narrator seems suspiciously uncomfortable (like Mr. Osborne looking back over his shoulder) with his own ironic revelation that the formidable barriers between traditional male power structures and female subordination may rest only upon the tenuous regulations of social heterodoxy and politeness. Becky's behavior is threatening here because it makes a calculated but covert assault on an etiquette system that Charles William Day and other conduct writers called "the *armour* of society" (1844: 90). The fact that she has nothing to lose makes Becky particularly well suited to test the coverage and thickness of this weakening social armament, though.

There is surely a sleight of tongue in the narrator's observation that it is "a mercy ... women do not exercise their power oftener."[13] The "threat" that men "go down on their knees" in the face of so small a gesture of female

Fig. 12. **Old Crawley's proposition.** *Vanity Fair*, 152.

assertiveness seems humorously overstated in its early context—especially after Jos elects to return to India rather than pursue a life with Becky. As George Levine has correctly noted about *Vanity Fair* in general: "the more telling irony is that the narrator's ironies might not be ironic at all" (2008a: 72). Indeed, the legitimacy of Becky's agency becomes more real (and narratologically realized) at the moment Thackeray depicts Sir Pitt Crawley's pathetic proposal in illustration (fig. 12) and prose:

> "Say yes, Becky," Sir Pitt continued ... "you shall have what you like; spend what you like; and 'av it all your own way. I'll make you a settlement. I'll do everything reglar ..." and the old man fell down on his knees and leered at her like a satyr. (152)

Fig. 13. Becky leading Old Crawley through Queen's Crawley. *Vanity Fair*, 70.

Here the armor of social etiquette appears quite porous. The baronet's prostrate position literally fulfills the seemingly ironic projection the narrator makes following Becky's initial interaction with Jos that "men go down on their knees at once" for a woman who "show[s] ever so little inclination" (27). Moreover, the tacit association the narrator draws between female gesture and "inclination" should remind us of Mary Poovey's assertion that the "problem" of female aggression at midcentury "could be conceptualized as female sexuality" (1988: 15). Thackeray's illustrated depiction of Becky's earliest contact with the elder Crawley reveals the validity of Poovey's point (fig. 13):

Her clutching of the baronet's hand here suggests an escalation of the gestural assertiveness she employed at the Sedley dinner table. The escalating threat Becky poses to hierarchical life at Queen's Crawley also shows up in the movement of the illustration: Becky leads her aristocratic employer through his *own* house just moments after meeting him and the rest of the staff for the first time.

Within the past decade there has been a revival of critical discussion about the ways Thackeray creates "intratextual narrative irony" through his inconsistent prosodic and illustrated depictions of *Vanity Fair*'s events.[14] I will address some of these inconsistencies later on in the chapter. For now, though, I want to stress how the importance of Becky's hands in her campaign to rise in social status appears far more literally than ironically threatening. The narrator refrains from recounting Becky's specific maneuvers in the above scene, but the illustrations—including the hyperliteral rendition of Crawley's bended knee proposal—confirm her ability to transform polite physical contact into social leverage. Thackeray therefore uses Becky's hands to register the sexual strategies that his readership and her gender typically forbid. They specify and also complicate Arnold Kettle's keen observation from long ago that Becky "uses consciously and systematically all the men's weapons plus her one natural asset, her sex, to storm the men's world" (1954: 164). We are unlikely to have considered the hand as "natural asset" of either gender, yet Thackeray's portrayal of Becky shows it to be a remarkably generative site for female agency in the world of *Vanity Fair*.

With the rapid increase of industrialization, traditional class categories became more fluid and, as James Eli Adams has noted, the process created "crises of interpretation" for the Victorians (2005: 52). Etiquette authors responded to the expanding boundaries of social intercourse by devoting entire sections of their books to the specification of rules for proper hand behavior in public settings. The manuals were precise and detailed, offering exact directions, particularly on the most sensitive areas of etiquette: introductions and salutations. One manual commented that "no idiosyncrasy of character [was] more important than the manner of salutation" (Simms 1872: 388). "As is the salutation," the chapter begins, "so is the total of the character" (388). Another contemporary manual asserted that "the charm of the hand, as a saluting member, lies in the fact of its grasping power, which enables the shaker to vary the salute" in strict accordance with class and gender discrepancies (Anonymous 1859: 324). By the early 1840s, etiquette manuals which concerned themselves with the fastidious choreography of drawing room interaction had become so pervasive that *Punch* commissioned Albert Smith to compose a ten-part illustrated series entitled "The Physiology of London Evening Parties." This piece's popularity led to its reissue in book form in March 1846—just a year before Thackeray started publishing *Vanity Fair.*

Given the contemporary surge in the popularity of etiquette literature, it is hardly surprising that Thackeray devotes so much narrative attention to the subject. In one particularly revealing instance, he spends an inordinate amount of space (in both prose and illustration) recounting the moment where the young George Osborne meets Becky at a Queen's Crawley dinner party. The scene occurs after Jos has spurned Becky but before she marries Rawdon Crawley. This means that Becky's precarious status as a governess situates her in one of the most vulnerable positions in Victorian fiction—a position that makes Becky's control of the introduction to George Osborne even more impressive. Thackeray's choice to embed the illustration of the meeting within his narrative only further dramatizes Becky's capacity to direct social interchange as staged drama. Indeed, the placement of this crucial illustration (fig. 14) within a single sentence of the prosodic narrative constitutes an exemplary instance of what J. Hillis Miller calls a "parabasis, an eternal moment suspending . . . any attempt to tell a story through time" (1992: 60):

> Miss Sharp put out her right fore-finger—
> And gave him a little nod, so cool and so killing, that Rawdon Crawley, watching the operations from the other room, could hardly restrain his laughter as he saw [George's] entire discomfiture.

Critics of Victorian illustration seldom miss an opportunity to point out Thackeray's deficiencies as a visual artist. Regarding this particular illustration, John Harvey cites Osborne's "wooden body" as evidence that Thackeray "has not 'seen' the incident at all, but is merely making a kind of hesitant visual guess" (1970: 80). Harvey goes on to suggest that an illustration "in the style of John Leech" would be more desirable for such a dramatic scene (80). I wish to focus on this illustration precisely *because* of what Harvey objects to as inferior artistry, though. It is true that George appears wooden and unnatural; but this is the way that Thackeray depicts him in the prose surrounding the illustration. Rather than interpreting George's woodenness as a deficiency in Thackeray's draftsmanship, we should consider Becky's role

Fig. 14. Inset of *Vanity Fair*, 148.

in provoking his awkward stiffness. George's visible discomfort is the result
of the *politeness* of Becky's aggressiveness—an idea Thackeray ingeniously
emphasizes by locating the illustration of her pointed forefinger directly
beneath the textual dash with which he introduces it (148).

George appears flustered in the middle of this most routine of social
rituals, but it is critical for my argument that Becky asserts control of this
interaction within the boundaries of propriety. As the illustration indicates,
George is shocked by Becky's manual audacity; his surprise ripples through

his entire ("wooden") body. The angle of his torso, the placement of his foot, and the direction of his open hand and fingers all suggest that he had expected a measure of physical deference from the seated governess. George assumes that his social superiority will automatically grant him what etiquette manuals called "the right of recognition" (Curtin 1987: 81). This "right" stipulates that it is George's decision—as a member of the higher class— whether to acknowledge Becky with a handshake or with the less intimate bow. As one manual clarified:

> On a first introduction, it is not customary to shake hands; both parties bow to each other only. It is not until some intimacy has arisen that shaking hands is practiced either at meeting or parting. Whatever the difference of rank may be in parties of opposite sexes, the gentleman is always introduced to the lady. (Anonymous 1861: 22)

The prose immediately preceding the illustration makes George's arrogant etiquette violations explicit:

> [George] walked up to Rebecca with a patronizing, easy swagger. He was going to be kind to her and protect her. He would even shake hands with her, as a friend of Amelia's; and saying, "Ah, Miss Sharp! How-dy-doo?" held out his left hand towards her, expecting that she would be quite confounded at the honour. (147)

When Becky counters with her right forefinger, Thackeray gives us a verbal rendition of George's discomfiture by describing "the start he gave, the pause, and the perfect clumsiness with which he at length condescended to take the finger which was offered for his embrace" (148). Becky had learned this brand of gestural vocabulary from her parting with Miss Pinkerton at Chiswick. There, the narrator informed us that Pinkerton gave "Miss Sharp an opportunity of shaking one of the fingers of the hand which was left out for that purpose" (7). Becky's triumph even at this earlier stage is manual; she wins the "little battle between the young lady and the old one" by "declining to accept the proffered honour" (7). George, to his detriment, neither thinks nor acts as quickly as Becky.

Following Foucault's account of the sublimation of power in the anatomo-politics of the body, Thackeray's choice of hands is a small but critical detail. George's decision to offer his left hand in the shake adds another (manual) dimension to his general condescension toward the female governess. Etiquette books stressed the universal fact that the right hand was to be used *always* in handshakes—even when one offered the fingers alone. Becky's determination to counter George's left hand with only her right forefinger thus reflects a conscious choice on her part as well. She might have easily offered her left hand to George's left hand, a move that could have challenged both his classed and gendered arrogance. Becky's offering of her *right* forefinger, however, has the effect of inducing an embarrassing anatomical awkwardness because of the simple fact that fingers alone cannot embrace each other gracefully. They do not fit anatomically into the traditional masculine-biased model of "upper-hand" heterosexual contact outlined in publications like the *Punch* evening party series (fig. 15). Furthermore, the slackness apparent in George's finger placement is met with Becky's aggressively pointed single finger so that both the prose and the illustration partake of the parry-and-thrust movement characteristically associated with the (aristocratic) male institution of the sword duel.

Thackeray's invocation of the duel in this scene is important for several reasons. Not only was Thackeray personally interested in the hotly contested debates about the morality of dueling in the nineteenth century,[15] but he also saw the surprising similarities between the emergence of etiquette literature for the lower and middle classes and the waning of duels among the upper classes; both were essentially performative and both attempted to apply social regulation to a kind of warfare he viewed as ridiculous. The key difference in *Vanity Fair* is that Becky's aggressiveness disrupts the pattern

Fig. 15. "The Physiology of London Evening Parties." *Punch* 2 (1842): 43.

where etiquette and duels are fought *over* women, inserting instead one where they are fought *by* them.[16]

Perhaps most importantly, the narrator does not conceal the effectiveness of Becky's drawing room maneuver. We immediately learn that "George was quite savage. The little governess patronized him and *persifflèd* him until this young British Lion felt quite uneasy ... Thus, was George utterly routed" (149). The terms of this "rout" are decidedly gestural, but they draw support from the facial and the verbal. Becky's impassive expression denies what her hand intends and, in fact, achieves. The discrepancy between the actions of the hands and the faces is what brings irony to the scene (and a blush to George's face). The portrait on the wall above Becky also instructs the viewer to *notice* the hand by prominently concealing it—all while the painting's face observes the encounter below. This interchange also marks an important stage in the development of Becky's escalating, but still permissible, aggressiveness. Her delicate hand-squeeze at the outset of the novel proved too light to win Jos Sedley, in part because of George's intervention. The pointed finger here, then, reflects Becky's desire to revenge George's role in her foiled attempt to marry Jos, but it also hints at the violence her hand is capable of performing in the role of the dagger-wielding Clytemnestra and beyond.

Maria DiBattista has discussed how a woman in Becky's position had few options to exercise self-assertiveness, especially in a drawing room full of people where she could quickly become the subject of damaging negative attention (1980: 827–37). My point is that Becky may defend and even assert herself gesturally while maintaining an otherwise cordial conversation. Her right-handed gesture becomes a (barely) acceptable paralinguistic mode through which she can contest traditional Victorian gender politics. Thackeray's treatment of Becky's hands directly anticipates Marcel Mauss's "Techniques of the Body" (1973) where gesture becomes simultaneously a biological, social, and psychological phenomenon. As Carrie Noland has noted, Mauss sets out an agenda for a truly phenomenological constructivism, "one that places gestural performatives, as opposed to discursive performatives, at the center of cultural theories of subjectivation and resistance" (2009: 21).

The residual charge of gender transgression originating in Becky's gesture galvanizes the entire scene. The anatomical maladroitness created by the fingers suggests a refutation of the lock-and-key model of heterosexual contact, thereby implicitly debunking the politics of gender determinism that George and so many of his contemporaries took for granted. Directed as it is to the concave posture of George's midsection, Becky's aggressively pointed finger resembles a visual analogy of the phallus of which George's body positioning clearly deprives him. Even the inversion of traditional gender codes represented in this scene must be masked by congeniality, though. The verbal and facial depictions of the event suggest a circuit of propriety, but crucially, a circuit that diverts the current of attention away from problematic discourses which remain latent in the gestural. Thus the decorous facial and conversational aspects of the scene exist to repress the physical and sexual energies of the hand. And yet the Victorians were fascinated by the hand, precisely because through its movements they could illustrate if not articulate the disavowed discourses (manual labor, sexuality, gender insurrection) that were so often the batteries of middle-class anxiety.

If we consider the "handshake" scene in the context of Becky's previous interactions with Jos and Sir Pitt Crawley, it becomes possible to identify how Becky's manual dexterity prompts a desire that men find difficult to resist but that polite women also cannot detect. Becky's aggressiveness, as deflating as it is for George, generates within him a lustful desire to pursue her sexually. We know from the novel's early chapters that George and Becky meet during Jos's short-lived courtship, but George, at that time, appears content with his fiancée Amelia. After the bungled handshake scene, however, George boldly pursues a sexual relationship with Becky. He confides in Rawdon that Becky is "a sharp one," "a dangerous one," and most revealingly, "a desperate flirt" on the day following Becky's "rout" (149). Far from being put off by Becky's actions, George quickly experiences sexual exhilaration: "throbbing with triumph and excitement" at the ball in Brussels where he secretly asks Becky to run away with him despite his one-week-old marriage to Amelia (290). Commentary by Martha Vicinus, Carol Christ, and others forms part of a long tradition of inquiry that envisions Victorian males resolving their ambivalence vis-à-vis sexuality and aggression by idealizing feminine passivity in the domestic "angel."[17] Just the opposite seems to be true in *Vanity Fair*, though. George comes to dislike Amelia's passive (and perhaps asexual) nature most at exactly those moments when it is juxtaposed with Becky's sexually charged hands.

Indeed, Amelia's manual submissiveness seems to act as an extension of her passive personality in general. At the moment George leaves for the war from which he will never return, for example, the narrator focuses our attention not on Amelia's sleeping face, but on the innocence of her hand: "God bless her! God bless her! [George] came to the bed-side, and looked at the hand, the little soft hand, lying asleep" (292). To George (and many of his contemporaries), it probably seemed only "natural" that such a hand would belong to a stereotypical female: one who "would cry over a dead canary-bird or over a mouse that the cat haply had seized upon, or over the end of a novel were it ever so stupid" (5). Thackeray inverts many of the aspects of George's farewell to Amelia's sleeping hand when the young Rawdon Crawley enters his mother's room hoping for maternal affection but finds appropriately only a "mystic bronze hand on the dressing-table, glistening all over with a hundred rings" (380). The contrasting images of Amelia's "little soft hand" and Becky's "mystic bronze hand" raise subtle but threatening questions about the "nature" of Victorian femininity. George's attraction to Becky reflects more of Simone de Beauvoir's notion that men project ideals of women that they themselves would like in some way to possess or incor-porate. Though this is no doubt inflected by the virgin/whore dichotomy where the latter becomes alluring despite or because of the former's ideal-ization, George's sudden attraction to Becky may also be seen as an attempt to recuperate the sense of masculine authority that he so clearly lost in the salutation scene. Any recuperation in this sense—sexual or otherwise—fits Foucault's notion of the sexual mosaic, where power itself operates as the mechanism of attraction (1978: 45–47).

The success of the encounter with George allows Becky to recognize that she possesses the ability to transform innocuous social rituals into combat-ive gestures—ones in which she is able to scramble traditional notions of class and gender without the consequences of doing so openly. The routing of George therefore inaugurates a pattern of behavior on which Becky relies even while operating under the most extreme social scrutiny at other points in the narrative. For example, during her first official visit to the Marquis de Steyne's Gaunt House estate, Becky finds herself attacked by high-ranking guests of both genders. But Thackeray describes her simultaneously aggres-sive and polite responses to these attacks as physical rather than verbal in nature. "The younger ladies of the House of Gaunt," the narrator tells us, "set people at [Becky], but they failed" (505). In the same paragraph we learn that "the brilliant Lady Stunnington tried a passage of arms with her, but was routed with great slaughter by the intrepid little Becky" (505). Perhaps most interesting in light of George's earlier fate, Mr. Wagg is called upon to vanquish Becky when her deft conversational skills prove unflappable to the women. Thackeray's narrator describes the scene this way:

Mr. Wagg, the celebrated wit, and a led captain and trencher-man of my Lord Steyne, was caused by the ladies to charge [Becky]; and the worthy fellow, leering at his patronesses, and giving them a wink, as much as to say, "Now look out for sport,"—one evening began an assault upon Becky, who was unsuspiciously eating her dinner. The little woman, attacked on a sudden but never without arms, lighted up in an instant, parried and reposted with a home-thrust, which made Wagg's face tingle with shame. (506)

Like the Osborne scene, Becky's aggressiveness is figured manually, but, in this instance, Thackeray provides no corresponding illustration to corroborate her success for the reader. The efficacy of Becky's verbal and gestural agency remains potent in an ekphrastic sense, though. With the Osborne scene, Becky's recalcitrance was figured literally in the determinative illustration of her pointed finger. With the above scene at Gaunt House, however, the fact that we do not *see* a representation of the interaction with Lady Stunnington and Mr. Wagg only serves to increase the threat of feminine intractability because Thackeray's ekphrastic representation encourages the reader to envision such an image anyway—having just read about (and looked at) a similar event in the dual mediums of prose and image in the Osborne tableau. As W. J. T. Mitchell has keenly observed, "the very idea of an 'idea' is bound up with the notion of imagery" once we see it with our eyes (1987: 5). Having seen the way Becky routs people with her hands, we need only read associative words like "attack," "parry," and "home-thrust" to invoke the image of her bellicosity in other contexts.

At Gaunt House, even though the physical has become the visual sphere of reference, Becky's activity is rendered verbally (in prose), but still crucially, within the metaphors of manual combat that we observed with George Osborne. So powerful is this referent as an index of social leverage that Becky's dueling hand actually replaces what we could assume would be the antagonistic content of adjacent conversations. The unrevealed dialogue between Becky and Wagg, suffused as it is with metaphors of hand-to-hand combat, becomes heteroglossic as it registers the tiniest shifts and oscillations of the social atmosphere (Bakhtin 1981: 300). The larger consequence of this focus on Becky's hands, even when they are not illustrated, is that the gestural assumes a place of primacy in Becky's social confrontations. The declarative discourse Becky is forbidden to use is articulated through a uniquely acceptable but potent manual discourse—a process that adds another dimension to Elaine Showalter's formulation of a feminine "gender-lect."[18] But Becky's gestural language in such a lexicon thrives in a place that is not overpopulated—in the Bakhtinian sense—with male intentionality precisely because it simultaneously challenges and adheres to conventional codes of social conduct.

Judith Butler's work has demonstrated that all gendering, at some level, emerges through the discursively determined activity of stylized acting.[19] This formulation applies to Becky in the sense that there is no moment in *Vanity Fair* when Becky is not performing her gender from within the boundaries of proper etiquette. "The best of women," the narrator recalls his grandmother say,

> are hypocrites. We don't know how much they hide from us: how watch-ful they are when they seem most artless and confidential: how often those *frank smiles* which they wear so easily, are traps to cajole or elude or disarm. (175, emphasis added)

The particular body part identified here in the "hypocritical" act, though, does not apply to Becky. As we have seen in many of Thackeray's illustra-tions, Becky's facial expressions actually betray her in the sense that they broadcast what is otherwise undetectable in the rest of her bodily demeanor. It is the performance of Becky's hands that often helps her evade crushing social defeats by both women and men of the classes higher than her own.

Just one example of this kind of manual performance occurs when Becky deflects the eminent Lady Steyne's deliberately frigid salutation with the utmost felicity and composure (so the Lady's aloofness will go undetected by onlookers). The narrator tells us that Becky takes Lady Steyne's hand, though it is "as cold and lifeless as marble," and "perform[s] a reverence which would have done credit to the best dancing master" (488). Here, as in many other key parts of the novel, Becky's dexterous manipulation of social eti-quette exists in conjunction with the threat she represents to normative gen-der and class relations—the culmination of which we witness in her charade performance as Clytemnestra (fig. 16).

The illustration freezes Becky in the act of sweeping "the prettiest little curtsey ever seen" but the violent image of the dagger charges the scene with palpable danger (511). The charades are particularly germane to my focus on Becky's hands because, as DiBattista has noted, their generic imperative is never to expose reality in the direct light of representation

Fig. 16. "The Triumph of Clytemnestra." *Vanity Fair*, 512.

(1980: 834). Thackeray's appropriation of the Agamemnon myth allows him to acknowledge, but also to displace, the contemporary threat of female autonomy from a Victorian domestic setting to a classical tragedy. Such a setting, according to DiBattista, "accumulates into itself all Thackeray's previous suggestions in the novel that beneath England's treatment of women—hypostasized in the angelic cult of Victorian womanhood—abides an unregenerate barbarity, a 'Turkish' lust for mastery" (1980: 830). Deborah Thomas (1993) and Micael M. Clarke (1995) have more recently connected this theme to Thackeray's 1844 trip to the Islamic Near East, where the almost universal subordination of women generated his interest in historical cycles of feminine reprisal. Taking these views into consideration, Becky's performance as Clytemnestra, like her interactions with Jos, Osborne, and Wagg, represents an escalation in the threat that lay coiled underneath the narrator's early and deeply ironic relief that "women do not exercise their power oftener!" (26–27).

PUPPETRY'S AUTHORIAL COLLISION AND COLLUSION

Thackeray's treatment of Becky's hands becomes even more remarkable if we consider the way they operate in relation to *Vanity Fair*'s formal structure. By connecting the important relationship between Becky's manual activity and Thackeray's narrative strategy, I hope to illuminate a new line of interpretation regarding what many consider to be the collusion or sympathy between the author and his novel's "lead puppet." Just as Becky calibrates her aggressiveness to the codes of Victorian propriety, the narrator-showman boasts of his ability to present the novel's sordid plot in a "perfectly genteel and inoffensive manner" (637). "Above the water-line," the narrator directly challenges us, "has not everything been proper, agreeable, and decorous?" (638). Apropos of this challenge is Walter Bagehot's 1858 appraisal of Thackeray's slippery narrative technique:

> No one can read Mr. Thackeray's writings without feeling that he is perpetually treading as close as he dare to the borderline that separates the world which may be described in books from the world which it is prohibited to describe. No one knows better than this accomplished artist where that line is, and how curious are its windings and turns. The charge against him is that he knows it but too well; that with an anxious care and a wistful eye he is ever approximating to its edge, and hinting with subtle art how thoroughly he is familiar with, and how interesting he could make the interdicted region on the other side. He never violates a single conventional rule; but at the same time the shadow of immorality that is not seen is scarcely ever wanting to his delineation of the society that is seen. (qtd. in Tillotson 1954: 68)

The "guiding sovereignty" of Thackeray's manipulative voice, to use Wolfgang Iser's phrase, undoubtedly stems from his claim to be the *sole* "Manager" of *Vanity Fair*'s complicated marionette production (1987, 54). My contention in this part of the chapter is that the puppetry motif is as generically functional and culturally relevant as it is merely aesthetic for Thackeray.[20]

The marionette fascinated Thackeray because of *Vanity Fair's* focus on the concealed origins and modalities of social control. Like the indeterminacy encoded in Becky's manual behavior and the manager's ironic narration, the generic imperative of the marionette is to expose and conceal simultaneously. It animates doll figures with human movement from a hidden place above the stage and, therefore, depends as much on what is seen by the audience as on what is unseen. Thus the parallel relationship between Becky's "discernable" propriety and the narrator's withholding style is pivotal. The threat Becky poses as a marionette becomes magnified in this schema. Amidst the entangling relationships Thackeray sees as characteristic of nineteenth-century English society, the authority of the smug narrator-showman, as with Osborne and Wagg, is constantly under siege by Becky's threatening but socially acceptable appropriation of the novel's "leading-strings" (679).

I raise these points because they counter decades of interpretation related to the structure of *Vanity Fair*. There is an overwhelming critical consensus that Thackeray simply tacked on the verbal and pictorial puppet to the first and last sections of *Vanity Fair* in his preparation of the final double number in June 1848. The resoluteness with which Joan Stevens makes this argument characterizes the almost universal agreement among critics since the late 1960s:

> Puppetry . . . is not emphasized in either words or illustrations until the very end of the novel . . . it does not appear in the text until the last sentence of book; it appears in "Before the Curtain," written at the same time; the only illustrations embodying the idea are those in the cluster of three drawn, also at the end, for the decoration of the final double Number. (1968: 394–95)

In part from Eyre Crowe's recollection of a discussion with Thackeray,[21] Stevens concludes that "*only* in June 1848, while he was working on the sheets of Numbers 19 and 20, did Thackeray realise the usefulness of the puppet show for his purpose" (396, emphasis added). This has become the default view of how puppetry works in the text ever since.[22]

The narratological complexity in so many sections of *Vanity Fair*, however, is the result of the characters' manipulation of each other even while they are themselves subject to the literal manipulation of the Manager of the Performance. Throughout the novel, not only in the 1848 material, frequent interchanges between the roles of character-puppet and puppet-master form an important part of Thackeray's view of English social culture. In such a society, control is always part of an illusion that conflates seemingly opposite subject positions of puppet and puppet-master. Like so many critics, Roger Wilkenfeld takes Thackeray's narrator at his word in claiming that "the Manager of the puppet-show is its sole proprietor and manipulator" (1971: 314). This is true to a certain extent. But my contention is that Becky challenges this authority by taking over the controlling "hand" of the puppet-master at crucial junctures in the narrative. More specifically, Becky's dramatic strength, as I see it, lies in her manipulative performance of the control she seizes. We learn of Becky's affinity for such manipulation very early in the novel when Thackeray provides a prose and pictorial depiction of the entertainment she offers to the men of the artist's quarter (fig. 17).

This illustration appears only thirteen pages into the novel. The illustration, along with the accompanying prose describing how Becky would entertain the artists on Newman and Gerard streets, gives us a convincing introduction to Becky's performing hands at a very early point in the narrative. Stevens defends her position by arguing that this illustration "pictures ordinary dolls, not puppets" (1968: 395). She is correct; they are not marionettes in the definitive sense. But they are also not ordinary dolls as the prose suggests. The illustration shows Becky's hands controlling the puppets' movements from the *inside* of the dolls, her fingers clearly operating the movement of the figures' heads and arms. Kenneth Gross's recent work on this topic captures the electrifying possibilities of even the simplest of hand puppets: "The madness [of the puppet] lies in the hidden movements of the hand, the curious impulse by which a person's hand can make itself into the animating impulse, the intelligence or soul, of an inanimate object" (2011: 1). In Gross's estimation, the puppet "is an extension of the more basic wonder by which we can let this one part of our body become a separate, articulate whole, capable of surprising its owne[r] with its movements, the stories it tells" (1). Considering puppetry as containing this kind of influence should make us wary of taking the narrator's description of his relationship to the puppets at face value. If nothing else, the movement from the narrator's confident assertion of Becky's "uncommonly flexible" joints to puppet-master in this

Fig. 17. Hand puppets. *Vanity Fair,* 13.

early scene reveals the deceptive nature of control in the social realm. The person who seeks control in the tangled world of *Vanity Fair*, as the narrator and Becky both do, is always subject to control by others in different circumstances.

The threat embodied in Becky's controlling hand becomes decidedly more explicit only two chapters after she entertains the artists from Gerard Street with the hand puppets. During the final scene of *Vanity Fair*'s first Number (chapter V), Jos and Becky are left alone in the drawing room shortly after Becky has performed her first hand-squeezing maneuver at the

Sedley dinner. In the prose rendition of the scene, Thackeray reports that the "shining needles" of Becky's knitting "were quivering rapidly under her white slender fingers" as she completes the silk purse:

> "I must finish the purse. Will you help me, Mr. Sedley?" And before [Jos] had time to ask how, Mr. Joseph Sedley, of the East India Company's service, was actually seated *tête-à-tête* with a young lady, looking at her with a most killing expression; his arms stretched out before her in an imploring attitude, and his hands bound in a web of green silk, which she was unwinding. (36)

The only problem is that the illustration of this number-ending "*tête-à-tête*" is missing several of the scene's most crucial props. This discrepancy qualifies as a representative example of what Judith Law Fisher appropriately calls the "interpretive collision" between the verbal and the visual in Thackeray's fiction (2002: 70). The prose and the illustration are consistent in so far as they depict Jos with his arms stretched out before Becky in an imploring attitude ("doing his best to make a killing expression") while George and Amelia look on from outside the room. However, the "shining needles" that were quivering rapidly under Becky's fingers in Thackeray's prose, as well as her skein of silk, are entirely absent from the illustration entitled "Mr. Joseph entangled" (36–37) (fig. 18).

What we have is not a representation of Becky "unwinding" the green silk, but instead an illustrated scene that gives us considerably more information about Becky's hands than the prose does on its own. In what is perhaps Thackeray's most famous full-page illustration, Becky is shown not only holding, but also controlling, the two ends of string as it binds Jos's hands. She is holding the two ends of the string independently, but her raised hand suggests movement in a way that makes Jos's hands appear *controlled* rather than "entangled."

Unlike the weaving motion employed by the knitter of Thackeray's prose, the illustrated Becky appears to be pulling the silk back and forth in the manner of a puppeteer—an act that shifts the focus decidedly from "*tête-à-tête*" to *main-à-main*. The controlling effect on the hapless Jos, and also on the rest of the novel's plot, underscores the thematic and narrative convergence of Becky's social manipulation that will become so problematic in later parts of the text. Author, narrator-showman, and puppet are linked by the same strings, pulled by the same motives. In this sense, Becky's

Fig. 18. "Mr. Joseph entangled." *Vanity Fair*, 37.

hands allow her to move swiftly and simultaneously beyond her narratively inscribed position as a marionette *and* her ideologically assigned role as a submissive woman. The gendered relation of the puppet to the controlling hand is all the more compelling considering how Victorian puppet show-men—and they were most often men—were called "manipulators" by their contemporaries. The scene also incorporates an additional realistic detail from the material world of the marionette stage: puppets were controlled by green strings because of the color's supposed invisibility on a variety of multicolored background staging.

Recalling the needlework of chapter 3, the nonaggressive and almost exclusively middle-class female activity of knitting here in *Vanity Fair* becomes invisibly encoded in feminine gesture not only above and below the surface of polite social discourse, but also more subversively, embroidered *within* it. Thackeray's choice to include the marionette was certainly not as hastily employed as *Vanity Fair* criticism has so far adduced. Gross's recent theoretical observations on the historical place of marionette theater has only made this more clear. "Puppets," Gross says, "have often been asked to say things or to show things otherwise not permitted; it is a theatrical mode whose words and actions are more able to slip under the radar of official censorship, something too trivial to be taken quite seriously by the authorities" (2011: 17–18). The "things" unpermitted in *Vanity Fair* are expressions of female agency, and the "authorities" are nothing less than the entire male establishment.

It seems fair to conclude—at least tentatively—that Thackeray's construction of *Vanity Fair* is part of a larger critique of gendered power in the social sphere at midcentury. I would like now to probe that tentativeness by looking specifically at the novel's 1848 title page (fig. 19) and tail-piece (fig. 20), which Thackeray produced after completing the novel. What Thackeray calls "the puppet-box illustrations" (title page and tail-piece) have prompted readings that traditionally diminish Becky's place in the narrative to that of a simple puppet—easily shut up and dismissed.[23] At first glance, the new title page (fig. 19) seems to support these readings, which have held sway for more than half of a century. The proportionality of the illustration would link the puppet, the doll, and the woman in a seemingly implicit hierarchy of representational and gendered subordination. Becky's general diminution reinforces the manipulability that the narrator identifies as making her so "uncommonly flexible in the joints and lively on the wire" during the novel's "Before the Curtain" section (xvi).

I have maintained that we should be suspicious of these comments all along. If we examine the illustration more closely, we encounter some additional reasons to be skeptical of the narrator's glibness: Thackeray draws Becky with her hands extending outward in poses of physical struggle in both the title page and tail-piece. It is fitting that Gross subtitles his recent book "*An Essay on Uncanny Life*" because this is exactly the kind of (after) life we witness in the drawings of the shut-up and put-away Becky puppet.

Fig. 19. Engraved vignette title page (1848). *Vanity Fair.*

Gross's comments on the lingering life of put-away puppets indeed have an uncanny applicability to the illustrations of Becky in the title page and tail-piece illustrations. "In some shows I have seen," says Gross, "the most fascinating life resides in a puppet left untouched, laid on the ground ... A puppet in its very stillness and abandonment may be charged with potential motion, becoming an object of reverie, patiently awaiting some further life."

Fig. 20. 1848 Tail-piece illustration. *Vanity Fair*, 689.

(2011: 66). This is precisely how Thackeray draws the Becky puppet in the 1848 title and tailpieces.

These narrated/illustrated gestures of defiance seen on the Becky puppet add thematic depth and formal coherence to the complex struggle for control in *Vanity Fair*. Thackeray's employment of the mirror-wielding narrator has been amply discussed elsewhere.[24] Less attention, however, has been paid to the object next to the narrator, which reflects the dynamism and potency we see exhibited throughout the novel in Becky's hands (fig. 19). While the manager looks in the mirror, the Becky puppet reaches her arm in the direction of the crossed wood by her side. Critics traditionally identify this piece of crossed wood as one of two logical possibilities: as either a toy sword or as a marionette control bar.[25] Interpretations of the former undoubtedly comply with the farce of military glory that Thackeray sustains throughout the narrative; the latter becomes an obvious extension of the puppetry motif. Either way, the angle with which the narrator holds the mirror recalls the attitude we saw illustrated in the elder Osborne's over-the-shoulder glance back at the females of his family very early on in the narrative. The angle more specifically expresses the anxiety that Becky's appropriation of the sword or marionette bar produces. The narrator is indeed trying to look at himself, trying to believe in the vanity that his gender affords him, but he is deeply mistrustful of the validity of his position despite his obvious (size) advantages. Hence the angle of the mirror registers the threat posed by the proximity of Becky's hand to the sword or marionette control bar below.

In light of Thackeray's treatment of Becky's hands throughout the novel, it is crucial to consider the ways in which the sword and the control bar are *not* mutually exclusive. They are actually psychic *and* physical corollaries for Thackeray, and the narrator is concerned about both. The violent defense of one's self-interests and the puppet-master's abrogation of another's selfhood are at bottom merely different expressions of the same basic impulse to gain social leverage. Therefore, Becky's hand at the end of the novel is as *equally* indistinguishable from manipulative control as it is from physical violence; it partakes of them both. Its suspension between both violence and control in the 1848 title page, composed at the end of the novel is really a culminating instance of how her hands operate in *Vanity Fair* all along. In fact, what we might call Becky's "manipulative violence" reaches its highest dramatic pitch with Thackeray's illustration of her "second appearance" as Clytemnestra in the closing pages of the novel (fig. 21).

The hand's nearly imperceptible transformation from an instrument of mock-epic warfare (with Jos, Osborne, and Wagg) to an agent of dire physical violence locates the tension latent in nineteenth-century social interaction. The aggressiveness of Becky's hands throughout the text makes whatever it is she is holding behind the curtain similar to Merleau-Ponty's sense of *motility* in the overall body schema, where objects attached to the body transform into organic extensions of the limbs themselves (1969: 234). The fact that critics have long been unable to agree on the specificity of the instrument that Thackeray places *in* Becky's hand during her second appearance of Clytemnestra is also telling.[26] Even a close examination of the original illustration under a magnifying glass makes it no easier to discern if the object is a poisonous phial or a miniature dagger.[27] Either way, her hand itself is the locus of threat and the source of male anxiety. Whether or not Becky actually murders Jos

Fig. 21. "Becky's second appearance in the character of Clytemnestra." *Vanity Fair*, 686.

by poison or by stabbing is secondary if not irrelevant for the text's affectivity. More important is Thackeray's depiction of the violent nature of Becky's control over Jos. She appears capable of and willing to use violence as a means to gain ultimate control no matter what the form.

The collapsing of the combative into the dramatic in either the marionette paddle or the sword parallels the instability of whether Becky clutches a phial or a knife. Any combination of these scenarios reveals *Vanity Fair's* preoccupation with the controlling influence of Becky's hands—an effect that literalizes her manipulative temperament. The placement of the control mechanism *between* the Becky doll and the Manager in the title page is emblematic of a larger narrative tension, but its crossed shape is also crucial to the escalating violence located in Becky's previous maneuvers. Her mock-heroic squeeze of Jos's hand in the opening number gives way to fingers that act like miniature swords, even in the most tightly regulated drawing room encounters at Gaunt House. The threat of violence surrounding insurrectionary women, of course, is literalized in her hand during both of Becky's appearances as Clytemnestra. Thus as Becky reaches for the crossed wood on the title page—whether it is viewed as a sword, a marionette paddle, or a combination of both—she is reaching for a kind of feminine control which, in *Vanity Fair*, is always an entangling mixture of individual aggression and social propriety. It is useful in this sense to follow Foucault's reasoning that power is essentially a form of manipulation. What is so fascinating and yet so unnoticed is how literal the manipulation in *Vanity Fair* turns out to be.

One could say that Thackeray's method of composition in novel writing was inclined to give characters more authority than was typically the case with other novelists of his time. According to J. C. Jeaffreson, his method was "to create mentally two or three of his chief characters, and then to write away from time to time, with intervals of repose between the times of industry, and to go onwards from chapter to chapter, with only a general notion of the course he would be taking a few chapters later" (1894: 196). "I don't control my characters," Thackeray told Jeaffreson, "I am in their hands, and they take me where they please" (196). This vision of characterization fits Robert Lougy's appraisal:

When we first enter the fair, Thackeray is its manager, exhibiting before us a creation of his own making, one he understands and is thus able to control. However, we are not far into it before we are aware that we are

Fig. 22. "Virtue rewarded. A booth in Vanity Fair." *Vanity Fair*, 688.

witnessing the unfolding of an artistic vision at once more profound and frightening than even its creator may have anticipated, and consequently, one that Thackeray is at times barely able either to comprehend or control. (1975: 256)

I have argued up until this point that it is Becky who gradually and almost imperceptibly takes over the controlling strings of *Vanity Fair*. Although I have endeavored to show how Thackeray's critique of contemporary gender ideology attendant upon this narrative scheme was unique among male novelists writing in the 1840s, it would be unrealistic not to heed its substantive textual limitations. Becky Sharp goes from attending riotous dinner parties with England's most noble families to occupying herself in works of piety and church, ironically reduced, in a sense, to fulfill Sarah Stickney Ellis's normative definition of woman's role as the "foundation for England's moral worth" (1839: 69). Becky's place at the charity booth (fig. 22) in the novel's final pages is very different than the position she occupied at the height of her popularity in Lord Steyne's circle, the submissive posture of her hands ostensibly reflecting that "fall."

This is still more complicated by the fact that Thackeray clearly sees much of himself in Becky's previous combativeness. As a Cambridge man "writing for his life," in Carlyle's words,[28] with years of financial desperation and a growing family, Thackeray aligned himself—for better or for worse—with the oppressive social institutions and attitudes which Becky does battle against. Like her creator, Becky doesn't rebel against the system proper, but only against the system's treatment of her. Bernard Paris has articulated the inner conflict that Thackeray's simultaneous like and dislike for Becky caused him:

> [S]he is the incarnation of the submerged half of Thackeray's personality. In her character structure, value system, and world view Thackeray has perfectly embodied the aggressive trends that he consciously repudiates but longs to express. Thackeray protects his compliant value system and his public image by his overt condemnation of Becky, but his tendencies to *move against* manifest themselves in his structuring of the action in such a way that Becky is the protagonist. They are expressed in so hidden and subtle a way that Thackeray can ignore them or can pretend ignorance. (1974: 87)

A closer examination of Becky's hands in Thackeray's final full-page illustrations (fig. 23) reveals precisely this sort of subtlety.

Here, Thackeray draws Becky's innocuous hands (fig. 22) in the exact same compositional space as her rapier or phial-wielding hand in her "second appearance as Clytemnestra" (fig. 21). This means that the portrayal of her hands in these radically contrasting postures, only a single page apart and in the very same place on the page, appear through thin paper (or one quick

Fig. 23. Insets of Figures 21 and 22. *Vanity Fair*, 686, 688.

turn of the page) as a *composite* of the violence and propriety in females that Thackeray longs to repudiate and endorse throughout *Vanity Fair*. Endowing her most regular and repetitive social actions with a threatening sense of gender and class insurrection, Thackeray's depiction of Becky attests to, and indeed more directly anticipates, the deeply charged subjective anxiety surrounding hands as England approaches the Darwinian era of the mid- to late 1850s.

PART III

Handling the Perceptual Politics of Identity after Darwin

CHAPTER 5

The Evolutionary Moment in Dickens's Great Expectations

Just after the publication of *Vanity Fair*, in September 1848, *Punch Magazine* responded to a new wave of interest in the hand with a comical entry entitled "Handy Phrenology" (fig. 24). The piece satirizes the Victorian penchant for reading the legibility of character in the materiality of the body with a characteristically playful flair:[1]

> We dare say that the hand of WERTHER will be distinguished by its Werts; and we can imagine that the wrist will be found fully developed in A-WRISTOTLE, A-WRISTIDES, and the rest of the a-wristocracy of genius that the world has contained.

As is the case so often with *Punch*, however, its blunt humor reveals significant cultural preoccupations. The commercial success of texts such as Richard Beamish's *Psychonomy of the Hand* (1843) and *The Hand Phrenologically Considered* (1848) reflected the enthusiasm with which midcentury readers came to associate the material features of their hands with the social components of their identities.

Since no Victorian novelist relied more heavily on the material aspects of characterization than Charles Dickens, it should come as little surprise that the hands of many Dickensian characters operate as extensions of their general dispositions: Fagin's dirty fingernails, Miss Pecksniff's lily hand, Stephen Blackpool's steady grasp, and Uriah Heep's sweaty palms represent just a few notable instances. Some of these defining attributes show Dickens's familiarity with popular pseudoscientific texts reprinted throughout the 1850s. Thomas Gradgrind's "squarely pointing square forefinger" in *Hard Times* (2001 [1854]: 6), for example, draws on Beamish's explicit notion that

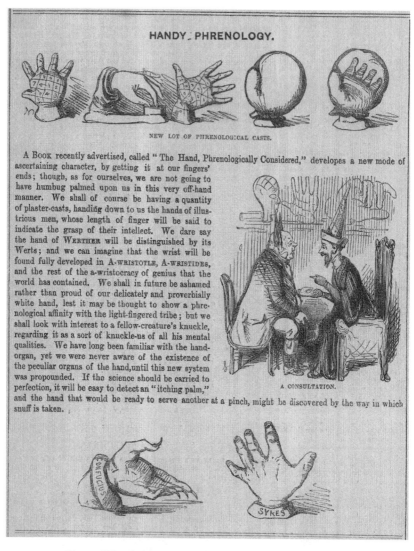

Fig. 24. "Handy Phrenology." *Punch* (9 September 1848): 104.

"the square form on the ends of the fingers [was] the index of precedent, custom, and routine" (1843: 8). The sheer number of hand-related references in *Great Expectations* (1860–61) puts this Dickens novel in a category all its own, though.[2] It is difficult to miss the more than 450 allusions to the word "hand" alone as many appear regularly in the novel's tragi-comedic undercurrent: Mrs. Joe refuses to let anyone forget that she has reared

Fig. 25. Inset from title page of Richard Beamish's *Psychonomy of the Hand* (1843). Courtesy of Ebling Library, Rare Books and Special Collections, University of Wisconsin–Madison.

her little brother "by hand" (1999 [1860–61]: 12); Pumblechook wants his nephew "bound out of hand" as a blacksmith but then cannot later curb his desire to shake Pip's gentlemanly hand (84, 153–54); Jaggers bites "his great forefinger" and throws his exceedingly "large hand" at his opponents (106); Miss Havisham nearly always follows her imperious commands with a curiously "impatient movement of her right hand" (51); Estella wields a "taunting hand," and Joe a "great good hand" (55, 349).[3] I grant that by isolating these examples in this way, I am plucking them from the flow of the narrative. That, however, is just my point.

   This chapter argues that, unlike other novels, Dickens's hands in *Great Expectations* are not merely extensions of their characters' personalities. A particular focus on hands in relation to evolutionary science will show how they function as starkly visible but barely noticeable features at the core of the novel's identity politics. For the contemporary reader, hands operate in the text like a trope so worn away by use and repetition that we hardly notice the attention they call again and again to the series of urgently interrelated Victorian debates about evolution, class, and political economy in which they participate.[4] We have seen in previous chapters how new modes of production catalyzed new modes of relation in the Victorian social sphere. Here, we will consider how a new model of evolutionary change made the hand the most crucial body part for understanding the interconnectedness between nature and culture that Dickens so adeptly probes in his first post-Darwinian novel.

ANIMALS WITH HANDS

The affiliation between the lower classes and lower animals converges in the fictional hand because this body part had begun to lose its privileged status as the primary site of physical differentiation between humans and other animals in the two decades before Dickens penned *Great Expectations*. Almost without exception, Western secular philosophical tradition dating to Aristotle's *De Partibus Animalium* (350 BC) celebrated the hand as an essential feature of human beings. The line of what we might call "hand privileging" among anatomists and philosophers runs remarkably straight from Galen and Bulwer to Kant and Heidegger. Jacques Derrida's coinage of the term *humainisme* ("humanualism") for this tradition brilliantly identifies the importance of the hand to wide-ranging philosophical conceptions of human identity in the Western imagination.

At the outset of *Changing Hands* we saw how Mary Shelley positioned the subject in relation to Genesis through the creature's reading of *Paradise Lost*. In chapter 2 we saw how Charles Bell's 1833 Bridgewater Treatise reasserted the hand's divine connections in response to both factory accidents and impinging materialist science from Germany and France. One strain of this materialist science could be traced back to Rousseau who, in his *Second Discourse* (1755), not only presented the radical view that humans could have evolved from an asocial, animal-like state of nature, but he also speculated (in one of his footnotes) that some of the great apes were humans in a more natural state (Cantor 8). Lord Monboddo (1714–99) picked up on Rousseau's ideas and included discussion of the orangutan in his works. Dickens's early novels, specifically *Martin Chuzzlewit* (1843), treated man's possible relation to apes comically.[5] Even so, as Laura Brown has shown more recently, the ontological shock experienced by humans upon the "discovery" of hominoid apes—from the publication of Edward Tyson's *Anatomy of a Pygmy* (1751) through Shelley's *Frankenstein* (1818)—was focused not on the likeness of hands but on the similarities of heads and faces (2011:

2–63). Throughout the eighteenth century, those familiar with scientific travel books were shocked to learn of a "Monster with a human face"(30).[6]

This facial location changed rather dramatically in the 1840s when a tandem of scientific and fictional work brought anxieties about the human-ape relationship to a far greater swath of the English public. In 1844, Robert Chambers anonymously published *Vestiges of the Natural History of Creation*—one of the first English works to popularize a theory of evolution for the history of the world (Lightman 1997: 207). Because the text provided an organic theory for species creation and because it was published anonymously, *Vestiges* had many detractors in the conservative and established scientific community. Nonetheless, criticism of the book seemed only to publicize and to increase its popularity. The more *Vestiges* "was dissected at public scientific meetings, [and] condemned from pulpits and lecture platforms," the more it was "borrowed from circulating libraries, and read" (Secord 2000: 37). A passage that would have been alarming to this wider audience was the text's assertion that human "hands, and other features grounded on by naturalists as characteristic . . . do not differ more from the simiadae than the bats do from the lemurs" (1994 [1844]: 266). Chambers's use of a double negative here jumbles (perhaps unconsciously) his central point that the hand may not be so characteristic of humans after all.

As fate would have it, a horrifying piece of fiction preceding the publication of *Vestiges* by several years amplified this uneasy notion that lower animals could possess hands. The April 1841 installment of *Graham's Magazine* contained Edgar Allan Poe's "The Murders in the Rue Morgue." This new kind of detective story chronicled a gruesome double murder, one of which involved a young woman "strangled to death by manual strength" (1985: 262). Auguste Dupin solves the murders only by eventually recognizing that "the dark bruises, and deep indentations of finger nails" match Cuvier's "minute anatomical and generally descriptive account of the large fulvous Ourang-Outang" known for its "gigantic stature . . . prodigious strength and . . . wild ferocity" (252, 264).[7] These narratives featuring what Susan David Bernstein appropriately calls the *"anxiety of simianation"*— in both their scientific and fictional iterations—reveal that the discomfort about the possibility of evolutionary proximity between humans and other primate species clearly existed before the watershed event of Darwin's 1859 *Origin of Species* (2001: 255).

Man's superiority over animals was contested throughout the 1850s by what the Victorians referred to as the "Development Hypothesis." But it was not until the publication of Darwin's *Origin of Species* that a mechanism (natural selection) for evolution seriously challenged the notion of a uniform law created by an almighty lawgiver. One of the very few passages containing explicit reference to human beings in the *Origin* discusses (with considerably more confidence than *Vestiges*) how the hand resembles the extremities of presumably "lower" animals: "the framework of bones [is] the same in the hand of a man," writes Darwin, as in the "wing of a bat, fin of the porpoise, and leg of the horse" (1996 [1859]: 387). Aside from this sentence, Darwin famously excluded humans from his original formulation of natural selection, yet their conspicuous absence from the text only made the subject more prominent to Victorian readers who considered the *Origin* to be "centrally concerned with man's descent" (Beer 1983: 59–60). Theories of racial degeneration multiplied as reports of the newly discovered gorilla began to circulate among Victorian scientists in the late 1840s and 1850s. Two gorilla skulls reached the British Zoological Society in 1846, followed by a full skeleton in 1851, and finally, a gorilla body (pickled in alcohol) in 1858. These developments, along with the popular African travel books of Paul du Chaillu, helped make the existence of gorillas known to the general public in England during the late 1850s. Propelled by Darwin's theory of evolution, the preoccupation with a "missing link" had developed into a full-fledged cultural phenomenon. Virtually every British newspaper and magazine carried stories referencing "man's nearest relation" by 1860.

What propelled the Victorian interest in gorillas was how much like humans the animals looked and behaved. Du Chaillu's account of his first gorilla sighting confirms the extent to which their general stature invoked comparison to humans: "they looked fearfully like hairy men" (1861: 60). Du Chaillu was even more shocked to discover how closely gorillas resembled humans from a skeletal perspective (fig. 26). His detailed comparisons revealed differences in the cranium, the spine, and the pelvis but they also repeatedly called attention to the same number of bones (twenty-seven) in the human and gorilla wrist and hand (418).[8]

As I have suggested in discussing Chambers's *Vestiges* and Poe's "The Murders in the Rue Morgue," the Victorian fascination with the gorilla was heightened by the fact that the animal's ferocity was not solely a matter of redness in tooth or claw. The reports coming to England in the late 1850s dramatized how the gorilla attacked not with its formidable teeth, but rather with its bare hands. Du Chaillu had described this method of attack in considerable detail in *Explorations and Adventures*:

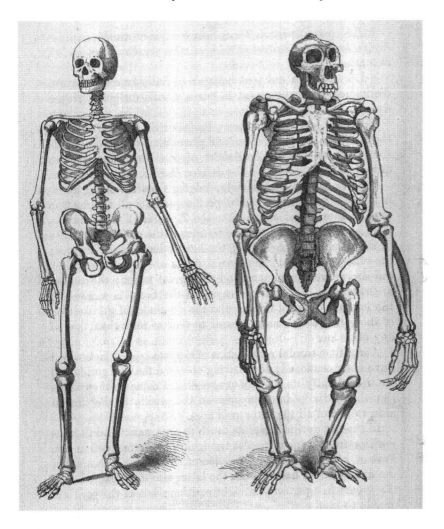

Fig. 26. "Skeletons of Man and the Gorilla." *Explorations and Adventures* (418).

[T]his animal lies in wait in the lower branches of trees, watching for people who go to and fro; and, when one passes sufficiently near, grasps the luckless fellow with his ["lower hands"], and draws him up into the tree, where he quietly chokes him. (62)

In May 1859, only a year and a half before the publication of *Great Expectations*, Dickens's own magazine (*All the Year Round*) set this aspect of the

gorilla's manual savagery against the backdrop of middle-class industriousness, in "Our Nearest Relation":

> The honey-making, architectural bee, low down in the scale of life, with
> its insignificant head, its little boneless body, and gauzy wing, is our type
> of industry and skill: while this apex in the pyramid of brute creation,
> the near approach to the human form, what can it do? *The great hands
> have no skill but to clutch and strangle.* (114, emphasis added)

A feature in *Punch* entitled "The Missing Link"[9] reveals how quickly
Britons co-opted contemporary evolutionary theory for colonial purposes
in order to help differentiate themselves from their Irish subjects:

> A gulf, certainly, does appear to yawn between the Gorilla and the
> Negro. The woods and wilds of Africa do not exhibit an example of any
> intermediate animal. But in this, as in many other cases, philosophers
> go vainly searching abroad for that which they would readily find if they
> sought it at home. A creature manifestly between the Gorilla and the
> Negro is to be met within some of the lowest districts of London and
> Liverpool by adventurous explorers. It comes from Ireland, whence it
> has contrived to migrate; it belongs in fact to a tribe of Irish savages.
> (October 18, 1862)

An unguarded letter Charles Kingsley wrote to his wife in 1860, however,
captures the spirit of deep anxiety Britons felt about their hollow justifica-
tions for colonial subjugation in Ireland:

> I believe that there are not many more of them than of old, but they
> are happier, better, more comfortably fed and lodged under our rule
> than they ever were. But to see white chimpanzees is dreadful; if they
> were black, one would not feel it so much, but their skins, except where
> tanned by exposure, are as white as ours. (1877, 107)

L. Perry Curtis and Patrick Brantlinger have demonstrated that the Victorians readily adopted this rhetoric of biological hierarchy to draw connections
between the simian and the Irish—a "race" regarded as subhuman in the
English imagination long before Darwin. The idea of an intermediary animal seemed to fit particularly well given the supposedly Irish predilection for

violence and physical labor. Their status as Europe's only white "savages" was deeply entrenched by the time Thomas Carlyle wrote in *Chartism* that the Irishman "is there to undertake all work that can be done by mere strength of hand and back—for wages that will purchase him potatoes" (1840: 124). What many Victorians thought of as a uniquely Irish combination of racial otherness, violence, and capacity for manual labor may be seen in the life-size "tracings of living hands," which accompany Richard Beamish's popular work *Psychonomy of the Hand* (1843) (fig. 27).

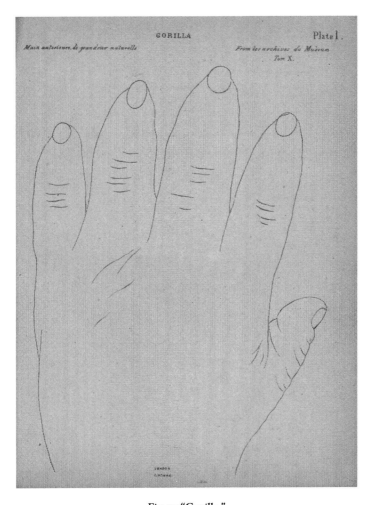

Fig. 27. "Gorilla."

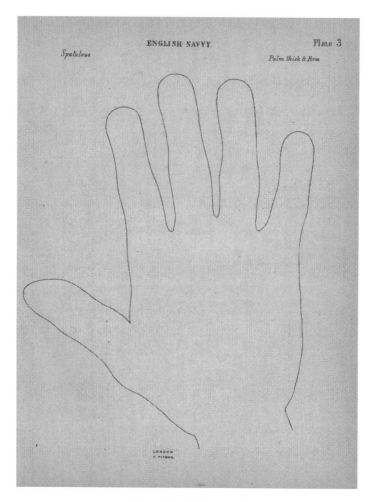

Fig. 28. "English Navvy."

These full-page plates appeared at the end of Beamish's text, and readers were encouraged to trace their own hands on top of them as a means of direct comparison. The above affiliation between the gorilla and the navvy is implied by proximity (plate numbers 1 and 3 of 30), and also by shape and nationality. Beamish states that "the more the palm dominates over the fingers in the hand of man, the more the character approaches to that of the brute, with instincts low and degrading" (6). Since the discovery of gorillas (fig. 27) and the influx of Irish navvies (fig. 28) into the British workforce occurred more or less simultaneously, large palms and short fingers were interpreted not only as indicators of a propensity to handle shovels, pick-axes, and barrows, but as signs of animality itself. Barbarism and manual labor—concepts linked long before Darwin—thus became biologically con-stituent in the Victorian imagination immediately before Dickens began to compose *Great Expectations* at the end of 1859. It is useful, here, to recall Alexander Welsh's warning not to "underestimate the degree to which Dick-ens was aware of the intellectual ferment of his time" (1971: 117).

Indeed, just eighteen months after his magazine published the piece describing "the portentous power of grasp" in the gorilla hand, Dickens created in his new novel a working-class Irish character (Molly) that mur-ders a woman twice her size by strangling her with her bare hands. Such parallels would be less worthy of remark if Dickens did not conspicuously emphasize Molly's Irishness throughout *Great Expectations*. Most obvi-ously, her name is a lower-class Irish nickname for Mary, and Wemmick's assertion that she has "some gypsy blood in her" (293) only confirms Terry Eagleton's observation that Gypsy blood in the nineteenth-century novel was "simply an English way of saying that [the character] is quite possibly Irish" (1995: 3). Brantlinger also reminds us of how often the English saw rebelliousness in general "as an Irish character flaw" (2011: 138). Therefore, the convergence of Molly's nationality, capacity for rebellion, and violent "nature" reaches its most ideological and subjective distillation in the dra-matic scene where Jaggers pins her hands to the table for Pip and the other gentlemen-in-training to view:

> "There's power here," said Mr. Jaggers, coolly tracing out the sinews [of Molly's hand] with his forefinger. "Very few men have the power of wrist that this woman has. It's remarkable what force of grip there is in these hands. I have had occasion to notice many hands; but I never saw any-thing stronger in that respect, man's or woman's, than these." (166)

Jaggers's compulsive admiration of Molly's hands further anatomizes the novel's general association of criminal behavior with animality. In particular, the scene's figuration of Molly's social deviancy in evolutionary terms serves to collapse the disavowed discourses of gender, labor, and criminality into a single bodily organ. The "remarkable force of grip" in Molly's hands alludes to her previous crime but, as we have seen, the method she uses in the per-formance of this criminal act reflects contemporary anxiety regarding the fragility of the barrier between the human and the animal.

This barrier becomes further destabilized by Molly's direct affiliation with manual labor. Since the narrative mentions her presence solely at Jaggers's dinner parties, it would be easy to overlook how Molly's status as the household's *only* servant makes her a "maid-of-all-work" in the 1850s—that "unfeminine and rough" housekeeping class whose daily chores included hauling coals, bundling wood, and scouring grates (Beeton 1861: 1485). Far from rendering her "a wild beast tamed" as Wemmick surmises, then, Molly's domestic servitude actually forms a necessary part of what Jaggers calls her "wild violent nature."

EXPRESSIONS AND REPRESSIONS OF LABOR

It is crucial to consider the ways in which Jaggers's outward domination of Molly's untamed working hands underwrites his attraction to them. Dickens figures this attraction as a class and racial affiliation that would have been immediately apparent to a readership familiar with manual typologies like Beamish's *Psychonomy*, which drew explicit correlations between race, occupation, and hand size.

According to Beamish, "the one [fig. 29], by force of character raised himself to respectability and wealth; the other [fig. 30] remains in his original depression, a labourer at two shillings and sixpence a day" (1843: 11). What is implied, of course, is the Lamarckian notion that the hand's biological structure wills itself to suit its owner's social stature—a point more subtly implied by the blankness of the "respectable" hand (fig. 29) in comparison to the marked palm of the laborer (fig. 30). Thus the emphasis on Jaggers's "exceedingly dark complexion" and "correspondingly large hand[s]," combined with his compulsive desire to keep them *un*marked by his labor, paradoxically forms a kind of perceptual politics that align him with the very qualities he attempts to tame out of Molly (68).[10]

In fact, it is possible to view the novel's uncanny insistence on the material presence of Jaggers's hands as constitutive of the ideological contradictions at the heart of middle-class subjectivity at midcentury. Edgar Rosenberg (Dickens 1999) and Daniel Tritter (1997) have demonstrated how Jaggers's training in a lawyer's office (as opposed to at a university) makes his work more like a trade than a genteel profession. I would like to press this point a bit further, though. The *way* Jaggers uses his ponderous hands even in his middle-class job as a solicitor suggests a more immediate

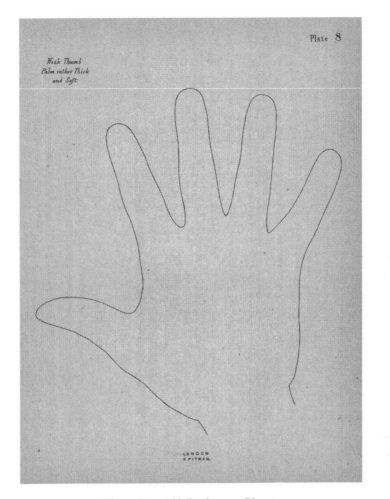

Fig. 29. Beamish's *Psychonomy*, Plate 8.

connection to manual labor. Jaggers's occupation clearly situates him in a class above common laborers, yet nearly all of the professional "work" he accomplishes in the novel depends directly on his abnormally large hands. For instance, his habit of biting his hands and throwing his "great forefinger" frightens clients and magistrates alike in every scene the reader witnesses in connection to his profession (107).

Jaggers's "ceremonious" use of his handkerchief also allows him to induce fear by forcing his opponent to focus on his most recognizable physical attribute (185). Even his reliance on the silk handkerchief is shot through

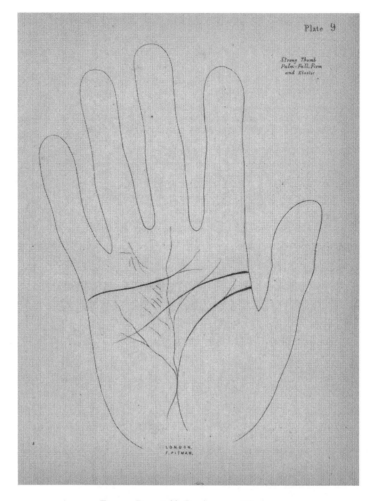

Fig. 30. Beamish's *Psychonomy*, Plate 9.

with internal and professional contradiction, though. Evacuated as it is of
the functional value it would have for laboring hands, the handkerchief
communicates social divisions by simultaneously invoking and invalidating
the most common anatomical site of work in the nineteenth century. By
contrast, "real" laborers wore handkerchiefs around their necks and in their
pockets. There they were used for protection against the sun and for wiping
away sweat from the face and hands when performing manual work of the
kind we later learn Magwitch performs in New South Wales. Given these
cultural associations, Jaggers's ownership of the silk handkerchief marks

him as genteel, but his actual *use* of it points to working-class origins—especially since Dickens repeatedly emphasizes how the handkerchief's "imposing proportions" correspond directly to the size of his hands (185).[11]

Elizabeth Grosz's view of the body as a live theater of sociocultural life (1994) is germane to *Great Expectations* in the sense that the scenes involving the aestheticization of Molly's hands stage Jaggers's complicated personal relationship to society's lowest classes. Since Jaggers orchestrates Molly's "hand trap" to interrupt a discussion of the arm size and rowing prowess of his genteel clients, the scene offers a dramatic commentary on class from an unlikely, and otherwise robotically-neutral, source. It is precisely when Pip's group is "wound up . . . to a pitch little short of ferocity," "baring and spanning [their] arms in a ridiculous manner" that Jaggers traps and displays Molly's hands for his genteel clients (166). Not only does the timing of the action make it a pronouncement to Pip and his friends about the authenticity of the labor she performs but, more importantly, it draws attention to a form of labor that Jaggers's middle-class profession prohibits him from claiming as his own.

What we witness in Jaggers's eccentric behavior is the complex and often vexing presence of work in Victorian England. James Eli Adams (1995), Kaja Silverman (1992), and Herbert Sussman (1995) have demonstrated the multiform ways in which masculinity operated as a locus of anxiety rather than as a monolithic and stable source of power for Victorian men. In particular, the Victorian ideology that defined masculine "work" as physical and muscular induced an anxiety in middle-class males who no longer worked with their hands amidst a society transformed by bourgeois industrialization. A new valorization of manliness—unsteady though it was—emerged around a model of discipline and self-regulation in the face of what was seen as the libertinism and idleness of the gentry and the irregularity and sexual license of the working class. As we see with Jaggers, though, even a rigid application of "control" offers not a unitary consolidation of masculinity, but rather one beset by contradictions that James Eli Adams correctly refers to as "the energies and anxieties of masculine self-legitimation" (1995: 1).[12]

The fact that Wemmick can reliably predict Pip's experience of the hand-trapping spectacle during his visit to Gerrard Street means that the exhibition of Molly's hands is a ritualized part of Jaggers's fragile identity. It reveals the "anxious conjunction of discipline and performance in middle-class constructions of masculinity" (Adams 1995: 10). Wemmick's fulfilled prediction indicates that Jaggers routinely performs this "show" for new visitors. Such a "show" relates to Peter Stallybrass and Allon White's view concerning the contradictory psychological effects that rapid economic transition had on the middle-class subject: "The bourgeois subject continuously defined and re-defined itself through the exclusion of what is marked as 'low'—as dirty, repulsive, noisy, contaminating . . . Yet the very act of exclusion was constitutive of its identity" (1986: 191). More recently, Janice Carlisle has linked this line of inquiry to a particular "melancholic condition" in Victorian manhood; what she calls a "nearly pathological insubstantiality" affecting recently mobile men who "unconsciously long for the sensuous, material reality characteristic of traditional forms of trade" (2004: 20, 62). It is for exactly these reasons that the language of Molly's "taming" so accurately describes the fractured nature of Jaggers's subjectivity. In both cases the ever-present possibility of eruption of the "low" must be "kept down," as Jaggers himself admits, by a repetitive process designed to stop even "an inkling of its breaking out" (307).

I refer here to a mechanism of psychic repression that is not solely Freudian. Like many Foucauldian-influenced critics, I seek to recast behavior that has been ahistorically aligned with fear, anxiety, or avoidance as a Victorian response to the unstable and contradictory boundaries of normative bourgeois masculinity. By this logic, the episodic taming of Molly's hands provides a necessary environment for facilitating the *controlled return* of all that Jaggers represses in his own hands.[13] It is a paradoxical process of acknowledgment and negation that ultimately links Molly's wildness with other textual indicators of Jaggers's anxiety: his insistence on casual rather than "ceremonious" dinner attire and his preference for "Brittania metal" rather than silver (163, 160).[14] And since anxiety protects by obscuring what would otherwise be intolerable to contemplate, the "training" sessions at the dinner table with Molly allow Jaggers to touch yet control the qualities that middle-class Victorian men were most anxious about: their proximity to manual labor, "unmanly" intellectual labor, and racial degeneration. The aestheticization of Molly's hands in terms of Irishness, animality, and labor becomes a way for Jaggers to retain physical and psychological contingence with the most socially interdicted realms of middle-class Victorian manhood. "These low domains," according to Stallybrass and White, predictably "return as the object of nostalgia, longing and fascination" (1986: 191).

However, *Great Expectations* represents only one instance of a cultural trend after the publication of *Origin of Species* where the physical site of such longing and fascination was figured in the human hand. What we might call Dickens's "attraction to repulsion" from working hands also formed the basis of the bizarre relationship between the real-life Arthur Munby and his servant-turned-wife Hannah Culliwick. The Cambridge-educated Munby never worked with anything heavier than a pen, yet his diaries are replete with an attraction to the animalistic features of working female hands. Recent historians and literary critics have acknowledged the value of Munby's diaries to constructions of mid-nineteenth-century gender and class anxieties, but surprisingly not in relation to *Great Expectations* where these concerns surface as a particular form of evolutionary uneasiness in the wake of the publication of *Origin of Species*.[15]

Consider the eerie similarity between the dramatic hand-trapping scene in *Great Expectations* and Arthur Munby's diary recollection of an encounter with a servant in 1861:

> I asked her to show me her hand. Staring at me in blank astonishment, she obeyed, and held out her right hand for me to look at. And certainly, I never saw such a hand as hers, either in man or woman. They were large and thick & broad, with big rude fingers and bony thumbs—but that was not very remarkable . . . It was in her *palms* that she was unrivalled: and such palms! The whole interior of each hand, from the wrist to the finger-tips, was *hoofed* with a thick sheet of horn . . . What must be the result to a woman of carrying about her always, instead of a true human hand, such a brutal excrescence as this? (Reay 2002: 99–100, 128)

Since there are no documented links between Dickens and Munby (not to mention the near simultaneousness of *Great Expectations* and this particular account), it would be a mistake to dismiss their focus on rough female hands as isolated instances of social deviance. Instead, if we view this kind of "manual" perversion as a culturally *central* phenomenon, it is possible to see the ways in which the deviant hand emerged as an important site of tension between new scientific theories of interconnectedness and a social heterodoxy that assigned innate, unalterable characteristics to gender, class, and animality. The staging of what Judith Halberstam calls "female masculinity" (1998) is riveting for Munby and others like him precisely because it offers a privileged glimpse into how masculinity is constructed as masculinity. This anxious pluralizing of gender categories productively complicates the pervasive academic model that often situates nineteenth-century gender conflicts solely within the binary of masculine/feminine. In a novel deeply concerned about the pre-cariousness of many identities, *Great Expectations'* attention to hands exposes the disturbingly relational—not immutable—nature of such categories.

SLEIGHTS OF HAND

The fact that the novel's most "wild" hand is biologically connected to its most refined hand makes this body part a prime agent in the novel's plot as well as a site of collapsed social signification. Here I wish to extend Peter Brooks's influential claim that plotting is "the central vehicle and armature of meaning" in *Great Expectations* by exploring how the novel's aesthetics of embodiment make meaning not only carnal but, even more specifically, manual (1984: 24). The semioticization of the body eventually converges with what Brooks calls "the somatization of the story" in Pip's sudden real-ization that Molly's "hands [are] Estella's hands" (1993: 21). The improbabil-ity of their biological association, of course, rests on the putative difference between what their respective hands mean in the era's symbolic perceptual economy: if Molly's hands connote animality, violence, and labor, then Estel-la's signify refinement, beauty, and leisure.

Yet for much of the novel, Dickens actively abets and even endorses the misinterpretation of these categories as separate, self-contained enti-ties through its depiction of female gesture at Satis House. He often figures Miss Havisham's class leverage, for example, as a barely perceptible but con-sistent combination of verbal and manual directive. Over and over again, Miss Havisham's orders for Pip to play, to sing Old Clem, and to walk her around the bridal table are accompanied by the same "impatient movement of the fingers of her right hand" (51, 77, 70). What complicates Pip's mistake is the fact that Estella appears to inherit a capacity for similar behavior as she uses her "white," "taunting hand" to reinforce her inaccessibility during Pip's tortuous early visits to Satis House (55, 181). This narrative red herring apparently affiliates Satis House hands with a Ruskinian notion of gentility as an organic sensibility where the "fineness of nature" is figured as a category of breeding. Unable even to consider the notion of a less-than-aristocratic Estella, Pip is blinded by the Victorian ideology that tended to convert dif-ferences in the acquisition of culture into differences of nature.[16]

Dickens highlights this inability to comprehend relationships between high and low in Pip's repeated failure to identify the connection between

Estella's and Molly's hands. After the taming scene at Jaggers's house, the text subtly but regularly aligns Molly's animality with Estella's recalcitrance almost exclusively by way of gestural similarity. Estella's insistence that she possesses "no softness, no—sympathy—[no] sentiment," for instance, becomes acutely unsettling to Pip because it is accompanied by "a slight wave of her hand" (183, 182). The proclamation of insensitivity, combined with the movement of her gesturing hand, sends Pip into the novel's most puzzling meditation:

> As my eyes followed her white hand, again the same dim suggestion that I could not possibly grasp, crossed me. My involuntary start occasioned her to lay her hand upon my arm. Instantly the ghost passed once more and was gone.
>   What *was* it? (183)

Similar to what we will encounter in chapter 7 where Lady Dedlock's recognition of her lost lover's handwriting in *Bleak House* touches her "like the faintness of death," the question in *Great Expectations*—"What *was* the nameless shadow?"—revisits Pip each time he observes Estella's hands in any capacity (202).

Pip's failure to identify the connection between Estella's and Molly's hands provides narrative suspense but it also exposes his crucial misunderstanding of the relationship between nature and culture. Estella's beauty and inaccessibility lead Pip to assume that there is something "natural" about her class position, an assumption that exemplifies Bourdieu's notion that social values become invisible as acts of culture. Indeed, Pip suffers from a form of habitus which legitimates (and delimits) categories in a society that encourages people to recognize as valid the kinds of everyday ritual, dress, and actions which make particular individuals appear to be the flesh-and-blood incarnation of social roles. Pip exhibits this blindness most notably as he objects to Estella's professed incapacity for feeling by alleging that such emotional deficiency "is not in Nature" (271). Estella's double-sided response more accurately summarizes the interconnectedness between origin and culture that Pip repeatedly fails to see: "It is in *my* nature . . . It is in the nature formed within me" (271, emphasis added).

The formation of the latter nature, or what we might call personality, is antedated by Estella's biological kinship with Molly and Magwitch. Beneath her genteel aloofness and apparent refinement there are important parts of

Estella's identity that link her disposition, as well as her hand movements, to Molly's "wild" nature. Not only does she exhibit the violent capacity of her mother's hands as she slaps Pip's face "with such force she had," but she also appears *attracted* to the atmosphere of physical aggression itself.[17] Watching Herbert and Pip fistfight delights Estella so much that she offers Pip her only unsolicited amatory advance in the moments after the altercation:

> There was a bright flush upon her face, as though something had happened to delight her. Instead of going straight to the gate, too, she stepped back into the passage, and beckoned me.
> "Come here! You may kiss me if you like." (75)

Interestingly, Estella shows her attraction to Pip not when he learns to act like a gentleman, but after he cuts his hands on Herbert's teeth and confesses to feeling like a "species of young wolf, or other wild beast" (75). The attraction of Estella to physical violence, apparent also in her inscrutable decision to marry the horse-beating Drummle, suggests the emergence of a long-buried barbarism that opens deeper connections to her mother Molly. Yet only in the "action of their fingers," does Pip register a Darwinian truth that he, along with middle-class culture at large, deeply abhors: that criminality and civilization, violence and refinement, wealth and poverty are inextricably linked.

THE LABOR OF HAND TRANSFORMATION

The Darwinian model of interconnectedness frames the entire novel in the sense that Pip's *bildung* turns out to be the process by which he learns to appreciate the social, economic, and emotional value of his own (and others') hands. This development poses a figurative corollary to the literal transformation of Pip's hands from coarse instruments of labor in the forge to bejeweled appendages of leisure in London. Nowhere does the contrast between laboring and genteel hands appear more starkly than when Magwitch returns to London at the end of the novel's second volume. Here, Magwitch's proclamation that he "lived rough, that [Pip] should live smooth" is not simply highlighted, but brilliantly *embodied* by the physical interplay of Magwitch's "heavy brown veinous" hands and Pip's ringed and recoiling hands (241). On seven different occasions in this brief reunion chapter, Magwitch attempts to embrace Pip's hands while Pip responds by "recoil[ing] from his touch as if he had been a snake" (241).

Like Molly, Magwitch's class and criminality evoke a fear of barbarity that is located principally in the action of his hands. The reader shares with Pip, for instance, the frightening image of Magwitch's "manacled hands" shaking Compeyson's "torn hair from his fingers" from one of the novel's earliest scenes (33). In the convict's return to Pip's apartment, Dickens extends this conflation of animality, labor, and criminality. Magwitch's membership in the penal colony of Australia necessarily classifies him as both a criminal and a manual laborer in the eyes of the state. Pip registers his "repugnance" and "abhorrence" for Magwitch in his remark that "there was Convict in the very grain of the man" (253–54, 252). But Pip seems to object, both consciously and unconsciously, more to the wild unrefinement of Magwitch's class than to the barbarity of his unknown crimes. The observations Pip makes in the paragraph immediately following his contention that there was "Convict" in the very grain of the prisoner reveal his entrenched prejudices: "In all his ways of sitting and standing, and eating and drinking . . . there was Prisoner, Felon, Bondsman, as plain as could be" (252–53).

Likewise, the tone of indictment Pip uses to describe Magwitch's bearing resonates with his disgust for Joe's clumsiness upon first visiting London. Joe, of course, remains antithetical to all things criminal, but the working-class life he represents becomes criminalized nonetheless once Pip arrives at his new status as a gentleman. In this sense, the genteel requirement to stay away from work, home, and forge is represented most poignantly by Pip's sobbing farewell to the finger post at the end of his village lane. Pip either touches or mentions the finger post every time he comes back to the marshes as a gentleman. Thus, if the finger post is "the pastoral equivalent of Jaggers's forefinger," as Douglas Brooks-Davies has suggested, then the manual labor it points to becomes criminalized like everything else to which Jaggers directs his great index finger (1989: 57).

Rightfully so, a host of critics have explored the complex array of forces that make labor particularly resistant to representation in the Victorian novel.[18] In *Great Expectations*, though, we encounter work in the most likely and obvious (surface) places: in the hands of its working characters like Biddy, Joe, the Aged P., and Molly. It is true that *Great Expectations*, like the majority of other Victorian novels, conceals much of the actual work performed within its pages. With Magwitch, however, Dickens makes up for the deficit of narrative space devoted to his sheep-farming operations in Australia by repeatedly inscribing it on Magwitch's hands. Marx's physiological model of labor power as a commodity which exists only in the worker's living body becomes dramatized in Magwitch's account of his life as he sits before Pip and Herbert. Within this scene, crucially, even the act of recounting the narrative of labor is laborious. Pip remarks how Magwitch often "spread his hands broader on his knees, and lifted them off and put them on again . . . took out his [cotton] handkerchief and wiped his face and head and hands, before he could go on" (262–63). So powerful is Dickens's presentation of manual work—even if it occurs outside of the novel—that any account of it partakes of its strenuousness.

Furthermore, Magwitch's hands appear "large," "heavy," "brown," "knotted," and "veinous" only when he returns from New South Wales and knocks on Pip's door in London (240). This characterization seemingly fulfills Engels's postulation that "the hand is not only the organ of labour, *it is also the product of labour*" (1968 [1876]: 253, emphasis original). As we saw with Jaggers and Molly, the size of Magwitch's hands would indicate wildness and criminality to nineteenth-century readers. But the narrative's insistence on the color, shape, and texture of his hands reflects manual labor's unwillingness, as it were, to go away even in the Victorian novel where it is rendered textually and often geographically invisible. In a Marxian sense, Dickens's emphasis on the materiality of Magwitch's hands highlights the physiological fact of human labor behind a money commodity that could not have been more abstract to Pip. As Pip tells Herbert, "It has almost made me mad to sit here of a night and see him before me, so bound up with my fortunes and misfortunes, and yet so unknown to me" (358).

Rather than recognize labor in Magwitch's hands, or perhaps *because* he recognizes it, Pip confuses a hand that is "stained with blood" with a hand that is marked by work (242). His unwillingness to acknowledge a hand so marked engages the more central problem of work's invisibility in the rapidly industrializing capitalist economy in the decade before *Great Expectations*. Thomas Richards has argued that the Great Exhibition of 1851 inaugurated an "era of the spectacle" where the display of Victorian commodities became physically and semiotically separated from their actual manufacture (1990: 3). Pip confirms his culture's investment in this imaginative separation of work and commodity when he laments that the only thing worse than being a manual laborer is being seen in the act of performing such labor:

> What I dreaded was, that in some unlucky hour I, being at my grimiest and commonest, should lift up my eyes and see Estella looking in at one of the wooden windows of the forge. (87)

In an ironic twist on Marx, Pip's ignorance of where his money comes from is perhaps never so fraught with alienation than on the night he perceives the hands that actually produced it. The agitation with which Pip receives Magwitch's avowal that "I worked hard, that you should be above work," therefore, comes not so much because Magwitch is or was a criminal, but rather because the producing hand has become literally visible. Up until this point, Pip has maintained a state of agitated unawareness regarding the connection between the money that sustains him and the labor that supports him. The "social hieroglyphic" that Marx sees connecting labor and money, though, becomes immediately decipherable when Magwitch enters Pip's apartment with his hands outstretched (132). Magwitch's "large brown veinous hands" finally materialize the "mystical character" of the commodity that Marx attributes to its ability to embody human labor (240, 132). The size and color of his hands, along with their veins and knots, serve as the text's most important reminder that the idleness and prosperity of the privileged classes are dependent on the labor of others.[19]

Dickens could not mark the end of Pip's time as an idle gentleman more aptly. He renders physically useless the very hands upon whose *dis*engagement Pip's Victorian gentility had been defined. The fact that Pip burns his hands in a fire while trying to save Miss Havisham further emphasizes how far his quest for gentlemanly status has taken him from his original apprenticeship as a blacksmith—a vocation that required him to handle fire, coals, and molten iron on a daily basis. Regaining "the use of [his] hands" so that he can row Magwitch to safety thus becomes the most important object in Pip's life and one necessary for him to recognize the immediate power and value of the burned hands he had earlier disowned as "coarse and common" appendages (301).

If Pip's emotional search for Estella's true identity is a displaced search for his own identity, as Carolyn Brown has usefully suggested, then the specific location of the disclosure of Estella's history within the scene where Pip receives treatment for his burned hands merits closer scrutiny (71). This displacement becomes pivotally highlighted by the text's juxtaposition of Herbert's family's knowledge of Molly with the physical convalescence of Pip's hands:

"It seems," said Herbert, "—there's a bandage off most charmingly, and now comes the cool one—makes you shrink at first, my poor dear fellow, don't it? but it will be comfortable presently—it seems that the woman was a young woman, and a jealous woman, and a revengeful woman; revengeful, Handel, to the last degree." (302)

Herbert's dialogue may appear routine given his task, but something remarkable happens in this passage's treatment of Pip's "shrinking." The reaction is at once a physical response to having bandages removed from his blistered hands and an emotional flinch from learning of Estella's low, criminal heritage—a scenario that confirms Beer's notion that "many Victorian rejections of evolutionary ideas register a physical shudder" (1983: 9). The causes of physical and emotional pain are the same for Pip at this moment, and their convergence in the novel's most important body part draws attention to the ways in which Victorian anxieties about the fragility of the barrier between human and animal were transferred—often via the hand—to the period's eroding social boundaries.

The novel eventually mitigates some of this anxiety by figuring the hand as the principal instrument of sympathetic feeling between Pip and Magwitch. In a sequence at the end of the novel that Harry Stone has influentially referred to as a "secret freemasonry of hands," (1979: 330) Pip yearns for contact with the criminal hands he so desperately sought to keep separate from his own. Many subsequent critics have followed Stone's lead, consciously or not, in attempting to decode Dickens's emphasis on hands in *Great Expectations* as part of a "fugitive," "covert," and "textually-established scheme" (MacLeod 2002: 127, 129); as the site of "encryption for homosocial desire" (Cohen 1993: 221); or simply as "the end point of the novel's metonymic logic" (Woloch 2003: 201). As I have endeavored to show, however, the meaning behind the pantomime of imagery that ends *Great Expectations* is far from secret or "magical" (Stone 1979: 333). Instead, it offers a quite fitting resolution for a novel composed at the unique cultural moment when the hand was diagnostic of biological, social, and moral identity.

Historicizing hands in the context of contemporary discourse allows us to evaluate how this particular part of the body became a site where scientists and novelists alike could reimagine progress and transformation. This is where I think Dickens acts in characteristic fashion in his good-spirited use of Darwinian evolutionary material. In the world of this novel, those who fail to adapt and to change never truly make any social or moral progress, and

Dickens clearly revels in this idea as he concludes. People like Pumblechook conspicuously offer "the same fat five fingers" in the text's beginning and its end, while Joe, over the same course of time, develops not only his laboring hand but his writing one as well (351). Likewise, Pip's moral development actually becomes manual development; the sensitivity of Pip's character eventually merges with the sensitivity of his hands as he learns to understand, among other things, the feel of "pretty eloquence" in Biddy's ringed hand and the exquisite meaning of the "slight pressures" of Magwitch's hand while his benefactor lay on his deathbed (341). Even his ability to thwart Jaggers's "powerful pocket handkerchief" develops concomitantly with his ability to distinguish between criminality and manual labor, between hands that forge bank notes and hands that forge iron, and ultimately between hands that "work" and hands that work (305).

CHAPTER 6

Racial Science and the Kabbalah in Eliot's Daniel Deronda

Previous chapters have shown how the human hand became a lightning rod for a host of nineteenth-century anxieties related to the shifting categories of manufacture, gender, class, animality, and religion. George Eliot, in relation to these anxieties, was both an author very much of her time and yet a thinker far ahead of her time. Like just about every serious scientist and intellectual of the 1870s, she maintained a physiological understanding of the development of organic life. But unlike many of her contemporaries, she remained relatively unmoved by the anxieties about the hand that swept through the post-Darwinian world.[1] Even at the height of the "gorilla-mania" that followed Du Chaillu's *Explorations* (1861), Eliot's fiction emphasized the uniquely human attributes of the hand's sensitivity, receptiveness, and connection to sympathetic feeling.

Eliot composed *Romola* (1862–63) when, as we saw in the previous chapter, all of London was transfixed by the evolutionary tension figured in gorilla hands. In contrast to this tension, *Romola* highlights the hand's ability to act as an extension of both sight and soul. Take, for example, Eliot's description of the blind scholar Bardo's request to envision Tito's character through touch:

> Bardo passed his hand again and again over the long curls and grasped them a little, as if their spiral resistance made his inward vision clearer; then he passed his hand over the brow and cheek, tracing the profile with the edge of his palm and fourth finger, and letting the breadth of his hand repose on the rich oval of the cheek. (1913 [1862–63]: 76)

Or her description of Savonarola by way of his hands:

[Romola's] eyes fell at once on his hands, which were folded across his breast and lay in relief on the edge of his black mantle. They had a marked physiognomy which enforced the influence of the voice: they were very beautiful and almost of transparent delicacy ... the face was hidden, and the hands seemed to have an appeal in them against all hardness.... Then [he] stretched out his hands, which, in their exquisite delicacy, seemed *transfigured from an animal organ for grasping into vehicles for sensibility too acute to need any gross contact*: hands that came like an appealing speech from that part of his soul which was masked by his strong passionate face. (165, 522–23, emphasis added)[2]

These examples from early in Eliot's career as a novelist establish two points upon which this chapter will build. First, they show that even an author as aesthetically, philosophically, and intellectually superior as George Eliot engaged (albeit in a very different way) with her culture's unusual fascination with hands. Second, and more specifically, Eliot's preference for emphasizing the physical characteristics of hands instead of faces (Savonarola's hands have a "marked physiognomy") crystalizes her participation in the sustained scientific and cultural interest in hands after Darwin. We will see in this chapter how Eliot's tendency to prioritize hands—to continue to find uniqueness in them despite new evolutionary revelations—makes her final novel, *Daniel Deronda* (1876), both a realist masterpiece and a model for twentieth-century conceptions of bodily subjectivity.

MANUAL KINSHIP

In a letter to John Blackwood in November 1875, G. H. Lewes, in consultation with George Eliot, resolved that Volume I of *Daniel Deronda* should conclude with a very specific scene because of the "strong *expectation* [it] excited" (Eliot 1954: vi. 189, emphasis original). The scene with which they decided to end the first volume was the one where Deronda formally parts with Mirah after rescuing her from drowning in the Thames. The final two paragraphs of the first volume appear below:

"Good-bye," said Deronda, looking down at Mirah, and putting out his hand. She rose as she took it, and the moment brought back to them both strongly the other moment when she had first taken that outstretched hand. She lifted her eyes to his and said with reverential fervour, "The God of our fathers bless you and deliver you from all evil as you have delivered me."

Deronda could not speak, but with silent adieu to the Meyricks, hurried away. (170–71)

If the "expectation" excited by Mirah's bold speculation of Deronda's Jewishness ("the God of *our* fathers") is as strong as Eliot and Lewes envisioned, exactly how it achieves such an expectation remains unclear. After all, Deronda's failure to speak is not in itself remarkable. He fulfills his conversational duty by saying "good-bye" once. Is, then, Eliot's notion of expectation at the end of this first volume generated merely by the narrator's hypothetical assurance that he "*could* not speak" (had it been required)?

Eliot and Lewes likely assumed that readers would be far more concerned with Deronda's inability to speak than with the particulars of conversational etiquette. We sense that Deronda's silence—required or not—must be related somehow to Mirah's failure to complete her end of the salutation according to English social custom. Instead of meeting Deronda's "good-bye" with one of her own, she offers him a fervent blessing and, more particularly, a liturgical bond of Jewish kinship. Because this scene occurs just after we learn that Deronda's physical appearance matches none of the Mallinger family portraits, the narrative expectation becomes conspicuously rooted in the question of how the God of Mirah's father and the God of Deronda's father could be linked. But this is not the only question that readers would have thought about as they waited for Volume II to resume. The other question they would have pondered during the entire month of February 1876 is one that continues to influence critical appraisals of the novel's realism today. Phrased differently, this question asks how anyone without prior knowledge of Deronda's parentage could possibly, and realistically, have any inkling of his Jewishness by simply shaking his hand.

It is well known that nineteenth-century narratives often uncover the body in order to expose truths that must appear in the flesh.[3] This is all the more vexing in Eliot's final novel, though, because of the difficulty readers inevitably encounter in trying to "see" Deronda's body with any degree of physical specificity. In the Mallinger portrait gallery, for instance, the narrator fastidiously lists the features of the family physiognomy ranging from the time of Elizabeth to George IV: "arched eyebrows," "rosebud mouths,"

and "full eyelids" (140). Yet on the facing page, this litany of physical description yields nothing specific about Deronda's body beyond the narrator's
vague assurance that he "was handsomer than any of [the Mallingers]" (141).
Since the novel's publication this conspicuous withholding of his physical
attributes has been a major source of critical frustration, and it remains
one reason why the question of Deronda's corporeal Jewishness has had so
much traction (or slippage, depending on one's theoretical allegiances) for
generations of critics. Henry James was among the first to voice the critical
frustration that continues even in current assessments of the novel. James
felt strongly that Deronda's vague handsomeness rendered the Jewish part
of the novel "admirably studied" but "not embodied" (1876: 687). In James's
estimation, Eliot's deliberate ambiguity on the topic of Deronda's appearance made him "a person outside of Judaism—aesthetically" (687).[4] I revisit
this well-known controversy because it most fully reveals what is at stake
in *Daniel Deronda*'s treatment of realism, religiosity, and bodily representations of sympathy.

Critics of virtually every stripe since James have used Deronda's physical
abstraction as the cornerstone for a myriad of disparate interpretations.[5] Perhaps the most notable and enduring has been Cynthia Chase's influential—
and what some consider "virtuoso"—contention that the plot, and with it
the novel's realism, "goes aground" on the issue of Deronda's circumcision
(Duncan 2014: 31). It should be noted that Chase's argument works brilliantly because of its premise that Deronda's illegibility could theoretically
appear everywhere *but* on his penis (1978: 222). For all its deconstructive
hallmarks, though, Chase's reading paradoxically operates on a somewhat
historicized notion of permanency regarding Deronda's genetic origins—
origins that must be both physiologically and metonymically signified by
his circumcised penis. This chapter first explores the validity of such a position in terms of scientific formulations of racial affiliation in the nineteenth
century, and then contends that—given the unlikely combination of Victorian identity politics and Eliot's orientation with Jewish mysticism—*Daniel
Deronda* criticism for far too long has focused on body parts that have preoccupied contemporary critics (as opposed to those that mattered most to
Victorians). I argue that interpreting the body parts that were foremost in
the Victorian consciousness offers us not only a way through the problematic representation of Jewishness in the nineteenth century, but also a completely new and alternate way of thinking about Eliot's realism, sympathy,
and theory of race.

SCIENTIFIC DETERMINISM AND JEWISH INHERITANCE

It is clear that Eliot's racial understanding of Jewishness in *Daniel Deronda* was deeply embedded in the intellectual and scientific culture of which she was very much a part. Like Charles Darwin, Herbert Spencer, John Tyndall, and G. H. Lewes, Eliot was drawn to issues of inheritance, and particularly to what Mary Jean Corbett accurately terms "the historical/cultural/ biological production of difference" that Darwin's *Descent of Man* brought to the fore in 1871 (2004: 116). Though Eliot distanced herself from the explicitly determinist notions of phrenology she held at the end of the 1840s, she nonetheless maintained organicist assumptions regarding the subject of physical difference throughout her career. Her reformulation of Wilhelm Riehl's ideas in "The Natural History of German Life" in 1856, for example, stakes out a distinctly physiological basis for national, ethnic, and class "type." Here Eliot writes:

> In Germany . . . it is among the peasantry that we must look for the historical type of the national *physique*. In the towns this type has become so modified to express the personality of the individual, that even "family likeness" is often but faintly marked. But the peasants may still be distinguished into groups by their physical peculiarities. In one part of the country we find a longer-legged, in another a broader-shouldered race, which has inherited these peculiarities for centuries. (1992 [1856]: 267, emphasis original)

While Eliot was reviewing Riehl, Lewes was solidifying this "fixed type" model of historical and biological development for inclusion in his *Physiology of Common Life* (1860). Both authors were keenly interested in pursuing questions of inheritance among historically, culturally, and biologically isolated populations. As a result, Jewish history became an obvious subject of interest for both Lewes and Eliot. Lewes wrote in *Physiology of Common Life*:

> We will not say that it is a mere coincidence which preserves intact the various "breeds" of animals: which makes the bull-dog resemble the bull dog, and the bull-dog and terrier; which makes the Jews all over the world resemble Jews, because they keep their race free from admixture, by never marrying into other races. (315)

He concluded that if "both parents have the Jewish physiognomy, the off-spring will be unmistakably Jewish" (317). Eliot, for her part, was committed to a belief in the retention of what she called "physical peculiarities" (among historically affiliated people) for the duration of her writing career. In "The Natural History of German Life," she notes the "long faces, with high fore-heads, long, straight noses, and small eyes with arched eyebrows and large eyelids" that "subsisted unchanged" on the "old Hessian type of face" (1992: 267). Similarly, in "The Modern Hep! Hep! Hep!" she asserts that "every Jew" possesses common attributes passed down by "ancestors who have transmit-ted to them" a particular "physical and mental type" (1994 [1879]: 164).

Eliot's and Lewes's shared belief in the fixity and persistence of racial types, combined with *Daniel Deronda's* otherwise literal alignment of Jewishness and "visibility" (the Meyricks' desire to "watch for Jewish par-ticularities"), makes the absence of Deronda's physicality a crisis in the text's realism—assuming, as we should, the nineteenth-century belief that Deronda's Jewishness *had* to be legible somewhere on his body (191). Deconstructionist arguments about the presence of a hidden but circum-cised penis have remained an influential way to explain the apparent dis-connect between Eliot's scientifically informed views and her "featureless" description of Deronda. The problem is that these interpretations, though often ingeniously articulated, run counter to Eliot's well-documented bio-logical understanding of inherited physiological type. As John Plotz com-ments on Eliot's position, "circumcision, arguably, is what inscribes custom *on* the body" (2008: 211, emphasis added).[6] Eliot's scientific perspective made her far more interested in bodily demarcation that had already "naturally" inscribed itself on the Jewish body—via the kind of inheritance Darwin, Lewes, Spencer, and Tyndall were investigating.

Therefore, my contention is that Eliot locates Deronda's Jewishness nei-ther on his face nor on his penis but on his hands. She does this for several reasons that link up with the broader claims I have been making about the Victorian preoccupation with hands throughout the century. One reason for Eliot depends on the fact that her readership, even focused as they were on hands, was unlikely to have been familiar with what I will show were the overwhelmingly *positive* biblical connections between Jews and hands. Thus, such a location's everyday familiarity allows for a physiologically determina-tive body part to go virtually unnoticed as either a presence or an absence in the narrative (readers of this novel must not know with certainty that Deronda is a Jew too early in the narrative). The demarcation of Jewishness

in hands also fit her larger objective to replace unfortunate Jewish stereotypes with more historically informed connections between Judaism and
Christianity. Eliot noted that her contemporaries "hardly k[new] that Christ
was a Jew" and quipped that she could "find men educated at Rugby supposing that Christ spoke Greek" (Turner 1981: 72).

Eliot, unlike the majority of her readers, was aware of the myriad positive
biblical representations of Jewish hands. Therefore, Victorian readers would
have been as unlikely to suspect that Deronda's outstretched hand indicates
his Jewishness to Mirah in the closing scene of Volume I as they would be
in the novel's opening scene at the Leubronn gaming table to connect the
"bony, yellow, crab-like hand [of the Jewish pawnbroker] stretching a bared
wrist to clutch a heap of coin" with "the white bejewelled fingers of an English
countess" (4). In paying closer attention to the materiality of hands in *Daniel
Deronda*, it becomes possible to identify an alternate version of realism in
Eliot's fiction, and in the Victorian novel more generally: one based on the
legibility of signs that literary criticism—even its Marxist, historicist, and
postcolonial iterations—has overlooked.[7] These criticisms likely recognize
so little of the cultural work done by actual hands in the nineteenth century
precisely because of the taken-for-granted status of hands in the twentieth
and twenty-first centuries.[8] Like everyone else in the nineteenth century who
lived through heaving industrial and scientific change, though, George Eliot
thought far more literally than metaphorically about human hands.

JEWISH STEREOTYPES AND THE PROBLEM
OF NARRATIVE REALITY

Unfortunately, Eliot's readership would have been all too familiar with offen-
sively determinist representations of Jewish identity that appeared throughout the nineteenth century (figs. 31 and 32). Jewish hands often appeared in
contemporary discourse as "bony, yellow, [and] crab-like" because they were
thought to steal children, as well as money—a stereotype Dickens consolidated to great effect early in the Victorian era in his descriptions of Fagin's
clutching "yellow fingers" in *Oliver Twist* (194). Something very unusual happens in Eliot's treatment of the subject, however. After the opening scene at
the gaming table in *Daniel Deronda* (where the "yellow, crab-like hand" *is*
meant to signify Jewishness), Eliot turns this stereotype completely upside
down. The Anglican Grandcourt's "throttling pincer" quickly replaces the

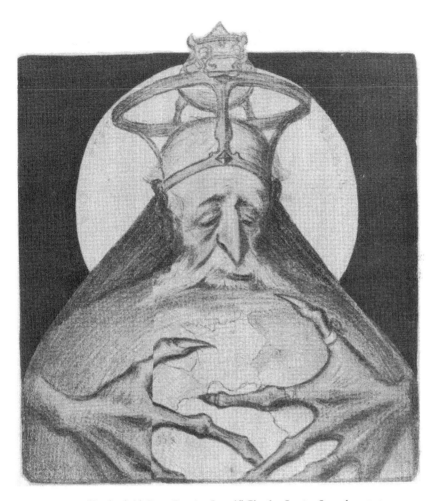

Fig. 31. "Rothschild: Dieu Protège Israel," Charles-Lucien Leandre, 1898.

"perfect [English] hand" that Gwendolen thinks he possesses upon meeting him for the first time (483, 91). Once they marry, the narrator repeatedly configures Grandcourt's brutal "delight in dominating" his wife in manually descriptive terms: Gwendolen fears that any quarrel could "end with throt-tling fingers on her neck," and wonders "if the thumb-screw and the iron boot were being placed by creeping hands within sight of the expectant vic-tim" (289, 483, 292).

By contrast, the narrator's notoriously vague descriptions of Deronda's facial appearance materialize quite explicitly in the positive description of

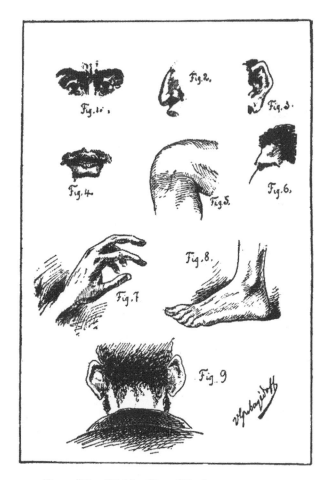

Fig. 32. "How We May Know Him," anonymous, 1888.

his extraordinary hands. For the first sixteen chapters of the novel, as we have seen, the closest the narrator comes to revealing anything specific about Deronda's physicality occurs when we learn that he "might have served as a model for any painter who wanted to image the most memorable of boys" (141). The penultimate chapter of Volume I (the same in which Deronda saves Mirah from drowning in the Thames), however, issues forth the novel's single most descriptive paragraph of Deronda's "terrestrial" embodiment:

> Rowing in his dark-blue shirt and skull-cap, his curls closely clipped, his mouth beset with abundant soft waves of beard, he bore only disguised

traces of the seraphic boy "trailing clouds of glory" ... The voice, sometimes audible in subdued snatches of song, had turned out merely high
baritone; indeed, only to look at his lithe powerful frame and the firm
gravity of his face would have been enough for an experienced guess that
he had no rare and ravishing tenor such as nature reluctantly makes at
some sacrifice. *Look at his hands*: they are not small and dimpled, with
tapering fingers that seem to have only a deprecating touch: they are long,
flexible, firmly-grasping hands, such as Titian has painted in a picture
where he wanted to show the combination of refinement with force. And
there is something of a likeness, too, between the faces belonging to the
hands—in both the uniform pale-brown skin, the perpendicular brow,
the calmly penetrating eyes. Not seraphic any longer: thoroughly terrestrial and manly; but still of a kind to raise belief in a human dignity which
can afford to acknowledge poor relations. (157–58, emphasis added)

The "abundant soft waves of beard" appear faintly Mosaic, but there is
still nothing specific about "the firm gravity of his face." Were we "only to
look at" his face, the narrator assures us, we would discover nothing out
of the ordinary.[9] This changes immediately when the narrator enjoins us
to "Look at his hands," though. The description moves swiftly through the
unremarkable, stops abruptly, and then lingers on Deronda's only physically
noteworthy body part. Garrett Stewart sees the reader, at this moment, "conscripted by second-person grammar" to notice an "overt prosopopoeia—the
textual giving face to an absent person" (1996: 304). Such a reading crystalizes one of the central points of *Changing Hands*: that even the sharpest
contemporary critics so often look only to faces for meaning—even when
they are directed explicitly to notice hands.[10]

Catherine Gallagher's identification of Eliot's triptych movement
between the typical and the unusual is more useful here. In Gallagher's view
of Eliot's oeuvre, a narrator's direct address to the reader often signals the
onset of a triptych that breaches the threshold of typicality, focuses briefly
on the unusual, then moves back again to the general (2005: 63–65). In this
case, the narrator's direct appeal to "look at [Deronda's] hands" acts as a reassurance of the subtle links between the ideational and specific. Eliot's particular reference to Titian's painting, *Man with the Glove* (fig. 33), makes the
passage all the more important to her realist narrative.

In Titian's portrait, the dark, indeterminate background, black garments,
and resplendent white cuffs focus by contrast on details of the hands that,

Fig. 33. *Man with the Glove*. Titian (1519–23?). Louvre, Paris. Used by permission from Art Resource.

for Eliot, most effectively reveal the subject's compelling persona. This parallels the narrator's unique description of Deronda, within both painting and prose, where "the faces belon[g] to the hands" and not the other way around as we might normally expect in literary and art criticism (158). It is not the sitter's face but his ungloved hand that suggests a willingness to "acknowledge poor relations" just as its "terrestrial and manly" shape hints at Deronda's willingness to accomplish something on behalf of those relations in the future (158).[11]

Despite the concentrated focus on Deronda's hands at this very specific point in the narrative, the fact that Eliot provides *only* a hint about his future is pivotal for my argument about the way hands operate in the world of this novel. No amount of praise for Deronda's hands in this early scene could guarantee his Jewishness for anyone, including Deronda himself. Indeed, the narrator explicitly emphasizes as much. Deronda has "no thought of an adventure in which his *appearance* was likely to play any part" as he rows beneath the Kew bridge just minutes before encountering the drowning Mirah (158, emphasis added). Yet in order to fulfill this novel's particular set of narrative requirements, Deronda's future and—by the logic of Eliot's physiological/organicist/genetic understanding of Jewish identity—his past must be detectable by some (select characters) but not by others (Deronda and readers). All the while, the legibility of such Jewishness must also surmount the double difficulty of either depicting Jews as invisible through assimilation or as too visible as a stigmatized type. These exigencies make for an extremely tenuous set of narratological circumstances. Eliot's persistent acceptance of an organicist determinism only makes her narrative tightrope trickier to walk. Perhaps Gillian Beer characterizes this problem best as she defines it as a matter of "how to liberate the future into its proper and powerful state of indeterminacy and yet make it part of the story" (1983: 185).

My argument is that this narrow set of limitations helps explain why Eliot was drawn to the convergence of determinism and prophecy in the Kabbalah; it offers her a realistic mode of prediction that is to a large degree hidden. C. D. Ginsburg's *The Kabbalah: Its Doctrines, Development, and Literature* (1863), a book that Eliot studied and took extensive notes from in the 1870s, accurately describes how the Kabbalah's religious theosophy "rests solely on signs which are scarcely perceptible" (181). Ginsburg observes how the Kabbalah's *"secret wisdom"* is "only handed down by tradition through the initiated, and is indicated in the Hebrew Scriptures by signs which are hidden and unintelligible to those who have not been instructed in its mysteries" (86, emphasis original). The point is that, as a dedicated practitioner of the Kabbalah, Mordecai possesses the religious and mystical training to decipher Deronda's Jewishness despite having no knowledge of his parentage. Mordecai's Kabbalistic orientation allows all of the text's other narrative exigencies to exist: Deronda may be Jewish without either him or the reader knowing it too soon. Analyzing the Kabbalah's relationship to prophecy is also an intervention on behalf of the novel's realism. An understanding of how the Kabbalah works eliminates the need for what so many critics see as detrimental to the text's realism; namely, its supposed reliance on the trope of metalepsis (the transference of effects into causes).[12]

A KABBALISTIC REALISM

To cite the novel's own words, the viability of Mordecai's "second-sight" has long been "a flag over disputed ground" for those interested in evaluating Eliot's formal realism (404). Critics often see Mordecai's seemingly unfounded insistence on Deronda's Jewishness as an odd, "wish-fulfillment aspect" of the plot (Loesberg 2001: 139). Audrey Jaffe captures the spirit of a line of critical interpretation running fairly straight between U. C. Knoepflmacher and Deborah Epstein Nord when she claims that "before Mordecai's 'wishful vision,' Deronda is the Jew even the most discerning of observers can't discern" (2000: 125).[13] A few critics have offered notable exceptions to this prevailing view. These seek to account for Mordecai's prophetic insight by viewing him as a type of scientist with a working "hypothesis" that Deronda is a Jew.[14] This view of Mordecai as "a type of scientist, so rigorously demanding of reality that he literally forgets himself and his body" no doubt adheres to Eliot's interest in the unlikely connections between rationality and mysticism (Shuttleworth 1984: 32).[15] I would agree, but would add that something else is at issue here as well, and that we can see what it is by considering how Eliot's interpretation of Kabbalistic philosophy reconciles the apparently divergent scientific and religious strains of thought. But even recent criticism of this sort misses the mark in terms of identifying Eliot's narrative commitment to the Kabbalistic principles she so earnestly studied before composing the novel.[16] For instance, Jules Law remarks that the novel's two powerful epiphanic scenes (the one in which Deronda discovers Mirah and the one in which Mordecai discovers Deronda) "appear to accord almost occult power to the gaze" (2010: 116). Ian Duncan sees Mordecai's belief in Deronda's Jewishness become self-verifying "in a shamanistic blaze of enthusiasm" (2014: 32). This view, combined with the commitment to the trope of metalepsis, compels Duncan to view *Daniel Deronda* as "press[ing] beyond the bounds of realism into a kind of science fiction" (18). However, if we consider Eliot's scholarly immersion into the doctrines of the Kabbalah, combined with her organicist understanding of race, these scenes of visual encounter and discovery are not quixotic, occult, or even purely "scientific"; rather, they are pivotal parts of a realistic portrayal of Jewish mystical thought and racial representation.

It is significant that Mordecai's Kabbalisitic inclination to "read outward facts" reaches its highest narrative pitch in the scene where he hails Deronda from atop Blackfriar's bridge (438). In fact, Mordecai's belief that Deronda matches "the long-conceived [Jewish] type" becomes incontrovertible or infallible (in Mordecai's view) *only* when he inspects the rowing Deronda from above. We should recall that Eliot's staged viewing of Deronda's body from the vantage point on the bridge resonates with the narrator's earlier exhortation to "look at his hands" in the moments before he saves the drowning Mirah. By this point, Eliot has already emphasized the connection between Deronda's Titian-like hands and Mordecai's Kabbalistic interpretation of them by revealing how Mordecai's extreme "sensitiv[ity] to physical characteristics" causes him to linger "in the National Gallery in search of paintings" containing "noble types" belonging to "men of his own race" (405). Mordecai's Kabbalist search for such racialized types both inside and outside of the National Gallery adds an important additional dimension to what Hugh Witemeyer calls Eliot's "literary pictorialism" (1979, 32). Critics tend to assume that Mordecai's interest in portraiture at the National Gallery limits his investigation to faces. As we have seen over and over again in *Changing Hands*, and in the Titian portrait in particular, though, the hands are often as conspicuous as the faces—a fact that likely also would have applied to any individual portrait in the National Gallery since portraiture, almost by definition, focuses on the faces and hands of its subjects.

This previously unexplored dimension of Eliotic realism depends on the fact that the hand is a crucial component in the relationship that the Kabbalah identifies between Jewish texts and Jewish bodies. Eliot Wolfson has put it succinctly in his assertion that the "literal body [in Kabbalah] is embodied in the body of the book" (2005: 191). Sections of the *Zohar*, for instance, explicitly focus on how the "supernal mysteries" of the hand reveal the unbroken line of Jewish descendants from Biblical times onward (Matt 2007: 411).

Although the *Zohar* does not isolate only hands in its identification of Jewish ancestry, human limbs appear nonetheless "fashioned as symbols of hidden, supernal *realities*" (Matt 2007: 81, emphasis added). Eliot is not likely to have missed such formulations in her fastidious scholarly preparations—especially since they aligned with her own (and Lewes's) organicist understanding of legibility in general and of racial typology in particular. In 1875, just one year before the publication of *Daniel Deronda*, Lewes had commented that "internal workings must be legible in the external symbols" (98–99). It is common for Kabbalists to recognize these "external symbols" in a complex isomorphic dimension linking the physical structure of the hand to the sacredness of the Torah. Moshe Idel records a representative passage from a Kabbalist in which each finger of the human hand represents a book of the Torah:

> Genesis corresponds to the thumb, is divided into three topics: the creation of heaven and earth, the events related to the forefathers, and the matter of exile. And the second finger corresponds to Exodus, and just as there are three joints in a finger, so is the book divided into three topics: it tells of the events of Moses bringing the people of Israel from Egypt, the laws and rules, and the matter of the Tabernacle. And the book of Leviticus, which corresponds to the third finger, so is this book the middle of the Pentateuch, and it is divided into three topics corresponding to the three joints of the middle finger. They are the law of sacrifices, and the law of leprosy, and the blessings and curses. The book of Numbers corresponds to the fourth finger and is divided into the topics of the census, the priesthood, and the issue of the spies. The fifth book corresponds to the fifth finger and is called Deuteronomy, which explicates the wonders and miracles, the commandments, and Moses' death. (2002: 72)

Shabbetai Horowitz's iconic representation (fig. 34) demonstrates this relationship in the legibility of Jewish hands by those trained to interpret them. Horowitz's illustration makes it possible to see what Geoffrey Hartman calls "a combinatory art that questions the canonized letters before us" (2011: 92). "While these letters have a received meaning on the *grammatical* level of word and sentence," Hartman notes, "they are taken to be, at the same time, *anagrammatic*, in the sense of constituting the elements of a divine name coterminous with the Torah and guaranteeing every mark in it" (92).

The practicing Kabbalist actually sees the fifteen words of Aaron's Hebrew blessing in direct correlation to the fifteen parts of the hand (fourteen joint sections plus the palm). This anthropomorphic and symbolic correlation is highlighted also by the inscriptions appearing on the hands and fingers, with each of the letters of the twenty-two-letter Hebrew alphabet

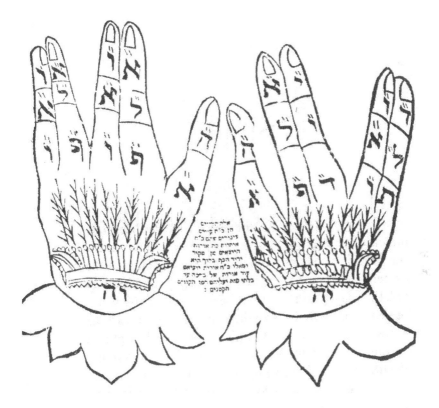

Fig. 34. Shabbetai Horowitz, *Shefa Tal* (1612).

retaining a specific numerical equivalent by way of *gematria*. The letters at
the base of each hand in the *Shefa Tal* thus meet to spell the unutterable
name of God in the Bible: YHWH (the tetragrammaton). Partly because
the four letters of the word (*yod, he, vav, he*) have the same numerical value
(45) as the letters of the name Adam in esoteric gnosis, Kabbalists interpret
hands as an important site of divine inscription where "the science of permu‐
tation of letters" becomes decipherable.

It is the recognition of Deronda's hands within this mystical system of
physiological interpretation—rather than what critics tend to interpret as
wishful vision or shamanic enthusiasm—that accounts for the swiftness
and unswerving confidence of Mordecai's identification of Deronda as a Jew
while he looks on from the parapets of Blackfriar's bridge. In this sense,
Mordecai's capacity "to measure men with a keen glance" paradoxically
(but nonetheless realistically) culminates in his ability to see what others

cannot—a skill that he confidently assures a bewildered Deronda that he possesses. Mordecai, having observed Deronda row from above (the same perspective from which the narrator encourages the reader to "Look at his hands"), tells him:

> I know the philosophies of this time and of other times: if I chose I could answer a summons before their tribunals. I could silence the beliefs

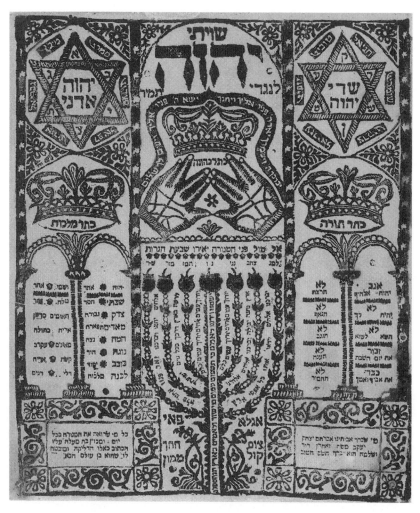

Fig. 35. Shiviti. "Hands over Menorah." Reprinted with permission from the Library of the Jewish Theological Society of America.

which are the mother-tongue of my soul and speak with rote-learned language of a system, that gives you the spelling of all things, sure of its alphabet covering them all. (430–31)

This inclusion of an "alphabet covering them all" is a direct reference to the divine inscription that Kabbalists see inscribed on hands. They believed that the holy name of God should always be placed before the eyes of their followers—a practice constantly reinforced by Kabbalistic iconography showing Jewish hands in the intermediary position between the divine and earthly realms (fig. 35).

Not only did Eliot take notes on *gematriatic* symbolism while studying Ginsburg's *Kabbalah*, but she was also familiar with this particular kind of Hebrew hand iconography from her visits to the Okopowa Street Jewish Cemetery in Prague during the 1860s (Irwin 1996: 456). There, as is often the case in older Jewish cemeteries, many of the 200,000 marked graves are graced with hands in exactly the same position as those in the *Shefa Tal* and "The Holy Name of God" shiviti inscribed and facing up to heaven at the top section of the tombstone (fig. 36).

Fig. 36. Tombstones in the Okopowa Street Jewish Cemetery. Prague, Czech Republic. Used by permission of the Photograph Archive at the Jewish Museum of Prague].

"STARS AND CONSTELLATIONS OF THIS SKIN"

The epigraph to the chapter first introducing the reader to Deronda resonates with the combination of transparency and inscrutability that characterizes the Kabbalah. It begins by asserting that "Men, like planets, have
both a visible and an invisible history" (139). More specifically, the epigraph
situates the observable past—both human and planetary—in a determinative relationship with the present and the future: "The astronomer threads
the darkness with strict deduction, accounting so for every visible arc in the
wanderer's orbit; and the narrator of human actions, if he did his work with
the same completeness, would have to thread the hidden pathways of feeling
and thought which lead up to every moment of action" (139). This interfused
association of the physiological and the astronomical is also common in Kabbalistic discourse, and Eliot's inclusion of such a detail suggests her familiarity
with the connections between astronomy and physiology in Jewish mystical
writings. The *Zohar*, in particular, often imagines the two simultaneously:

> In the heaven covering all, impressions were made, thereby showing and
> revealing—through inlaid impressions—concealed matters and secrets.
> Those are impressions of stars and constellations inlaid in this heaven cov-
> ering outside. Similarly, skin—external covering of a person—is a heaven
> covering all, containing impressions and traces. Those are stars and con-
> stellations of this skin, a covering heaven, through which concealed mat-
> ters and secrets are shown and revealed—stars and constellations eyed by
> the wise of heart, gazing upon them to know. (Matt 2007: 410)

> Lines of hands and lines of fingers, inside, all inhere in other mysteries,
> revealing concealed matters. These are stars shining, to gaze into constel-
> lations in supernal aspects . . . Hands in supernal mysteries. (411)

In many ways this relationship between "bodies" and hands is just a more
specialized iteration of what each one of my earlier chapters already demonstrates. Mordecai simply exhibits a more precise, Zoharic level of perspi-
cacity in his identification of Deronda's "concealed matters and secrets" at
Blackfriar's bridge.

Moreover, immediately after expressing complete confidence in his ability to converse "with the rote-learned language of a system" covering "the

spelling of all things," the narrator informs us that Mordecai sees Deronda as a "strong man whose gaze was sustainedly calm and [whose] finger-nails [were] pink with health" (431). The movement of the narrator's gaze from Deronda's face to his hands recalls not only Mordecai's inspection of the portraits in the National Gallery, but also the Titian portrait in which the narrator frames Deronda's hands from the initial meeting with Mirah. The two powerful scenes of encounter and discovery share other similarities as well. Just as in the earlier rowing scene where Deronda seems blissfully igno-rant of a situation where his appearance could play any part, in the latter scene with Mordecai at Blackfriar's, Deronda's musings about the instability of "out-ward signs" ironically (and repeatedly) take the hand as their focal point:

> After all, [thought Deronda], what was there but vulgarity in taking the fact that Mordecai was a poor Jewish workman, and that he was to be met perhaps on a sanded floor in the parlour of the *Hand and Banner,* as a reason for determining beforehand that there was not some spiritual force within him that might have a determining effect on a white-handed gentleman. There is a legend told of the Emperor Domitian, that having heard of a Jewish family, of the house of David . . . sent for its members in alarm, but quickly released them on observing that they had the hands of work-people. (437)

Eliot read about this event in Heinrich Graetz's *History of the Jews* (1863–75) at the beginning of her research on Judaism, and it impressed her sufficiently enough to underline *"their workmen's hands"* in her written notes (Irwin 1996: 267). While the Domitian story she retells in *Daniel Deronda* at first appears to endorse a distrust of the reliance on outward signs for inward truths, it also dramatizes Mordecai's position, unlike Domitian, as a Kabbalah-trained interpreter of such signs—a scenario that allows Morde-cai to link Deronda's hand with its (racial) banner.

Even the choreography Eliot uses to construct the recognition scene at Blackfriar's bridge parallels the earlier scene at the Meyricks, where Mirah first speculates on Deronda's Jewishness. At Blackfriar's, Mordecai's con-viction that Deronda's "resemblance to the preconceived type" fulfills "an inward prophecy" has the same awkward silencing effect as Mirah's volume-ending Hebrew blessing: "Deronda did not speak. He felt himself strangely wrought upon" (411, 422–23). Unlike the scene at the Meyricks', Deronda eventually resumes conversation with Mordecai, but the narrator's specificity concerning the chapter-ending handshake makes it nonetheless strikingly similar to Mirah's recognition scene: "[Deronda] put out his ungloved hand. Mordecai, clasping it eagerly, seemed to feel a new instreaming of confidence, and he said with some recovered energy—'This is come to pass, and the rest will come.' That was their good-bye" (433). Just as conversational etiquette becomes overshadowed by a recognition of Jewishness, in this instance as in the earlier one with Mirah, the reference to the "ungloved hand" indicates more than mere politeness on Deronda's part; it also recalls the narrator's initial characterization of Deronda's hands by way of the Titian portrait. Whereas the reader has only Mirah's seemingly unfounded reaction (in the form of her blessing) by which to assess her experience of Deronda's handshake at the end of the novel's first volume, we learn here that Mordecai's contact with Deronda's ungloved hand catalyzes a "new instreaming of confidence" and "recovered energy." This is significant because, to this point in the narrative, Mordecai's mystical training has allowed him only to see Jewish affiliation in Deronda's hands. With the description of this dramatic handshake, though, Eliot reveals yet another dimension of her faithfulness to the central tenets of both contemporary science and Jewish mysticism. Eliot knew well that Herbert Spencer had staked his entire view of human psychology on the principles of voluntary touch (*Principles of Psychology* [1872]). This contemporary scientific notion also uniquely fits the Kabbalah's emphasis on transmission through touch. Mordecai now *feels* Deronda's Judaic ancestry in a way that is consistent with what Gershom Scholem has characterized as the "magnetic act of communication" in Kabbalah (1990: 290). The *Zohar* specifies that the discovery of "secrets" appear in "flashes of intuition" (Matt 2007: 27).

This electric sense of religious unification may be seen also in the *Zohar's* account of what transpires when Jewish hands touch in conjunction with the *Shema* prayer (Deut. 6:4). The combination of five fingers on two sides allows God's emanations to flow freely through all ten *sefiroth*, reuniting what Kabbalists call "the primordial ten." The hand is of particular importance in the Kabbalah because of its numeric association with divine agency: the ten digits of the human hand correspond to the ten sefirotic utterances with which God created the world, the Ten Commandments, the ten plagues (brought on by "the finger of God"), Moses's ten raised fingers in the battle against Amalek, the ten bars supporting the lateral sides of the tabernacle, Aaron's ten priestly fingers raised up to heaven, etc.[17] Thus Mordecai's eager clasp of Deronda's hand renews his confidence and infuses him with

an influx of generative power that acts as a channel for the terrestrial mani-
festation of divine energy. It is specifically this kind of sacramental embrace
that prefigures the dramatic moment of metempsychosis later in the novel:

> [Deronda's] dominant impulse was to do what he had once done before:
> he laid his firm gentle hand on the hand that grasped him. Mordecai's
> [hand], as if it had a soul of its own—for he was not distinctly willing
> to do what he did—relaxed its grip, *and turned upward under Deronda's.*
> As the two palms met and pressed each other, Mordecai recovered some
> sense of his surroundings. (464, emphasis added)[18]

Daniel Hack correctly notes how such scenes work to uncouple the dualism
established earlier in the novel in Mordecai's plea that Deronda be "not only
a hand [to him], but a soul" (2005: 170). This is exactly the point for the
trained practitioner of the Kabbalah for whom the hand is the most visible
and also the most tangible extension of the Jewish soul.

CONTEMPORARY SCIENCE AND THE CONTEXT OF RACIAL INHERITANCE

It is critical to emphasize how well Eliot's knowledge of the Kabbalah
aligned with her scientific understanding of race and Jewish religiosity. The
publication of Darwin's *The Descent of Man* in 1871 shifted the focus of Victorian evolutionary debate to more immediate questions regarding man's
specific physiological inheritances. Gillian Beer has shown how in the 1870s
"the search for origins, the enquiry into their nature and into their relationship to development had become an intellectual obsession" for Eliot and her
circle of acquaintances (1983: 181). In "The Belfast Address" (1874), Eliot's
and Lewes's friend John Tyndall publicly codified the prevailing scientific
belief in "ancestral experience"—where man "carries with him the physical
texture of his ancestry" even in the absence of experiential knowledge (1984
[1874]: 180). Tyndall was of course building on Herbert Spencer's pioneering
evolutionary work from *The Principles of Psychology* (1872) and on Darwin's
The Variation of Animals and Plants Under Domestication (1868). Spencer
developed the notion that the mind inherits through the nervous system the
legacy of its predecessors' adaptations, a topic Darwin would elaborate on
in *Variation* and *Descent*. Eliot's persona makes clear in "The Modern Hep!

Hep! Hep!" the desire for Jews to retain just this sense of racial cohesion based on historical, religious, and inherited memory:

> Every Jew should be conscious that he is one of a multitude possessing common objects of piety in the immortal achievements and immortal sorrows of ancestors who have transmitted to them a physical and mental type strong enough, eminent enough in faculties, pregnant enough with peculiar promise, to constitute a new beneficent individuality among the nations. (1994 [1879]: 164)

This transmission of physical and mental "type," when combined with what Tyndall called "ancestral experience," becomes a separate racial category in *Daniel Deronda.*

This category depends as much on the biological as on the social. Deronda inherits his grandfather's papers, but they take on religious meaning because he also possesses an "inherited yearning—the effect of brooding, passionate thoughts in many ancestors" which have lain dormant within him as a "dim longing for unknown objects and sensations" during the years when he was cut off from his Jewish heritage (642). Here, Eliot's view of Deronda's racial heredity is closely aligned with contemporary scientific opinions on heredity. Take, for example, Lewes's statements in *Problems of Life and Mind*:

> No physiologist will deny that the organism has an inherited structure which causes it to react in particular ways, and that this structure has been determined by ancestral modifications; that is to say, ancestral modes of reaction, and the stored-up wealth of experience enriches the experience of succeeding generations. (1879: 173)

Darwin similarly imagined the body of any organism as a living vault, which both stored and transmitted successive physical states of its ancestors for possible recurrence:

> Inheritance must be looked at as merely a form of growth, like self-division of a lowly-organised unicellular organism. Reversion depends on the transmission from the forefather to his descendants of dormant gemmules, which occasionally become developed under certain known or unknown conditions. (1898 [1868]: 398–99)

Eliot had also previously explored this contemporary notion of "organic memory" vis-à-vis racial ancestry in her verse poem *The Spanish Gypsy* (1868). Such a preconscious, biological, and ultimately material kinship with race surfaces in *The Spanish Gypsy* when Fedalma discovers a gold necklace inscribed with Zíncala characters:

> And these twisted lines—
> They seem to speak to me as writing would,
> To bring a message from the dead, dead past.
> What is their secret? Are there any characters?
> I never learned them; yet they stir some sense
> That once I dreamed—I have forgotten what. (2008 [1868]: 280)

Fedalma has no experiential knowledge of the Zíncala alphabet, yet the letters still "speak" to an imbedded Zíncala soul shaped by her ancestors' lives; she "bears no marks/That tell of Hebrew blood," and yet she displays a Zíncala subconscious which is figured as "a longing that haunts [her] in [her] dreams" (258, 277).

Deronda has a strikingly parallel experience in the moments immediately after Sir Hugo informs him that he lost his parents while very young:

> Daniel then straining to discern something in the early twilight, had a dim sense of having been kissed very much, and surrounded by thin, cloudy, scented drapery, till his fingers caught in something hard, which hurt him, and he began to cry. (139–40)

Deronda's fleeting memory here recalls Tyndall's belief that man "carries with him the physical texture of his ancestry" in what Darwin calls "dormant gemmules." The repressed and preverbal element of this particular memory suggests that Deronda's ancestral experience allows him, in Tyndall's words, to "organically remember" his experiences in the synagogue for which he has neither words nor rational explanation. This does not make it any less real, however. The seemingly inscrutable memory realistically places him in a synagogue prayer service when the Torah scroll is carried around and touched by the community—a practice which interested Eliot enough to record how "the year-old infant's hand" was made to touch the silver pinnacles of the Torah-roll in her *Deronda* notebooks (Irwin 1996). Deronda's fingers react to the feeling of the Torah crowns, which, because of their elaborate filigree, would have been both attractive and sharp to a child's touch.[19] Thus race—either Jewish or Zíncala—for Eliot meant that the body, and to some extent the soul, was a priori; its existence the determined performance of what the *Daniel Deronda* narrator calls a "spell-bound habit" within "inherited frames" (642). In this way, Deronda's dim preverbal experience in the synagogue prefigures Mordecai's belief that "the heritage of Israel . . . is the inborn half of memory, moving as in a dream among writings on the walls, which it sees dimly but cannot divide into speech" (457).

The scenes involving Jewish hands in *Daniel Deronda* offer Eliot a chance to explore more fully the psychological, material, and filial implications of such ancestral experience within a contemporary scientific framework. Harry Shaw has commented on the degree to which Eliot's realism depends on the norms and values of her own historical situation (1999: 267). We see such a situation emerge in another notable instance where Mordecai and Deronda embrace each other's hands. Here the narrator observes how "the lines of what may be called their emotional theory touched" (466). For Eliot, "emotional theory" is always an offshoot of organic ancestry, as when Mordecai asks his fellow Jew, "have we not from the first touched each other with invisible fibres—have we not quivered together like the leaves from a common stem with stirrings from a common root?" (489).

The hand is so often the catalyst for connections among Jews in *Daniel Deronda* that Eliot's sense of manual Jewish affiliation also extends beyond Mordecai and the Kabbalah. Take, for instance, Klesmer's dramatic evaluation of Mirah's musical talent not by listening to her voice, but by inspecting her hand:

> [Klesmer's] long hand, back uppermost, was stretched out in quite a different sense to touch with finger-tip the back of Mirah's, and with protruded lip he said—
> "Not for great tasks. No high roofs. We are no skylarks. We must be modest." (415)

Himself a "felicitous combination of the German, the Sclave, and the Semite," Klesmer's ability to discern Mirah's musical capabilities by "reading" her hand seems to combine the Guidonean method of "hearing with the hand" and the nineteenth-century cultural tendency to see identity in the materiality of the hand.[20] In another oddly revealing instance, Eliot has Deronda unconsciously link Jewishness to hands while he probes for links between the Cohen family and the recently discovered Mirah. Deronda asks Ezra's mother, "which side of the family does [Jacob] get [his hands] from?" (443). We may extrapolate that this question is meant as a comparison of the young boy's hands to Mirah's because of Deronda's thoughts immediately following the ambiguous response from Cohen: "'I shall never know anything decisive about these people until I ask Cohen point-blank whether he lost a sister named Mirah when she was six years old'" (444). The similarities Deronda thinks he sees between Jacob's hands and Mirah's are likely related to the Darwinian notion of "adaptive resemblances" in animal species.

MANUALS OF THE MATRILINEAL

The long-awaited reunion of Deronda with his mother is undoubtedly the most poignant example of the novel's tendency to locate Jewishness in hands, though. Upon seeing her son for the first time since his infancy, the Alcharisi, like so many others in the novel, is preeminently drawn to Deronda's most extraordinary physical attribute:

> "—there is something of your own father in you; and he made it the labour of his life to devote himself to me: wound up his money-changing and banking, and lived to wait upon me—he went against his conscience for me. *Let me look at your hand again*: the hand with the ring on. It was your father's ring."
>
> [Deronda] drew his chair nearer to her and gave her his hand. *We know what type of hand it was: her own very much smaller was of the same type.* (543, emphasis added)

In this pivotal moment of mother-son reunion, Eliot's racialized view of heredity, her commitment to disabuse Britain of negative Jewish stereotypes, and her successful negotiation of problematic narrative requirements all converge on the figure of Deronda's hand in a singular moment of "haptic visuality"—William Cohen's interpretation of "seeing on the model of touch" (1993: 17).[21] The "type" of hand shared by mother and son fits Eliot's and Lewes's sense of the fixed organic model—especially in relation to Jewish endogamy and its laws of matrilineal descent. Moreover, the Alcharisi's desire to look at "the hand with the ring" is unquestionably physiological.

That is, her primary interest is in assessing the degree to which the hands of her former husband and those of Deronda resemble each other when they wear a common object.[22]

The Alcharisi's biblical (oddly Jacobesque) request to inspect her son's hands also links up with Eliot's larger aim to reacquaint her audience with the positive connections between Judaism and Christianity. Just as many Britons (much to Eliot's dismay) "hardly kn[e]w that Christ was a Jew," many who perpetuated negative stereotypes about "bony, yellow, crab-like hand[s]" were wholly ignorant of the sacred status of Jewish hands in the Bible—let alone the Kabbalah (1954: 6:302; 1984 [1876]: 4). For Jews, as Eliot was well aware, the "hand of God" was not merely a scriptural allusion to divine power in the Hebrew Bible; it was the body part through which God worked most directly: Moses leading the Israelites out of Egypt by stretching his hands over the Red Sea (Exod. 14:21) and later leading Joshua's army to victory by raising and lowering his hands in the battle against Amalek (Exod. 17: 10–13).[23] Barry Qualls correctly ties this element of Eliot's biblical typology to her realist project when he remarks that Eliot's "art of naturalization of the sacred" requires the use of traditional iconography and typology to create the moral territory for her realism (2001: 125).

In a paradoxical and deeply compelling way, then, Eliot to some degree bets on the expectations of her readers' ignorance in the novel's opening gambling scene at Leubronn—hedging in a sense, on a prediction that such ignorance would be shaped by nineteenth-century imagery and discourse around a reliably unattractive Jewishness. By situating "the white bejewelled fingers of an English countess" next to "a bony, yellow, crab-like hand" in the novel's opening scene, Eliot leaves open to her readers the possibilities of seeing in hands either "a striking admission of human equality" or the "very distant varieties of European type" (4). She perhaps tilts the scales to the latter, negative side by making the Jewish gambler's yellow hand "easy to sort with the square, gaunt face, deep-set eyes, grizzled eyebrows, and ill-combed scanty hair which seemed a slight metamorphosis of the vulture" (4).

If we invoke what Irene Tucker calls "the politics of racial seeing," the description of the Jewish gambler reads as a near point-for-point commentary on the unattractive Jewish body found in the nineteenth-century illustration entitled "How We May Know Him" (fig. 32) [2012: 12]. It is this evidentiary dynamic that Sander Gilman refers to as "tainted" in regard to [Jewish] signifiers (63). Yet it is just these signifiers that prevent the reader from associating Deronda with Jewishness at (too) early narrative junctures—including during the handshake scene between Deronda and Mirah that ends the first volume. Eliot has been hedging on these racialist boundaries throughout the novel. Consider how she embeds an unappealing description of Lush's "fat hands" around images of Klesmer's elegant, "long" piano-playing hands (94). Think, also, back to the scene where Deronda sees none of his own facial features in the Mallinger portrait gallery. The narrator reveals that the artist of Sir Hugo's portrait "had done something more than justice in slightly lengthening the nose, which was in reality shorter than might have been expected in a Mallinger" (140–41). The large nose, of course, was thought to be a universal negative feature of Jews—but here is Eliot discussing the *lengthening* of an aristocratic Anglican nose! (see note 4). The set of positive Jewish associations that emerge over the long course of the novel is then usefully complicated by new contexts, new iconography, and new discourses centered on the reevaluation of what a positively connoted Judaism could mean—especially in an English population made up of, in the narrator's words, "a miscellaneous people" (85).

Likewise, the Kabbalah vector of the novel adds a prophetic arc to the narrative, but one that can function perfectly well (i.e. "realistically") without a full understanding of its mystical significance. This is because Eliot can still bank on the fact that, like Domitian, non-Jews will look for the wrong things in Jewish hands—or not look at them at all—despite her narrator's sometimes blunt encouragements to do so. In this case, the physicality of the Jewish hand in *Daniel Deronda* becomes a racially, religiously, and narratologically indispensable piece of what John Plotz calls "portable property"; a unique scenario wherein "any nation's portable culture will be visible only to those already within the charmed circle that such a national culture generates . . . a national culture going so far inward as to be either invisible or illegible to those on the outside" (2008: 73, 75).

An exploration of what happens in this "charmed circle" may provide the most logical basis yet for questioning whether the novel's realism actually hinges on the immutability of Deronda's circumcision, as so much criticism has assumed. Contra this strain of criticism, several recent critics have drawn on contemporary medical discourse to highlight the somewhat surprising possibility that a Jewish male could have remained uncircumcised in the Victorian period.[24] My larger point, however, is that Eliot's treatment of Jewish hands obviates the need to look outside the text at all to make an assessment of what criticism since the 1970s has taken to be the novel's most thorny issue. Deronda's mother seldom misses a chance to express her contempt for outward signs of Jewish separateness:

> I rid myself of the Jewish tatters and gibberish that make people nudge each other at the sight of us, as if we were tattooed under our clothes, though our faces are as whole as theirs. I delivered you from the pelting contempt that pursues Jewish separateness. (544)

Her marriage to a malleable husband, combined with her orthodox father's death *before* Deronda's birth, make it not only possible but probable that she could have avoided the most basic of Jewish rituals for her son. This probability is strengthened by the Alcharisi's almost boastful remark that her weak husband "went against his conscience for [her]" (543). Under these circumstances, the narratological movement between an avoided circumcision and the Alcharisi's requests to inspect Deronda's hand upon reunion—from "he went against his conscience for me" to "let me look at your hand"— reveals the extent to which Deronda's Jewishness could be marked by a body part that Eliot saw as a positive indicator of religiosity in particular and of characterization in general throughout her career. Think, for instance, of the characteristically "hands-first" description of *Romola*'s Savonarola with which this chapter began.

SYMPATHETIC HANDEDNESS

Deronda's hands mark him as a Jew in the world of this novel but, crucially, they do not perform *only* this function. The "consecrating power" of his sympathy for others—Jew and non-Jew alike—manifests itself throughout the narrative in scenes that make a spectacle of the firm but gentle touch embodied in the Titian example (141). Nowhere is the "flexible sympathy" of Deronda's touch more apparent than in his reaction to Gwendolen's suffering (307). This appears particularly as Gwendolen recounts the harrowing story of Grandcourt's death:

> Her quivering lips remained parted as she ceased speaking. Deronda could not answer; he was obliged to look away. He took one of her hands,

and clasped it as if they were going to walk together as two children: it was the only way in which he could answer, "I will not forsake you." . . .

That grasp was an entirely new experience to Gwendolen: she had never before had from any man a sign of tenderness which her own being had needed, and she interpreted its powerful effect on her into a promise of inexhaustible patience and constancy. The stream of renewed strength made it possible for her to go on as she had begun—with that fitful, wandering confession where the sameness of experience seems to nullify the sense of time or of order in events. (592)

The restorative impact of Deronda's hands so transcends its Jewish realm that the narrator ultimately renders even his dialogue with Gwendolen in the rhetoric of manual intervention: "[His] words were like the touch of a miraculous hand to Gwendolen" (659). This Feuerbachian and Comtean mode of transcendence is fitting since the narrative does not lead to a discovery that Deronda is no longer English; it instead shows that he is also a Jew. It confirms why Eliot's inclusion of Titian's *Man with a Glove* in Deronda's first description resonates so subtly yet so appropriately throughout the course of the novel. Titian's one-gloved sitter approaches a modern sensibility precisely because the treatment of his hands reveals a sense of multiform allegiance. There is no doubt that the sitter's gloved hand marks him as an (Christian) aristocrat, but his ungloved hand—by Eliot's lights— is "of a kind to raise belief in a human dignity which can afford to acknowledge poor relations" (158). This belief in human dignity is exactly what Eliot accomplishes in the connections between Deronda and people ranging from the Cohens to the Harleths. Such remarkable contrasts allow Eliot to transform the possibility of multiple class and religious allegiances into multiple racial, ethnic, and national possibilities. Critics have traditionally drawn parallels of Eliot's universalized religiosity to Comte's "religion of humanity." Her immersion in Jewish mysticism for her final novel, though, is simply a more specific instantiation of her belief in the divine's interdependence on the human. Daniel Matt's description of this interdependent relationship in the *Zohar* is uniquely applicable to the model of active divination that Eliot endorses throughout *Daniel Deronda*: "God is not static being, but dynamic becoming. Without human participation, God remains incomplete, unrealized. It is up to us to actualize the divine potential in the world. God needs us" (2007: 1–2).

Peter Stallybrass and Ann Rosiland Jones have remarked, in another context, how "[Titian's] painting stages the unpairing of hands" (2001: 123). Applied to *Daniel Deronda*, though, its "unpairing" provides an important dimension of materiality to recent pioneering discussions of Eliot's commitment to what Amanda Anderson has influentially called "reflexive dialogism" (2001: 121, 138, 143). Important work by Bryan Cheyette (1993), Michael Ragussis (1995), Daniel Novak (2004, 2008), and Anderson correctly attempts to reconcile Jewish identities that are simultaneously given and constructed. Yet just as the linguistic expression "on the one hand … on the other hand" rhetorically unpairs different parts of a single idea, both *Man with a Glove* and *Daniel Deronda* suggest how those differences might be contained within one body—indeed, even within one set of hands. The novel quite literally enacts this multiplicity on the level of plot where Deronda's hands connect what critics have long referred to as the "English" and "Jewish" halves of the novel: he becomes a sacred priest to the Christian Gwendolen even as he prepares to help build a Jewish homeland in the East.[25] Ultimately, Eliot sacramentalizes Deronda's hands not only because they are Jewish, but because they are the appendages through which human sympathy flows most directly. Prayer, as Derrida observes, does not know of right or left hands; instead, it is "the gesture in which two hands join together to make themselves one in simplicity" (2007: 42). It is for this reason that Eliot prefigures modern and twentieth-century philosophers who have continued to find new ways for the hand to be uniquely human. Daniel Deronda is therefore a fitting character upon which to make the transition to the uniqueness of handwriting that is the subject of chapters 7 and 8. It is he, after all, who deciphers God's handwriting on the wall (Daniel 5: 26–28).

Plotting the Novelty of Manual Narratives

CHAPTER 7

Handwriting and the Hermeneutics of Detection in Dickens's Bleak House

In chapters 1 and 2 we saw from a scientific perspective how the eighteenth-century interest in faces eventually shifted to the nineteenth-century concern for life and limb. To underscore the staying power of these changed circumstances, I want to return now to a facet of this same shift, but from a different angle and by using a different genre of fiction. Part IV will eventually settle in to a discussion of the shared manual thematics of several key Victorian detective novels but, to do so, it is necessary to think about their relation to the eighteenth-century novels that preceded them.

Over the course of the eighteenth century in Britain, the epistolary format became the dominant mode of fictional representation. Novelists as varied as Samuel Richardson and Frances Burney composed their novels entirely within letters shared back and forth between their characters. Oddly enough, even though these authors predicated their fiction on the exchange of handwritten letters, there is little—if any—emphasis on what their various characters' penmanship looked like. This lack of specificity is all the more odd when we consider Eve Tavor Bannet's recent finding that the proliferation of eighteenth-century discourse outlining the proper "manual architectronics" of letter writing became almost as popular as the fictional representations of this epistolary world itself (2005: 54). Given the widespread cultural interest in what Bannet calls "letteracy" during the eighteenth century, how do we account for its novelists' lack of interest in the materiality of the handwriting in their fictionalized letters? The issue becomes even more puzzling when we think of how different this is from the scenario in the nineteenth century, where authors fetishize handwriting's material properties. Think, for instance, of Charles Dickens's *Bleak House* (1853–54), Mary Elizabeth Braddon's *Lady Audley's Secret* (1862), and

Robert Louis Stevenson's *Dr Jekyll and Mr Hyde* (1886). The plots of these novels, each from different decades of the second half of the nineteenth century, explicitly hinge on the material features of their characters' handwriting. Considering this raises another question in relation to the earlier one: how do we account for the Victorian novel's preoccupation with what Janet Altman calls the "epistolarity" of a no longer epistolary genre? (1982: 4).

My argument in this chapter may at first seem as counterintuitive as these questions themselves. One would think that eighteenth-century novelists, working as they did within the established epistolary framework, would have a great deal to say about their characters' penmanship. But they don't. Conversely, it would appear logical that Victorian novelists would think less, not more, about the handwriting in their fiction at a time when the hands around them were becoming less and less exceptional in economic and evolutionary contexts. Likewise, this isn't the case. I will respond to this paradox by arguing that anxieties about the hand appear most strikingly in British fiction when this previously essential human appendage becomes threatened, destabilized, or toppled from its place of uniqueness in the cultural imagination. Like the overarching contention of *Changing Hands*, then, these final chapters will expose how anxieties about the body appear only when a part of it becomes threatened. We have seen how this plays out in fiction concerned with mechanization, gender ideology, and evolution. What we will see now in the comparison of several eighteenth- and nineteenth-century texts is a return to how Victorian novels continually align hands with unique individual identity as a reaction to industrializing processes and evolutionary theories that were rendering them less and less exceptional.

EPISTOLARY HANDS AND
THE EIGHTEENTH-CENTURY NOVEL

One reason why people in the eighteenth century paid so little attention to hands was because of the fact that they were more interested in faces. Deidre Lynch's *The Economy of Character* (1998) links ideas about human physiognomy to the ways plots were constructed throughout the eighteenth century. More recently, Juliet McMaster has shown how eighteenth-century novelists knew the respectable classical origins of physiognomy and, therefore, stories about reading and misreading faces became a staple of the period's fiction well before English translations of Johann Lavater's "face-oriented" work began to appear in the late 1770s (2004: 45). Reading the classical origins of physiognomy was buttressed by the work of contemporary philosophers and visual artists alike. James Parsons's *Human Physiognomy Explain'd* debuted at the Royal Society in 1749 and William Hogarth's *The Analysis of Beauty* provided "a lineal description of the language written" in the "expressions of the countenance" in 1747 (127). McMaster notes how these popular cultural texts and others like them helped the face become "a sufficient and effective synecdoche for the whole personality" in the eighteenth century (2004: 96).

It is as important for my argument to analyze what is *missing* from descriptions of the hand's materiality in the eighteenth century as it is to notice what is provided about the face—especially in novels containing epistolary components where attention to the work of writing hands would seem to be a place of logical interest for novelists. Eliza Haywood's *Fantomina* (1725), for instance, is a fiction of mistaken identity par excellence but its focus is characteristically on faces, not hands. The novel contains many handwritten letters yet Haywood's emphasis remains on how Fantomina takes on different costumes, hair colors, accents, and make-up to satisfy the unsuspecting Beauplaisir's desire for multiple lovers. "So admirably skill'd in the Art of feigning," Haywood's narrator tells us, "that [Fantomina] had the Power of putting on almost what Face she pleas'd" (2004 [1725]: 57). Near the end of the story Fantomina writes Beauplaisir a lengthy (and anonymous) letter soliciting his amorous attention, which she signs only with the name "INCOGNITA." Beauplasir asks the letter carrier if the writer "were a Wife, or a Widow, and several other Questions" but then becomes convinced "that nothing but doing [what Incognita asks], could give him any Light into the Character of the Woman who declar'd so violent a Passion for him" (63–64). My point in recounting this part of Haywood's text is to note how the handwriting in Fantomina's/ Incognita's letters is in no sense revelatory. The written epistles are simply an assemblage of alphabetic "letters"; nothing about them reveals anything concerning the writer's subjective identity.

Very little changes by the middle of the eighteenth century when the epistolary form comes to dominate fictional representation. For instance, Samuel Richardson spends over 1,500 pages and 537 letters telling the story of Clarissa Harlowe's attempts to retain her independence from Robert Lovelace and other suitors in *Clarissa* (1748). Yet handwriting is so divorced from individual subjectivity in this novel that Lovelace is able to forge successfully several letters to Clarissa in the name of her friend Anna Howe under the most facile of disguises. In one of these forged letters, Lovelace provides a fictional postscript to cover for any potential discrepancy Clarissa may notice in her "friend's" handwriting: "I have written all night. *Excuse indifferent writing. My crow-quills are worn to the stumps, and I must get a new supply,*" writes the feigning Lovelace to Clarissa (814, emphasis added). Furthermore, the actual handwriting is so far from Richardson's consciousness that, even in the famous letter where Lovelace inserts manual indice marks on Anna Howe's original letter, it goes completely unmentioned. Before sending the forged letter to Clarissa, Lovelace intercepts a crucial warning letter on its way to Clarissa from Anna Howe telling her of the villain's true designs. Lovelace sends his friend Belford a copy of Anna's warning letter but he "crowd[s] with indices [the symbol ☞]" the margins of the copied letter. The myriad of tiny hands in the margin (103 of them in all) is meant to highlight Anna's remarks that Lovelace finds particularly aggravating (fig. 37). Terry Castle has argued that,

---

[Letter 229.1: Anna Howe] to Miss Laetitia Beaumont

                                                    Wednesday, June 7
My dearest friend,
You will perhaps think that I have been too long silent. But I had begun two letters at different times since my last, and written a great deal each time; and
☞ with spirit enough, I assure you; incensed as I was against the abominable wretch you are with; particularly on reading yours of the 21st of the past month.*

☞ The *first* I intended to keep open till I could give you some account of my proceedings with Mrs Townsend. It was some days before I saw her: and this intervenient space giving me time to re-peruse what I had written, I thought
☞ it proper to lay that aside, and to write in a style a little less fervent; for you would have blamed me, I know, for the freedom of some of my expressions
☞ (*execrations*, if you please). And when I had gone a good way in the *second*, the change in your prospects, on his communicating to you Miss Montague's letter, and his better behaviour, occasioning a change in your mind, I laid that aside also. And in this uncertainty, thought I would wait to see the issue of affairs between you, before I wrote again; believing that all would soon be decided one way or other.

I had still, perhaps, held this resolution (as every appearance, according to your letters, was more and more promising), had not the two past days furnished me with intelligence which it highly imports you to know.
☞ But I must stop here, and take a little walk, to try to keep down that just

---

Fig. 37. Inset from *Clarissa* (743).

for the reader, "the effect of the hands is fetishistic, oppressive, disturbing" (1982: 112). If this is so, it is because Lovelace's unconstrained orthographic repetition of his own indexical hands so close to Anna Howe's writing also prefigures the ease with which he forges Anna's "hand" just pages later in his false letter to Clarissa.

The epistolary novels of Tobias Smollett and Frances Burney exhibit a similar (non)treatment of handwriting. Smollett's *The Expedition of Humphry Clinker* (1771) is a novel composed of more than 85 individual letters with only a single mention of handwriting. In the closing pages of the novel, Matthew Bramble mentions the pleasure with which he recognizes Dr. Lewis's "hand-writing, after such a long cessation" (1929 [1771]: 411). Even in this single instance, though, the handwriting is characterized more by the doctor's occupation than it is by any sense of individuality. Bramble writes to Dr. Lewis, "Heaven knows, I have often seen your hand-writing with disgust—I mean, when it appeared in abbreviations of apothecary's Latin" (412). Likewise, Burney's *Evelina* (1778) contains no commentary on its characters' handwriting even as it turns on forged letters and issues of mistaken identity. When Sir Clement Willoughby confesses that he was the one who wrote the infamously offensive and "ever-to-be-regretted letter" to Evelina, he says simply, "I [wrote] it, therefore, in Orville's name" (2002 [1778]: 282, 388). There is no commentary whatsoever about how his handwriting comes to be taken for another person's—even at a crucial moment in the novel's plot. My point is that handwriting in the eighteenth-century novel is a relatively unremarkable subject because handwork had not yet become seriously threatened. It only stands to reason that people would not express anxiety about something they had not yet experienced. In Bill Brown's theorization, we only begin to confront "the thingness" of an idea, a concept, or an object when such a thing stops working (4).[1]

As we've seen in the opening chapters of *Changing Hands*, anxieties about the mechanization of manual labor—from Luddite rebellions to factory accidents—pervaded the English imagination at the beginning of the nineteenth century. This chapter argues that we may also trace these lines of tension to nineteenth-century novelists' treatment of handwriting and, further, that a new preoccupation with handwriting in the construction of fictional plots coincides with mechanized developments in general, but within the book industry in particular. It must be stressed that this stark change in the attention novelists pay to handwriting in the nineteenth century does not occur neatly or overnight, as many nonindustrial and extraliterary factors necessarily contribute to such a change. For this reason, I concentrate in this chapter on fiction that has no immediate or explicit connection to industrial expansion but whose preoccupation with the handwritten word nevertheless depends on the effects of mechanization in print culture construed more broadly. But a substantial part of my argument concerns authors who were connected to facets of the book trade (either as investors or editors) that brought them into immediate contact with revolutionary change in nineteenth-century machine culture as it pertained to the changing material conditions of literary labor.

THE ORIGINS OF HANDWRITING ANALYSIS
IN THE NINETEENTH CENTURY

Most discussions of handwriting analysis begin with the work of the Swiss pastor and physiognomist, Johann Kaspar Lavater (1741–1801). From 1775 through 1778 Lavater published what would eventually become known in English translation as *Essays on Physiognomy*. Lavater devoted the majority of this text (and its accompanying illustrations) to a detailed exposition of his physiognomical theory, but the later editions contained what Bradley Deane has called a "brief and somewhat tentative" chapter on handwriting as an index of character (2003: 74). In these few pages devoted to handwriting, Lavater did little more than propose an argument for the analysis of penmanship. He did, however, illustrate his approach with ten "specimen signatures," and this was enough to pique the interest of many commentators beyond the continent.

For the purposes of this chapter, I am interested in the clustered amplification of Lavater's theories as they emerged closer to England in conjunction with what we have already seen was its rapid and unprecedented industrial expansion during the first decades of the nineteenth century. In France in 1812, for example, Edouard August Hocquart (1789–1870) published a more fully developed treatise than Lavater's entitled (in English translation) *The Art of Judging the Mind and Character of Men and Women from Their Handwriting*. This more specialized analysis of handwriting had reached England by 1823 when Thomas Byerley (n.d.–1826), under the pseudonym Stephen Collet, published "On Characteristic Signatures" in *Relics of Literature*. Writing during the decade of England's most rapid industrial expansion, Byerley says:

In all other actions . . . *some share* of guile and deception *may* lurk, which it requires penetration, experience, and skill to be able to detect; but in using his pen, a man acts unconsciously, as the current of his blood impels him; and there, at all times, nature flows unrestrained and free. Hence, in common language, we talk about finding out *what vein a man is in*; and that he has *got his wits at his finger ends*; speaking like physiologists, without being aware of the secret truth to which we are paying homage. (369–70, emphasis original)

As we have seen in other contexts in previous chapters, Byerley's work is yet another index marking the nineteenth-century's shifting interest from faces to hands. "I have reached that point of physiognomical skepticism," Byerley writes, "that I would no more form an opinion of a man from the mode of his wearing his face . . . than I would from the shape, size, or colour of any article of his apparel" (369). A year later, Isaac Disraeli (the father of future Prime Minister Benjamin Disraeli) strengthens this changed focus on the hands by including a section devoted to "Autographs" in his *Curiosities of Literature* (1824). Disraeli surmises that "Nature would prompt every individual to have a distinct sort of writing" because "the flexibility of the muscles differs with every individual, and the hand will follow the direction of the thoughts" (1834 [1824]: 279–80). It is not coincidental that these arguments for the importance and individuality of handwriting gain momentum in congruence with the displacement of human hands in British textile industries.

This pattern of manual displacement appeared not only within the textile industry, but also within an industry much more pragmatically connected to the production of fiction at the turn of the nineteenth century: paper manufacture. Before the nineteenth century, all paper on the continent and in England was rag woven—by hand. The first industrially produced paper was made in France by Nicolas Louis Robert in 1799, but Robert's mechanical venture proved to be unsustainable. The English brothers Henry and Sealy Fourdrinier made several mechanical improvements and built the first paper mill in Hertfordshire in 1803. This development made paper-making machines commercially successful in England as early as 1805 (Gaskell 1995: 228). Such progress should help us recall Kevin McLaughlin's point that "paper is a historical, as well as a philosophical, subject" (2005: 11). In describing the new machine capable of producing as much paper as fifteen men "without the intervention of manual labour," John Murray (1981 [1829]) compared the apparatus and the process to automatic cotton manufacture. Murray's important comparison sheds light on the fact that, in a far less visible industry, but one nonetheless more practically connected to fiction, hand labor was undergoing a similar process of supersession by industrial machinery.

In the early decades of the nineteenth century, the first novelists to emphasize the originality and subjective uniqueness of handwriting were those with some immediate knowledge of how mechanization affected the publishing process. This is perhaps why, for instance, we see Walter Scott and not Jane Austen begin to show a sustained interest in fictional characters' penmanship. Austen was quite far removed from the mechanization of the paper, press, or textile industries and so she predictably adheres to what we have seen as a more eighteenth-century model of indifference in the fictional representation of her characters' handwriting. Think of Frederick Wentworth's memorable "you pierce my soul" love letter to Anne Eliot at the end of *Persuasion* (1817). Despite the letter's dramatic composition where Wentworth drops his pen out of sheer nervousness, Austen reveals nothing of Wentworth's penmanship in this crucial letter—except that it was "hastily" composed (2003 [1817]: 222).

Walter Scott presents us with a very different relationship to writing. Though he refused to admit it until much later, Scott was enmeshed in the commercial aspects of book production as a part of the Ballantyne brothers' publishing and printing business (Deane 2003: 12). In 1802 Scott was investing heavily in the mechanical paper and printing operations and became a partner the new publishing firm of Ballantyne & Co. in 1809. It was this involvement on both the authorship and the commercial sides of novel production that led to Scott's unique, market-oriented view of the industry. As Bradley Deane points out, Scott answered Adam Smith's distinction between the unproductive work of men of letters and the seemingly more directly beneficial products of other branches of manufacture by contending that novels should be considered functionally equivalent to other commodities (2003: 15).

In the "Introductory Epistle" to *The Fortunes of Nigel* (1822), composed at a key moment in England's industrial expansion, Scott writes that "a successful author is a productive labourer, and that his works constitute as effectual a part of the common wealth, as that which is created by any other manufacturer" (1853 [1822]: 22). This is the decade that Thomas Carlyle had dubbed "the Age of Machinery" in 1829 and, as we saw in chapter 2, economic historians agree with the accuracy of Carlyle's designation. An intimate awareness of how the process of industrialized production was supplanting manual labor, combined with the heightened cultural responsiveness in England to contemporary theories of writing where the hand was *still* relevant, likely influenced Scott to employ what was then the budding pseudoscience of graphology in his own fiction. For example, in *Chronicles of Canongate* the narrator of the Croftangry family history, angry that his "great-grandsire" squandered most of the inheritance, nearly throws the grandfather's diary into the fire. Just before doing so, Scott's narrator reconsiders on the basis of the relationship between handwriting and individual identity:

> A little reflection made me ashamed of this feeling of impatience, and as I looked at the even, concise, yet tremulous hand in which the manuscript was written, I could not help thinking, according to an opinion I have heard seriously maintained, that something of a man's character might be conjectured from his handwriting. That neat, but crowded and constrained small hand, argued a man of good conscience, well regulated passions, and, to use his own phrase, an upright walk in life. But it also indicated narrowness of spirit, inveterate prejudice, and hinted at some degree of intolerance, which, though not natural to the disposition, had arisen out of a limited education. The passages from Scripture and the classics, rather profusely than happily introduced, and written in a half-text character to mark their importance, illustrate that peculiar sort of pedantry which always considers the argument as gained, if secured by a quotation. Then the flourished capital letters, which ornament the commencement of each paragraph, and the name of his family and of his ancestors, whenever these occurred in the page, do they not express forcibly the pride and sense of importance with which the author undertook and accomplished his task? I persuaded myself, the whole was so complete a portrait of the man, that it would not have been a more undutiful act to have defaced his picture, or even to have disturbed his bones in his coffin, than to destroy his manuscript. (1827: 33–34)

Here a "good conscience," "well regulated passions," and "an upright walk in life" become legible in the grandfather's "neat, but crowded and constrained small hand." The shift I have been tracking in emphasis from the face to the hands is also here: penmanship provides the narrator with "so complete a *portrait*" of his grandfather that destroying the manuscript would have been tantamount to "defac[ing] his picture."

It becomes possible to pinpoint in Scott's detailed analysis of handwriting an early response to what becomes fairly standard in the Victorian novel with writers like Charles Dickens, Mary Elizabeth Braddon, and Robert Louis Stevenson—all writers who were similarly familiar with technological and scientific change. The desire to become in Kathryn Sutherland's terms "both master-manufacturer" and "workman" in an increasingly industrialized world has the effect of making authors as well as their readers hyperfocused on a form of manual labor (handwriting) that still remained untouched—so to speak—by mechanization (1987: 101). The basic printing processes from papermaking to typesetting the press become fully mechanized and eventually merge with the culture's larger experience of industrialization in, for example, the railway distribution network at the end of the 1830s.[2]

A closer look at the homogenizing forces of industrialism in the early decades of the nineteenth century reveals complexities and contradictions even within the seemingly "untouched" world of penmanship in England. Indeed, contemporary developments such as the refinement of the factory system, the increasing anonymity of urban life, and the frenetic pace of the marketplace inevitably led to major changes in how the handwritten word was taught, read, and executed. Although there was no compulsory writing curriculum in England until the Elementary Education Act of 1870, earlier changes in penmanship training generally conformed to the rapid expansion of Britain's merchant class. Students from wealthier families would often spend three to four years acquiring proper penmanship before putting these skills on hold as they studied (and copied) Latin and Greek, only to arrive at an irregular hand as they left their schooling. This process often produced a formal, stiff, "text-hand" ill-suited for practical and faster-paced business correspondence. As a result, a new market opened for penmanship masters such as Joseph Carstairs who promised to teach, in a matter of months, a fast and legible script called the mercantile "runninghand," which was developed specifically for middle-class business communication. His *Lectures on the Art of Writing* proclaimed the "invention and perfection of a new mode of writing" fit for "the day-book and ledger" of a merchant's office (1816: 2, 18).

Mirroring contemporary industrial modes of production, Carstairs and others aimed at "teaching writing by a mechanical process, founded on systemic principles" that would yield "uniform advancement toward practical perfection" (1816: 18). Such precision in writing was accomplished not only by repetition, but also by mechanical intervention:

> The pen ought to point exactly to the shoulder and to be held so as to come between the second and the third joints of the fore-finger, the extremity of the thumb to be kept directly opposite the first joint of the fore-finger.
>
> Those who find it difficult to keep the pen pointing to the shoulder, may take a small cane about a yard long, and fix it to the barrel of a short pen, and hold it so as to let the upper end of the cane rest on the shoulder. If any difficulty should be found in making the cane rest easily on the shoulder, let an open loop be fixed to the shoulder, so as to admit the upper end to run freely within the loop. The loop may be made of broad tape or a slip of paper . . . and fastened with a pin. (16–17)

The device designed to bring handwriting "nearer to perfection" that Carstairs describes here (fig. 38) is a precursor to the mechanical "tantalograph" (fig. 39) he includes in later editions of his book (36).

What we see, then, is not a monolithic and stable account of handwriting as the last refuge of manual handicraft but a more contradictory story where the individuality of penmanship itself is challenged. Even commentators who believed in the somatic connections between handwriting and human character like Thomas Byerley and Isaac Disraeli expressed doubts about the possibility of doing so in an increasingly industrial future. "The great mass of people," wrote Byerley, "may be said to consist of mere negatives; of persons who act as they are desired, think as they are taught, and *write after the copies set before them*; and the utmost that you can expect to discover from handwriting of such persons is, that they have no individual character at all" (1823: 370–71, emphasis original). In 1824, Disraeli expressed a similar,

Fig. 38. The "tantalograph"

Fig. 39. Mechanical "tantalograph"

if more industrially inflected, sentiment: "But regulated as the pen is now too often by a mechanical process, which the present race of writing-masters seem to have contrived for their own convenience, a whole school exhibits a similar handwriting; the pupils are forced in their automatic motions, as if acted on by the pressure of a steam-engine . . . all appearing to have come from the same rolling press" (1834 [1824]: 279). This uniformity in writing was enhanced in 1842 when England's Committee of Council on Education endorsed the Mulhauser Method for use in its schools—a method adopted in Switzerland and Germany in the 1830s to teach young middle-class students the proper mechanics of penmanship.

PLOTTING HANDS IN *BLEAK HOUSE*

There may be no work of fiction in the nineteenth century that so adamantly dramatizes the tensions between mechanized and individualized modes of writing as Charles Dickens's *Bleak House* (1853–54). Over twenty years ago, J. Hillis Miller began a chapter dedicated to this novel in *Victorian Subjects* with an aptly provocative sentence: "*Bleak House* is a document about the interpretation of documents" (1991: 179). I would like to press this interpretation of the novel's documents to its most tangible incarnations. Unlike the eighteenth-century epistolary texts with which this chapter began, the entire plot of *Bleak House* turns on the uniqueness of a single handwriting sample—a trace of individuality in a written format that is supposed to eradicate uniqueness. Lady Dedlock recognizes her former lover's "hand" amidst the "legal repetitions and prolixities" that the lawyer Tulkinghorn presents to Sir Leicester Dedlock (26). "'Who copied that? . . . Is it what you people call law-hand?' she asks." These two uncharacteristically animated questions from Lady Dedlock set the whole of the novel's detective plot into motion. Tulkinghorn responds, saying "Not quite. Probably . . . the legal character it has, was acquired after the original hand was formed" (26–27). Tulkinghorn's response elevates this exchange from the level of passing non-chalance to one of arresting significance for *Bleak House*'s central concerns with individuality in an age of modernizing homogeneity.

The "legal character" to which Tulkinghorn refers is the arcane style of penmanship (fig. 40) that survived in English Chancery papers through the nineteenth century despite its disappearance from ordinary writing by the beginning of the seventeenth century.

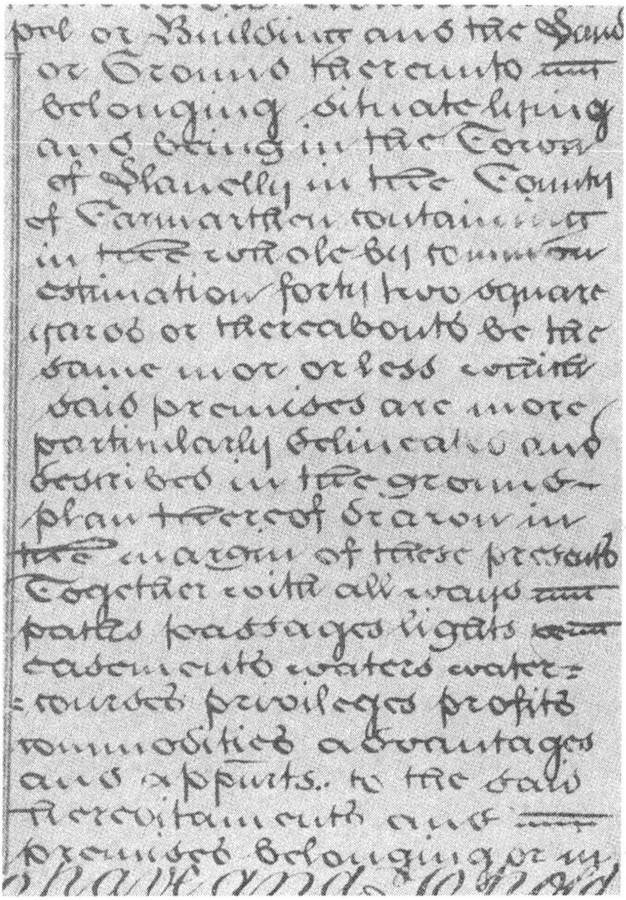
pel or Building and the Land
or Ground thereunto
belonging situate lying
and being in the Town
of Llanelly in the County
of Carmarthen containing
in the whole by common
estimation forty two square
yards or thereabouts be the
same more or less which
said premises are more
particularly delineated and
described in the ground
plan thereof drawn in
the margin of these presents
Together with all ways
paths passages lights
easements waters water=
=courses privileges profits
commodities advantages
and appurts. to the said
hereditaments and
premises belonging or ap

Fig. 40. Deed enrolled in Chancery, 1830.

Thus "Chancery-hand," because of the extent of its difference from all other forms of nineteenth-century handwriting, becomes for Dickens an incredibly effective medium through which to illustrate the effects of mechanization on the human body. In an interesting case of anachronistic irony, the mechanical rigidity of the much older and rarified writing form amplifies the cultural anxieties toward industrialization represented in the contemporary drive to systematize a new "clerical hand"—of the kind Carstairs promoted.[3] Hawdon's livelihood depends on his ability to copy affidavits with such precision that each iteration looks exactly like every other one he or anyone else produces—a self-conscious process of "disappearance into writing" that he perpetuates through his advertised name of "Nemo" (Jackson 2009: 80). Nemo's disappearance, therefore, depends on the invisibility conferred by the mechanical task of copying. Under pressure from Tulkinghorn, Snagsby admits that he knows Nemo only by the way his speed, accuracy, and automated indefatigability stand out even in a profession of mechanical copiers: "he gradually fell into job-work at our place; and that is the most I know of him, except that he was a quick hand, and a hand not sparing of night-work; and that if you gave him out, say, five-and-forty folio on the Wednesday night, you would have it brought in on the Thursday morning" (170).

And yet the novel's plot depends on the ability of some characters (Lady Dedlock, Esther, and possibly Tulkinghorn) to see individuality as minute orthographical digressions from the purely mechanical task of copying. For instance, shortly after Lady Dedlock recognizes lingering traces of Hawdon's hand in his Chancery affidavit, Dickens reinforces such a prospect in the other, first-person (Esther) narrative voice at the outset of the novel. Esther has spent very little time in London but she proves remarkably astute in reading the various signs that bombard her during her first outings in the city. As she stands in front of Krook's "Rag and Bottle Warehouse," one particular sign catches her attention:

> Some of the inscriptions I have enumerated were written in law-hand, like the papers I had seen in Kenge and Carboy's office, and the letters I had so long received from the firm. Among them was one, *in the same writing*, having nothing to do with the business of the shop, but announcing that a respectable man aged forty-five wanted engrossing or copying to execute with neatness and dispatch: Address to Nemo, care of Mr Krook within. (68, emphasis added)

If Dickens were to leave it at this, we could only surmise that the *style* of writing (law-hand) Esther recognizes on these signs matches that of a profession rather than an individual within that profession. However, we know that Esther wrote biannually to Mr. Kenge (the lawyer acting on behalf of her guardian) for the six years she was in school informing him of her status as "happy and grateful" (39) and that, in response, she "always received by return of post exactly the same answer, *in the same round hand*; with the signature of Kenge and Carboy in another writing" (40, emphasis added) (fig. 41).

Old Square, Lincoln's Inn.

Madam,

Jarndyce and Jarndyce.

Our cĺt Mr Jarndyce being aƀt to rece into his house, under an Order of the C̄t of Chy, a Ward of the C̄t in this cause, for whom he wishes to secure an elḡble compn̄, directs us to inform you that he will be glad of your serces in the afsd capacity.

We have arrn̄gd for your being forded, carriage free, p' eight o'clock coach from Reading, on Monday morning next, to White Horse Cellar, Piccadilly, London, where one of our clks will be in waiting to convey you to our offe as above.

We are, Madam,

Your obed¹ Servˢ,

Kenge and Carboy.

Miss Esther Summerson.

Fig. 41. Legal (Non-Chancery) "Hand." *Bleak House* (40).

This additional knowledge means that Esther unwittingly makes the connection that the writer of the sign soliciting copy work from Krook's shop is the same person who writes her twice a year. Perhaps Dickens intends for his readers to miss this deeply embedded clue; only upon re-reading the novel could anyone guess the implication of this handwriting match. For what such a match means is that Esther was receiving letters not necessarily *from* her father but *in* her father's unique style of "law-hand"—a hand that we can assume, as in the case of the individuality embedded in his "Chancery-hand," stands out despite cases of rigid legal formatting.

Though the plot is propelled by a hunt for "a specimen of [Hawdon's] handwriting," and later by the search to discover whether the letters in his possession are in Lady Dedlock's hand, the novel remains fixated on the tension between mechanical standardization and human variation in several other ways. The most obvious example involves the relationship between Mrs. Jellyby and her eldest daughter, Caddy. Dickens presents this relationship not as one between mother and daughter but rather between oral dictator and amanuensis; Mrs. Jellyby "perseveringly dictat[es]" correspondence related to Borrioboola-Gha to Caddy who copies them out exactly (79). Such mechanical copying leaves Caddy feeling paradoxically alienated from her labor despite its direct connection to her hand. She complains to Esther that she "can't do anything hardly, except write" (60).

No one in *Bleak House*, though, is more alienated from the work of writing than Krook. His illiteracy makes him an ideal copyist (and the most mechanistic one) because he is completely unencumbered by the meaning of the words he chalks out on the wall of his shop in front of Esther (75–76). His inability to read also ensures that each cluster of lines will appear as a perfect copybook example of the letter it represents, a fact underscored by Krook's "very curious manner" of "beginning with the end of the letter and shaping it backward" (75). Krook forms each letter "as any clerk in the Messrs Kenge and Carboys office would have made," telling Esther that he possesses "a turn for copying from memory" despite the fact that he "can neither read nor write" (76).

Although Krook stubbornly distrusts any form of external instruction, his method of letter formation reflects contemporary models of penmanship acquisition in England. Carstairs's *Lectures in the Art of Writing*, for instance, sought to establish "a mechanical process, founded on [the] systematic principles" of seventeen elementary pen-strokes (fig. 42) rather than on the phonetic comprehension of the twenty-six letter alphabet in its "universal advancement towards practical perfection" (1816: 18).

After memorizing the seventeen pen-strokes or characters (and their corresponding numbers), the student may be taught to join the different

Fig 42. Plate B. Carstairs, *Lectures on the Art of Writing* (80).

strokes together to form the letters in the alphabet: "the characters under the numbers 1 and 2, form the letter *a*,—those under 3, 2, and 4, form the letter *b*,—5, 6, and 7, the *c*.—1, 3, and 2, the *d*," etc. (76). This important step committed to memory, "the master should [be able to] exercise his pupils in writing any word that he may chuse to dictate by the numbers of each character until the word is completed" (80). In the plate above, Carstairs takes the word *contemplation* as an example of this process: the letter *c* is number 5; and the *o*, number 1; the *n*, 10 and 8; the *t* 16; the *e* 7 and 5; the *m* 10, 10, and 8; and so on for the rest of the word. The emphasis is thus not on the comprehension of the word's meaning, but its form and proportion—elements of spelling that Krook has mastered despite his illiteracy.[4]

By 1840 England's Committee of Council on Education was identifying the effectiveness of similar methods for the teaching of penmanship throughout Europe. The committee found that Germany, Holland, and Switzerland were all using a system called the "Letter Case" or "Reading Machine" where young students imitated "straight lines . . . or curves resembling those used in writing" (*Minutes* 1841: 40). In so doing, "with the aid of a careful arrangement of the written characters, in the order of their comparative simplicity, the children learn to write *before* they learn how to read" (40, emphasis added). England's Council on Education unanimously decided to adopt this method of "systematising" English writing education with its endorsement of Mulhauser's Manual (41). Krook's method, therefore, was more representative than anomalous in teaching handwriting to midcentury English youth.

Despite the mechanizing forces of mid-nineteenth-century culture in general and writing instruction in particular, *Bleak House* stubbornly emphasizes the individuality and uniqueness buried in one's handwriting.[5] This is true in part because, as J. Hillis Miller notes, Dickens always "stresses the material, bodily base of all writing" (2001: 54). We see this in examples ranging from "the trying business" of Charley's attempts to copy the letter "O" to the individuality embedded within Nemo's law-hand. As Tony Jackson says of the latter instance, "the purely visible signs of [Hawdon's] flesh and blood hand show up in spite of, and in conflict with, the uniformity required by law-hand" (2009: 83).

This emphasis on the uniqueness of handwriting reappears in other, seemingly unrelated places in the novel. For instance, Dickens follows Lady Dedlock's recognition of Hawdon's/Nemo's handwriting with Esther's recollection of reading from the Gospel of John where Jesus stoops down and writes with his finger in the dust when the Pharisees bring an adulteress before him. This scene is odd because we never know (in both the Bible and in *Bleak House*) what exactly Jesus writes in the sand; the emphasis instead rests on Jesus's repeated act of writing as a response to the Pharisees' sustained assertion that Mosaic Law requires adulterous women to be stoned (John 8:1–11). Again, though, Jackson's shrewd interpretation of the scene makes sense of the oddity both in the Bible and in *Bleak House*: "In Jesus's eyes the old Mosaic Law has become dehumanized and rigid," "inhuman" and "mechanistic" when "implemented only according to its written letter, not its originating spirit" (2009: 1, 84). Therefore, Jesus's finger-in-the-dust writing is important not for what it says, but rather what it *is*. Writing with the hand—no matter what it says—suggests an individuality that fundamentally differs from anything wrote, copied, or mechanically applied. Jesus emphasizes this by continuing to offer his individual handwriting in the face of a mechanical law that concedes nothing for individual circumstance.

It would be difficult (and ultimately unproductive) to discern Dickens's exact views on the relationship between handwriting and character that captivated his Victorian audience. The topic was of such popular concern, for example, that *Punch* was regularly poking fun at it by the late 1840s. The "Handy Phrenology" piece we saw at the start of chapter 5 represents one example of this phenomenon. Another one, a short piece entitled "Handwriting and Character," expresses skepticism toward the "undertaking by sundry advertising experimentalists on public credulity to tell the character by the handwriting in return for a certain amount in silver or in postage stamps" (1849: 231). The "Bleak House Advertiser," which accompanied each number of the novel as it was originally published, for instance, contains several advertisements from a "Mr. Warren" who promises to "delineate the Character of Individuals from their Handwriting" for thirteen postage stamps (No. 1, March 1853, 17; No. 2, April 1852, 14). Advertisements such as this one sought to connect the outward sense of character represented in the physical letters of the alphabet and the inward sense of a person's moral character. A *Punch* piece from 1850 also satirizes this practice (fig. 43).

However, a comparatively longer piece called "Mr. Van Ploos on Penmanship" in Dickens's own *Household Words* from the same year reveals a more nuanced portrait of handwriting interpretation at midcentury. In this short story version, the son of a family of celebrated writing-masters in Amsterdam reflects on the public's fascination with handwriting analysis:

Fig. 43. "A Sketch of Character By Professor Milkansop, the Celebrated Graphiologist." *Punch* 19 (1850): 154.

The question of how far the character of men is to be known by their
handwriting, involves many very curious and interesting considerations.
By some it has been regarded as a matter of divination or conjuring;
but in any case there is *something* true to be made of it. We see advertisements, from time to time, in the newspapers, offering to divine and
divulge the character of any unknown person whose handwriting is
brought to them, at the small charge of five shillings per character. By
these means men, about to engage in partnership, or to have important
transactions with anyone, may know before-hand the character of the
person with whom they will have to do . . . Is this all nonsense? Not *all*;
but it is simply pushing, as we commonly see, a fact beyond its legitimate

bounds, till it becomes an absurdity, and no fact at all worth a pinch of snuff. (1850: 40; emphasis added)

Although Mr. Van Ploos is somewhat ambivalent about direct connections between handwriting and character, his most important observation about handwriting as it pertains to *Bleak House* is his emphatic resolution that "no two [hands are] exactly alike" (38). Indeed, the uniqueness of an individual character's handwriting propels *Bleak House*'s plot at every turn: first, and most importantly, with Hawdon's identity emerging from the exactitude of Chancery-hand and the subsequent search for a handwriting sample in trooper George's possession, but also with Smallweed's matching of Lady Dedlock's hand to the love letters left at Krook's (823–24), Esther's identification of her mother's penmanship in her final letter, and the discovery of the "Will of later date . . . all in the Testator's handwriting" (948).

It is important of to recall that Dickens began writing *Bleak House* during a time of heightened and officially sanctioned public consciousness of mechanical progress. He started composing the novel in 1851—the year England's Great Exhibition of industrially produced products at the Crystal Palace mesmerized hundreds of thousands of visitors with its comprehensive display of contemporary machine culture. Exhibition goers walking up the Main Avenue saw railway engines, steam boilers, mill machinery, and hydraulic presses in full working order. They also saw the hopeful predictions of early industrialists such as Andrew Ure come to fruition in machinery where improved equipment truly did begin to substitute "the iron arms and fingers of the machinery, for [human] bone and sinew" (qtd. in Pettitt 2004: 95). According to the *Official Descriptive and Illustrative Catalogue*, for example, De la Rue's envelope-folding machine utilized its "magic finger" to fold and gum 2,700 envelopes per hour. Without this machinery, an experienced manual worker was unlikely to fold this amount in an entire day using the rudimentary "folding stick" method (Golden 2009: 133).

Perhaps most importantly for its relation to *Bleak House*, even that most basic and longest lasting technology—the pen quill—had become mechanically updated by midcentury. Manufacturers of steel pen nibs sprang up around Birmingham to produce a perforated artificial tip that had the flexibility of the traditional goose quill (Hensher 2012: 148). And the pen industry was hardly as small as the products it churned out. As Sonja Neef has noted, English manufacturers began to process Sheffield steel by the ton in gigantic works equipped with steam-powered, smoking blast furnaces in

enormous factory spaces (2011: 109). It was within this atmosphere, satu-
rated with mechanized culture right down to the very writing instruments
used to "pen" fiction, that Dickens composed *Bleak House*—a novel whose
plot hinges on the uniqueness of the human hand's written form.

THE MECHANICS OF LITERARY LABOR

I will return later on to the significance of pens both inside and outside
of the world of this novel. For now, though, I would like to consider *Bleak
House* in relation to mid-nineteenth-century novel production in general.
John Sutherland has commented that by 1852 the English novel was as much
a triumph of industrial progress as anything in the Great Exhibition (1976:
66). David Napier's double platen printing machine was used widely to produce thousands of copies at a time with minimal problems such as jam-
ming and ink blots that had hindered earlier versions of this machine. This
development flourished in part because the slow and expensive process of
casting type by independent handicraftsmen was also replaced around 1850
by mechanized foundries that produced five times as much type (Dooley
1992: 48). Before this, printing firms did not own enough type to produce
an entire novel at once. These new developments in book production meant
that authors were increasingly pressed by what E. P. Thompson inaugurated
as new industrial "time-routines" both to create and to compose (write out)
their novels (1990: 382).

The vexed role of the novelist as artist in the age of mechanical reproduction inevitably led to the "Dignity of Literature" debates within the novel-
writing profession at midcentury. On one side was William Thackeray's
entirely unsentimental characterization of the hired writer in the age of
rapid textual reproduction as a profession that could be perilously close to
the industrial monotony endured by factory workers in *Pendennis* (1848–
50). "We know how the life of any hack, legal or literary," writes Thackeray's
narrator, "is dull of routine, and tedious of description" (1991 [1848–50]: 353).
At least publicly, Dickens balked at such unflattering, mechanized views of
the profession for a combination of reasons. He was deeply affected by the
Carlylean and Romantic notions of the author as a heroic "man of genius"
for whom writing was effortless. However, Dickens's previous experience—
from putting labels on boot blacking to learning shorthand for parliamentary
court reporting—predisposed him to align work of any kind with manual

labor. We see this in *David Copperfield* (1849–50), the novel Dickens was writing contemporaneously with Thackeray's *Pendennis*, where the young David repeatedly characterizes his path to economic self-sufficiency with the rhetoric of strenuous manual labor. "What I had to do," he says, "was, to take my woodman's axe in my hand, and clear my own way through the forest of difficulty, by cutting down trees" (1981 [1849–50]: 505). Dickens felt quite earnestly about this laborious representation of writing. His earnestness was likely rooted in the fact that, despite all the technological advances in book production, writing (for any author) was still the most manual of occupations.[6] We saw this in chapter 2 where his 1850s letters to Forster emphasize the difficulty of composing fiction for weekly or monthly periodical deadlines. Indeed, Dickens's account of the printing processes involved in the production of *Household Words* refers directly to "the ponds of writing ink, [and] the mileage of finger movement that precede the issue of each week's allowance to the world" (16 April 1853, 7: 145–49, 147). We should bear this in mind when considering Dickens's physical (manual) relationship to his longest novel—one that contains "tens of thousands" of hand-copied Chancery papers (17).

Juliet John has recently probed the complexity of the relationship between imagination and industry by claiming that Dickens occupies a "threshold position" in cultural history because his works and philosophies employ "both a mechanical *and* an organicist conception of art" (2010: 158). To bolster her point about what she calls Dickens's "'halfway house' or creative fusion" between mechanism and creativity, John correctly concludes that Dickens was opposed not to mechanization universally, but to the use of mechanization without a larger commitment or emotional investment in community and human relationships (2010: 171). It is important to trace the origins of these relationships to the contradictory components of Dickens's changing professional life as well. He was no longer only an author, as he was in *David Copperfield*. It was during the 1850s that Dickens began editing his weekly magazine *Household Words* in addition to his composition of fiction. As Bradley Deane has noted in *The Making of the Victorian Novelist* (2003), editorship in the nineteenth century was not a creative or original endeavor. The culling and arranging of a periodical's contents week after week quickly resembled a mechanized routine as monotonous and rigidly scheduled as any other industrial occupation (34). It was during this time that Dickens also began to criticize the recently formed National Association of Factory Occupiers for doing nothing more than aggregating to pay fines for fencing violations under the 1844 Factory Act. In Sally Ledger's view, Dickens's changing attitude to mechanization during this period provides a context for his great social novels of the 1850s—of which *Bleak House* is exemplary (2010, 186).

Another factor complicating matters was Dickens's very public and aggressive stance toward international copyright laws. His advocacy for stricter copyright laws was part of an effort to exchange an enduring romantic perception of the artist as an effortless creator for that of a hard-working bourgeois professional. This does not mean that Dickens switched his allegiances in the "Dignity of Literature" debates with Thackeray and others. It means, however, that the boundaries of Dickens's artistic views were often unclear and sometimes contradictory. Acknowledging these aspects of Dickens's life, in connection with the broadly mechanizing spirit of the 1850s, helps us get a better view of the central issues at stake in *Bleak House's* extraordinary focus on handwriting. The fact that *Bleak House* was produced during a time when mechanization was beginning to affect even the work of creative novelists offers us, I think, a privileged glimpse into broader cultural anxieties about authenticity in a world becoming increasingly dependent on automatic manufacture.

For concrete examples of midcentury Britain's agitated and unresolved relationship to industrialization, we need look no further than to the contents of the "Bleak House Advertiser"—that cultural apparatus literally and figuratively closest to the anxieties contained with *Bleak House* itself.[7] Here we can trace the unresolved (and almost schizoid) social meanings of "manufacture" in the mid-nineteenth century to facing pages of the text attached to the beginning of *Bleak House*. On page three there is an advertisement for Hugo Reid's *The Steam Machine* (1838), the full title of which reveals its appeal to a general audience: *The Steam-Engine; Being a Popular Description of the Construction and Action of that Engine; With a Sketch of Its History, and of the Laws of Heat and Pneumatics.* Yet on the very next page of the Advertiser (page four), there is an advertisement for a *"New Edition"* of Charles Bell's *"THE HAND; ITS MECHANISM AND ENDOWMENTS, as evincing design"*—which, as we saw in chapter 2, was a panegyric for the handmade. This interpolation of the automatic and the handmade may be seen as well in another section from the Advertiser where the top of the page features an ad for "Waterlow's Patent Letter Copying Presses" while the bottom of the page features ads for "Metallic Pens" and individual "Glass Cone Inkstands" (fig. 44).

WATERLOWS'
PATENT AUTOGRAPHIC PRESS,
OR PORTABLE
PRINTING MACHINE,
FOR THE COUNTING-HOUSE, OFFICE, OR LIBRARY,
BY MEANS OF WHICH
EVERY PERSON MAY BECOME HIS OWN PRINTER.

The Process is simple, and thousands of copies may be produced from any writing, drawing, piece of music, or design (previously made on paper), and the requisite number of copies being finished, the subject may be effaced and another substituted.

The attention of MERCHANTS and SHIPPERS is particularly called to the importance of this invention, for the Colonies and Foreign Countries: and when it is considered that in many places no printer is to be found, and that in some countries, especially in the East, the complication of the numerous Oriental characters renders it necessary for all documents to be multiplied by the tedious process of transcribing, the peculiar advantages of the Autographic Press become manifest.

The Autographic Press will be found of great utility to *Railway Companies, Joint Stock Banks, Merchants and Brokers,* and to *all persons engaged in Business,* for printing their own *Circulars, Invoices, Statements, &c.*

The Press is now in use in some of the first establishments in this country and abroad, and may be seen at work at the Patentees. The following prices include everything pertaining to the Press, and full instructions for using it:—

				Improved.	Improved, on Mahogany Stand.
To Print a Subject	11 × 9	- £4 4 0	- £7 7 0	- £9 9 0
Ditto	16½ × 10½	- 5 5 0	- 8 8 0	- 10 10 0
Ditto	18 × 13½	- 6 6 0	- 9 9 0	- 12 12 0

PATENTEES—WATERLOW AND SONS,
65 TO 68, LONDON WALL, LONDON.

From the City Article of "The TIMES."

A very useful invention has been patented by Messrs. WATERLOW & SONS, which will be productive of great convenience to Banking Establishments and other concerns requiring to send out circulars with despatch. It is called the Autographic Press, and a letter written on prepared paper with which it is furnished, can be transferred by a short process to a metallic plate, from which any number of copies may afterwards be taken on common paper and by ordinary pressure. In the colonies and other places where facilities for such operations are now scarce, and in all cases where the documents to be copied are of a confidential nature, it is likely to prove particularly valuable.

"MORNING CHRONICLE."

AUTOGRAPHIC PRESS.—An invention has been patented which is likely to prove of great utility to public companies and men of business generally. It will become a great desideratum to merchants in the colonies, and will be found very useful at the chief offices of banks, in suspending the necessity for copying any number of circulars which it may be necessary to send to the Branches from time to time. We understand it has received the patronage of His Royal Highness Prince Albert, and it is the invention of Messrs. WATERLOW and SONS, London Wall, by whom it has been patented.

Fig. 44. "The Bleak House Advertiser." Waterlow's Autographic Press. Courtesy of Special Collections, Spencer Research Library, University of Kansas Libraries.

If we extend Jennifer Wicke's insight that "literature and advertisement are cultural kindred," and consider these early advertisements for books on steam machinery and human hands in connection with the opening pages of *Bleak House* itself, the effect is nothing short of astonishing (1988: 3). Lady Dedlock scans the mechanical form of Chancery writing and recognizes within it the individual "hand" of her former lover (26–27).

Like Tony Jackson's point about the Gospel of John, here we have another, and perhaps more striking, example of *Bleak House* enacting its own extraliterary version of itself. I say that it may be more striking (and thus more representative of the broader cultural context) for two reasons. First, if we assume that Bradbury and Evans lined up their advertising clients independently according to market rates for available space, Dickens, unlike the insertion of the Gospel of John, would have had nothing to do with the uncanny connection we see here between life (nonfiction advertising) imitating art (fictional tension between the mechanical and the handmade). Second, the schizoid toggling between the mass-produced and the unique individual does not end with this one example. The supplemental Advertiser contains ads for handwriting analysts, ink, penmanship manuals, envelopes, bankers' checks, portable printing machines, manufactured steel pens, fireproof safes, and mutual life insurance, among other goods and services. This wide array of ads is interesting but, for the purposes of this chapter, not nearly as interesting as the repeated interplay within these ads between the mechanistic and the manual. We have already seen both in and outside of the novel, for example, how various routinizing systems of handwriting sought to eliminate variation and individuality by making penmanship appear more uniform. We have also seen how individuality and uniqueness cannot be fully divorced from one's handwriting—how identity always lies in wait in an individual's "characters." The same is true in the layout of the Advertiser where ads for "Mr. Carstairs' Writing Rapidly Improved" share the same page as ads for "Mr. Warren's" ability to decipher "Character from Handwriting" (17).

Just as in the fictional novel, the Advertiser reveals the contradictory elements of handwriting in the industrial age. Mr. Carstairs "rapidly improve[s]" writing precisely by making it adhere to a mechanical, copy-book template while Mr. Warren professes an ability to locate individual "character" from seemingly undifferentiated "characters" of the printed alphabet. This process only becomes more complicated with the development of mechanized letter reproducibility. "Waterlows' Patent Autographic Press, or Portable Printing

Machine (fig. 44), which appears numerously throughout the Advertiser, for example, promises that "every man can become his own printer" by producing "thousands of copies" of any written document. Such a process uncannily echoes Nemo's decline as a subject exposed to mechanical reproduction.

A more detailed look at the entire contents of the Advertiser appears at first to reveal a lopsided emphasis on mechanization over the manual. The precision of Stone's Patent "bankers cheques" and "account books" is ensured "by a machine of ingenious and novel construction, worked by STEAM POWER, which produces a clear and bold figure, of an unequalled regularity" (17). The Advertiser attached to the seventh installment of *Bleak House* (September 1852) contains a prospectus for *The Practical Mechanic's Journal*—a four-volume set with 1,200 engraved illustrations listed alphabetically. A sample of "Specimens" listed under the letter "B" includes Findlay's Bobbin Turning Machine, McNaught's High-Pressure Boiler, Hill's Self-Acting Brake for Railway Inclines, and Randell & Saunders' Brick, Tile, and Pipe Machine (4). What is so interesting about the Advertiser in relation to the tensions contained in *Bleak House*, though, is that despite this overwhelming emphasis on mechanization, the individual hand always remains stubbornly visible. Just under a three-quarter-page ad for Waterlow's "Patent Letter Copying Presses" sits an ad for "Turkey Quills" and "Porcupine [Quill] Holders." Moreover, one of the most frequently occurring ads in the nineteen *Bleak House* installments is for a pen (fig. 45) made by Joseph Gillott. The prominent and uninterrupted inclusion of this ad (in every number from September 1852 through September 1853) shows that handwriting was still essential to mid-nineteenth-century life.

Even so, it would be misleading to argue that this recurring pen ad reflects an unmitigated connection to handicraft. As we have seen earlier in this chapter, pen *making* from rolled steel was as industrial a process as any other, and Gillott's ad characteristically touted this: "by a novel application of his unrivalled Machinery for making Steel Pens, and in accordance with the scientific spirit of the times, [Gillott] has introduced a *new series* of his useful productions" (No. VII; 8). My point is that there may be no better or more germane example of the unresolved and contradictory nature of "manufacture" in the nineteenth century than the steel pen itself. It is simultaneously a mass-produced instrument and yet the one most commonly used to produce a kind of subjective authenticity only to be found in the handwritten. Mechanical rammers would stamp the firm's name and trademark into the flat steel blanks—a process by which the same unmistakable signature

Fig. 45. Joseph Gillott Metallic Pen Advertisement. "The Bleak House Advertiser." Courtesy of Special Collections, Spencer Research Library, University of Kansas Libraries.

would vouch for the quality of their company's product (Neef 2011:109). The Gillott ad is shot through with exactly this rhetoric of authenticity: "each pen bears the impress of his name as a guarantee of quality." In connection with *Bleak House*, Emily Steinlight has shown how the novel's crises invariably "follow from various modes of copying and reproduction" and, further, "how these processes can seem to produce disastrous effects and insoluble problems of subjective agency" (2012: 138).

The anxiety compacted in these insoluble problems of agency for the author of a nineteenth-century novel resides in the uneasy relationship between the machine-stamped signature *on* the pen and the hand that *uses* such a pen to manufacture, as it were, an original work of fiction.[8] Jenny Hartley's recent conclusion that "the process of writing" was as important to Dickens as its "appearance" should make it unsurprising that he "groaned when he had to 'write with a steelpen'" (2012: xv). According to Hartley's observation of Dickens in her recent selection of his letters, "your writing does not just express you, it *is* you" (xvi, emphasis added). This observation rings true for even minor characters in *Bleak House*. Think, for instance, of the orphan Charley. When we first meet her, the thirteen-year-old washes clothes to support her two young siblings, and her hands tell the story plain enough. Esther notices that constant exposure to "soap-suds" has made Charley's "fingers ... white and wrinkled with washing" (245). Later in the novel, when Charley enjoys the much less laborious position of maid-servant to Esther, we learn that her hands have become "plump and round" (486). As is the case with so many in *Bleak House*, though, her handwriting retains the traces of her original, material (dis)position as a prematurely aged young washerwoman: "It was very odd," Esther remarks, "to see what old letters Charley's young hand had made; [the letters], so wrinkled, and shrivelled, and tottering" (486).

Perhaps no hands give away their owner so fully and so fantastically than do those of Lady Dedlock, though. The great lady's hands reveal her identity at three important plot junctures in the novel. On the first occasion, she visits the burial site of Nemo/Hawdon in the disguise of her servant, Hortense. Inspector Bucket's suspicions lead him to ask Jo to confirm Hortense's identity as "the lady" who asked to be shown to the nameless grave. Jo apparently does so through his recognition of "the wale, the bonnet, and the gownd" of the woman paraded before him in Tulkinghorn's office (363). When Bucket presses for Jo to look also at the woman's hands, the street sweeper immediately notices his mistake, saying "It an't her hand ... [her] Hand was a deal whiter, a deal delicater, and a deal smaller" (364, 363). On the second occasion, grandfather Smallweed examines a bundle of love letters stashed in Nemo's quarters above Krook's shop. He then proceeds to make the connection between the uncommon name signed "Honoria" and "the same hand" as Lady Dedlock (824). The third occasion occurs at the very end of Lady Dedlock's life, when she manages to elude inspector Bucket by disguising herself once again as another woman. This time she throws Bucket and Esther off by walking through a snowstorm from London to St. Albans and back again only to have her disguise blown by what we have come to see as the nineteenth century's most undisguisable body part: her hand.

Having wrestled the letter away from Guster, Bucket demands—in a scene that eerily parallels the opening affidavit one—to know "Whose writing is that?" (909). Despite the letter's hasty composition in "pencil-writing, on a crushed and torn piece of paper, blotted with wet," Esther confirms that it is in fact her mother's handwriting (909). Perhaps most tragic of all is Lady Dedlock's belief that she has "nothing about [her] by which [she] can be recognised" (910). She *has* shed all the physical trappings of her life as a baronet's wife; she wears a brickmaker's wife's dress, no jewels, no cold-weather clothing. And yet it is upon her "unshedable" written hand, like that of her former lover, that her identity is confirmed most definitively. Both Hawdon and Lady Dedlock eventually come to literalize the cliché of characters who destroy themselves by their own hands,[9] living out Hegel's belief that the hand "is the living artificer of [a person's] fortune" (1807:189).

It is important to point out that in this novel where individual identity traced through the hand so often leads to disaster, it also leads to hope. The discovery of "a Will of later date than any in the [Chancery] suit" depends on the fact that it appears "all in the Testator's handwriting" (948). After-thought though it may seem in a novel of such misery, the discovery of the will in the testator's handwriting allows Ada, and by extension Esther, to live in comfort for the rest of their days. *Bleak House*'s consistent interest in handwriting and its connection to individuality represents an earlier instantiation of what we saw culminate in *Great Expectations*, where the physicality of the hand stands for the person. Unlike *Great Expectations*, though, *Bleak House* is anxiously preoccupied by the hand in relation to mechanical rather than biological reproduction.

CHAPTER 8

Narrative Red-Handedness in Braddon's Lady Audley's Secret *and Stevenson's* Dr Jekyll and Mr Hyde

It has been said that Mary Elizabeth Braddon's early fiction, reworked, re-packaged, and "sensationalized" the stylistic strategies of Dickens's detective novels.[1] Although there is no doubt that Braddon took a great deal from the narrative strategies on display in *Bleak House*, this does not mean that Braddon was merely a purloiner of plots. I will argue nonetheless that she *was* a purloiner of a particular form of corporeal narratology that came to prominence in the nineteenth century.[2] The narrative thrust of *Lady Audley's Secret* (1862), just like *Bleak House*, depends almost entirely on hands and handwriting. As was the case with Dickens, Braddon was both an author and an editor in a time of enormous change within the publication industry. Perhaps more importantly, she was a member of a larger culture undergoing unprecedented mechanized expansion and modernization. Despite our knowledge of this, generations of critics have overlooked—like the purloined letter that sits in plain sight on the mantel piece—the most obvious corporeal expression of anxiety regarding industrialization in the nineteenth century. I have suggested throughout my study that the reason why even historically minded critics overlook hands in Victorian fiction is, ironically enough, a problem of literary and cultural historiography. It has not occurred even to historicist critics, who live in a culture almost completely changed by the metaphorical treatment of its manual connections, to revisit a time when the very status of a body part so routine as hands was in such anxious flux. This, combined with the lopsided critical tendency to study nineteenth-century embodiment through the overdetermined lens of physiognomy, makes the hand all too easy to overlook even in the narratives like *Lady Audley's Secret* where it plays such a crucial role.

Braddon foregrounds the relationship between hands and industrial-ized modernization in a seemingly simple object described in the novel's second sentence. As the reader approaches Audley Court—"this glorious old place"—the narrator describes "a clock tower, with a stupid, bewildering clock, which had only one hand; and which always jumped straight from one hour to the next" (1998 [1862]: 8, 7). This clock has only one hand because an hour was as specific as time needed to be in this old and rural part of Eng-land—a point reinforced by the narrator's almost comical use of the word "old" six times within the opening two pages. In a novel so heavily predicated on far more specific instances of "railroad time" (trains leave the station at precise minutes, not hours) there is a sense that this clock is truly *missing* a hand. This missing hand, I think, taps into a deeper root of Victorian anxiety present throughout the nineteenth century about the interaction of people and industrialized mechanisms. The fact that the narrator personi-fies the Audley clock as "bewildering" hints at the sense of a broken body. As we have seen, the missing hand haunts not only temporally, but also corpo-really, so many new industrial spaces in the Victorian world.[3]

Since *Lady Audley's Secret* is a narrative based on the collision of old and new ways of life, it seems apt to consider the Audley clock tower in terms of what its older eighteenth-century "face" prevents us from seeing in its important but absent nineteenth-century hand.[4] The tendency in criti-cal appraisals to focus on the "unmasking" of Lady Audley certainly follows "contemporary taste" in so far as it relates to the Victorian interests in pre-Raphaelitism and physiognomy, but it does so at the expense of the other routinely visible body part that we know by now also captivated the nine-teenth-century imagination (Pykett 1992: 101).

Ultimately, as we shall see, though, the narrative drive to unmask Lady Audley hinges on the recognition of authenticity not in Lady Audley's face but in the legibility of her handwriting. Here we have another example of a narrative red herring where Braddon follows Dickens quite closely. At the outset of *Bleak House*, Guppy becomes "absorbed by the portrait" of Lady Dedlock because of its resemblance to Esther Summerson (111). He even goes so far as to stake a marriage proposal to Esther on the resemblance he sees in the portrait. As we saw in the previous chapter, though, Lady Ded-lock's ultimate identification comes not via her face but her handwriting. The same scenario plays out at the start of *Lady Audley's Secret*, where the narrator ascribes the minute facial detail in Lady Audley's painting to the compositor's pre-Raphaelitism:

No one but a pre-Raphaelite would have painted, hair by hair, those feather masses of ringlets with every glimmer of gold, and every shadow of pale brown. No one but a pre-Raphaelite would have so exaggerated every attribute of that delicate face as to give a lurid lightness to the blonde complexion, and a strange, sinister light to the deep blue eyes. No one but a pre-Raphaelite could have given to that pretty pouting mouth the hard and almost wicked look it had in the portrait. (72)

There is no question that George Talboys makes the identification of his former wife through the facial features of this portrait, but he exits the novel early on without telling anyone—least of all Robert—of his realization. As is the case in so many Victorian novels, though, hands become far more revelatory than faces in Braddon's text. The revelations they provide are perhaps most impressive in *Lady Audley's Secret* because details about the facial often appear by way of the manual. Robert Audley, for example, sees Lady Audley's face in her hand(writing). He makes the following observations upon receiving a written note from his step-aunt:

> It is the prettiest, most coquettish little hand I ever saw ... I never believed in those fellows who ask you for thirteen postage stamps, and offer to tell you what you have never been able to find out yourself; but upon my word I think that if I had never seen your aunt, I should know what she was by this slip of paper. Yes, here it all is—the feathery, gold-shot, flaxen curls, the pencilled eyebrows, the tiny straight nose, the winning childish smile, all to be guessed in these few graceful up-strokes and down-strokes. (66)

Beginning with this cavalier association between the manual and the facial, this chapter aims to demonstrate how dependent Lady Audley's "unmasking" is on her hands and handwriting, and then it goes on to explore how deeply this dependency is intertwined with anxieties about women in an increasingly industrialized society.

SENSATION'S GRIP

The grouping of a particular kind of sensation fiction at the beginning of the 1860s, like many other literary appellations before it, emerged from the consensus not of authors but of critics. In the case of the new sensational genre, critics acted almost immediately to denounce the supposedly harmful effects that sensation fiction inflicted upon its readers. An article in the April 1863 *Quarterly Review* entitled "Sensation Fiction" by the Dean of St. Paul's, H. L. Mansel, provided the sharpest and most noteworthy criticism of its kind:

> No divine influence can be imagined as presiding over the birth of [this genre's] work, beyond the market-law of demand and supply; no more immortality is dreamed of for it than for the fashions of the current season. *A commercial atmosphere floats around works of this class, redolent of the manufactory and the shop.* The public wants novels, and novels must be made—so many yards of printed stuff, sensation-pattern, to be ready at the beginning of the season. (495–96; emphasis added)

Embedded in Mansel's criticism is the realization that an exponentially increasing class of readers were attracted to a kind of fiction which was affiliated with industrial expansion, and, hence, with the democratizing forces of modernization. Not only were women increasingly filling factory positions previously held by men, but they were also composing and consuming the majority of sensation fiction. Thus lower-class female readers were drawn to this type of fiction because they played a major role in the industrial expansion of mills and factories.

There is little doubt that the removal of stamp and paper duties in 1855 contributed to what Wilkie Collins famously called a new "monster audience" of readers. However, Mansel's criticism reveals a general concern for the relationship between mass literacy and industrial production, and it explicitly shows a more specific unease with women's role in the "manufactory" of sensational fiction. In 1862, E. S. Dallas had written in *The Times* that "This is the age of lady novelists" (18 November 1862: 4). Mansel's comparison of sensation fiction to "so many yards of printed stuff . . . to be ready at the beginning of the season" confirms a larger cultural fear that women were dominating both production and consumption in this new literary industry. And this is true: *Lady Audley's Secret* went through nine editions in the three months after it was issued in book form in 1862. Part of the reason for the novel's success in acquiring new female readers was the way it synchronized the progressive forces of industrial modernity with the escalation of women's autonomy. Indeed, Henry James had conceded that "innovation, specifically technological innovation, undertaken by a female character, [was] one of the defining attributes of sensation fiction" (1865: 593–94).

The anxiety that novelists such as Dickens felt toward the mechanization of their craft in the 1850s became tolerable and even desirable for Braddon and other sensation novelists in the 1860s precisely because the industrial rhythm in fiction was its most appealing (and best-selling) characteristic. In this regard, Jonathan Loesberg's insightful comment about the intersection of fiction with the political atmosphere of the 1860s applies equally to the period's industrial atmosphere. "One reason for the popularity of sensation fiction," Loesberg writes, "was that those novels were telling a story, in one version or another, that all Victorian society was telling itself" (2001: 128). Women were gaining traction in society at least in part because of their participation in its industrial economy. We shall see that what G. H. Lewes pejoratively referred to as the "breathless rapidity of movement" so characteristic of sensation fiction's narrative armature by 1862 actually helped stabilize a new British reading populace that was struggling to make sense of its rapid and disorienting ascent to an increasingly industrialized modernity (1866: 894).

To read with rapidity, suspense, and mystery—speeding on trains all over metropolitan England—in order to discover the truth of Lady Audley's past becomes part and parcel of living in a world conditioned by industrialized time rituals and urban anonymity. *Lady Audley's Secret* does this and more, though. It extends the threat of female capability inside the factory to the mastery of modern technology outside the factory walls. The novel is such a compelling and unique sensation text because the mechanized pace and modernizing forces of contemporary life are repeatedly aligned with (lower-class) female independence. The principal anxiety of the text, therefore, emanates not so much from mechanization per se but from a woman's autonomous employment of it to achieve an improved lifestyle. It proclaims that women as well as men may stand to benefit from the forces of modernization. The eventual containment of such anxiety depends on the secret buried in the decidedly "old" technology of her handwritten letters. This scenario underscores how heavily the Victorian novel depends on embodied handedness.[5] Despite all of the industrial and modernizing components that Lady Audley utilizes to transform her life, it is, like with Lady Dedlock, the invariability and uniqueness of her hand (penmanship) that eventually betrays her. The remainder of this chapter will analyze the relationship between the literal legibility of Lady Audley's past and her incarcerative future.

TECHNOLOGY AND FEMININE AUTONOMY

The stark contrast between Robert Audley's preindustrial, aristocratic idleness and Lady Audley's modernized, class-conscious mobility forms the core of the novel's narrative tension. In effect, the rational and logistical "work" behind Lady Audley's secretive rise from obscurity to ladyship embodies the independent and technologizing spirit of modernity itself. The anxiety that Robert feels radiating from Lady Audley has its source in the simultaneity of what she represents as an autonomous, technologically inclined woman beneath the performative role she enacts as Sir Michael Audley's "childish" wife. Indeed, there would be no threat in the text if Lady Audley arrived at her position as the wife of a baronet via the traditionally passive process of the marriage market that she affects to have followed. To invoke the language of the novel, though, Helen Maldon/Helen Talboys/Lucy Graham/Lady Audley had to "*do* a great deal to accomplish such a change" (121, emphasis added). Unlike Thackeray's Becky Sharp who similarly marries up, Braddon predicates Lady Audley's rise on an active participation in the modernizing world of industrial mechanization. Lady Audley adheres to temporal precision as she crisscrosses England on a network of trains, orchestrates the sending and receiving of newly developed telegraphic messages, choreographs her own death, and exhibits a mastery of the newspaper industry by reading, placing, and responding to advertisements in *The Times*—all extremely independent and progressive actions for a woman in 1862.

Braddon deliberately portrays Robert Audley in opposition to these progressive forces at the outset of the novel in order to dramatize the anxieties of the privileged upper classes who are threatened by a rapidly industrializing and democratizing Victorian world. The narrator informs us that he "had never either had a brief, or tried to get a brief, or even wished to have a brief" in his five years as a barrister (35). Rather than practicing the law, the "listless, dawdling, indifferent, irresolute" young barrister prefers to live comfortably ("smoking his German pipe, and reading French novels") on the £400 a year left to him by his father (35). Jenny Bourne Taylor rightly points out that Robert Audley's "entire being becomes the embodiment of passive spectatorship" (1998: 36, xxxiv). This listlessness changes very quickly with the disappearance of George Talboys and with the "honest purpose" the investigation adds to Robert Audley's idle life, however (147). We learn just how entrenched Robert's idleness has been, though, when the narrator reports early in the novel that "the young barrister was worn out by a day spent in hurrying from place to place [tracking Lady Audley]. The usual monotony of his life had been broken as it never had been broken before in his eight-and-twenty tranquil, easy-going years" (99).

Although Robert's new investigative life has a purpose, it is also marked by a deep ambivalence and even hatred for women with whom he constantly associates the faster-paced, industrialized forces of modernity. This becomes more apparent as we learn that Robert does not enjoy the rapid change his lifestyle undergoes as he pursues the circumstantial evidence pointing to Lady Audley's guilt. In one particularly revealing moment, he laments that he has "been false to the leading principle" of his aristocratic lineage in being forced to "submit to all the dreary mechanism of life" (205, 207). As Robert's meditative digressions move from his own specific circumstances to a more generalized misogyny, his thoughts repeatedly and disdainfully link women to the new, modernizing conditions of England's industrialized economy:

> I've been acting for myself, and thinking for myself, for the last few months, and I'm tired of the unnatural business . . . What the devil am I doing in this *galere?* . . . A man might lie in the sunshine and eat lotuses, and fancy it "always afternoon," if his wife would let him! But she won't, bless her impulsive heart and active mind. She knows better than that. Whoever heard of a woman taking life as it ought to be taken? Instead of supporting it as an unavoidable nuisance, only redeemable by its brevity, she goes through it as if it were a pageant or a procession . . . She drags her husband on to the woolsack, or pushes him into Parliament. She drives him full butt at the dear, lazy machinery of government; and knocks and buffets him about the wheels, and cranks, and screws, and pulleys; until somebody, for quiet's sake, makes him something that she wanted him to be made . . . It is because women are never lazy. (207–8)

Robert baldly expresses a fear that women's industriousness is better suited for the increasingly faster-paced and mechanized public world of the 1860s. His thinking here represents a nearly complete reversal of the traditional separate-sphere ideology that we saw so restrict the lives of women in chapters 3 and 4. Such a stance is no doubt inflected by Robert's social positioning above the cares of the getting and spending of a middle-class life. Nonetheless, Robert confirms his preference for such a reversal in his oft-voiced desire to shrink from "the fatigues of [his] troublesome life" tracking Lady Audley's history (123). Shrinking from this new active life would eventually allow him to return to the aristocratic idleness the narrator enumerates in the "half-a-dozen French novels" and "three pounds of Turkish tobacco" that he lugs around with him in his portmanteau while attempting to keep pace with his young aunt (117). Robert's sense that industrious women secretly act as the force behind the public endeavors of professional men, of course, conceals the far deeper fear that women may be no longer satisfied with passive participation in a modernizing world through male surrogacy. This threat, like any other, increases proportionally with its proximity to contemporary reality. Lower-class women had already proven their capacity to work alongside men in mills and factories. Throughout the 1850s Harriet Taylor, Barbara Leigh Smith, and others were beginning to successfully challenge the nature and fixity of middle-class gendered categories. By the end of the decade the *Englishwoman's Domestic Magazine* ran an article entitled "Is Woman Superior to Man?" (qtd. in Palmer 2011: 33). All of this attests to how much has changed, in Braddon's view, from the debates of the 1840s, which focused merely on the capabilities of woman. Now that woman had proven herself capable of participating in a middle-class world, the question appropriately began to shift to one of opportunity.

In Braddon's fictional world, the specter of such feminine competence surfaces and resurfaces in Robert's constantly articulated anxiety that "a stronger hand than his own point[s] the way which he was to go" (159). His reluctance, in this regard, is rhetorically figured not in terms of a disembodied providential hand, but the earthly feminine one of Lady Audley. This formulation easily becomes the novel's most dominant trope as Robert repeats variations of it at many key narrative junctures:

> "I try in vain to draw back or stop short upon the road, for a stronger hand than my own is pointing the way to my lost friend's unknown grave." (169)

> "[H]ow pitiless I am, and how relentlessly I am carried on. It is not myself; it is the hand which is beckoning me further and further upon the dark road whose end I dare not dream of." (174)

> "A hand which is stronger than my own beckons me on." (174)

"A hand that is stronger than my own is beckoning me onward upon the dark road." (200)

"A hand that is stronger than my own is beckoning me onward on the dark road that leads to my lost friend's unknown grave." (255)

The "hand stronger than [his] own" that Robert fears is crucially linked to literalness in the novel. Not only does Robert fear that Lady Audley has managed to throw George Talboys down the well, but he also fears (rightly so) that she has a better grasp on the hyperactive technology of the industrializing British landscape. Therefore, the trepidation echoed in this trope of "a hand stronger than my own" operates as a fearsome bass note continually sounding the alarm of feminine competency, especially after it becomes clear midway through the novel that the proof of Lady Audley's crime will depend absolutely on connecting her true identity to "the evidence of [her] handwriting" (268).

Following the traces of evidence that lead him to the Talboys estate in hopes of finding handwriting samples of Helen Maldon/Helen Talboys, George asks himself a question that specifically identifies Lady Audley's hand as the source of his ongoing trepidation: "Why did my relentless Nemesis ever point the way to that dreary house in Dorsetshire?" (390). His "Nemesis" is Lady Audley, but the lack of evidence in the form of her handwriting as Helen Maldon or Helen Talboys only identifies the equally disturbing incarnation of female agency that resides in George's sister, Clara. Braddon brilliantly transfers this threat from Lady Audley to Clara Talboys by way of the same manual trope. When no older handwriting samples turn up at the Talboys estate in Dorsetshire, the investigative dead end leaves Robert feeling relieved that his work finally may be over. Relief for the diffident Robert proves to be short-lived, however, as Clara immediately challenges him to continue the investigation with a stark warning that she will act in the event of his inaction. It is necessary to cite a longer section of their dialogue in order to demonstrate Braddon's tendency to couple manual anatomy and female autonomy:

A quarter of an hour before, he had believed that all was over, and that he was released from the dreadful duty of discovering the secret of George's death. Now this girl, this apparently passionless girl, had found a voice, and was urging him on towards his fate.

"If you knew what misery to me may be involved in discovering the truth, Miss Talboys," he said, "you would scarcely ask me to pursue this business any further."

"But I do ask you," she answered, with suppressed passion—"I do ask you. I ask you to avenge my brother's untimely death. Will you do so? Yes or no?"

"What if I answer no?"

"Then I will do it myself!" she exclaimed, looking at him with her bright brown eyes. "I myself will follow up the clue to this mystery; I will find this woman—yes, though you refuse to tell me in what part of England my brother disappeared. *I will travel from one end of the world to the other to find the secret of his fate, if you refuse to find it for me.* I am of age; my own mistress; rich, for I have money left me by one of my aunts; I shall be able to employ those who will help me in my search, and I will make it to their interest to serve me well. Choose between the two alternatives, Mr. Audley. Shall you or I find my brother's murderer?"

He looked her in the face, and saw that her resolution was the fruit of no transient womanly enthusiasm, which would give way under the iron hand of difficulty . . . "Oh, my God," she cried, suddenly clasping her hands and looking up at the cold winter sky, "lead me to the murderer of my brother, *and let mine be the hand to avenge his untimely death!*" (200–201, emphasis added)

Clara's resolution to "let [hers] be the hand to avenge [George's] untimely death" presents Robert with a dilemma hauntingly familiar to the one embodied by Lady Audley. In fact, the independence Clara threatens to exercise in the case of Robert's inaction would be facilitated by the same industrialized components of modern life to which Lady Audley has so effectively availed herself: namely, independent travel, as she says, "from one end of the earth to the other" by way of locomotive and steam.

Braddon also barbs the specific threat of independent action on Clara's part by connecting it to the original agentic vector that sets the narrative in motion even before the novel begins. The entire narrative problem of this novel stems from the fact that the deserted Helen Talboys has already *acted* independently to secure a livelihood for herself and her son because her absent husband did not; George has not written a single letter in three years away from his wife and child (27).[6] Becoming a governess and marrying again were not Helen Talboys's first actions. Mrs. Barkamb, the landlady at Wildernsea, tells Robert that Helen "tried to support herself after her husband's desertion by giving music lessons" (246). The landlady speculates that Helen would have "succeeded pretty well" had it not been for "her father [who] took her money from her, and spent it in public-houses" (246). Thus Robert's preferred inertia (and misogyny) fits into the broader scenario Braddon establishes in *Lady Audley's Secret* that Pamela K. Gilbert has referred to as "alienated patriarchy"—where its women appear far more motivated and capable of action than its men (1997: 94). This pattern applies almost universally to men in the novel: to George's complete lack of communication with his wife, to Helen's father's drunkenness, to Robert's constitutional laziness, and to Luke Marks's dependence on Phoebe for the acquisition of his public house at Mount Stanning.

Under these conditions, the ever-present specter of female autonomy—emphasized by the repeated association of femininity with mechanized modernity and rhetorically figured as "a hand stronger than [Robert's] own"—operates as the novel's principal source of narrative unease. The anxious struggle to uncover the truth of George's disappearance through the excavation of Helen Maldon's/Lady Audley's literal hand (handwriting) becomes reiterated in Robert's constant concern with Clara's metaphorical hand. In the scene where Clara shows her willingness to make good on her threat to find her brother's murderer by traveling alone to Essex, for instance, Robert's anxiety is not only palpable, but also palpably preoccupied with Clara's hands:

> Of all the people in the world she was the last whom Robert either expected or wished to see ... That the sister of his lost friend should be here—here where she could watch his every action, and from those actions deduce the secret workings of his mind, tracing his doubts to their object—made a complication of his difficulties that he could never have anticipated. It brought him back to the consciousness of his own helplessness, in which he exclaimed—
> "*A hand that is stronger than my own is beckoning me onward on the dark road that leads to my lost friend's unknown grave.*" (255, emphasis added)

And only one page later:

> "*What am I in [Clara's] hands?*" he thought. "*What am I in the hands of this woman? ...* How unequal the fight must be between us, and how

can I ever hope to conquer against the strength of her beauty and her wisdom?" (256, emphasis added)

Robert's outward confidence in his assemblage of "circumstantial evidence"—and thus his ability to prove Lady Audley's guilt—is always shot through with inward doubt occasioned by the general competence of women in the text. Contemporary reformers such as Harriet Taylor had ramped up male uneasiness toward the prospect of female capability by pushing the fixity of gender spheres to their logical extremes. In the *Westminster Review* (July 1851) Taylor (anonymously) wondered why, if women were so "naturally" incapable of making a living beyond the domestic sphere, prohibitive laws were needed to limit them at all:

> There is no need to make provision by law that a woman shall not carry on the active details of a household, or of the education of children, and at the same time practise a profession or be elected to parliament. Where the incompatibility is real, it will take care of itself: but there is gross injustice in making the incompatibility a pretense for the exclusion of those in whose case it does not exist. (153–54)

The space for female capability that these formulations open up perhaps explains why Robert's uneasiness reaches its highest narrative pitch at those moments when the evidence against Lady Audley seems strongest. For example, while examining the labels on Lucy Graham's traveling box at Mrs. Vincent's home, Robert thinks to himself: "What a world it is, and how these women take life out of our hands. Helen Maldon, Lady Audley, Clara Talboys, and now Miss Tonks—all womankind from beginning to end" (236). Robert's misgivings about his own capacity to overpower Lady Audley run so deep partly because he continues to associate assertiveness of any "womankind" with mechanized industry. We have already seen how Clara's challenge necessarily links her to the potential use of rail and steam. It is no coincidence, then, that Robert interprets Miss Tonks's industriousness educating women with the rhetoric of modernized industry: "She was no age in particular, and looked as if she had never been younger, and would never grow older," Robert says, "but would remain for ever working backwards and forwards in her narrow groove, like some self-feeding machine for the instruction of young ladies" (233).

Yet Robert's consideration of women's professional actions often send him careening into delusional meditations on what can only be seen as attempts on his part to reassure himself of their essential domesticity—domesticity of the kind we saw embodied in the separate-sphere ideology in novels of the 1840s. Take, for instance, Robert's extended thoughts on the necessarily gendered connection between femininity and tea making just as he begins to suspect Lady Audley's formidable role in George Talboys's disappearance:

> Lucy Audley looked up from her occupation amongst the fragile china cups . . . She looked very petty and innocent, seated behind the graceful group of delicate opal china and glittering silver. Surely a pretty woman never looks prettier than when making tea. The most feminine and most domestic of all occupations imparts a magic harmony to her every movement . . . At the tea-table she reigns omnipotent, unapproachable. What do men know of the mysterious beverage? . . . How hopelessly they hold the kettle, how continually they imperil the frail cups and saucers, or the taper hands of the priestess. To do away with the tea-table is to rob woman of her legitimate empire . . . Better the pretty influence of the teacups and saucers gracefully wielded in a woman's hand than all the inappropriate power snatched at the point of the pen from the unwilling sterner sex. Imagine all the women of England elevated to the high level of masculine intellectuality; superior to crinoline; above pearl powder . . . above taking the pains to be pretty, above making themselves agreeable; above tea-tables. (222)

The first two sentences of the next paragraph consolidate the domestic innocuousness of which Robert tries so earnestly to convince himself: "My lady was by no means strong-minded. The starry diamond upon her white fingers flashed hither and thither amongst the tea-things, and she bent her pretty head over the marvelous Indian tea-caddy . . . with as much earnestness as if life held no higher purpose than the infusion of Bohea" (222–23). Robert's meditations on Lady Audley's small, "tea-capable" hands (and even smaller intellect) appear here almost ridiculously talismanic when we recall his repeated skittishness about the prospect that "a hand stronger than [his] own" caused George's untimely death (169, 174, 200, 255).

This is why Robert's self-doubt manifests itself in his oft-expressed desire for Lady Audley to admit her guilt. If she admitted as much, he could simply cease the work of his investigation: "If I *could* let the matter rest if—if I could leave England forever, and purposely fly from the possibility of ever coming across another clue to the secret, I would do it—I would gladly, thankfully do it" (174, emphasis original). Robert even appears genuinely nonplussed when Lady Audley, whom he calls a "pretty, childlike . . . poor little creature," stands firm and refuses to do what he himself would prefer to do: "Why doesn't she run away while there is still time? I have given her fair warning, I have shown her my cards, and worked openly enough in this business, Heaven knows. Why doesn't she run away . . . Why doesn't she run away?" (250).

As a reactionary and aristocratic male, Robert is constitutionally incapable of understanding why Lady Audley prefers "a duel to the death" to "run[ning] away and repent[ing] [her] wickedness in some foreign place" (272). Lady Audley inverterately refuses to go backward as she meditates out loud on the choice Robert has presented before her: "No, Mr. Robert Audley . . . I will not go back—I will not go back. If the struggle between us is to be a duel to the death, you shall not find me drop my weapon" (312). For the male aristocrat in the 1860s, to "go back" is to turn back the clocks, to withdraw from the "busyness" of the business life and, in Robert's own words, to "shrink from the turmoil of the race-course—the tumult and confusion of the struggle" (279). He already feels that actively pursuing George's disappearance has caused him to lose "all sympathy with the pleasures [smoking] and occupations [reading French novels] of his class" (211). For women such as Lady Audley, though, going back means a return "to the old life, the old, hard, cruel, wretched life—the life of poverty, and humiliation, and vexation, and discontent" (312). In the age of fledgling female autonomy, where claims about female emancipation, a woman's right to education, and to own her own income were becoming more frequent, to go back was to return to the decidedly old and unprogressive definitions of femininity. Lady Audley puts it best when she says that a retreat on her part would mean that she "should have to go back and wear [her]self out in that long struggle, and die—as [her] mother died" (312).

In fact, the novel's entire narrative movement depends on Braddon's portrayal of the different gender and class experiences of Robert and Lady Audley as differences between the old and the new, between idleness and productivity, and between the preindustrial and the modern. Only by learning to follow Lady Audley's technologized movements throughout London and by learning to decipher her use of new modes of telegraphic communication does Robert train himself to live in a fast-moving, middle-class world. On this issue, I would add one point of further specificity to Nicholas Daly's notion that the sensation novel "trained its readers to live within the temporality of the railway age" (2004: 50). The way it accomplished this task was by exhibiting that training process as it unfolded for its major characters. Crucially, it is the threat of a woman's mastery of this new modernizing world that spurs Robert into action, and the "training" he receives by following Lady Audley is so effective that he can hardly recognize himself at the end of the novel:

> Was it I who was one of the boys who sit at ease upon the wooden horses, while other boys run barefoot in the mud, and work their hardest in the hope of a ride when their work is done? Heaven knows I have learned the business of life since then. (394)

It is deeply ironic that it takes an inversion of the traditional separate spheres for Robert to learn the "business" side of life from women. Even Robert's description of his change, though, hints at the process of mechanization that helped bring it on: tracking Lady Audley has required that he trade the ease of his wooden horses for the mechanically synchronized iron horses of networked industrialization.

PLAYING THE HAND THAT'S DEALT

Kate Flint and others have argued that the swiftness of the critical uproar over sensation novels occurred because of their chiefly female readership (1995: 274). If this is true, then Robert's gradual modernization as he attempts to "catch up" with Lady Audley's movements (and her past) provides Braddon's novel with its most riveting sense of narrative tension. Lady Audley counters with a mastery of several new technologies that allow her to outmaneuver Robert on more than one occasion. She beats him to London, for instance, by taking faster trains and expedites (as well as camouflages) her communications with her conspirators by sending telegraphic messages while Robert tries to locate her older, handwritten correspondence. As Robert begins to make progress in his investigation, the underlying question fueling the narrative becomes this: will Robert learn enough about the business side of life and modernize fast enough to expose Lady Audley's machinations?

Assuming the scandalous premise that a newly modernized Robert and a technologically resourceful Lady Audley are evenly matched three-quarters of the way through the novel, the central drama of the text stalls out in some ways as it comes to focus on which combatant can prove madness in the other. The long association of female criminality with insanity eventually plays out in Robert's favor but, for several chapters, the narrative teeters on the brink of uncertainty. A "shiver of horror, something akin to fear, chill[s] [Robert] to the heart" as he evaluates Lady Audley's capabilities: "'She would be capable of any new crime to shield her from the consequences of the old one,' he thought. 'She would be capable of using her influence with my uncle to place me in a mad-house'" (271).

It is very important for the modernizing spirit of *Lady Audley's Secret* that the resolution of this stalemate does not hinge on any particular strength or weakness on Robert's or Lady Auley's part. Instead, the narrator appropriately describes the outcome as a "rigged" contest:

> The game had been played and lost. I do not think that my lady had thrown away a card, or missed the making of a trick which she might by any possibility have made: but her opponent's hand had been too powerful for her, and he had won. (365)

Here it is useful to recall Lyn Pykett's argument that a feminist analysis of sensation fiction must also be "a properly historical analysis" (1992: 50). Applied directly to *Lady Audley's Secret*, the narrator's metaphor of the rigged game is perfectly in keeping with the historical moment in the 1860s when women were beginning to make legal and political headway, but when men still held many of the deck's best cards. The narrator's card-game description of Lady Audley's defeat also deliberately invokes the source of Robert's constant preoccupation with female "hands stronger than [his] own."

The anxiety of "a hand stronger than [Robert's] own" never completely diffuses, even at the conclusion of the novel. By orchestrating such an abrupt and hollow conclusion to a fear that, as I have suggested, sounds a bass line in the novel's narrative score, Braddon's conclusion is not so bleak for women as it may seem. Here I agree with Gilbert, Tromp, and Haynie that Braddon's resistance to normative Victorian standards throughout the novel continues to call into question issues of gendered identity and the domestic order (2000: xvii). In the line of inquiry I have been tracing, there is a palpable sense that the patriarchal hold on the game's best cards will not last very much longer. If "the game of life is something like the game of ecarté," the sense that "the best cards are sometimes left in the pack" suggests that, in a democratized and technologized future, the male consolidation of power will have to depend on something more substantive than mere tradition or the luck of the draw (279). After all, Dr. Mosgrave's diagnosis reveals Lady Audley not to be mad but "dangerous!" (372). This dangerousness, moreover, is underwritten by her capable grip on the levers of technological modernity—what Dr. Mosgrave obliquely identifies as her "employ[ment of] intelligent means" (370). It is no surprise then that Mosgrave's antidote for containing such a dangerous and technologically capable woman is "to send her *back* to her first husband" (370, emphasis added).

This notion of going back, of reversing the forces of technological modernization, leads us straight to the material evidence of Lady Audley's guilt. The production and reproduction of her identities as Helen Maldon, Helen Talboys, and Lucy Graham finally ends because of the evidence contained in the least modernized part of her existence: her handwriting. It is quite fitting that an older and unchanged "hand" lands Lady Audley in the *maison de santé* in Villebrumeuse, which is described as situated in an "old world place," "out of the track of all railway traffic," in an "old ecclesiastical town" (377, 376). But the hint of fear generated by Lady Audley's capabilities is part and parcel of her punishment. Putting Lady Audley in her place is tantamount to putting her in a place where her capability is negated by her isolation; where her grasp of the industrialized present will be out of her reach. Just like in *Bleak House*, the chain of circumstantial evidence that puts her in this place eventually ends in handwriting—that most unique expression of individualized human identity still left in a world transformed by mechanical reproduction.

JEKYLL AND HYDE'S STRANGE HANDWRITING

Robert Louis Stevenson recalled his admiration of Mary Elizabeth Braddon in a Wordsworthian vein before his death in 1894: "I remember reading *Lady Audley's Secret* when I was fifteen, and I wish my days to be bound each to each by Miss Braddon's novels" (Wolff 1979: 9). It turns out that Stevenson's admiration for *Lady Audley's Secret* was more than a passing teenage fancy, however. *Lady Audley's Secret* and *The Strange Case of Dr Jeykll and Mr Hyde* (1886) share important thematic and formal features. Both texts explore the nature of multiple identities and employ lawyers as lead investigators in the detection of their crimes. Ian Duncan has argued recently for the distinctiveness of Stevenson's fiction despite its broad similarities with the sensational and escapist entertainment that followed the chasm in the high Victorian novel left by the deaths of George Eliot and Anthony Trollope. "We should understand Stevenson's works of fiction," Duncan says, "in terms of a series of choices and experiments which involved a critical refusal of the Victorian novel and its protocols, rather than a failure to master them" (2010: 15). I agree with Duncan, but I want to make the point that, even in Stevenson's radical "virtuoso formal refinement" of the sensational novella, the hand (and especially handwriting) maintained its place as a marker of individual identity and narratological tension. Duncan's point about Stevenson's difference from other Victorian novelists reinforces to the point I aim to make in this section: Stevenson is stylistically very different from the Victorian novelists who preceded him and yet the narrative armature of his most famous work still depends on the manual themes and topics that dominated nineteenth-century discourse. And it did so in spite of the various deforming pressures of a late nineteenth-century modernity that splintered human subjectivity into new and fluid social, economic, and psychological categories.

Nearly thirty-five years separate *Bleak House*, *Lady Audley's Secret*, and *Jekyll and Hyde* but they all rely solely on the physical characteristics of handwriting to propel their very different narrative structures. In a democratizing and urbanizing culture where the search for definitive indicators of identity had become more anxiously contested, the analysis of handwriting offered stability; it allowed the hand to continue to be associated with human uniqueness despite the blows delivered to that sense of uniqueness throughout the century by urbanization, mechanization, and shifting evolutionary paradigms.

Jekyll and Hyde's narrative dependence on handwriting seems fairly straightforward at first. It begins after Hyde runs down a young girl in the street and emerges "with another man's cheque" to pay off the threat of blackmail (8). Enfield reports of the handwriting that "the figure was stiff; but the signature was good for more than that, if it was only genuine" (2002 [1886]: 8). The fact that the bank accepts the note as genuine sets in motion the central mystery of the text: why a respectable and upstanding doctor chooses to associate himself with such a miserable degenerate as Hyde. This unseemly association becomes even more troubling for Utterson because of his knowledge of Jekyll's will, which stipulates that "all [Jekyll's] possessions were to pass into the hands of his 'friend and benefactor Edward Hyde'" upon the doctor's death or disappearance (11). The order in which Stevenson orchestrates Utterson's response to this mysterious situation is especially germane to the shifting emphasis on bodily features that I have been tracking throughout *Changing Hands*. Utterson at first believes that a personal inspection of Hyde's face will yield a rational explanation—even though others have looked on that face and been unable to describe him accurately. The narrator tells us that "there sprang up and grew apace in the lawyer's mind a singularly strong, almost inordinate, curiosity to behold the features of the real Mr Hyde":

> If he could but once set eyes on him, he thought the mystery would lighten and perhaps roll altogether away, as was the habit of mysterious things when examined . . . And it would be a face worth seeing: the face of a man without the bowels of mercy: a face which had but to show itself to raise up . . . a spirit of enduring hatred. (13–14)

The emphasis here on the information Utterson believes will be legible in the face only heightens the sense of elusiveness in Hyde's character when he finally does have the opportunity to look upon it. Like Enfield and others, Utterson is at a loss to describe "any nameable malformation" in a face that unequivocally induces "unknown disgust, loathing and fear" in anyone who perceives it (16).

Stevenson's treatment of the body is so compelling in *Jekyll and Hyde* because he does not immediately shift the narrative suspense from the face to the hands upon describing the illegibility of Hyde's facial features. Instead, he conflates the two in a brilliant narrative sequence (reminiscent of Scott, Eliot, and Braddon) where Enfield and Utterson actually see *hands* in Hyde's face. Discussing his baffling inability to describe Hyde despite having a distinct memory of his deformed face, Enfield resorts to the rhetorical use of an oddly manual expression: "He's an extraordinary man, and yet I really can name nothing out of the way." "No, sir," Enfield says, "I can make no *hand* of it; I can't describe him" (10, emphasis added).[7] Not only does Enfield's inability to make a "hand" of Jekyll's face prefigure the body part upon which this story will turn, but it also confirms the surprisingly inverted circuit of identification that I have been tracking in Victorian detective fiction more generally.[8] Utterson, for his part, has a similar but even more intriguing response to the illegibility of Hyde's countenance. After exhausting his attempts to identify a "namable malformation" on Hyde's head, Utterson states that he can surely "read Satan's signature upon [his] face" (16). The evil he sees "signed" on Hyde's face, of course, points quite literally to Hyde's handwriting—a hand that Utterson becomes convinced contains "a murderer's autograph" (29).

The narrative tension also depends on the central conceit that Jekyll and Hyde have nearly identical handwriting. This tension increases midway through the text when Jekyll presents Utterson with a letter from Hyde that claims to sever his connections to the doctor (27). Utterson's clerk, "being a great student and critic of handwriting," compares Jekyll's handwriting side-by-side with Hyde's and determines that "the two hands are in many points identical: only differently sloped" (29). The similarities between the two handwriting samples thus give readers the first clue that Jekyll and Hyde may in fact be the same person. As we have seen in a variety of contexts throughout this study, Victorian readers thought they were quite well informed about the relationship between handwriting, individuality, and character. Just two years before the publication of *Jekyll and Hyde*, Henry Firth published *A Guide to the Study of Graphology* (1884), which previewed several topics relevant to Stevenson's treatment of handwriting. Specifically, Firth sought to claim new levels of accuracy and scientific objectivity for graphology by "propos[ing] to dispense with all assistance, other than handwriting" (8). "We . . . desire no assistance," Firth wrote, "from photographs or description of hair and eyebrows, eyes, nose and complexion" (8). These are the very aspects of Hyde's appearance which no one can accurately describe. A "haunting sense of unexpressed deformity" is the closest any character comes to describing Hyde's face, partly because "he had never been photographed" (24–25). Moreover, Firth asserts that a backward sloping hand "shows a weak and easily influenced person" (69):

> Selfishness is generally to be recognized in an upright, *angular* hand, combined with a "throw back" of the capital letters, such as C or M. These letters and their terminating loops will turn to the left, backwards. (70, emphasis original)

We know from "Henry Jekyll's Full Statement of the Case" that the doctor employs exactly this technique when writing as Edward Hyde: "by sloping my own hand backward, I had supplied my double with a signature" (61).

Given these specific parallels to contemporary graphological discourse, it is odd that Frederick H. W. Meyers took exception to Stevenson's treatment of the subject. Meyers wrote in a personal letter to Stevenson that "Handwriting in cases of double personality (spontaneous ... or induced, as in hypnotic cases) *is not* and *cannot* be the same in the two personalities" (Stevenson 1981: 214, emphasis original). Here, it is crucial to point out that Meyers's graphological reading is correct, but his literary interpretation is not. If there were no point of connection between Jekyll and Hyde, their written hands—by the late nineteenth-century tenets of graphology that Meyers invokes—would have to be fundamentally different. However, Jekyll specifically acknowledges that his "two natures had memory in common" (63), and this memory leads directly to the handwriting vector of the plot. While in the body of Hyde, he can still write in the hand of Jekyll; Jekyll (in the body of Hyde) says, "I remembered that of my original character, one part remained to me: I could write my own hand" (66).

The fact that Hyde can write in the "character" of Jekyll only confirms the two-way traffic between the two personas' handwritings: "Hence," Jekyll complains, "the ape-like tricks that [Hyde] would play me, scrawling in my own hand blasphemies on the pages of my books" (69). Judith Halberstam succinctly summarizes the confusion built into the novel via its handwriting:

> Here autographs and signatures become the inscriptions of a dual identity and one is assumed to be a forgery of the other. But of course, both identities and neither of them are forged; each one depends upon the hidden presence of the other and each must perform and inscribe the doubleness and instability of the identity they share. Moving back and forth between these two tales, one of Dr. Jekyll and one of Mr. Hyde, the text alternates between the two differently sloped handwritings as one tale constantly disguises or writes over the other. (1995: 60)

There is a biographical explanation for this phenomenon. It turns out that Robert Louis Stevenson had several different types of handwriting. According to Edwin J. Beinecke (the benefactor of Yale University's collection), "Stevenson's writing, while always retaining certain fundamental characteristics, varied more than any other author's." It contained a "forward-flowing type" as well as "backward ... and vertical styles." Beinecke points out that, "to the confusion of some, the same [Stevenson] manuscript has been found to contain more than one distinct type of writing" (1940: n.p.). We witness

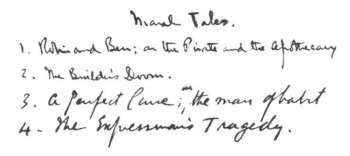

Fig. 46. "Moral Tales" Outline. *Robert Louis Stevenson's Handwriting,* Edwin Beinecke (24).

this discrepancy in Stevenson's outline for a series of poems called "Moral Tales" (fig. 46).

The title of this writing sample, "Moral Tales," as well as the first two numbered entries, "Robin and Ben: On the Pirate and the Apothecary" and "The Builder's Doom," appear in Stevenson's upright, backward-leaning penmanship. Entries three and four, "A Perfect Cure" and "The Expressman's Tragedy," appear in Stevenson's forward-sloping hand. It is important for my argument that despite the different sloping angles of Stevenson's handwriting (and by extension, Jekyll's and Hyde's), the penmanship always maintains what Beinecke calls "certain fundamental characteristics."

The kind of narrative of discovery that works backward from an "end point"—which, in this case is the fundamental characteristics shared by both Jekyll's and Hyde's handwriting—is not at all a new idea in narratology. A number of prominent theorists have posited that, in essence, this is the logic of all narrative—realist, detective, sensation, or otherwise. Narrative derives its coherence from the knowledge that "an end lies in wait, to complete and elucidate whatever is put in motion at the start" (Brooks 2011: 125).[9] My point is that for detective fiction composed during the second half of the nineteenth century, the end that is so often lying in wait is the uniqueness of a (previously mistaken) character's penmanship.

What we encounter, therefore, in the mirrored penmanship of Jekyll and Hyde is the same principle we saw in *Bleak House* and in *Lady Audley's Secret*: that the deepest seat of individuality resides in one's handwriting. Years of legal training cannot totally alter the hand of Nemo from the hand of Hawdon just as gaping social chasms do not change the hand of Helen Maldon from the hand of Lucy Audley. That Edward Hyde's handwriting "mirrors" Henry Jekyll's might be the most impressive of all these scenarios, however, since Stevenson explicitly draws our attention to the stark differences in their hands' materiality: "Now the hand of Henry Jekyll … was professional in shape and size: it was large, firm, white and comely. But the hand [of Hyde] which I now saw, clearly enough … lying half shut on the bed clothes, was lean, corded, knuckly, of a dusky pallor and thickly shaded with a smart growth of hair" (61). Here we see the evolutionary point from *Great Expectations* reprised in a different, handwritten context thirty-five years later. Just as the gap between gorilla "hands" and human appendages in *Great Expectations* is linked by the Darwinian theme of interconnected animality, so too are the differences between Hyde's and Jekyll's hands collapsed into the shared category of sloped penmanship.

Thus, Mr. Guest's conclusion that "the two hand[writings] are in many points identical" speaks very strongly to a desire for human hands to remain unique despite the deforming modern pressures of industry and evolution. We might even measure the depth of this Victorian desire in the twentieth century's rapid and almost unshakable belief in the individuality of the fingerprint (even though DNA evidence is exponentially more accurate). As Ronald Thomas has commented, "the fingerprint showed the human body to be a mechanism always already writing itself into absolute uniqueness" (2003: 203). If this is true, then, as I have been arguing throughout Part IV, before the discovery of the science of fingerprinting (dactyloscopy) at the turn of the twentieth century, one's handwriting *was* the body's fingerprint.[10]

Conclusion

The Victorians, the Twentieth Century, and Our Digital Present

I have aimed to show how, despite unprecedented changes in industry and evolutionary theory, hands continued to matter in a myriad of new ways for people living through the nineteenth century in England. It is beyond the scope of this book to analyze all of the ways that hands continue to matter (in still yet changed ways) through the twentieth and twenty-first centuries. What I would like to do as I conclude, though, is to consider a few of the ways that changes in the nineteenth century continue to affect us and our relationship to our hands. The hope is that my historically contingent study of Victorian hands has shown the body to be an entity always in flux, where contests between competing factions had outcomes that were far from inevitable or obvious. And I want to stress that, with the staggering pace of technological invention and anatomical engineering, the hand's meaning in relation to the body will continue to change. The flesh-and-blood hand may eventually live out all its half-lives. That time, though, has not yet come. A sampling of contemporary issues ranging from philosophy to phones will help demonstrate this final point.

Looking briefly at developments in philosophical thinking reveals how much twentieth-century phenomenology is indebted to Victorian hand debates. One of the founding documents of this discipline, Edmund Husserl's *Ideas Pertaining to a Pure Phenomenology* (1928), returns again and again to the hand as the primary indicator of the body's simultaneous objective and subjective "Being in the world." Husserl prefigures the phenomenology of sensation (physical feeling) in Heidegger, Merleau-Ponty, and Derrida by exploring the uniqueness of the hand's ability to act both as a touching and feeling organ. Husserl says that, "in the case of one hand touching the other . . . we have then two sensations, and each is apprehendable or experienceable in a double way" (1989 [1928]: 154). Only the hands allow for this "double apprehension" where "the same touch-sensation is apprehended as a feature of the 'external' Object and is apprehended as a sensation of the Body as Object" (155). Husserl dubs the hand the "real organ of touch" because the other senses offer no such subject-object "analogon" (155–56). As a result, Husserl returns to the hand in nearly every part of his discussion about the phenomenology of the body: "The 'far' is far from me, my Body; the 'to the right' refers back to the right side of my Body, e.g., to my right hand" (166); "I experience the mechanical movement of the Body as the movement of a material thing like any other thing in the case of spontaneity, and I find it characterized at the same time as a spontaneous movement in the sense, 'I move my hand,' etc." (167); "the physical [heating] process, 'red illumination of my hand,' is not followed by the sensation of red in the same way that the sensation of warmth follows the heating of my hand, and the physical process to which the sensation of the color is linked—red light rays striking my eyes—is not given to me at all" (168).

Perhaps the hand-privileging that Husserl's student, Martin Heidegger (1889–1976) exhibits is even more compelling because of the latter's direct confrontation with Darwinian evolutionary issues. Heidegger boldly states in *What Is Called Thinking?* that "apes, too, have organs that can grasp, but they do not have hands" (1968: 16). For Heidegger, the hand is an essential aspect of the human being in the world; the body part crucial to human beings' understanding of historicity and meaning. The being of the Heideggerian hand is not determined by its bodily operation of prehension. Rather, the hand is the essence of humanity because it "reaches and extends, receives and welcomes—and not just things: the hand extends itself, and receives its own welcome in the hands of others. The hand holds. The hand carries. The hand designs and signs" (16). The context of Heidegger's ideas about the exceptionalism of human hands is grounded in thought. The deep etymological connection in German between manual grasping (*greifen*) and intellectual comprehension (*begriefen*) is thus not lost on Heidegger. As Jacques Derrida points out in his work on "Heidegger's Hand" (*Geschlect II*), "thinking is not cerebral or disincarnate" for Heidegger; "[thinking, *das Denken*] is a craft, a 'handicraft,' a work of the hand in two words" (2007: 38).

Derrida's writing on Heidegger and Jean-Luc Nancy does not so much justify as it does explain how the hand arrived at what he calls its place of "phenomenological nobility" (2005a: 164). Tracing the ideas of thinkers from Maine de Biran to Merleau-Ponty, Derrida discusses this "nobility" of the hand in a typical phrase of ingeniously appropriate word play. The hand, according to Derrida, has enjoyed this special status in phenomenological thought precisely because it is "at the joint of two faculties; touching and feeling" (149). In terms of touch, it "occupies an *ideal* region of effort poised between passivity and activity" (155, emphasis original). Here Derrida extends Husserl's sense of the "double-apprehension" to what he calls the "touching-touched" (159).

Rather than rehash all the ways that Derrida's thinking aligns with phenomenological thinkers, I want to focus for a moment on a telling instance where he differs—where, in effect, we see his far stronger allegiances to the deconstructive program. For instance, Derrida outlines the primacy of the "sub-objectivity" in Husserl's hand only to question it:

> And is it also true that this cannot be said of every external part of the body. But why only the hand and the finger? Why not my foot and toes? Can they not touch another part of my body and touch one another? What about the lips, especially? All of the lips on the lips? And the tongue on the lips? And the tongue on the palate and many other parts of 'my body'? How could one *speak* without this? . . . And the eyelids in the blink of an eye? And, if we take sexual differences into account, the sides of the anal or genital opening? (164).

Derrida's litany of questions regarding the possible importance of other body parts deserves a response. *Changing Hands*, I hope, has been responding to these questions from the start. Derrida's questions are valid and each has their own connection to his important work on speaking, writing, and sexuality (to name only a few related topics). The point his deconstructive questioning fails to account for, however, is the historically contingent story of how the hand's importance came to be so altered in the nineteenth century. None of the body parts mentioned by Derrida underwent a radical destabilization, physically or ontologically, except the hand.

Certain parts of the hand's destabilization follow us into our twenty-first-century present. In fact, there are many parallels between the nineteenth century's production of new ways for the hand to be important and what we see occurring now in cultural contexts construed more broadly. A strong case could be made that recent advances in technology, including but not limited to the palpable sense that machines could take over human jobs in both the general population and in the academy, have inspired twenty-first-century responses pertaining to the hand's uniqueness. But these responses are not altogether different from the ones that emerged in the nineteenth century when this "problem" first arose (chapters 1–3). For instance, contemporary media outlets ranging from *60 Minutes* to the *New York Times* have reported (and, of course helped to produce) a renewed tension in our culture about the blurring line between machines and human beings.[1] Academe has not been immune from this, either. *The Chronicle Review* recently published a lead article on "The New Industrial Revolution" exploring how "a coming wave of robots" could redefine not only jobs but also people themselves. This special issue included pieces on whether robots can commit crimes, on the machine's inability to perform "critical thinking," and on how MOOCs could mean the obsolescence of the professoriate. Though each of these articles are important in their own right, I am interested in the iconography *The Chronicle* selects to represent this contemporary machine-human moment (fig. 47).

The Chronicle's cover shows a laboratory worker reaching up to touch the chain-linked "hand" of an enormous robot. The robot's appendage appears clunky and, for that reason, perhaps makes less threatening the machine work the special issue attempts to assess. This is misleading, however. On the page (B2) opposite this cover image, the very first article is one by Joseph Harris somewhat defensively titled "Teaching 'by Hand' in a Digital Age." In it, Harris argues for the continued need—now more than ever in the age of MOOCS and on-line instruction—for an instructor's individual and uncybernetically mediated attention to the writing process. He likens such an approach to " 'teach[ing] by hand,'" where a professor's "pencil [remains] poised" to mark up a student's work (B2). As Harris himself acknowledges, there are digitized "feedback systems" that offer similar services to the student taking an on-line course (not to mention the fact that many of us use similar software programs even when we electronically comment on and grade papers in traditional "face-to-face" courses). What is so interesting about Harris's article is how clearly it resonates—even in 2013—with powerful nineteenth-century articulations of the relationship between individuality and handedness. Indeed, in the final paragraph of his article Harris says that he takes the phrase "'teach[ing] by hand' . . . to mean that we teach not subjects or courses but *individuals*" (B2, emphasis mine). Just as in the

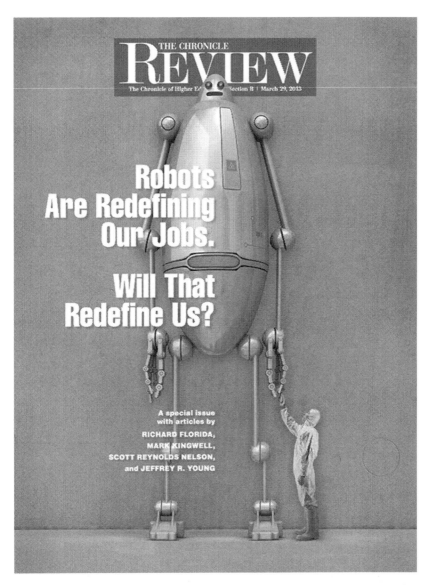

Fig. 47. Cover Page of *The Chronicle Review*, March 29, 2013. Used by permission from Science Source and *The Chronicle of Higher Education*.

Victorian debates about industrialization and evolution, the hand is once again at the center of issues concerning twenty-first-century individuality (and digitality). The difference now, though, is that the hand is becoming metonymically invoked to stand in for the whole person with a *positive* flourish: surely Harris and others in favor of traditional "face-to-face" instruction have the whole instructor in mind—not simply the instructor's grading or commenting hand.

Of course *The Chronicle*'s coverage of this topic is hardly meant to suggest that there are tiny digital hands within word processing software programs performing the work of the instructor's pencil. A recent installment of the *Smithsonian* reveals a more accurate state of current robotic development vis-à-vis the hand, though (fig. 48). Aside from its unmistakable compositional similarity to the Sistine Chapel, the image gives a sense of

Fig. 48. *Smithsonian* Cover Image. September 2013, Reprinted by permission of Kiernan Dodds.

how far the field of robotics has come in developing a mechanical hand that possesses the dexterity and functional capabilities of a human hand.[2]

The specter of this particular occurrence, combined with the general cultural interest in robotic supersession even in traditionally "nonmanual" job sectors, has generated a renewed interest in the hand's (still) unique connection to our being in the world. I have suggested that there are parallels in this scenario to what occurred in the nineteenth century. However, I want to be clear that these are parallels far more related in kind than degree. *Changing Hands* has argued that the Victorians were the first people to be jarred into developing new ways for the hand to be important in the face of enormous change. There is a host of contemporary cultural evidence suggesting that we have extended this nineteenth-century impulse to find new ways to emphasize the importance of the manual in an increasingly industrialized digital world. The exponential growth of farmer's markets, farm-to-table movements, and the elevation of artisanal craftwork of all kinds in the last fifteen years reveal as much.

But there is an important difference in our contemporary culture that is something like the historical flip side of our tendency to overlook literal hands in the nineteenth-century novel. Elaine Freedgood has succinctly identified the attraction of artisan markets to early-twenty-first-century consumers: "the special consolation ... [in the occasional] purchase of a 'hand-made' good affords a much-needed relief from the alienation, reification, and fetishism from which we both suffer and benefit because of our inescapable participation in commodity exchange" (2003: 644). Consider how opposite this experience is from Pip's in *Great Expectations* when he becomes horrified at seeing the hands (Magwitch's) that produced his wealth. The meanings we now attach to hands could hardly be more different; where we have been incapable of seeing the materiality of nineteenth-century hands, we now actively search out such embodied connections. Our almost purely metaphorical experience with commodities makes it a "special consolation" to see (and even shake) the hands of those whose livelihoods afford them a more literal relationship with their hands. Farmer's markets provide a carnival atmosphere for these kinds of consolations. The consolation of "handmade" has struck a chord so deep that people are attracted to it even in the digital marketplace. The expansion of Etsy—an electronic commerce web site dedicated to selling handcrafted items—has become popular so rapidly that it recently became embroiled in a quandary of whether to sell goods that have been made in part by machinery. We may measure our culture's continued (or renewed) interest in the hand made by the scope of the Etsy controversy: Etsy's decision, made in October 2013, to include the sale of "unique" factory-made products on its site has been the source of considerable uproar.[3]

This paradoxical commercialization of the handmade has also caught on in one of the most rapidly changing technological sectors: mobile phones. Advertisers for these most ubiquitous handheld devices are seeking new ways to render their products' technological advancements in terms of manual affiliation. No doubt tech companies have anatomic incentives for such "manual" marketing: touch screens, finger scrolling, etc. Their most prominent advertisements, however, reveal concerted efforts to associate the technologically digital with the anatomically digital. Take, for example, a recent advertisement for Apple's iPhone 5. The late 2013 ad touts the trademarked "Touch ID," where the user's "finger is the password." This technology makes accessing the phone easier than punching in a numerical password but it also emphasizes the uniqueness of the hand in terms of its fingerprint. The consolation for having a device that looks like every other device is that this one somehow knows your hand is different from all the other hands that may touch it. As if sensing the emotionally (and economically) powerful pull of a deeply human basis for this new technology, LG released a new series of ads similarly focusing on the uniqueness of the human index finger. Perhaps LG executives believed that the only thing that could rival the fingerprint for uniqueness in the handheld device market was the whole finger upon which the print is only its outermost extremity (fig. 49).

LG has the index finger pointing to the central controlling position on its phone, but the phone's semitransparency in the ad ensures that the finger also points (through the phone) at the holder of the device. Whether LG is aware of it or not, they have struck upon one of Heidegger's further distinctions between man and ape via the hand. Heidegger claimed that animals, unlike humans, never use their prehensile organs to point. The issue hinges in part on the idea that self-pointing registers a being in the world ("ego sum") that Heidegger believes animals do not possess.[4]

The only problem with this is that LG's ad is clearly not concerned with animality. Instead, it focuses on erasing (and perhaps easing) the potential buyer's perception of the human-technology divide through the machine's cognition of human individuality. It is the phone which says to the purchaser, "To me, you are perfect"—a phrase which, when combined with the image, locates this perfection in the hand and index finger. Although it is clear that

Fig. 49. Advertisement for LG G$_2$ Phone. *New Yorker*, December 16, 2013. Used by permission from LG Electronics.

the "you" of the advertisement is the consumer, it is far from certain who the "me" is meant to be. One not-so-concealed possibility is that LG wants to invoke a God-like figure. Emerging as it does from complete blackness, and unconnected to a body, the hand that suddenly sheds light on the phone appears more than faintly divine. Now that we have seen how deeply notions of "perfection" were connected to nineteenth-century mechanical and evolutionary debates, we are perhaps more likely to notice the enormity of the shift from divine craftsmanship to a mobile telephone.

Finally, the "Goblin Market"-like closing caption, "Come see how we are learning from you," simultaneously entices the consumer to buy "smarter" technology even as it reassures the buyer that such advanced digital technology has its origins in the human hand.[5] The televised version of LG's ad only reinforces these messages, but with an added twist. Despite all the ways fingers are used to operate technological devices, LG's television ad banks on its viewers taking their hands for granted. As the ad announces the new phone's "easy control" feature, it reminds its audience that "you use your index finger for almost everything." The ad then cuts to a long series of "everyday" activities meant to highlight its message: a baby pointing from its crib, fingers on a laptop keyboard, on a light switch, tapping on a steering wheel of a car, writing in the sand, a woman playing with her hair on a subway car, a basketball spinning on an index finger, adults pointing while hiking, an index finger reading Braille (itself a nineteenth-century invention), etc.—in short, a partial list of literal uses that LG is betting its consumers already overlook without a second thought. So the ad invokes the hand as something both more simple and more original.

Advertisements such as Apple's and LG's, though removed from Victorian debates about industrialization and evolution by more than one hundred years, nonetheless tap into a similar cultural impulse to develop new ways for the hand to stay relevant. It appears that this impulse may be more of a yearning for hands to continue to matter—albeit in very changed ways. Think, for instance, of Peter Brooks's recent conclusion in *Enigmas of Identity* that "our criminal justice system, and our culture at large, are not ready yet to do without fingerprints" (2011: 12). Brooks reassesses the nature of our dependence on a technique of identification whose claim to scientific status is more a matter of cultural myth than tested fact. "Although the reliability of fingerprint evidence has yet to be given a thorough, probative test," Brooks writes, "both professional techne and the popular imagination clearly believe that fingerprints are revelatory of identity" (13). Science still looks to the hands for determinative information more than any other body part. First-rate laboratories currently conduct longitudinal research on sex differences by comparing finger length ratios in infants, adolescents, and adults.[6] The newest computers go considerably further than the iPhone's fingerprint recognition. Many companies are now experimenting with biometric devices that identify vein patterns in the palm of the hand for security purposes.[7]

As we have seen, advertisements for new technological devices attempt to connect the anatomical uniqueness of the hand to our emotional purchase on the cultural constructions of that individuality. The Apple and LG ads provide a window into the place of hands in the popular imagination, but there are additional windows—perhaps all the more transparent because of their dissociation from their strictly commercial enterprise. Consider recent bulletins for the Leukemia & Lymphoma Society (fig. 50) and Nebraskans Against the Death Penalty (fig. 51).

Fig. 50. Cancer Ends with Me. Used by permission from the Leukemia & Lymphoma Society.

Fig. 51. NADP Flyer. Used by permission from NADP and Karissa Vieth.

These bulletins provide another example of the historical inversion of the literal/figurative representations of hands. The system of representation, here, is so familiar to our cultural lexicon that we are unlikely to notice the metonymical ways in which hands become iconographic for organizations whose missions are dedicated to saving *entire* human bodies—not just their hands. It is in many ways a reversal of the nineteenth-century scenario we encountered in *Hard Times* where "Hand" represented not the entire human being, but only that part of it which was required to facilitate industrial processes.

This kind of reversed (or positive) metonymy has also played a significant role in recent attempts to politicize meanings related to the body. In one instance of such a case, the German Chancellor Angela Merkel's nearly automatic hand placement has become iconographic for a stability-starved European Union (fig. 52). We have already seen how the twentieth century killed off many of the literal meanings embedded in hand-based language. Just like in commercial advertising for the technological, though, the hand has seen a resurgence in the contemporary politicization of the body. The

Fig. 52. Angela Merkel Photomontage.

so-called "Merkel rhombus," for instance, became a rare instance of a *living* metaphor (the steady hand) during the run-up to her September 2013 re-election campaign in Germany. The "safe pair of hands," as *The Economist* magazine dubbed them, was meant to convey a spectacular political message in the heart of Berlin—on an enormous billboard between Germany's train station and parliament buildings (fig. 53). Super-sized and without commentary or contextualization of any kind, the manual image assures the German public that it is "in good hands" with Merkel at the helm.

I have endeavored nonetheless to show how the seemingly universal tendency to emphasize hands has itself changed over time. Representations of hands appear in different forms in different periods precisely

Fig. 53. Christian Democratic Union (CDU) Billboard. Berlin, Germany. Image used by permission from Shutterstock.

because the meanings attached to the hand are as ideological as they are anatomical. Placed side by side, for example, the hands in the leukemia and anti-death-penalty flyers above have very different meanings from the hand plates we encountered in Richard Beamish's 1843 *Psychonomy of the Hand* (chapter 5). I draw attention to these varied meanings to emphasize that my identification of the hand's primacy since the early nineteenth century does not mean that this will always be the case. Its primacy is contingent upon many factors, some predictable and others not. Touch-sensitive devices are certainly moving in the direction of voice command and identificatory paradigms may eventually rely solely on DNA or retina scans. Car makers are succeeding in automatizing some elements of the driving experience (rear-mounted cameras, sleep sensors) and Google is in the process of developing a vehicle capable of driving without human intervention of any kind. The day may come when hands are quite literally absent from all but a few essential activities and, if so, even newer and different meanings will then accrue around them. But that day has not yet come. New technological advancements are allowing hand amputees to use pattern-recognition software to move their prostheses more intuitively, but the industry (both private and military) is far from artificially replicating the touch impulses of the hand. As a recent article in the *New York Times* reported, the first robotic hand was designed at the Stanford Artificial Intelligence Laboratory in the 1960s. Since then, robotic append-ages have been designed to perform repetitive factory work, but they still cannot open a door or pull a coin out of a pocket (see Markoff 2014). Eti-enne Roesch, a senior researcher at the University of Reading's Centre for Integrative Neuroscience and Neurodynamics, has written recently on this subject: "What we've come to realize ... is that we are nowhere near pro-ducing a robot with humanlike motor abilities. Robotic hands are probably the best example of this failure: We build even more sophisticated robotic devices, but we cannot figure out how to use them in the type of seamless interactions with our world that they are meant to enact" (2013: 412). This is hardly for want of money or resources. The Pentagon has worked for decades on a prototype called the DEKA hand but it still cannot perform all of the functions of a human hand (see Dao, "Learning to Accept, and Master, a $110,000 Mechanical Arm" [2012]).

DIGITALITY

If the hand shows up frequently in contemporary popular culture, it, and the body more generally, have apparently all but disappeared in the cybernetic age of technological virtuality.[8] This is an issue unique to the digital domain. While philosophers such as Iris Marion Young ("Throwing Like a Girl," 2004 [1990]) have extended phenomenological analysis of embodied being-in-the-world into the late twentieth century, the cybernetic construction of the human has followed attempts to understand being human as a set of informational processes more aligned with Deleuze and Guattari's "body without organs." My brief discussion of what this perceived disembodiment means for work in the digital humanities has been heavily influenced by the work of N. Katherine Hayles—particularly by her account of how much of the body needed to be erased in order to arrive at a seemingly bodiless sense of cybernetic information flow.

It is useful to consider how far the discussions in *Changing Hands* have ranged by comparing the nightmares of Shelley and Hayles, two women living in very different technological eras. This study began with Shel-ley's nightmare of Victor Frankenstein's construction of a living subject that could not have been more embodied. I now conclude with Hayles's nightmare of a very different scenario. Her disquieting vision speaks for itself: "my nightmare is a culture inhabited by posthumans who regard their bodies as fashion accessories rather than the ground of being" (1999: 5). The brilliance of Hayles's work lies in its delivery on the provocative title's promise; she does not simply accept the disappearance of the body as a condition of technological determinism. Instead, she traces contingent events throughout the twentieth century to discover how we arrived at a time when informational patterns appeared to trump the material instantiation of the body.[9]

Hayles's choice of rhetoric is one of the interesting ways her work connects to the themes of my book. Specifically, she uses a manual metaphor to describe the "ancient game" of philosophy's tendency to privilege the abstract as the "Real" and downplay the importance of material instantiation. Hayles identifies two moves in particular that had important roles in constructing the information/materiality hierarchy. "Irreverently," Hayles says, she thinks of these two moves as "the Platonic backhand and forehand" (12). The "backhand," which is an old move dating back to the Greeks, works by inferring a simplified abstraction from the world's noisy multiplicity. Hayles sees the Platonic "forehand" as more recent because it requires the assistance of computers to move from simplified abstractions to specific algorithms in the creation of a nonbiological virtual world of ones and zeros. Irreverent though it may be, her formulation of this idea in terms of backhands and forehands certainly fits Hayles's sense of historical gamesmanship in the field of philosophical inquiry, but it is also a nod to the line of twentieth-century phenomenologists for whom the physicality of the hand was an integral part of the lived experience.

I would like to close by thinking about the recalcitrance of physical hands since they entered the literary and cultural imagination in what I have characterized as new ways since the nineteenth century. Their meanings, as well as their physical and ontological relations, have changed as much for the Victorians as they have for twenty-first-century academics. But they have not gone away. Katherine Hayles reminds us of this in *Writing Machines* (2002):

> If simulation is becoming increasingly pervasive and important, however, MATERIALITY is as vibrant as ever, for the computational engines and artificial intelligences that produce simulations require sophisticated bases in the real world. The engineers who design these machines,

Fig. 54. Posthumanites Series logo; Cary Wolfe, series editor. University of Minnesota Press. Used by permission of University of Minnesota Press.

the factory workers who build them, the software designers who write the programs for them, and the technicians who install and maintain them have no illusions that reality has faded away. (6)

To *main*tain anything—be it a digital archive, a software platform, a tool for computer-assisted data analysis, or a car—is still, to a very real extent, to do so with hands.[10] I am guided in this formulation by Derrida's dictum that "one cannot talk about the hand without talking about technology" (2007: 36). For Derrida, via Heidegger, there is no such thing as a handless technology. Even the emerging twenty-first-century academic field of the "posthuman" remains tied—at least representationally—to handedness. The field's leading research outlet, the University of Minnesota Press, uses a pixelated hand as the logo for its highly regarded "Posthumanities" book series (fig. 54).

Recent events in cutting-edge technological digitization eerily substantiate the representational and literal staying power of hands in the digital age.

Fig. 55. "Two Hands." *Hands on Literature* Tumblr. Used by permission from Brad Pasanek.

Hands refuse to go away, as it were, even in the most unprecedented electronic initiative ever undertaken: the Google Books scanning project. The only parts of the human body to appear in the millions of books scanned in the project are the fingers and hands of its scan operators, which sometimes accidentally appear in a tiny percentage of the scans (figs. 55 and 56).

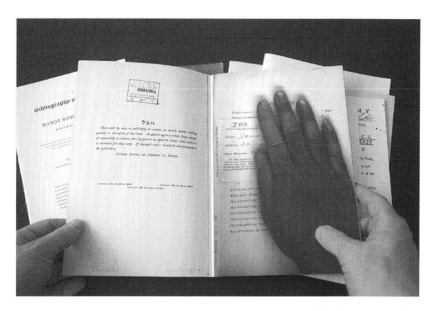

Fig. 56. "GOOGLE HANDS." 2009. Used by permission from Benjamin Shaykin.

The meaning of the idiomatic expression of "having something at one's fingertips" has come inadvertently but nonetheless aptly full circle in the "digital" information age. Hence the figurative and literal instantiations of having something "at hand" in a digital research environment merge with uncanny force. They remind us that our seemingly disembodied ability to scroll through a digitized text by tapping electronic buttons still relies on the human hands that first performed the function. It would be difficult to imagine a more fitting example of changing hands.

Notes

Introduction

1. 40,000-year-old hand paintings grace the walls of caves on almost every continent. The Greek philosopher Anaxagoras (510–428 BC) professed that human intelligence was rooted in the dexterity of the hands. About one hundred years later, Aristotle (384–322 BC) famously praised the hand as the "tool of tools" (1986: 209). The Hebrew Bible figures the hand as characteristic of man's singular relationship with God. Scholars of the medieval and early modern periods have shown how anatomists (such as Galen) and painters (such as Rembrandt) became enthralled by what they discovered when they witnessed the dissected hand. (For a detailed analysis of this topic, see Goldberg or Rowe). John Bulwer (1606–56) was so obsessed with hands that he named his adopted daughter Chirothea (Hand of God) and went on to publish two exhaustive works documenting human gesture, *Chironomia* and *Chriologia*, in 1644. Immanuel Kant (1724–1804) claimed the hand as the window onto the mind during the Enlightenment.

2. A simple search using Google's NGram Viewer reveals the spike in instances of the word "hand" between the centuries. I am indebted to the interest my departmental colleagues who work in digital humanities have shown in my project—specifically Steve Ramsay and Matt Jockers. Steve Ramsay helped in the comparison of Eighteenth-Century Collections Online (ECCO) and the Chadwyck-Healy database Nineteenth Century Fiction (NCF). The results were startling to both of us: the ECCO database, despite being four times the size of the NCF database (and despite the fact that it includes all major genres whereas the NCF obviously tracks only fiction) returned two times fewer instances of the word "hand." Aligning the results in these databases showed that nineteenth-century fiction mentioned hands at a rate of around eight times more than in all genres of the eighteenth century. This result was even more startling when Matt Jockers helped me move the comparison from the 250 novels in the NCF database to one containing around 3,500 novels written in the nineteenth century. Running similar searches returned roughly the

same results—far more instances of hands in the nineteenth century as compared to the eighteenth. I want to be very clear about how I have treated this data, though. Instances of a word do not in any way "equal" meaning. Distant reading the data like this hardly "proves" that hands were more important in the nineteenth century; I will allow my much closer analysis of the literature and culture of the Victorian period to accomplish this. The data mining strategy is just one way to demonstrate what this strange phenomenon (the spike in references to hands) is. Making sense of its strangeness undergirds the argument of my book. These computer-assisted results do not supply or confirm an answer so much as they frame important new questions about the period that we may not have previously considered. Some of the initial research informing *Changing Hands* sits, therefore, somewhat precariously between what I and many others see as shifting paradigms in the study of literary history. Early conversations with Matt Jockers about what he calls "macroanalysis"—both when he was at Stanford's Literary Lab and now at Nebraska—have convinced me that the future of literary study must blend both traditionally "close" and revolutionary new "distant" readings. This blended approach to computer analysis is shared by many in the field of digital humanities, including Tanya Clement, Alan Liu, and Ted Underwood. For this reason, I was encouraged to analyze the strange spike in hand references in the nineteenth century at the Digital Humanities Summer Institute (DHSI–University of Victoria, BC) in 2011. My confidence in the larger arc of the argument I make in *Changing Hands*, therefore, is due in part to the macro-scale analytics gleaned from using the SEASR components I learned at DHSI from Loretta Auvil and Boris Capitanu of the National Center for Supercomputing Applications (University of Illinois). That said, no one could mistake this project for one that incorporates the comprehensive data mining that specialists endorse. Put in bodily terms, it is a traditional project that has dipped one of its toes into current DH methodologies.

3. This trend is paralleled also by major journal publications. For a recent sampling, see Simon Goldhill's "A Writer's Things: Edward Bulwer Lytton and the Archaeological Gaze; or, What's in a Skull" (2012); Shalyn Claggett's "George Eliot's Interrogation of Physiological Future Knowledge" (2011); Sarah Winter's "Darwin's Saussure: Biosemiotics and Race in *Expression*" (2009); Josh Epstein's " 'Neutral Physiognomy': The Unreadable Faces of *Middlemarch*" (2008); and Ian Duncan's "Sympathy, Physiognomy, and Scottish Romantic Fiction" (2008).

4. Jonathan Goldberg's *Writing Matter* (1990) and Katherine Rowe's *Dead Hands* (1999) are exceptions to this general rule. These books obviously focus on the early modern period, however.

5. I am indebted to Helena Michie for this formulation. See *The Flesh Made Word* (1987: 88).

6. My understanding of these developments has been influenced by N. Katherine Hayles's analysis in *How We Became Posthuman: Virtual Bodies in Cybernetics, Literature, and Informatics* (1999).

7. The closest any come to doing this treat the sense of touch in its physiological incarnations. Very good studies that come to mind in this regard are William Cohen's

Embodied: Victorian Literature and the Senses (2008) and Constance Classen's *The Deepest Sense: A Cultural History of Touch* (2012).

8. Deleuze outlines the affection-image, how a close-up of the face is constituted as affect, power, and potentiality in chapter six of *Cinema 1*. Asa Briggs dedicates a chapter of his *Victorian Things* (1988) to this: "The Philosophy of the Eye: Spectacles, Cameras, and the New Vision" (Ch. 3; pp. 103–41). For a very specific recent example relating to photography, see Dan Novak's *Realism, Photography, and Nineteenth-Century Fiction* (2008). Photography's more general impact may be gauged by the attention it has received in the flagship journal for New Historicist studies, *Representations*. On average over the past ten years, *Representations* has published at least one article or more dealing with photography.

9. Here I have been influenced by Rita Felski's call for a mode of interpretation that responds to the question of "how texts resonate across time" ("Context Stinks" 2011:575).

10. Specifically, I have in mind here Bill Brown's *The Material Unconscious* (1996), "Thing Theory" (2001), and *A Sense of Things* (2003). In the field of Victorian studies, I have been influenced by Thad Logan's *The Victorian Parlour* (2006) and Elaine Freedgood's *The Ideas in Things* (2006).

11. This formulation is Felski's; see "After Suspicion" (2009:31).

12. For an explication of this methodology, see the Fall 2009 special issue of *Representations*. It includes critiques by Stephen Best, Sharon Marcus, Emily Apter, and Elaine Freedgood, among others.

13. See http://www.matthewjockers.net/macroanalysisbook/macro-themes/?topic =BODY_FEATURES. For a methodological explanation of how this topic word cloud was derived, see http://www.matthewjockers.net/2011/09/29/the-lda-buffet-is-now -open-or-latent-dirichlet-allocation-for-english-majors/.

Chapter 1

1. For a useful study of the relationship of Adam Smith's "invisible hand" to the nineteenth-century British novel, see Courtemanche (2011).

2. I concede that this is not solely a religious issue. The notion of eyes as "the windows to the soul" goes back to ancient times.

3. For an account of the ugliness of the creature's eyes in connection with Burkean aesthetic theory, see Gigante (2000).

4. Percy Shelley refers to Paley's work in an 1811 letter. See I: 200 of the Jones edition of *The Letters of Percy Bysshe Shelley* (1964).

5. For a more detailed exploration of Lawrence's treatment of eye disorders, see Martha Stoddard Holmes's *Fictions of Affliction: Physical Disability in Victorian Culture*, especially chapter 1 entitled "Melodramatic Bodies" (2004:16–33).

6. George Levine has argued influentially that Victor's process of creation means that "we are confronted immediately by the displacement of God and woman from the acts of creation and birth" (1979: 8). It is true, as Levine contends, that "the whole

narrative of *Frankenstein* is . . . acted out in the absence of God" (1979: 7). My point is that *Frankenstein* is predicated on the vitalist debates, which themselves were debates about God's role in the physiological construction of "life." Therefore, since the vitalist debates were directly predicated on the question of God's role (or lack thereof) in the boundary between life and death, God—whether he or it is never mentioned—is still a constant figurative and rhetorical presence in *Frankenstein*. For example, at the moment when Victor believes that he has "succeeded in discovering the cause of generation and life," he concludes that even though "the stages of the discovery were distinct and probable," "some miracle might have produced it" (1818: 30). This conflation of "distinct and probable" materialist science and miraculous religion echoes John Abernethy's position in the sense that it simultaneously allows for a creation that is both supernatural and strictly natural.

7. For an alternate reading of this scene in terms of Enlightenment human rights, see Reese (2006: 52).

8. For a more detailed account of this discovery, see Raby's *Bright Paradise: Victorian Scientific Travellers* (1997), especially chapter 7.

9. I am in agreement on this point with Marilyn Butler who, in "*Frankenstein* and Radical Science" (1996), argues that Mary Shelley "deliberately avoided committing herself to the evolutionist hypothesis" in her depiction of the creature (qtd. in Shelley 2012a: 309). Other influential critics such as Chris Baldick point out that Victor's creation "is a fully human creature" (1990: 44–45). More recently, Timothy Morton, in *Shelley and the Revolution in Taste*, has argued that the creature's diet of berries, nuts, and roots (no meat) makes him in many ways more human than his maker 1994: 49).

10. Robert Mitchell's *Experimental Life: Vitalism in Romantic Science and Literature* provides perhaps the most concentrated case in point. In a six-page section of "Media Spaces in Shelley's *Frankenstein*," Mitchell uses the word "grasp" (or a variation of it) figuratively eighteen times in his brilliant discussion of the ways the novel's characters vary by "the differing degrees to which each can grasp . . . the natural, cultural, and communicational media that surround them" (2013: 177).

11. This religiously infused view of the dissected human body is what D'Oyly and others in the traditional medical establishment saw violated in Lawrence's teachings (and practices). Since Lawrence's materialism allows for no definitive or necessary relationship between "the contemplation of nature, to nature's God," the established medical profession saw Lawrence making a "conversion of the lecture-room of students in surgery into a school of infidelity" (1819: 5). Lawrence and other materialist physicians such as Thomas Southwood Smith and Thomas Wakley (the influential editor of the popular new medical publication *The Lancet*) viewed themselves as a younger and more scientifically informed generation of medical men who conducted their work free from Tory politics and old-fashioned ideas. Adrian Desmond notes the brazenness of this group by quoting Thomas Wakley's impersonation of the more dogmatic members of the Royal College who "never touc[h] a phalanx and its flexor tendon, without exclaiming, with

uplifted eye, and most reverentially-contracted mouth, 'Gintlimin, behold the winderful eevidence of *desin!*'" (1989: 112).

12. For Hunter's views, see the Introduction (xvii) of the second (2012a) Norton edition of *Frankenstein*. Alan Rauch, in *Useful Knowledge: The Victorians, Morality, and the March of the Intellect* (2001), wades into a delineation of perspective between Percy and Mary Shelley in terms of religion and science. Rauch concludes that "science for Percy was an unrestrained practice free from the superstitions of the church. But Mary Shelley's enthusiasm for the radical ideas espoused by Percy was tempered." "Like Percy," Rauch points out, "she was interested in advocating and encouraging scientific inquiry, but, where he was willing to trust the scientific community to participate in a 'link'd chain of thought,' she would have it answerable to a more familiar code of ethics" (2001: 127). Also related to this subject, John Williams, in *Mary Shelley: A Literary Life*, notes Mary Shelley's tentative return to attending traditional Anglican church services in 1822 (2000: 71). Even with this in mind, I would not go so far as David Hogsette recently has in "Metaphysical Intersections in *Frankenstein*," wherein he argues that Mary Shelley subscribed to a particularly Christianized "theistic vitalism" (2011: 537).

13. It would not be difficult to develop a list of critics who, in the last thirty years, see the interpretation of the novel in terms of a moral fable of presumption as fundamentally unnuanced. Two very influential critics who come immediately to mind are George Levine (1979) and Chris Baldick (1990).

14. It is worth noting that there were, in fact, three editions published: in 1818, in 1822, and in 1831. The 1818 edition was published anonymously (with a Preface by Percy and a dedication to Godwin). The 1822 edition was published virtually unchanged except for the attribution of Mary Shelley as the author after the success of Richard Peake's stage play *Presumption; or, the Fate of Frankenstein* (1822). The 1831 edition was published in Henry Colburn and Richard Bentley's *Standard Novels* series with a new "Author's Introduction" and several revised or added passages. These are the facts of *Frankenstein*'s publication history, so the only question—to which there are many interpretations—is what the motivating factors were in the decision to publish a significantly different version in 1831. Interestingly enough, D. L. Macdonald and Kathleen Scherf correctly argue that the 1818 and 1831 editions are best treated as two separate texts, yet they nonetheless endorse the 1818 edition as "closer to the imaginative act and atmosphere" that produced the novel (Shelley 2012:b 44). In terms of biographical perspectives, Mary Poovey has claimed that Shelley's revisions "extend her criticism of imaginative indulgence, already present in the 1818 text, and direct it much more pointedly at the blasphemy she now associates with her own adolescent audacity" (1984: 133). "Mary Shelley wants most of all," according to Poovey, "to assure her readers that she is no longer the defiant, self-assertive 'girl' who once dared to explore ambition and even to seek fame herself without the humility proper to a lady" (1984: 137). Anne Mellor agrees that Shelley's outlook changed radically from 1818 to 1831, but more so as a result of pessimism generated by the deaths of Clara, William, and Percy and by the betrayals of

Byron and Jane Williams (1988: 209). Mellor also suggests that Mary Shelley's severely constricted economic circumstances by the late 1820s played a role in her decision to publish a revised edition with Bentley. This latter point is especially relevant, considering that it was Shelley who approached Charles Ollier, chief literary adviser to the firm Colburn and Bentley, to test the interest in a revised version of *Frankenstein* for its Standard Novels series (Shelley 2007: 184).

15. For the remainder of this chapter, when I refer to the two editions of *Frankenstein*, I mean the 1818 and 1831 editions.

16. My understanding of the cultural atmosphere after 1818 has been distilled from Marilyn Butler's pioneering essay, "*Frankenstein* and Radical Science" (1996).

17. My interpretation of this part of the text has been enriched by conversations and suggestions from Stephen Behrendt, Charles Robinson, and, via Charles Robinson, Nora Crook.

18. The most influential interpretation of the creature as a machine representing the proletariat is Moretti's "The Dialectic of Fear" (1982).

Chapter 2

1. Bell's Treatise on *The Hand* was the fourth in the series. The others were, in the order of their publication, *The Adaptation of External Nature to the Moral and Intellectual Condition of Man*, by Thomas Chalmers; *On the Adaptation of External Nature to the Physical Condition of Man*, by John Kidd; *Astronomy and General Physics considered with reference to Natural Theology*, by William Whewell; *Animal and Vegetable Physiology considered with reference to Natural Theology*, by Peter Mark Roget; *Geology and Mineralogy considered with reference to Natural Theology*, by William Buckland; *On the History, Habits and Instincts of Animals*, by William Kirby; *Chemistry, Meteorology, and the Function of Digestion, considered with reference to Natural Theology*, by William Prout.

2. *The Hand*'s popularity was reinforced by more than 120 reviews that appeared in forty different periodicals during the 1830s (Topham 1998: 249).

3. This process, of course, does not occur overnight despite the rapid growth referred to by economic historians. As Elaine Freedgood has pointed out, the power loom, the steam engine, and the spinning frame "had not achieved the dominance in mid-Victorian imaginations that we might expect in part because they had not [yet] achieved that dominance in production" (2006: 2).

4. See Sussman's *Victorians and the Machine* (1968); Joseph Bizup's *Manufacturing Culture* (2003); Ketabgian's *The Lives of Machines* (2011).

5. The materialist instructor at Ingolstadt, M. Waldman, refers specifically to this kind of advancement when he mesmerizes Victor with talk about the "miracles" modern scientists are capable of: "They have acquired new and almost unlimited powers; they can command the thunders of heaven, mimic the earthquake, and even mock the invisible world with its own shadows" (1818: 28). It is interesting to note that Shelley later

added a section to her 1831 edition that seems to act as a counterweight to Waldman's materialist position. On visiting the valley of Chamounix after making the creature, Victor takes solace in the impressive and sublime "language" of the natural world: "The weight upon my spirit was sensibly lightened as I plunged yet deeper in the ravine of Arve. The immense mountains and precipices that overhung me on every side—the sound of the river raging among the rocks, the dashing of the waterfalls around, spoke of a power mighty as Omnipotence—and I ceased to fear, or bend before any being less almighty than that which had created and ruled the elements"(1831: 97). It is as if Victor, *avant la lettre*, gets the point Bell makes with his meteorological metaphor.

6. Most critics agree that the most canonized British "factory fiction" shows remarkably little of what occurs inside the walls of the factories themselves. The lack of attention to factories in Mary Gaskell's *Mary Barton* (1848) and *North and South* (1855), Charlotte Brontë's *Shirley* (1849), Charles Dickens's *Hard Times* (1854) are but a few examples that prove the rule. For another early example of one that does, see Frances Trollope's *Michael Armstrong, Factory Boy* (1840)—particularly the scene where Mary Brotherton discovers a factory worker with "a little shriveled right-hand, three fingers of which had a joint deficient" (128).

7. As Gallagher points out: "The novel contains no logical solution to this dilemma, but the narrator does find a stylistic device to cover the contradiction. She tells the events of Helen's life completely from Helen's viewpoint, filtering everything that happens in the factory through Helen's submissive and largely nonanalytical consciousness . . . most of the narrator's analyses of the factory system are thus separated from the recounting of Helen's providentially ordained experience" (1985: 46).

8. To fortify my interpretation that Tonna's noise-centered description of the factory is in direct conversation with pro-industrialist discourse, consider Ure's placid and, indeed, almost silent account of his experience on the factory floor:

> The spinning-factory of Messrs. Ashworth, at Egerton, which has been at work for several years, exhibits an elegant pattern of the engineering just described: for it has some subordinate shafts, hardly thicker than the human wrist, which convey the power of ten horses, and revolve with great speed, *without the slightest noise or vibration*. The prime-mover of the whole is a gigantic water-wheel of sixty feet diameter, and one hundred horses' power. I have frequently been at a loss, in walking through several millwright factories, to know whether the polished shafts that drive the automatic lathes and planing machines were at rest or in motion, *so truly silently did they revolve*. (35, emphasis added)

9. According to Gallagher, Thomas Carlyle was "the most influential and enthusiastic early Victorian chorister in praise of workfulness" (2008: 64). Carlyle's place as the strongest voice in this choir probably comes from his famous passage in *Past and Present* (1843): "[A]ll true Work is Religion . . . Admirable was that [phrase] of old Monks,

'*Laborare est Orare*, Work is Worship'" (1960: 206). The connection between Dickens's view of work and Carlyle's is reinforced by the former's dedication of the first book edition of *Hard Times* (1854) to the latter.

10. Since Mary Poovey's influential reading of *David Copperfield* in *Uneven Developments* (1988), critics have noted the ambivalence that mid-nineteenth-century writers felt toward their occupations as professional authors. No matter how each individual conceived of their work, the need for authors to produce copy for publishers ensured them an ambiguous position between the execution of mental and manual labor. Many critics, owing to the very public "dignity of literature" debates carried out in the contemporary press, assume that Dickens and Thackeray occupied opposite ends of the ideological spectrum concerning literary labor. In this common comparative scenario, Thackeray emphasizes the routine and tedious nature of writing for the periodical press while Dickens tries to maintain a Carlylean and heroic stance above the fray. Rarely is the truth ever so simple as this, but in the specific case of *David Copperfield*, I agree with Richard Salmon's recently articulated argument that this early, semiautobiographical novel "may also be read as a negotiation of the process by which the 'poet' is converted to the function of 'wage-labour' within modern society" (2013: 102–3).

11. For the most recent critic to do so, see Juliet John's interpretation in *Dickens and Mass Culture* (2010): "When David first tells the reader that he has begun to publish fiction, his emphasis is on money … As we have seen on the reading tours, Dickens's tendency (literally) to enumerate success—in money and people—was fundamental to his assessment of his own worth and of the value of his cultural labour" (183). It is not that I disagree with John on this point per se. I simply think that there's more going on in Dickens's choice of the chopped-off fourth finger than the merely monetary notation.

12. Charles Eastlake would make a similar Ruskinian point at around the same time (the 1851 Crystal Palace Exhibition). For Eastlake, "irregularity of form" is "evidence of human handiwork, and that to the end of time will always be more interesting than the result of mechanical precision" (1878: 106).

13. The interest in promoting the proper fencing of machinery is another connection between Bell and Dickens. Bell testified that his concern for the loss of life and limb from unfenced machinery prompted him to appeal to Francis Horner, one of the founders of the *Edinburgh Review* and an MP from Bell's native Scotland (1832: 605). Dickens, for his part, was upset that the nominal fine for having unfenced machinery allowed factory owners to pay fines and continue production with the improperly fenced machines. In effect, it was cheaper for factory owners to pay the fines than to shut down their machines and install proper fencing.

Chapter 3

1. For an explication of this methodology, which, I think, is an outgrowth of an even more heightened interest in materialism, see the introduction to the Fall 2009 issue of

Representations. Here, Best and Marcus outline an interpretive method meant to illuminate obvious textual feature that symptomatic (suspicious) interpretations render ironically invisible (7).

2. In the September 1969 issue of *Victorian Studies*, Patrick Brantlinger claimed that "understanding the conditions which led to Luddism is distinctly secondary" (42). In 1975, Terry Eagleton influentially argued that "Chartism is the unspoken subject of *Shirley*" (2005: 45). Eagleton's opinion that *Shirley*'s workers appear only in the text as "freaks or disembodied roars" allows him to make a now classic (and still compelling) argument that Brontë substitutes subversive Chartism for explicit Luddism (50). Similarly, feminist critics have built on these tropes of displacement by calling attention to the thematic connections Brontë makes between the plights of male woolen workers and middle-class homemakers. Sandra Gilbert and Susan Gubar (2000: 372–98), and more recently Anna Silver (2002: 81–115) and Beth Torgerson (2005: 39–57), have argued that starvation and cholera link the women of the novel to its unemployed workers. The staying power of these "symptomatic," displacement-based interpretations no doubt owes much to Catherine Gallagher's pioneering book *The Industrial Reformation of English Fiction*, which asserts that the "industrial conflict in *Shirley* is little more than a historical setting and does not exert any strong pressure on the form" (xi n.1). Rosemarie Bodenheimer also propelled this line of interpretation with her view, expressed in *The Politics of Story in Victorian Social Fiction*, that *Shirley* is tantamount to a "virtual abandonment of the industrial issue" (1988: 42).

3. In a letter to her publisher in February 1849, Brontë wrote that "in reading *Mary Barton* (a clever though painful tale) I was a little dismayed to find myself in some measure anticipated in both subject and incident" (1995).

4. It is quite obvious that those who categorize *Shirley* as a political novel have been influenced primarily by Brantlinger (1969) and Eagleton (1975). Those who see it as a "woman question" novel take their cue from Gilbert and Gubar (2000). While there is no clear derivative criticism for those who view *Shirley* as an "etiquette novel," this group has drawn either directly or indirectly on the work of Laurie Langbauer (*Women and Romance: The Consolations of Gender in the English Novel*, 1990) and, more recently, Elizabeth Langland (*Society in the Novel*, 1984, and *Nobody's Angels*, 1995).

5. I am not alone in making this general connection. Sally Shuttleworth (1996: 183), Susan Zlotnick (1998: 94), and others have also recognized the relationship between the disposed male weavers and middle-class women. My argument is unique in so far as it relies on aspects of the Luddites' and the middle-class women's "literal handedness." For example, I agree with Zlotnick that Brontë links middle-class women to working-class men through the common affliction of unemployment. Zlotnick, however, sees this analogy breaking down because "the interests of the male Luddites and those of the novel's women are not identical" (74). My larger contention beyond hands is that the loss of "a centuries-old way of life" (74), though not identical,

applies to both working-class men and middle-class women in the first decade of the nineteenth century. It should also be noted that Nancy Armstrong has argued in *Desire and Domestic Fiction* (1987) that *Shirley's* representation of reading is the novel's most important historical context. Mary Poovey's *Making a Social Body* (1995) ties the emergence of domesticity and class formation to Chadwick's 1842 *Sanitary Report*. My chapter seeks to uncover an earlier history of gender and class formation. More recently, John Plotz sees the relationship between women and workers as not completely analogous but makes a scintillating argument about how middle-class women's flight toward privacy is produced by the threat of the mob. See chapter 6 of *The Crowd: British Literature and Public Politics* (2000), entitled "Producing Privacy in Public" (154–93).

6. As Elaine Freedgood has noted, in the seventeenth and eighteenth centuries, handicraft and mechanical production resided unproblematically in the word "manufacture" (2003: 629).

7. Throughout this chapter I rely on the following histories of British industrialization: Sally Alexander's "Women's Work in Nineteenth-Century London; A Study of the Years 1820–1850" (1977), Brian Bailey's *The Luddite Rebellion* (1998), Maxine Berg's *The Age of Manufactures: Industry, Innovation, and Work in Britain, 1700–1820* (1994) and *The Machinery Question and the Making of Political Economy 1815–1848* (1980), Duncan Bythell's *The Handloom Weavers* (1969), François Crouzet's *The Victorian Economy* (1982), Phyllis Deane's *The First Industrial Revolution* (1965), Robert Gray's *The Factory Question and Industrial England, 1830–1860* (1996), Pat Hudson's *The Genesis of Industrial Capital: A Study of the West Riding Wool Textile Industry c. 1750–1850* (1986), Raphael Samuel's "Workshop of the World: Steam Power and Hand Technology in Mid-Victorian Britain" (1977), and E. P. Thompson's *The Making of the English Working Class* (1963).

8. Helena Michie (1987) has noted that sewing "takes on a sinister cast" in the lives of some fictionalized leisure-class heroines, including Caroline Helstone. However, where Michie's analysis focuses on repressed feminine bodily urges, I am interested in the specifically material relationship between industrial and domestic manufacture.

9. Not so ironically, it was in 1842 that the publication of a blue book by the Children's Employment Commission on Mines caused havoc due to its findings on the conditions of women's work.

10. For a reading that focuses on the symbolic importance of food in this early scene, see Janet Gezari's *Charlotte Brontë and Defensive Conduct: The Author and the Body at Risk* (1992: 90).

11. Perhaps the scene with Mrs. Gale also sheds some light on the tone and word choice Brontë uses in the bristled written response to her critical (male) publishers that I cite earlier in the chapter: "Say what you will—*gentlemen*—say it as ably as you will—Truth is better than Art" (1995: 185, emphasis added). There is no doubt a similar tension in the enactment of the distinctly male right to exercise criticism of female production.

12. For two excellent but very different discussions of the cultural relevance of handling the physical properties of books, see Leah Price's *How to Do Things with Books in Victorian Britain* (2012) and Andrew Piper's *Book Was There: Reading in Electronic Times* (2012).

13. I owe a debt to Kathryn Ledbetter for piquing my interest in this area of needlework. Her paper delivered at the 2010 Interdisciplinary Nineteenth-Century Studies meeting at the University of Texas first alerted me to this field of research. She has since published a book-length study on the topic, entitled *Victorian Needlework* (2012).

14. The relevant lines from Proverbs 31 (l.13–31) appear as follows:

> She seeks wool and flax,
>   and works with willing hands.
> She is like the ships of the merchant,
>   she brings her food from far away.
> She rises while it is still night
>   and provides food for her
>   household
>   and tasks for her servant-girls.
> She considers a field and buys it;
>   with the fruit of her hands she
>   plants a vineyard.
> She girds herself with strength,
>   and makes her arms strong.
> She perceives that her merchandise is
>   profitable.
>   Her lamp does not go out at night.
> She puts her hands to the distaff,
>   and her hands hold the spindle.
> She opens her hand to the poor,
>   and reaches out her hands to
>   the needy.
> She is not afraid for her household
>   when it snows,
>   for all her household are clothed in
>   crimson.
> She makes herself coverings;
>   her clothing is fine linen and
>   purple.
> Her husband is known in the
>   city gates,
>   Taking his seat among the elders of
>   the land.

She makes linen garments and sells
    them;
    She supplies the merchant with
    sashes.
Strength and dignity are her clothing,
    and she laughs at the time to come.
She opens her mouth with wisdom,
    and the teachings of kindness is on
    her tongue.
She looks well to the ways of her
    household,
    and does not eat the bread of
    idleness.
Her children rise up and call her
    happy;
    her husband too, and he
    praises her:
"Many women have done
    excellently,
    but you surpass them all."
Charm is deceitful, and beauty
    is vain,
    but a woman who fears the LORD
    is to be praised.
Give her a share in the fruit of her
    hands,
    and let her works praise her in the
    city gates.

15. Lamarck believed that the use or disuse of a bodily organ or appendage could increase or diminish its size—even within a single generation.

16. Many seamstress workers did not, in fact, work in solitary environments. As *The Times* reported: "Sometimes as many as five or six young girls occupy one small room in which they work and sleep and take their meals in common, plying their needles from morn to night, without a ray of hope to cheer them" (October 27, 1843, qtd. in Edelstein 1980). I agree with Edelstein that iconographic popularizers such as Redgrave made a conscious choice to use the single figure in their seamstress paintings. As a result, Brontë's solitary representation of Caroline invokes the seamstress within an iconographic vocabulary that would have been familiar to the popular understanding of the profession. There is an additional, more direct connection between female handiworkers

and factory production that Brontë is unlikely to have missed: in 1838, Daniel Foote-Taylor acquired control of an industrial patent to produce machine-made, one-piece pins. Pin-making machines in Birmingham subsequently manufactured pins at a rate of 200 per minute—almost 300,000 per day (Ledbetter 2012: 97).

17. See, for example, Lynn M. Alexander's *Women, Work, and Representation: Needlewomen in Victorian Art and Literature* (2003).

18. I am thinking here of Gilbert and Gubar, but also of critics such as Constance Harsh who, in *Subversive Heroines: Feminist Resolutions of Social Crisis in the Condition-of-England Novel* (1994), tries to square Brontë's conservative paternalism with a feminist interpretation. For another more recent example of the same critical impulse, see Rebecca A. McLaughlin's "'I Prefer a *Master*': Female Power in Charlotte Brontë's *Shirley*" (2004). For criticism advocating Brontë's feminine paternalism more broadly, see Bodenheimer's *The Politics of Story* (1988). For an excellent reassessment of Brontë's "domestic duty" in terms of Elizabeth Gaskell's biography of Charlotte Brontë, see Linda H. Peterson's *Becoming a Woman of Letters: Myths of Authorship and Facts of the Victorian Market* (2009), especially 131–53.

19. "The Winding-Up" is the title of the final chapter of the novel. I would argue that, even here, Brontë is playing with the plot threads of the working-class men and middle-class women that intertwine to make up the novel.

20. For a more recent and still more specific iteration of this interpretive blind spot, it is worth considering Jason B. Jones's assessment of "Causation and Interpretation in *Shirley*" in his *Lost Causes: Historical Consciousness in Victorian Literature* (2006). Jones writes: "Critics pursuing *Shirley*'s class and gender themes again *join hands* at the novel's end, arguing that the novel enforces paternalism as a solution to the myriad problems of English society (61, emphasis added). As is the case with so much twentieth- and twenty-first-century criticism, Jones treats a novel so deeply predicated on physical handedness with hand-based metaphors, or, in this more deeply disembodied instance, as an idiomatic expression describing the dual marriages.

Chapter 4

1. This quotation is from Brontë's Preface to the second edition of *Jane Eyre*, which she dedicated to Thackeray.

2. For a recent representative example of this approach, see Elizabeth Langland's "Dialogue, Discourse, Theft, and Mimicry: Charlotte Brontë Rereads William Makepeace Thackeray" (2002).

3. Michael Curtin, in *Propriety and Position: A Study of Victorian Manners* (1987), finds that there were no conduct manuals published between 1804 and 1828. In 1837 alone, though, the *Quarterly* reviewed more than ten etiquette books. Commenting on this phenomena, Elizabeth Langland has written that:

the rise in etiquette guides thus coincides with a period in British life inaugurated by the Reform Bill, a period marked by a drive to represent new forces in British politics and economics and a compensatory desire to stabilize the system along predictable lines . . . These guides, which highlighted the way "social status could be indicated through minute control of conventional behavior," differed substantially from the earlier courtesy or conduct books. (2001: 124)

Curtin has shown that whereas earlier conduct books focused on individual standards of moral behavior, etiquette books emphasized what to do in very specific social situations—a topic this chapter eventually analyzes.

4. Thackeray had a recent history of attacking such pretense and snobbery from both angles: his review of John Henry Skelton's *My Book; or, The Anatomy of Conduct*, entitled "Fashnable Fax and Polite Annygoats," appeared in *Fraser's* (1837) while "The Snobs of England" was serialized in *Punch* (1846–47). Thackeray's experience of comparative poverty in his early professional years, after having been raised a Charterhouse gentleman, made him uniquely qualified to satirize both the low and the high.

5. I am hardly alone in my suggestion regarding Thackeray's sympathy for the plight of female subordination. For book-length studies treating the subject of Thackeray's "feminism," see Richard Barickman, Susan MacDonald, and Myra Stark's *Corrupt Relations* (1982); Deborah Thomas's *Thackeray and Slavery* (1993); Micael M. Clarke's *Thackeray and Women* (1995). Kate Flint has more recently argued that *Vanity Fair* "is a novel fundamentally *about* women, and about their strategies for survival under adversity" ("Women, Men and the Reading of *Vanity Fair*" [1996: 261]).

6. My own interpretation of the opposition between the sexes in this chapter has been influenced most by Nancy Armstrong's *Desire and Domestic Fiction* (1987) and Mary Poovey's *Uneven Developments* (1988).

7. Despite the fact that many critics now consider Thackeray's illustrations to be, as Henry Kingsley said in 1864, "key to the text," it is surprising how many studies still underestimate their interpretive possibilities. Since Thackeray illustrated *Vanity Fair* at the time of its composition and publication (even subtitling its first serialized number as "Pen and Pencil Sketches of Society"), there is no conflation of multiartist intent as there is with, say, Charles Dickens and his various illustrators. For a recent discussion of how ambiguous it is to try to identify authorial intention when dealing with separate illustrators, see John Jordan's *Supposing Bleak House* (2011). In the Appendix of his study, Jordan attempts to argue for Lady Dedlock's ghost within an illustration by Hablot Browne and acknowledges the difficulties of parsing the level of intentionality between Dickens and his illustrator (147–60). Because Thackeray composed the illustrations as he produced the text of *Vanity Fair*, this problem does not exist. *Vanity Fair* is therefore the only major Victorian novel where the illustrations may be treated *as* unmitigated text.

8. As James Phelan has noted from rhetorical and feminist viewpoints, *Vanity Fair* "offers a powerful indictment of courtship behavior in [its] male-controlled society" (1990: 139).

9. See Helena Michie's *The Flesh Made Word* (1987: 10) and Lisa Jadwin's "The Seductiveness of Female Duplicity in *Vanity Fair*" (1992: 664).

10. Jadwin comes closest to my argument regarding a specifically manual discourse when she asserts that Becky's "trap" mode is "characteristically sub-linguistic—minimalistic or even silent—and often takes the form of a series of standard, theatricalized gestures or poses calculated to generate a certain response" (1992: 665).

11. The elder Osborne's positioning may therefore not only exercise but also emphasize his right to keep his own hands, like his thoughts and intentions, unobservable.

12. For a representative example of this line of interpretation applied to this specific passage, see Jadwin 1992. For the novel's more general "masculine biases" vis-à-vis male reading habits, see Flint 1996.

13. This apposite phrasing is Shillingsburg's (2001: 75).

14. See Fisher 2002: 60–75.

15. For a detailed study of dueling, see V. G. Kiernan's *The Duel in European History* (1998).

16. The fact that a "true" duel never takes place in the pages of *Vanity Fair* further supports my argument that Thackeray thoroughly transports physical combat from the (male) realm of the Napoleonic Wars to the domestic realm of the drawing room.

17. For an early example of this strain of criticism, see Martha Vicinus's *A Widening Sphere* (1977: xviii).

18. See Showalter, *The New Feminist Criticism* (1985: 254).

19. As Butler comments in *Gender Trouble*, acting or the performative can be defined as "a set of repeated acts within a highly rigid regulatory frame that congeal over time to produce the appearance of substance" (1990: 33).

20. The work of George Speaight (1990), John McCormick (2004), and Kenneth Gross (2011) has shown that the popularity of the marionette grew rapidly during the early Victorian period—a fact which would not likely have escaped Thackeray's attention.

21 Eyre Crowe's story of how Thackeray happened upon the idea of puppetry during his composition of the final numbers also remains one of the strongest arguments for critics who maintain that *Vanity Fair*'s puppetry is ornamental rather than organic. The following is Crowe's account of the events: "It occurred in June, 1848, one day when Thackeray came at lunch time to my father's house. Torrens McCullaugh, happening to be one of the party, said across the table to Thackeray, 'Well, I see you are going to shut up your puppets in their box!' [Thackeray's] immediate reply was, 'Yes, and, with your permission, I'll work up that simile'" (qtd. in Stevens 1968: 396).

22. For a representative example of this de facto critical position, see Aaron Matz's *Satire in the Age of Realsim* (2010). In a footnote to a discussion of Hardy, Matz

acknowledges that "'Puppet' is an essential word in *Vanity Fair*" (186). He then under-
cuts his own acknowledgment of puppetry's "essential" place by (1) referring to it only as
an "essential word" (rather than motif, or concept, etc.) and by (2) referring only to the
"tacked on" puppetry in the text. Here is Matz's comment in full: "'Puppet' is an essential
word in *Vanity Fair*. In the prelude to that novel, 'Before the Curtain,' Thackeray calls his
heroine 'the famous little Becky puppet'; and the final chapter concludes with an invitation to the reader: 'Come children, let us shut up the box and the puppets, for our play is
played out'" (186–87). My analysis of this framing device is meant to prove how essential
puppetry is to the *entire* novel. In effect, I attempt to answer the question Robyn Warhol
poses in *Gendered Inventions*: "What could be less vitally important, more trivial and
petty, than the activities or observations of puppets?" (1989: 84). A notable recent exception to this tendency of downplaying the puppetry *throughout* the text is David Kurnick's
chapter on *Vanity Fair* in *Empty Houses: Theatrical Failure and the Novel* (2012). Though
Kurnick focuses on the "miniaturization" of Thackeray's puppet theater, we agree that
the Becky puppet nearly "usurp[s] the plotting function of her narrator" (51).

23. See John Loofbourow, *Thackeray and the Form of Fiction* (1964: 31–32); Jack Rawlins, *Thackeray's Novels* (1974: 28).

24. See Robert Lougy's "Vision and Satire: The Warped Looking Glass in *Vanity Fair*"
(1975). For more recent treatments, see Heather Brink-Roby's "Psyche: Mirror and
Mind in *Vanity Fair*" (2013); Mario Ortiz-Robles's *The Novel as Event* (2010: 110–11);
and Sarah Rose Cole's "The Aristocrat in the Mirror: Male Vanity and Bourgeois Desire
in William Makepeace Thackeray's *Vanity Fair*" (2005).

25. See Catherine Peters, *Thackeray's Universe* (1987: 146); Wilkenfeld 1971: 308.

26. The identification of the object in Becky's hand remains in dispute. Robert Lougy
(1975) and Martin Meisel (1983) are examples of critics who identify the object as a sinister phial of poison. Maria DiBattista (1980) and Carol MacKay (2011) are examples
of critics who identify it as a knife.

27. I am indebted to Peter Shillingsburg (2001) for reminding me of the ambiguities
that exist even in the original illustration.

28. Quoted from Monsarrat (1980: 90).

Chapter 5

1. It is well known that the perceptual codes of physiognomy and phrenology perme-
ated psychological, aesthetic, and fictional conventions by the middle of the nineteenth
century. See Fahnestock 1981; Taylor 1988; Cowling 1989.

2. For a history of criticism related to this topic, see Forker 1961–62; Moore 1965;
Buckley 1974; Stone 1979; Reed 1981; Cohen 1993; Macleod 2002; Woloch 2003.

3. Not surprisingly, "hand" criticism took a deconstructive turn. It was J. Hillis Miller's brief discussion of the topic in *Charles Dickens: The World of His Novels* (1958) that
inspired Forker's more detailed article (1961–62). In 1979 Harry Stone noted that the

handshake ritual "is part of an elaborate network of hand imagery that links half the characters in *Great Expectations* in a secret freemasonry of hands. One is constantly astonished by the magical ceremony of hands, for though plain to view, it is virtually invisible; it merges with—one might almost say loses itself in—the book's compelling realism" (334). Walter L. Reed concluded that "a whole prototextual sign language is generated simply by attention to the physical detail of hands. These manual markers are not simply metaphors, a pattern of imagery in the traditional sense where literal phe-nomenon and figurative expression are relatively distinct. They are rather an example of the physically literal world shaping itself into rudimentary patterns of meaning, creating a primitive version of language which characters may speak and—occasionally com-prehend" (1981: 269–70). More recently, William A. Cohen has influentially extended Stone's notion of a "secret freemasonry of hands" to the encryption of sexuality in the novel's manual activity. According to Cohen, the "manual semiotics" of masturbation is covertly signaled yet "so starkly obvious as to be invisible" (1993: 221). I am interested in the same issue of invisibility as Stone and Cohen, but for very different reasons.

4. Where the majority of critics treating this subject focus on the symbolic or mimetic functions of the hands, I seek instead to historicize Dickens's treatment of them within specific cultural—and often scientific—debates about the expression and management of mid-Victorian anxieties vis-á-vis bourgeois subjectivity. To use Forker's expression, hands are "almost an obsession" in *Great Expectations* precisely because Victorians were indeed obsessed by them—but for a very specific set of scientific reasons (1961–62: 280).

5. George Levine makes this observation. See 1988: 127.

6. I agree with Brown's convincing argument, but show in chapter 1 how *Franken-stein* acts as a transition text where these fears move from the face, and eyes in particular, to the hands.

7. Ironically, the final line of "The Murders in the Rue Morgue" contains a partial quotation—in French—from Rousseau's *Julie* (1761). Dickens met Poe in Philadelphia during his 1842 trip to the United States, and would have certainly known Poe's famous short story of 1841. For the popularity of Poe's fiction in England, see Fisher 1999.

8. The Victorian public feared descent even as evolutionary biologists altered their definitions of anatomical species development to reassert human supremacy with differ-ent rhetoric. Herbert Spencer, for example, began to emphasize the "*perfection* of the tac-tile apparatus" in human as compared to ape hands while Richard Owen argued for the cerebral primacy of man—a position that would later form the basis of the vituperative public arguments between Wilberforce and Huxley (1872: 361, italics mine). It was this general anxiety, and the publicity of these debates in particular, that allowed the hand to emerge as a site where scientists, politicians, and novelists alike looked for a paradoxical kinship with and divergence from the variously imagined "lower orders" which dominate the cast of *Great Expectations*.

9. Steven Jay Gould calls attention to the fact that the scientific search for this "miss-ing link" was for a long time subverted by the search for the wrong body part (skull

rather than hand)—a mistake itself arising from a faulty (and according to Gould, ideologically stipulated) emphasis on man-as-intellect rather than on man-as-creator, man-as-maker, or man-as-worker. See 1977: 207.

10. The class anxiety manifested in Jaggers's hands may have been generated by events in Dickens's own life. It is well known that Dickens successfully suppressed any public knowledge of his own working-class experience in Warren's Blacking Factory. His father's incarceration in the Marshalsea Prison and his own sudden descent into manual labor formed in Dickens a lifelong desire to remove the taint of poverty and social disgrace. This process would have become quite literal for the young Dickens, whose ten-hour days ended by scrubbing black paste from his hands and nails. An overlooked fact, however, is that each of Dickens's adult professions—law clerk, stenographer, editor, and novelist—required hand washing as well. Though solidly above so-called "manual labour," his occupations were nonetheless implicated in such labor if only because of the tendency of ink to mark the hands of lowly "copy clerks"—a job Dickens held for eighteen months in the firm of Ellis and Blackmore. Dickens clearly associated the work of writing with the more physical occupations of manual labor. Consider, for example, the language of metaphorical labor that Dickens uses to describe his attitude toward copying documents for Spenlow and Jorkins in *David Copperfield* (1849–50): "What I had to do, was, to turn the painful discipline of my younger days to account, by going to work with a resolute and steady heart. What I had to do, was, to take my woodman's axe in my hand, and clear my way through the forest of difficulty, by cutting down the trees until I came to Dora" (505). Even as the most famous novelist in the world, Dickens's class status was insecure enough to make him grandiloquent about the novelist's calling. This is not to say that there was anything in the Victorian novelist's calling that prevented one from also being a "gentleman." Thackeray and Trollope had proven this beyond a doubt. But Charterhouse and Harrow provided a very different sort of training than Chatham dockyard and Warren's Blacking Factory.

11. The ambiguity of handkerchief deployment also directly affects Magwitch. Recounting his experience before the judge with Compeyson, Magwitch notes the skill with which Compeyson deployed his "white pocket-handkercher" during the trial, an obvious sign of his (fake) gentility in contrast to Magwitch, "a common wretch," against whom appearances remain heavily stacked (chapter 42). For a discussion of handkerchiefs in *Oliver Twist*, see Jordan 1989.

12. *Great Expectations* diffuses some of this anxiety in its comical treatment of hand ornamentation in other parts of the novel. For instance, the precariousness of Pip's rapid ascent from the forge may be seen in the way "the stiff long fingers" of his gloves constrain him from ringing the doorbell at Satis House upon his first visit as a "gentleman" (122). Similarly, the Aged P. struggles (against a tree!) to get his warehousing hands into kid gloves while his son, Wemmick, dons "at least four mourning rings" in Little Britain to decorate his "wine-coopering hands" (337, 135).

13. For a study of how production and consumption were conceptualized as forms of repetition and invoked to describe mechanical patterns of human behavior, see Vrettos 2000.

14. There are also several aspects of Jaggers's lifestyle which, taken together, reveal a deliberate attempt to remain true to his lower-class beginnings. We can infer from the constant demand on his services, and because he demands payment up front, that Jaggers enjoys a significant income. Yet he chooses to live in only three rooms of an unimpressive house in Soho (amongst the people he defends). As Pip ponders his invitation to have dinner at Jaggers house, Wemmick assures him that there is "no silver . . . Britannia metal, every spoon" (160). Once there, Pip takes notice that, though "the table was comfortably laid," there was "no silver in the service" (164). Just as Jaggers draws attention to his common dinnerware, he insists on common dinner attire even among his gentlemanly wards. "'No ceremony,' [Jaggers] stipulates firmly, 'and no dinner dress'" (163). Such comments suggest that Jaggers's harbors a deep ambivalence toward his role as a guardian for young men on the path to gentility—a path clearly not open to him when he experienced his own "poor dreams."

15. Although *Great Expectations* was composed in the immediate wake of *The Origin of Species* (1859), it has received surprisingly sparse Darwinian analysis. Gillian Beer's pioneering work *Darwin's Plots* (1983) does not discuss Dickens at all, as its focus is on George Eliot and Thomas Hardy. George Levine's *Darwin and the Novelists* (1988) still stands as the definitive work on Dickens in relation to Darwinism. However, Levine's chapter "Dickens and Darwin" in this work contains only two brief references to *Great Expectations*. He treats just about every other Dickens novel masterfully in terms of Darwin—concentrating the most on *Bleak House* and *Little Dorrit*. Most recently, Ivan Kreilkamp's chapter "Dying Like a Dog in *Great Expectations*" engages Darwin only in a footnote (2007: 88). For a recent exception, see Morgentaler (1998). The key texts in regard to Munby/Culliwick are Hudson (1972) and Davidoff (1979). More recent studies of this relationship, not in conjunction with *Great Expectations*, include Stanley 1986; Pollock (1993–94); McClintock 1995; Reay 2002. For another specific study of race in Dickens which does not treat *Great Expectations*, see Laura Peters's *Dickens and Race* (2013).

16. My formulation, of course, is indebted to Bourdieu. See 1984: 68.

17. Pip records much the same excited response in his sister, when she observes Joe fight with Orlick. Although she drops "insensible" at the window, Pip also notes, parenthetically—"(but who had seen the fight first, I think)"—and then records how she was carried back into the house and "laid down." After struggling and clenching her hands in Joe's hair, a strange hiatus follows. In Pip's words: "Then came that singular calm and silence which I have always connected with such a lull—namely, that it was Sunday, and somebody was dead—and I went upstairs to dress myself" (chapter 15). David Paroissien has convinced me that there is something decidedly postcoital about this intriguing scene (2010). If nothing else, it decidedly echoes the reaction of Estella to Pip's encounter with Herbert.

18. George Orwell famously searches in vain for a "realistic" portrait of the working class in *The Decline of the English Murder* (1965 [1946]). Bruce Robbins suggests the most realistically portrayed worker is the servant in *The Servant's Hand* (1986). Elaine Scarry has chronicled the ways in which work resists representation in *Resisting Representation* (1994). Alex Woloch treats labor in *Great Expectations'* representation of minor characters in *The One Vs. the Many* (2003). Most recently, Carolyn Lesjak interprets the "invisibility" of labor as an essential function of *Great Expectation's* imperial capitalism in *Working Fictions* (2006).

19. But because he does not extort the surplus value of his labor—he relinquishes it to Pip—Magwitch may be said to interrupt temporarily the antagonistic social relations of capitalism.

Chapter 6

1. This is because Eliot and others in her circle held a belief that would later characterize major twentieth-century scientific and philosophical views of the human hand's differentiation from those of the great apes. Her partner George Henry Lewes, for example, conceded that although "the ape has hands very much like man's," its "faculties are not a fiftieth part of those performed by the hand of man" (1879: I, 28). For Eliot, as this chapter will argue, the most important of these faculties was the human hand's ability to transfer sympathetic feeling between individual lives.

2. For a psychoanalytic interpretation of the concept of grasping, see Hertz 2003: 141–44.

3. See Peter Brooks's *Body Work: Objects of Desire in Modern Narrative* (1993). Brooks writes that "George Eliot, in her extraordinary last novel, *Daniel Deronda*, attempts to understand the woman's body, to make it something other than an object of vision, and to supplant the visual with another kind of narrative model" (222). I agree with Brooks in his estimation that the nineteenth-century body was thought to reveal essential "truths," but I disagree with Brooks in that my argument offers a new narrative model for *Daniel Deronda* that is based on the (mostly) male Jewish body in terms of its historicized place in nineteenth-century discourse generally, and in George Eliot's understanding of Jewish mysticism in particular.

4. Robert Knox's widely read *The Races of Men* claimed that the racial "unchangeability" of the Jew could be observed in the nose alone: "a large, massive, club-shaped, hooked nose, three or four times larger than suits the face" (1862: 197). George Jabet's *Notes on Noses* (1864) figured the Jewish nose as a physiological indication of an instinctual shrewdness that transformed "insight into profitable account" (11). It is in the context of this racialist discourse that Henry James's Pulcheria objected to the possibility of Deronda's handsomeness: "Never, my dear [Theodora], with that nose! I am *sure* he had a nose" (685, my italics).

5. David Kaufmann objects to Deronda's "stately inaccessibility" (1878: 65) and U. C. Knoepflmacher sees him as "fleshless and ethereal" (1965: 147). Robert F. Preyer addresses how a "hidden or non-perceptual" reality fits Eliot's commitment to realism (1960: 53). George Levine asserts that Deronda "is almost literally abstracted from the contingencies of the sensible world" (2008b: 43) and Bryan Cheyette claims that "it is difficult to 'see' Deronda . . . hence the need for certain defining traits, such as the routine 'grasping of his coat-collar,' as if the reader is continually meeting him for the first time" (1993: 45). Irene Tucker maintains that Jewishness in *Daniel Deronda* is "a condition of spectrality" (2000: 96). Bryan Cheyette persuasively interprets Deronda's "passive, featureless" body as a necessary precondition for Eliot's displacement of nationalist ideals on her eponymous hero (1993: 45). Talia Schaffer contends that Jewishness is "central yet virtually unshown" in *Daniel Deronda* (2011: 139). Daniel Novak argues that Deronda's "corporeal evacuation and abstraction" is the product of a literal reproduction of Francis Galton's "composite photography," which sought to isolate the pure "type" of family inheritance, pathology, and race of the Jew (2004: 60). For Novak, these typological composites—where anything and nothing are possible—make Deronda a "*model* Jew." Cynthia Scheinberg emphasizes Eliot's construction of Deronda's "idealized poetic identity" over his lack of physiological identity (2010: 829). Other critics continue to be drawn to Deronda's face despite its lack of physiological signifiers of identity. For example, Mikhal Dekel follows what he calls "the physiognomic grid of the novel" to Deronda's relatively dark skin color and his supposedly "Jewish" face for indications of his race (2010: 36). For a recent reading of Eliot's previous dedication to phrenology and, therefore, Mordecai's supposedly primary interest in Deronda's face, see Claggett (2011: 857).

6. On this point, I agree with John Plotz (2008), who builds on a previous formulation by James Buzard regarding Eliot's adherence to biological conceptions of ethnicity. Buzard formulates it this way: "While it is true that Daniel holds out a model of national belonging that preserves a space for the continuing reassessment and revision of one's cultural inheritance—for choice, in other words—it remains true as well that ethnic inheritance is regarded as setting down boundaries beyond which choice is not to pass" (2005: 296).

7. My interpretive methodology, here and in *Changing Hands* more generally, participates in the critical turn toward a kind of "surface"/"literal" reading which has emerged in the first decade of this century with works by Elaine Freedgood (*The Ideas in Things*, 2006), Margaret Cohen ("Narratology in the Archive of Literature," 2009), Ann Stoler (*Along the Archival Grain*, 2010), and Sharon Marcus (*Between Women*, 2007), among others. The difference with my approach, though, is that I do not privilege surface reading over "close reading." Instead, I employ a surface approach to identifying places in texts that need to be more closely read. My reading of Deronda's hands furthers this line of interpretation, arguing as it does that resituating a text within its discursive contexts can illuminate textual features that are obvious but which critics continually overlook. For a discussion of the turn to interpret the complexity of

literary surfaces, see the special issue of *Representations* dedicated to the topic of "'The Way We Read Now" (108; Fall 2009).

8. Even for cultural literary critics of the caliber of Bruce Robbins, the hand is always already metaphorical as in *The Servant's Hand: English Fiction from Below* (1986). For other examples of this kind of blindness to the materiality of hands, see Patricia Johnson's *Hidden Hands: Working-Class Women and Victorian Social Problem Fiction* (2001), and Eleanor Courtemanche's *The 'Invisible Hand' in British Fiction, 1818–1860* (2011).

9. The Titian painting, like Thackeray's illustrations in *Vanity Fair*, can be conceived as an example of what Peter Wagner calls an "iconotext": an "artifact in which the verbal and the visual signs mingle to produce rhetoric that depends on the co-presence of words and images" (1996: 16).

10. Peter Brooks provides another notable example of this critical blind spot. Even in his compelling argument that modern narrative is intent on uncovering the body in order to expose a truth that must be written in the flesh, Brooks focuses exclusively on the head in his assessment of the gaze in *Daniel Deronda*: "Gwendolen begins her novelistic existence in the manner of so many women in nineteenth-century fiction, subject to the male gaze, indeed defining her very position and nature as the coercive, magnetic object of that gaze: someone whose destiny will be determined by how she plays to the eyes of men" (1993: 253).

11. As William Baker has noted, the Palestine Exploration Society was at the time recruiting individuals who could both plan and execute rugged civic engineering projects: "engineers, surveyors and soldiers, . . . [such as] Claude Conder, Charles Warren, and Kitchener, were seconded by the British army in order to draw up surveys to prepare the way for the settlement of immigrants" (1975: 136).

12. This reversal of effects into causes is the reason, in Ian Duncan's view, that critics identify a modulation of the novel "from realism to romance or allegory" (2014: 31).

13. According to Ragussis, Mordecai "unaccountably" asks Deronda to accept a Jewish heritage (1995: 273). Nord contends that Mordecai "decides" to regard Deronda as a Jew "for his own quixotic reasons" (2006: 116).

14. Most notably, George Levine, Sally Shuttleworth, and Ian Duncan have suggested this formulation.

15. Levine's scientific formulation, which is shared to some degree with Sally Shuttleworth, contends that George Eliot "associates Mordecai's visions not with the vagaries of mysticism, but with the concrete realm of science" (Shuttleworth 1984: 180).

16. The most comprehensive study of Eliot's Judaic preparation is still William Baker's *George Eliot and Judaism* (1975).

17. Religious scholars have recently argued against the assumption that the Hebrew God's transcendence or sacrality necessarily resists embodiment. See Howard Eilberg-Schwartz, "God's Body: The Divine Cover-Up" (1995). For a discussion of God's deictic hands, in particular, see Daniel Boyarin's "The Eye in the Torah: Ocular Desire in Midrashic Hermeneutic" (1990).

18. Despite the fact that Mordecai never kisses Daniel before he dies (he dies holding hands with Mirah and Daniel), many critics, including Sarah A. Wilburn, often mistake Mordecai's mention of "the divine kiss" on his deathbed to stand in for the transmigratory kiss (Wilburn 2006: 20). This is yet another example where the hand has as much significance as the face.

19. For an alternate reading which interprets this as an unequivocal allusion to the moment of circumcision, see Jacob Press, "Same-Sex Unions in Modern Europe" (1997: 305).

20. Eliot took notes on the Guidonean Hand from John Pyke Hullah's *History of Modern Music* (1875).

21. Cohen's interpretation of "haptic visuality" is, as he says, based on Maurice Merleau-Ponty's posthumous essay entitled "The Intertwining—the Chiasm."

22. This is an inversion of the traditional Victorian relationship wherein the jewelry itself signifies family affiliation, as is the case in *Romola* (Eliot 1862–63) when the onyx ring signifies the nonbiological association between Baldessare and his "son" Tito. Interestingly, Deronda's Jewishness is never more positively affirmed than at the moment he *loses* his father's ring. Deronda asks Mirah to marry him at the exact narrative juncture that the ring disappears.

23. It is worth noting that the front cover image on Melvin Konner's *The Jewish Body* (2009) features mirror images of two very assertive fists—fitting Eliot's image of Titian's combination of "refinement and force" (157–58).

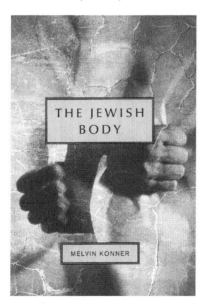

Fig. 57. *The Jewish Body*. 2009. Used by permission of Katya Evdokimova/ Archangel Images and Penguin Random House.

24. See K. M. Newton's *George Eliot* (1999), Jane Irwin's *George Eliot's Daniel Deronda Notebooks* (1996: 334), Deborah Nord's *Gypsies & the British Imagination* (2006: 116), and Jacob Press's "Same-Sex Unions in Modern Europe" (1997: 167).

25. I join several other critics in maintaining that Eliot was a product of her historical moment and that, therefore, she could not have foreseen the horrors of what such a project in the East would have meant in the twentieth century and beyond. Beer maintains that "the ending of the novel with its Zionist prospect reads very differently for us from the way it read to its first readers. To them it read like improbable dreams, to us as a dangerous reality" (1983: 234). Beer states the case with even more contextual precision, I think, in *Open Fields: Science in Cultural Encounter*: "To dismiss all Victorian writers as racist because they use vocabulary that offends us now, or because they all work within a developmental view of human history, has a further powerful disadvantage. It has the effect of absolving present-day readers and allowing us to feel enlightened. The rejection costs us no self-enquiry" (1996: 78). Levine also contends that Deronda "goes to Palestine not to establish the Jewish state but to inquire into its possibility. His relation to nationalism is 'reflective and dialogical' rather than visionary and essentialist (2001: 66).

Chapter 7

1. Ironically enough, Brown uses manual indices—of a hand holding a pen—to separate sections of this pioneering essay about "thingness" (2001).

2. As Clifford Siskin observes in *The Work of Writing*, "By 1830 the basic printing process, from papermaking to typesetting the press itself, are fully mechanized—a point reached by roughly 1830 after decades of largely British innovations that were followed, with the start of railroads during that same decade, by the mechanization of the distribution network" (1998: 11–12).

3. Like Tony Jackson, I take writing of any kind to be a historically specifiable technology that maintains as its ultimate goal the standardization of a system—be it copperplate, clerical, or italic—ideally meant to eliminate individual deviation (2009: 80). As Jacques Derrida puts it, "when we write 'by hand' we are not in a time before technology; there is already instrumentality, regular reproduction, mechanical iterability" (2005b: 20).

4. In the moments before Krook's "Spontaneous Combustion," Tony observes that the shopkeeper has been "spelling out words" in this way, "chalking them over the table and the shop-wall, and asking what this is, and what that is" for the "last quarter of a century" (515–16). This suggests that his "monomania" of mechanical letter copying finally reaches a point of white-hot friction that causes him to explode from within (515).

5. It is important to note that this identification of handwriting with individuality was not merely a British phenomenon. Georg Hegel, for instance, in his *Phenomenology of Spirit* (1807), has this to say about the relationship between handwriting and (inner) individuality: "Thus the simple lines of the hand, the timbre and compass of the voice as the individual characteristic of speech—this too again as expressed in writing, where

the hand gives it a more durable existence than the voice does, especially in the particular style of handwriting—all this is an expression of the inner, so that, as a *simple externality*, the expression again stands over and against the *manifold externality* of action and fate, stands in relation to them as an *inner*" (1977 [1807]: 189).

6. Putting pen to paper in order to produce a *manu*script would not change until authors gradually began to compose their work on typewriters at the very end of the nineteenth century.

7. Original readers of *Bleak House* received an advertising section made up of around fifteen pages of text and illustration that preceded each four-chapter, thirty-two-page monthly installment of the novel. My ideas on this topic have been informed by Daniel Hack's outstanding chapter on the subject in his book *The Material Interests of the Victorian Novel* (2005, chapter 2: "Reading Matter in *Bleak House* and the 'Bleak House Advertiser'").

8. I am cognizant of the fact that handwriting with any instrument—be it a natural quill or a metallic pen—is an inscription technology. As Walter Ong writes in *Orality and Literacy*, "[W]riting (especially alphabetic writing) is a technology, calling for the use of tools and other equipment: styli or brushes or pens, carefully prepared surfaces such as paper, animal skins, strips of wood, as well as inks or paint, and much more" (1982: 87). My concern in *Bleak House*, and in chapter 7 more generally, is with the hand's immediate connection to this technology and, hence, its individuality even within circumscribed systems of penmanship.

9. I am indebted to my colleague Priti Joshi (2011) for this insightful formulation.

Chapter 8

1. For a recent formulation of this idea, see Beth Palmer's *Women's Authorship* (2011: 50).

2. The wording, here, is Palmer's (2011: 52).

3. For a similar reading, see Eva Badowska (2009).

4. We encounter this tendency to overlook hands at the expense of faces even in the rhetoric of the novel's most influential historicist critics. Lyn Pykett, for example, in her foundational 1992 reading of the text, correctly identifies one of the major sources of narrative pleasure in the repeatedly postponed uncovering of Lady Audley's mysterious past (90–91). This uncovering, for Pykett, though, always takes place at the site of Lady Audley's face. Pykett's attention to "the construction of a narrative of unmasking" focuses almost exclusively on the viewing of Lady Audley's face in the famous scene where Robert Audley and George Talboys gain access to Lady Audley's unfinished portrait (91). This focus on Lady Audley's facial features works in direct connection with what Pykett refers to on five separate occasions as the text's "unmasking narrative" (91, 92, 103, 104, 113). Like the critical emphases traced in other chapters, Pykett's is far from alone in its focus on the face; many other influential Braddon critics, including Jenny Bourne Taylor,

Lynn Voskuil, and Louise Lee, follow suit. See Bourne Taylor's "Introduction" (1998: xxi–xxv), Voskuil (2001: 618), and Lee (2011: 135).

5. It is puzzling, though, how critics continue to read right past this dependence—especially when their interpretational rhetoric pinpoints the issue. Take, for instance, Louise Lee's recent formulation from Blackwell's *Companion to Sensation Fiction* (2011): "what makes the difference to Lady Audley's potentiality—what gives her a helping, or perhaps prosthetic, hand—is the mechanizing world of the 1860s" (138–39). As we have seen in every chapter of this study, Lee's purely metaphorical sense of Lady Audley's handedness is representative of a larger critical establishment that, by and large, seldom sees hands embodied in the ways the Victorians did.

6. The decision to have George's absence last three years is deliberate. The Divorce Act and Matrimonial Causes of 1857 stipulated two years as the official threshold for legal desertion. But, as Lillian Nayder has shown, the Indian Mutiny of 1857 was still fresh in the consciousness of many Victorians (2000: 32). This meant that "at the same time in which imperial rule was threatened in India, the sanctity of the marriage bond and its patriarchal privileges were challenged at home, as advocates of women's rights questioned the justice of English common law and the doctrine of *coverture*, which deprived women of property rights and legal identity upon marriage" (33).

7. For a more comprehensive discussion (but one that does not discuss hands) of Stevenson's use of weirdly unidiomatic expressions, unconventional verbal constructions and the skewing of words and phrases from their traditional usages, see Drury (2005).

8. I have been arguing throughout that in artistic renditions of characters ranging from *Bleak House* to *Daniel Deronda*, *Lady Audley's Secret* to *Jekyll and Hyde*, facial features often reveal far less than hands. It should be noted that portraiture from the early modern period onwards often revealed only the head and the hands of sitters. So, in effect, critics who fail to notice hands in portraiture do away with 50 percent of the interpretable body—a point that I elaborate on in my Introduction.

9. The line of narrative theorists on which Brooks is himself drawing includes Jean-Paul Sartre (*Nausea*, 1979), Frank Kermode (*The Sense of an Ending*, 1967), Roland Barthes (*S/Z*, 1974), and Gerard Genette (*Figures of Literary Discourse*, 1981).

10. Fingerprinting actually has more universal origins. The English civil servant Sir William Herschel in the 1840s and 1850s witnessed the natives of Bengal put their hands in clay and affix it to documents in a way that affirmed their intentions to make good on a proposed action.

Conclusion

1. *60 Minutes* aired an alarmist segment called the "March of Machines" on January 13, 2013. It was rebroadcast on September 8, 2013. The segment became the subject of *New York Times'* economics reporter Catherine Rampell's piece entitled "Raging (Again) Against the Robots" (February 2, 2013). A more specifically manual example

is John Markoff's reporting for the Science section of the *New York Times* in an article entitled "Making Robots Mimic Human Hands" (March 29, 2013). The article reports on the Pentagon's efforts to produce human-like prosthetics capable of changing an automobile tire.

2. It is worth pointing out that, in terms of prosthetic limb replacement, the hand is the last frontier. Humans without legs can now compete in the Olympics (Oscar Pistorius) and yet a fully functional hand is still not a reality. It should be noted, too, that this is not the case for lack of money or research. It is an issue of anatomical complexity. Researchers and engineers are confident that a fully functional mechanical hand will be developed by the end of the twenty-first century, however. An inventor cited in the *Smithsonian* article makes this claim. Just below it (the claim) is an image of a mechanical hand holding a single dice between its forefinger and thumb.

3. See National Public Radio's coverage of this controversy in their All Tech Considered segment. The story by Ashley Milne-Tyne, called "Etsy's New Policy Means Some Items Are 'Handmade in Spirit'" aired on October 29, 2013.

4. In *Michelangelo's Finger* (2010), Raymond Tallis has recently explored the role of pointing in relation to prelinguistic and linguistic states of humanity.

5. For a more detailed discussion of the hand in relation to electronic reading practices, see Piper 2012, especially chapter 3, entitled "Turning the Page (Roaming, Zooming, Streaming)."

6. I am thinking in particular of Matthew McIntyre and Peter Ellison's lab at Harvard. They, along with three other authors, recently published a study (2005) entitled "The Development of Sex Difference in Digital Formula from Infancy in the Fels Longitudinal Study."

7. In "Reading Your Palm, for Security's Sake," Anne Eisenberg reports on how new computers such as Fujitsu's Celsius H730 can be ordered with a palm vein sensor called Palm Secure (*New York Times*, December 28, 2013).

8. My definition of the posthuman comes from the historical sense of a distributed cognition outlined by N. Katherine Hayles in *How We Became Posthuman* (1999).

9. I acknowledge the leap of privilege I am making by discussing these issues from the perspective of a developed nation with a fully functioning cybernetic infrastructure. As Hayles shrewdly points out in 1999, "we are still talking about a world in which 70 percent of the population has never made a phone call" (20).

10 This point is only reinforced by the word's etymological meaning in French, from *main* (hand) and *tenir* (hold). Therefore, to maintain something is etymologically equivalent to holding it with the hand.

Bibliography

Adams, James Eli. 1995. *Dandies and Desert Saints*. Ithaca: Cornell University Press.

Adams, James Eli. 2005. "'The Boundaries of Social Intercourse': Class and the Victorian Novel," in *A Concise Companion to the Victorian Novel*, edited by Francis O'Gorman, 47–70. Oxford: Blackwell.

Akroyd, Peter. 1990. *Dickens*. New York: Harper Collins.

Alexander, Lynn M. 2003. *Women, Work, and Representation: Needlewomen in Victorian Art and Literature*. Athens: Ohio University Press.

Alexander, Sally. 1977. "Women's Work in Nineteenth-Century London: A Study of the Years 1820–1850." In *The Rights and Wrongs of Women*, edited by Juliette Mitchell and Ann Oakley, 59–111. New York: Penguin.

Altman, Janet. 1982. *Epistolarity: Approaches to a Form*. Columbus: Ohio State University Press.

Anderson, Amanda. 1997. "George Eliot and the Jewish Question." *Yale Journal of Criticism* 10 (1): 39–61.

Anderson, Amanda. 2001. *The Powers of Distance: Cosmopolitanism and the Cultivation of Detachment*. Princeton: Princeton University Press.

Anonymous. 1822. *Monthly Magazine* 53: 524–44. Microfilm.

Anonymous. 1848. *The Hand Phrenologically Considered*. London: Chapman and Hall.

Anonymous. 1859. *Habits of Good Society: A Handbook for Ladies and Gentlemen*. London: Carelton.

Anonymous. 1861. *Etiquette for All, Or Rule of Conduct*. Glasgow: George Watson.

Apple. 2013. iPhone 5 Advertisement. *The New Yorker*. December 2.

Aristotle. 1986 [350 BC]. *De Anima*. Edited by Hugh Lawson-Tancred. New York: Penguin.

Armstrong, Nancy. 1987. *Desire and Domestic Fiction*. Oxford: Oxford University Press.

"A Sketch of Character by Prof Milkansop, the Celebrated Graphiologist." 1850. *Punch* October 12. 154+.

Austen, Jane. 2003 [1817]. *Persuasion*. New York: Penguin.

Babbage, Charles. 1833. *Economy of Machinery and Manufactures*. London: Charles Knight.

Badowska, Eva. 2009. "On the Track of Things: Sensation and Modernity in Mary Elizabeth Braddon's *Lady Audley's Secret*." *Victorian Literature and Culture* 37, no. 1 (March): 157–75.

Bailey, Brian. 1998. *The Luddite Rebellion*. New York: New York University Press.

Baker, William. 1973. "The Kabbalah, Mordecai, and George Eliot's Religion of Humanity." *Yearbook of English Studies* 3: 216–21.

Baker, William. 1975. *George Eliot and Judaism*. Salzburg: University of Salzburg Press.

Bakhtin, Mikhail. 1981. *The Didactic Imagination: Four Essays*. Edited by Michael Holquist. Translated by Caryl Emerson and Michael Holquist. Austin: University of Texas Press.

Baldick, Chris. 1990. *In Frankenstein's Shadow: Myth, Monstrosity, and Nineteenth-century Writing*. Oxford: Clarendon Press.

Bannet, Eve Tavor. 2005. *Empire of Letters*. Cambridge: Cambridge University Press.

Banister, John. 1578. *Historie of Man*. London: Da Capo Press.

Barickman, Richard, Susan MacDonald, and Myra Stark. 1982. *Corrupt Relations*. New York: Columbia University Press.

Barker, Christopher. 1546. *Grant of Arms of the Royal College of Physicians*. Oil on canvas.

Barthes, Roland. 1974. *S/Z*. Translated by Richard Miller. New York: Hill and Wang.

Bartrip, P. W. J., and S. B. Burman. 1983. *The Wounded Soldiers of Industry: Industrial Compensation Policy 1833–1897*. Oxford: Clarendon Press.

Bate, Jonathan. 2000. *The Song of the Earth*. Cambridge, MA: Harvard University Press.

Baumgarten, Murray. 1960. *From Shylock to Svengali: Jewish Stereotypes in English Fiction*. Stanford: Stanford University Press.

Beamish, Richard. 1865 [1843]. *Psychonomy of the Hand*. London: Pitman.

Beer, Gillian. 1983. *Darwin's Plots*. London: Routledge.

Beer, Gillian. 1996. *Open Fields: Science in Cultural Encounter*. Oxford: Clarendon.

Beeton, Isabella. 1861. *The Book of Household Management*. London: S. O. Beeton.

Behrendt, Stephen. 2013. Written comments from a chapter draft. April.

Beinecke, Edwin J. 1940. *Robert Louis Stevenson's Handwriting*. New York: Private Printing.

Bell, Charles. 1832. Testimony from Select Committee on the "Bill to Regulate the Labour of Children in the Mills and Factories of the United Kingdom." August 7. *Parliamentary Papers* (1831–32 XV), Report. 604–5. Microfiche.

Bell, Charles. 1806. *Essays on the Anatomy of Expressions in Painting*. London: Longman.

Bell, Charles. 1821. *On Nerves*. Paper delivered to the Royal Society of London.

Bell, Charles. 1833. *The Hand: Its Mechanism and Endowments as Evincing Design*. London: Pickering and Chatto.

Bell, Charles. 2009 [1833]. *The Hand: Its Mechanism and Endowments as Evincing Design*. Cambridge: Cambridge Library Collections.

Berg, Maxine. 1980. *The Machinery Question and the Making of Political Economy 1815–1848*. Cambridge: Cambridge University Press.

Berg, Maxine. 1994. *The Age of Manufactures: Industry, Innovation, and Work in Britain, 1700–1820*. 2nd ed. New York, Routledge.

Bernstein, Susan David. 2001. "Ape Anxiety: Sensation Fiction, Evolution, and the Genre Question." *Journal of Victorian Culture* 6, no. 2 (Autumn): 250–71.

Best, Stephen, and Sharon Marcus. 2009. "Surface Reading: An Introduction." *Representations* 108(1): 1–21.

Bizup, Joseph. 2003. *Manufacturing Culture*. Charlottesville: University of Virginia Press.

Bodenheimer, Rosemarie. 1988. *The Politics of Story in Victorian Social Fiction*. Ithaca: Cornell University Press.

Bodichon, Barbara Leigh Smith. 1854. *A Brief Summary, In Plain Language, of the Most Important Laws Concerning Women*. London: Chapman.

Bourdieu, Pierre. 1984. *Distinction*. Cambridge, MA: Harvard University Press.

Bourdieu, Pierre. 1990. *The Logic of Practice*. Oxford: Blackwell.

Boyarin, Daniel. 1990. "The Eye in the Torah: Ocular Desire in Midrashic Hermeneutic." *Critical Inquiry* 16 (Spring): 532–50.

Braddon, Mary Elizabeth. 1998 [1862]. *Lady Audley's Secret*. New York: Penguin.

Brantlinger, Patrick. 1969. "The Case against Trade Unions in Early Victorian Factory Fiction." *Victorian Studies* 13, no. 1 (September): 37–52.

Brantlinger, Patrick. 1979. *The Spirit of Reform*. Cambridge, MA: Harvard University Press.

Brantlinger, Patrick. 2011. *Taming Cannibals: Race and the Victorians*. Ithaca: Cornell University Press.

Briggs, Asa. 1988. *Victorian Things*. London: Batsford.

Brink-Roby, Heather. 2013. "Psyche: Mirror and Mind in *Vanity Fair*." *ELH* 80: 125–47.

Bronstein, Jamie L. 2007. *Caught in the Machinery*. Stanford: Stanford University Press.

Brontë, Charlotte. 1985 [1849]. *Shirley*. Edited by Andrew Hook and Judith Hook. New York: Penguin.

Brontë, Charlotte. 1995. *The Letters of Charlotte Brontë: With a Selection of Letters by Family and Friends*. Vols. 1 and 2. Edited by Margaret Smith. Oxford: Clarendon.

Brooke, John Hedley. 1991. *Science and Religion*. Cambridge: Cambridge University Press.

Brooks, Peter. 1984. *Reading for the Plot*. New York: Knopf.

Brooks, Peter. 1993. *Body Work: Objects of Desire in Modern Narrative*. Cambridge, MA: Harvard University Press.

Brooks, Peter. 2011. *Enigmas of Identity*. Princeton: Princeton University Press.

Brooks-Davies, Douglas. 1989. *Great Expectations*. London: Penguin Critical Studies.

Brown, Bill. 1996. *The Material Unconscious*. Cambridge, MA: Harvard University Press.

Brown, Bill. 2001. "Thing Theory." *Representations* 28, no. 1 (Autumn): 1–22.

Brown, Bill. 2003. *A Sense of Things*. Chicago: University of Chicago Press.

Brown, Carolyn. 1987. "*Great Expectations*: Masculinity and Modernity," in *Broadening the Cultural Context*, edited by Michael Green, 60–74. London: Murray.

Brown, John. 1832. *A Memoir of Robert Blincoe*. London: Doherty.

Brown, John. 1977. *A Memoir of Robert Blincoe*. Firle: Caliban Books.

Brown, Laura. 2011. *Homeless Dogs & Melancholy Apes*. Ithaca: Cornell University Press.

Browning, Elizabeth Barrett. 1843. "The Cry of the Children." *Blackwood's Edinburgh Magazine* 54 (334): 260–62.

Buckley, Jerome. 1974. *A Season of Youth*. Cambridge, MA: Harvard University Press.

Buffon, Georges Louis Leclerc, Comte de. 1780. *Natural History*. Edinburgh: William Creech. (*Eighteenth-Century Collections Online. Gale*. University of Nebraska–Lincoln. Last accessed September 9, 2014.)

Burney, Frances. 2002 [1778]. *Evelina*. Oxford: Oxford University Press.

Butler, Judith. 1990. *Gender Trouble*. New York: Routledge.

Butler, Marilyn. 1993. "*Frankenstein* and Radical Science." In *Frankenstein*, edited by J. Paul Hunter, 302–13. New York: Norton.

Buzard, James. 2005. *Disorienting Fiction: The Autoethnographic Work of Nineteenth- Century Novels*. Princeton: Princeton University Press.

Byerley, Thomas. (Pseud: Stephen Collet). 1823. *Relics of Literature*. London: Thomas Boys.

Bythell, Duncan. 1969. *The Handloom Weavers*. Cambridge: Cambridge University Press.

Calder, Angus. 1965. "Introduction." *Great Expectations*. Middlesex: Penguin.

Caldwell, Janice McLarren. 2004. *Literature and Medicine in Nineteenth-Century Britain*. New York: Cambridge University Press.

Cancer Ends with Me. n.d. Leukemia & Lymphoma Society. Bulletin.

Cantor, Paul A. 1984. *Creature and Creator: Myth-making and English Romanticism*. Cambridge: Cambridge University Press.

Carlisle, Janice. 2004. *Common Scents: Comparative Encounters in High-Victorian Fiction*. Oxford: Oxford University Press.

Carlyle, Thomas. 1840. *Chartism*. London: Fraser.

Carlyle, Thomas. 1899 [1829]. "Signs of the Times." *The Works of Thomas Carlyle*. Vol. XXVII, 56–82. London: Chapman and Hall.

Carlyle, Thomas. 1960 [1843]. *Past and Present*. London: Oxford University Press.

Carstairs, Joseph. 1816. *Lectures on the Art of Writing*. 3rd ed. London: Molineux.

Castle, Terry. 1982. *Clarissa's Ciphers*. Ithaca: Cornell University Press.

Catalogue of the Library of Charles Dickens from Gadshill. 1935. Edited by John. H. Stonehouse. London: Picadilly Fountain.

Cawthon, Elisabeth A. 1997. *Job Accidents and the Law in England's Early Railway Age*. Studies in British History Vol. 43. Lewiston: Edwin Mellen Press.

Chadwick, Edwin. 1965 [1842]. *Report on the Sanitary Condition of the Labouring Population of Great Britain*. Edited by M. W. Finn. Edinburgh: Edinburgh UP.

Chambers, Robert. 1994 [1844]. *Vestiges of the Natural History of Creation and Other Evolutionary Writings*, edited by James A. Secord. Chicago: University of Chicago Press.

Chase, Cynthia. 1978. "The Decomposition of Elephants: Double-Reading in *Daniel Deronda*." *PMLA* 93(2): 215–27.

Chase, Karen, and Michael Levenson. 2000. *The Spectacle of Intimacy: A Public Life for the Victorian Family*. Princeton: Princeton University Press.

Cheyette, Bryan. 1993. *Constructions of 'the Jew' in English Literature and Society: Radical Representations, 1875–1945*. Cambridge: Cambridge University Press.

Christ, Carol. 1977. "Victorian Masculinity and the Angel of the House." In *A Widening Sphere*, edited by Martha Vicinus, 146–62. Bloomington: Indiana University Press.

Christ, Carol T., and John O. Jordan, eds. 1995. *Victorian Literature and the Victorian Visual Imagination*. Berkeley: University of California Press.

Claggett, Shalyn. 2011. "George Eliot's Interrogation of Physiological Future Knowledge." *SEL* 51, no. 4 (Autumn): 849–64.

Clarke, Micael M. 1995. *Thackeray and Women*. DeKalb: Northern Illinois University Press.

Classen, Constance. 2012. *The Deepest Sense: A Cultural History of Touch*. Urbana: University of Illinois Press.

Clayton, Jay. 1996. "Concealed Circuits: Frankenstein's Monster, the Medusa, and the Cyborg." *Raritan* 15, no. 4 (Spring): 53–69.

Clayton, Jay. 2003. *Charles Dickens in Cyberspace: The Afterlife of the Nineteenth Century in Postmodern Culture*. Oxford: Oxford University Press.

C. M. C. 1838. "Private Correspondence." *Times*, March 24: 2. *The Times Digital Archive, 1785–2008*. Web. October 7, 2014.

Cohen, Margaret. 2009. "Narratology in the Archive of Literature." *Representations* 108, no. 1 (Fall): 51–75.

Cohen, William A. 1993. "Manual Conduct in *Great Expectations*." *ELH* 60: 217–59.

Cohen, William A. 1996. *Sex Scandal*. Durham: Duke University Press.

Cohen, William A. 2008. *Embodied: Victorian Literature and the Senses*. Minneapolis: University of Minnesota Press.

Cole, Sarah Rose. 2005. "The Aristocrat in the Mirror: Male Vanity and Bourgeois Desire in William Makepeace Thackeray's *Vanity Fair.*" *Nineteenth-Century Literature* 61, no. 2: 137–69.

Corbett, Mary Jean. 2008. *Family Likeness: Sex, Marriage, and Incest from Jane Austen to Virginia Woolf*. Ithaca: Cornell University Press.

"Coroner's Inquest." 1830. *The Times* October 12: 3. *The Times* Digital Archive. Infotrac. Web.

Courtemanche, Eleanor. 2011. *The 'Invisible Hand' in British Fiction, 1818–1860*. New York: Palgrave Macmillan.

Cowling, 1989. *The Artist as Anthropologist: The Representation of Type and Character in Victorian Art*. Cambridge: Cambridge University Press.

Craft, Chistopher. 1992. *Another Kind of Love*. Berkeley: University of California Press.

Crary, Jonathan. 1992. *Techniques of the Observer: On Vision and Modernity in the Nineteenth Century*. Cambridge, MA: MIT Press.

Crook, Nora. 2013. Electronic Mail Message (forwarded by Charles Robinson). January 21.

Crook, Nora, and Derek Guiton. 1986. *Shelley's Venomed Melody*. Cambridge: Cambridge University Press.

Crouzet, Francois. 1982. *The Victorian Economy*. Translated by Anthony Foster. New York: Columbia University Press.

Curtin, Michael. 1987. *Propriety and Position: A Study of Victorian Manners*. New York: Garland.

Curtis, L. Perry. 1979. *Apes and Angels: The Irishman in Victorian Cariacture*. Washington: Smithsonian Inst. Press.

Dallas, E. S. 1862. "Lady Audley's Secret." *Times*, November 18: 4+.

Daly, Nicholas. 2004. *Literature, Technology, and Modernity, 1860–2000*. New York: Cambridge University Press.

Dao, James. 2012. "Learning to Accept, and Master, a $110,000 Mechanical Arm." *New York Times*, November 27: A1.

Darwin, Charles. 1898 [1868]. *The Variation of Animals and Plants under Domestication*. Vol. 2. New York: Appleton.

Darwin, Charles. 1996 [1859]. *On the Origin of Species*. Edited by Gillian Beer. London: Oxford.

Darwin, Charles. 2004 [1871]. *The Descent of Man*. New York: Penguin.

Darwin, Erasmus. 1804 [1803]. *The Temple of Nature*. Baltimore: Bonsal & Noles.

Datson, Lorraine. 2004. "Attention and the Values of Nature in the Enlightenment." In *The Moral Authority of Nature*, edited by Lorraine Datson and Fernando Vidal. Chicago: University of Chicago Press. 100–126.

Datson, Lorraine, and Peter Galison. 1992. "The Image of Objectivity." *Representations* 40, no. 4 (Fall): 81–128.

Davidoff, Leonore. 1979. "Class and Gender in Victorian England: The Diaries of Arthur J. Munby and Hannah Culliwick." *Feminist Studies* (5): 86–141.

Davidoff, Leonore, and Catherine Hall. 1987. *Family Fortunes: Men and Women of the English Middle Class 1780–1850*. Chicago: University of Chicago Press.

Davy, Humphry. 1839 [1802]. *Discourse, Introductory to a Course of Lectures on Chemistry*. London: Smith, Elder, and Company.

Day, Charles William. 1844. *Hints on Etiquette and the Usages of Society*. Boston: Otis, Broader and Company.

Deane, Bradley. 2003. *The Making of the Victorian Novelist*. New York: Routledge.

Deane, Phyllis. 1965. *The First Industrial Revolution*. Cambridge: Cambridge University Press.

De Bondt, Jakob. 1769 [1642]. *An Account of the Diseases, Natural History, and Medicines of the East Indies*. London: T. Noteman. *Eighteenth-Century Collections Online*. Gale. University of Nebraska-Lincoln. September 9, 2014.

Defoe, Daniel. 2008 [1719]. *Robinson Crusoe*. Edited by Thomas Keymer. Oxford: Oxford University Press.

Dekel, Mikhal. 2010. "Novel, Nation, and the Jews: The End of Realism in *Daniel Deronda*." In *Realism's Others*, edited by Geoffrey Baker and Eva Aldea, 27–47. Newcastle upon Tyne: Cambridge Scholars Publishing.

Deleuze, Gilles and Felix Guattari. 2004 [1980]. *A Thousand Plateaus*. London: Continuum.

Deleuze, Gilles. 2005. *Cinema 1: The Movement Image*. Translated by Hugh Tomlinson and Barbara Habberjam. London: Continuum.

Derrida, Jacques. 2005a. *On Touching—Jean-Luc Nancy*. Translated by Christine Irizarry. Stanford: Stanford University Press.

Derrida, Jacques. 2005b. *Paper Machine*. Translated by Rachel Bowlby. Stanford: Stanford University Press.

Derrida, Jacques. 2007. "Heidegger's Hand (Geschlecht II)," translated by John P. Leavey, Jr. In *Psyche: Inventions of the Other, Vol. II*, edited by Peggy Kamuf and Elizabeth Rottenberg. Stanford: Stanford University Press.

Desmond, Adrian. 1989. *The Politics of Evolution: Morphology, Medicine, and Reform in Radical London*. Chicago: University of Chicago Press.

DiBattista, Maria. 1980. "The Triumph of Clytemnestra: The Charades in *Vanity Fair.*" *PMLA* 95 (October): 827–37.

Dickens, Charles. 1843. *Martin Chuzzlewit*.

Dickens, Charles. 1859. "Our Nearest Relation." *All the Year Round*, May 28, 112–15.

Dickens, Charles. 1960. *The Speeches of Charles Dickens*. Edited by K. J. Fielding. Speech to the Conversazione of the Polytechnic Institution, Birmingham (February 28, 1844). Oxford: Clarendon Press.

Dickens, Charles. 1981 [1849–50]. *David Copperfield*. London: Oxford.

Dickens, Charles. 1999 [1860–61].*Great Expectations*. Edited by Edgar Rosenberg. New York: Norton.

Dickens, Charles. 2001 [1854]. *Hard Times*. Edited by Fred Kaplan and Sylvere Monod. 3rd Edition. New York: Norton.

Dickens, Charles. 2003 [1853–54]. *Bleak House*. Edited by Nicola Bradbury. New York: Penguin.

Dilnot, A. F. 1975. "The Case of Mr. Jaggers." *Essays in Criticism* 25: 437–43.

Disraeli, Benjamin. 1948 [1844]. *Coningsby*. London: J. Lehmann.

Disraeli, Isaac. 1834 [1824]. *Curiosities of Literature*. London: Edward Moxon.

Dodd, William. 1968 [1841]. *A Narrative of the Experiences and Sufferings of William Dodd, A Factory Cripple*. In *The Factory System Illustrated*, 267–319. New York: Augustus M. Kelley.

Dodds, Kiernan. n.d. *Robot Sistine Chapel*. Photograph.

Dooley, Allan C. 1992. *Author and Printer in Victorian England*. Charlottesville: University of Virginia Press.

D'Oyly, George. 1820. [Review of Eight Works on the Vitalist Issue]. *Quarterly Review* 22: 1-34.

Drury, Richard. 2005. "Strange Language of Dr Jekyll and Mr Hyde." *Journal of Stevenson Studies* 2: 33–50.

Du Chaillu, Paul. 1861. *Explorations & Adventures in Equatorial Africa*. London: John Murray.

Duncan, Ian. 2008. "Sympathy, Physiognomy, and Scottish Romantic Fiction." In *Recognizing the Romantic Novel*, edited by Jillian Heydt-Stevenson and Charlotte Sussman, 285–305. Liverpool: Liverpool University Press.

Duncan, Ian. 2010. "Stevenson and Fiction." In *The Edinburgh Companion to Robert Louis Stevenson*, edited by Penny Fielding, 11–26. Edinburgh: Edinburgh University Press.

Duncan, Ian. 2014. "George Eliot's Science Fiction." *Representations* 125, no. 1 (Winter): 15–39.

Eagleton, Terry. 1995. *Heathcliff and the Great Hunger*. London: Verso.

Eagleton, Terry. 2005 [1975]. *Myths of Power: A Marxist Study of the Brontës*. 3rd ed. Houndsmills: Palgrave Macmillan.

Eastlake, Charles. 1878. *Hints on Household Taste*. Boston: Osgood & Co.

Edelstein, T. J. 1980. "They Sang 'The Song of the Shirt': The Visual Iconology of the Seamstress." *Victorian Studies* 23 (2): 183–210.

Eilberg-Schwartz, Howard. 1995. "God's Body: The Divine Cover-Up." In *Religious Reflections on the Human Body*, edited by Jane Marie Law, 137–48. Bloomington: Indiana University Press.

Eisenberg, Anne. 2013. "Reading Your Palm for Security's Sake." *New York Times*, December 28. Web.

Eliot, George. 1913 [1862–63]. *Romola*. Oxford: Oxford University Press.

Eliot, George. 1954. *The George Eliot Letters*. Edited by Gordon Haight. New Haven: Yale University Press.

Eliot, George. 1984 [1876]. *Daniel Deronda*. Oxford: Oxford World's Classics.

Eliot, George. 1992 [1856]. "The Natural History of German Life." In *Selected Critical Writings*, edited by Rosemary Ashton. Oxford: Oxford World's Classics.

Eliot, George. 1994 [1879]. "The Modern Hep! Hep! Hep!" In *Impressions of Theophrastus Such*, edited by Nancy Henry. Iowa City: University of Iowa Press.

Eliot, George. 1994 [1871–72]. *Middlemarch*. New York: Penguin.

Eliot, George. 1996. *George Eliot's* Daniel Deronda *Notebooks*. Edited by Jane Irwin. Cambridge: Cambridge University Press.

Eliot, George. 2008 [1868]. *The Spanish Gypsy*. Edited by Antonie Gerard van den Broek. London: Pickering and Chatto.

Ellis, Sarah Stickney. 1839. *The Women of England*. New York: Appleton.

Ellis, Sarah Stickney. 1842. *The Daughters of England, Their Position in Society, Character and Responsibilities*. London: Peter Jackson.

Ellis, Sarah Stickney. 1843a. *The Mothers of England*. London: Fisher.

Ellis, Sarah Stickney. 1843b. *The Wives of England*. New York: Appleton.

Engels, Friedrich. 1968 [1876]. "The Part Played by Labour in the Transition from Ape to Man." In *Karl Marx and Frederick Engels, Selected Works*. Moscow: Progress.

Engels, Friedrich. 1993 [1845]. *The Condition of the Working Class in England*. Edited by David McLellan. Oxford: Oxford University Press.

Epstein, Josh. 2008. "'Neutral Physiognomy': The Unreadable Faces of *Mid-dlemarch*." *Victorian Literature and Culture* 36(1): 131–48.

Evelyn, John. 1697. *Numismata*. London: Benjamin Tooke.

Fahnestock, Jeanne. 1981. "The Heroine of Irregular Features: Physiognomy and Conventions of Heroine Description." *Victorian Studies* 24, no. 3 (Spring): 325–50.

Felski, Rita. 2009. "After Suspicion." *Profession* 2009. New York: MLA. 28–35.

Felski, Rita. 2011. "'Context Stinks.'" *New Literary History* 42, no. 4 (Autumn): 573–91.

Feltes, N. N. 1986. *Modes of Production of Victorian Novels*. Chicago: University of Chicago Press.

Fielding, Henry. 1837 [1751]. *Amelia*. New York: Harper.

Fielding, Henry. 1973 [1749]. *Tom Jones*. Edited by Sheridan Baker. New York: Norton.

Firth, Henry. 1886. *A Guide to the Study of Graphology*. London: George Routledge.

Fisher, Benjamin F. 1999. "Poe in Great Britain." In *Poe Abroad: Influence, Reputation, Affinities*, edited by Lois Davis Vines. Iowa City: University of Iowa Press.

Fisher, Judith Law. 2002. *Thackeray's Skeptical Narrative and the 'Perilous Trade' of Authorship*. Burlington: Ashgate.

Flint, Kate. 1995. *The Woman Reader, 1837–1914*. Oxford: Oxford University Press.

Flint, Kate. 1996. "Women, Men and the Reading of *Vanity Fair*." In *The Practice and Representation of Reading in England*, edited by James Raven, Helen Small, and Naomi Tadmor, 246–62. Cambridge: Cambridge University Press.

Flint, Kate. 2008. *Victorians and the Visual Imagination*. Cambridge: Cambridge University Press.

Flusser, Vilem. 2014. *Gestures*. Translated by Nancy Ann Roth. Minneapolis: University of Minnesota Press.

Forker, Charles R. 1961–62. "The Language of Hands in *Great Expectations*." *Texas Studies in Literature and Language* 3: 280–93.

Foster, B. F. 1843. *Practical Penmanship*. Albany: O. Steele.

Foucault, Michel. 1978. *The History of Sexuality: Volume I*. Translated by Robert Hurley. New York: Pantheon.

Freedgood, Elaine. 2003. "'Fine Fingers': Victorian Handmade Lace and Utopian Consumption." *Victorian Studies* 45, no. 4 (Summer): 625–47.

Freedgood, Elaine. 2006. *The Ideas in Things: Fugitive Meaning in the Victorian Novel*. Chicago: University of Chicago Press.

French, A. L. 1974. "Beating and Cringing: *Great Expectations*" Essays in *Criticism* 147–68.

Gallagher, Catherine. 1985. *The Industrial Reformation of English Fiction: Social Discourse and Narrative Form 1832–1867*. Chicago: University of Chicago Press. Print.

Gallagher, Catherine. 2005. "George Eliot: Immanent Victorian." *Representations* 90(1): 61–74.

Gallagher, Catherine. 2008. *The Body Economic*. Princeton: Princeton University Press.

Gargano, Elizabeth. 2009. "Utopian Voyeurism: Androgyny and the Language of the Eyes in Haywood's *Love in Excess*." *Eighteenth-Century Fiction* 21, no. 4 (Summer): 513–34.

Gaskell, Mary. 1997 [1848]. *Mary Barton*. Edited by MacDonald Daly. New York: Penguin.

Gaskell, Mary. 1996 [1855]. *North and South*. New York: Penguin.

Gaskell, Peter. 1833. *The Manufacturing Population of England*. London: Baldwin and Cradock.

Gaskell, Philip. 1995. *A New Introduction to Bibliography*. New Castle: Oak Knoll Press.

Gaujot, G. 1867. *Arsenal de la Chirurgie Contemporaine*. Paris: Bailliere.

Genette, Gerard. 1981. *Figures of Literary Discourse*. Translated by Alan Sheridan. New York: Columbia University Press.

Gezari, Janet. 1992. *Charlotte Brontë and Defensive Conduct: The Author and the Body at Risk*. Philadelphia: University of Pennsylvania Press.

Gigante, Denise. 2000. "Facing the Ugly: The Case of *Frankenstein*." *ELH* 67, no. 2 (Summer): 565–87.

Gilbert, Pamela K. 1997. *Disease, Desire, and the Body in Victorian Women's Popular Novels*. Cambridge: Cambridge University Press.

Gilbert, Pamela K. 2014. "The Will to Touch: David Copperfield's Hand." *19: Interdisciplinary Studies in the Long Nineteenth Century* 19: 1-15.

Gilbert, Pamela K., Marlene Tromp, and Aeron Haynie. 2000. *Beyond Sensation: Mary Elizabeth Braddon in Context*. Albany: State University of New York Press.

Gilbert, Sandra, and Susan Gubar. 2000. *The Madwoman in the Attic*. 2nd ed. New Haven: Yale University Press.

Gilman, Sander. 1991. *The Jew's Body*. New York: Routledge.

Gilmour, Robin. 1981. *The Idea of the Gentleman in the Victorian Novel*. London: Allen & Unwin.

Ginsburg, Christian D. 1863. *The Kabbalah: Its Doctrines, Development, and Literature*. London: Longman.

Goldberg, Jonathan. 1990. *Writing Matter*. Stanford: Stanford University Press.

Golden, Catherine J. 2009. *Posting It: The Victorian Revolution in Letter Writing*. Gainesville: University of Florida Press.

Goldhill, Simon. 2012. "A Writer's Things: Edward Bulwer Lytton and the Archaeological Gaze; or, What's in a Skull?" *Representations* 119, no. 1 (Summer): 92–118.

Gould, Steven Jay. 1977. *Ever Since Darwin: Reflections in Natural History*. New York: Norton.

Graetz, Heinrich. 1949 [1863–75]. *History of the Jews*. Translated by Bella Lowy. Philadelphia: Jewish Publication Society of America.

Gray, Robert. 1996. *The Factory Question and Industrial England, 1830–1860*. Cambridge: Cambridge University Press.

Gross, Kenneth. 2011. *Puppet: An Essay on Uncanny Life*. Chicago: University of Chicago Press.

Grosz, Elizabeth. 1994. *Volatile Bodies: Toward a Corporeal Feminism*. Bloomington, Indiana University Press.

Hack, Daniel. 2005. *The Material Interests of the Victorian Novel*. Charlottesville: University of Virginia Press.

Halberstam, Judith. 1995. *Skin Shows*. Durham: Duke University Press.

Halberstam, Judith. 1998. *Female Masculinity*. Durham: Duke University Press.

"Handwriting and Character." 1849. *Punch*, December 15. 231+.

"Handy Phrenology." 1848. *Punch*, September 9. 104+.

Hankins, Thomas L. 1985. *Science and the Enlightenment*. Cambridge: Cambridge University Press.

Haraway, Donna. 1989. *Primate Visions: Gender, Race, and Nature in the World of Modern Science*. New York: Routledge.

Harris, Joseph. 2013. "Teaching 'By Hand' in a Digital Age." *The Chronicle Review*, March 29, B2+.

Harsh, Constance. 1994. *Subversive Heroines: Feminist Resolutions of Social Crisis in the Condition-of-England Novel*. Ann Arbor: University of Michigan Press.

Hartley, Jenny. 2012. *The Selected Letters of Charles Dickens*, ed. Jenny Hartley. Oxford: Oxford University Press.

Hartley, Lucy. 2006. *Physiognomy and the Meaning of Expression in Nineteenth-Century Culture*. Cambridge: Cambridge University Press.

Hartman, Geoffrey. 2011. *The Third Pillar: Essays in Judaic Studies*. Philadelphia: University of Pennsylvania Press.

Harvey, John R. 1970. *Victorian Novelists and Their Illustrators*. New York: New York University Press.

Hayles, N. Katherine. 1999. *How We Became Posthuman: Virtual Bodies in Cybernetics, Literature, and Informatics*. Chicago: University of Chicago Press.

Hayles, N. Katherine. 2002. *Writing Machines*. Cambridge, MA: MIT Press.

Haywood, Eliza. 2000. *Love in Excess*. Edited by David Oakleaf. Peterborough: Broadview.

Haywood, Eliza. 2004 [1725]. *Fantomina and Other Works*. Edited by Alexander Pettit, Margaret Case Croskery, Anna C. Patchias. Peterborough: Broadview.

Hector, L. C. 1958. *The Handwriting of English Documents*. London: Edward Arnold.

Hegel, Georg W. F. 1977 [1807]. *Phenomenology of Spirit*. Translated by A. V. Miller. Oxford: Clarendon.

Heidegger, Martin. 1968. *What Is Called Thinking?* Translated by Fred D. Wieck and J. Glenn Gray. New York: Harper & Row.

Hensher, Philip. 2012. *The Missing Ink: The Lost Art of Handwriting*. New York: Faber.

Hertz, Neil. 2003. *George Eliot's Pulse*. Stanford: Stanford University Press.

Hockey, Susan. *Electronic Texts in the Humanities*. Oxford: Oxford University Press, 2000.

Hocquart, Edouard August. 1816. *The Art of Judging the Mind and Character of Men and Women from their Handwriting*. Paris: Saintin.

Hogarth, William. 1753. *The Analysis of Beauty*. London: Reeves.

Hogsette, David S. 2011. "Metaphysical Intersections in *Frankenstein*: Mary Shelley's Theistic Investigation of Scientific Materialism and Transgressive Autonomy." *Christianity and Literature* 60, no. 4 (Summer): 531–59.

Holmes, Colin, ed. 1978. *Immigrants and Minorities in British Society*. London: Allen & Unwin.

Holmes, Martha Stoddard. 2004. *Fictions of Affliction: Physical Disability in Victorian Culture*. Ann Arbor: University of Michigan Press.

Hood, Thomas. 2006 [1843]. "The Song of the Shirt." In *The Broadview Anthology of English Literature*, edited by Joseph Black et al. Vol. 5, 57–58. Peterborough: Broadview.

Horne, Richard H. 1850. "Mr. Van Ploos on Penmanship." *Household Words*. 2, no. 28 (May): 38-42.

Horowitz, Shabbetai. 1612. *Shefa Tal*. Hanau: Hanoviah.

Hudson, Derek. 1972. *Munby, Man of Two Worlds: The Life and Diaries of Arthur J. Munby 1828–1910*. London: Murray.

Hudson, Pat. 1986. *The Genesis of Industrial Capital: A Study of the West Riding Wool Textile Industry c. 1750-1850 (See p 266 fn #7)*. Cambridge: Cambridge University Press.

Husserl, Edmund. 1989 [1928]. *Ideas Pertaining to a Pure Phenomenology*. Second Book. *Studies in the Phenomenology of Constitution*. Translated by Richard Rojcewicz and Andre Schuwer. Boston: Kluwer.

Idel, Moshe. 2002. *Absorbing Perfections: Kabbalah and Interpretation*. New Haven: Yale University Press.

Instructions from the Central Board of Factory Commissioners to District, Civil, and Medical Commissioners. 1833. Factory Commission.

Irwin, Jane. 1996. *George Eliot's Daniel Deronda Notebooks*. Cambridge: Cambridge University Press.

Iser, Wolfgang. 1987. "The Reader in the Realistic Novel: Esthetic Effects in Thackeray's *Vanity Fair*." In *Modern Critical Interpretations of Vanity Fair*, edited by Harold Bloom, 37–56. New York: Chelsea.

Jabet, George. 1864. *Notes on Noses*. London: Bentley.

Jackson, Tony E. 2009. *The Technology of the Novel*. Baltimore: Johns Hopkins University Press.

Jadwin, Lisa. 1992. "The Seductiveness of Female Duplicity in *Vanity Fair*" *SEL* 32, no. 4 (Autumn): 633–87.

Jaffe, Audrey. 2000. *Scenes of Sympathy: Identity and Representation in Victorian Fiction*. Ithaca: Cornell University Press.

James, Henry. 1865. "Miss Braddon." *The Nation*, November 9, 593–94.

James, Henry. 1876. "*Daniel Deronda*: A Conversation." *The Atlantic Monthly* 38 (December): 684–94.

Jameson, Fredric. 1990. *Postmodernism*. Durham: Duke University Press.

Jeaffreson, J. C. 1894. *A Book of Recollections*. Vol. I. London: Hurst and Blackett.

Jean, Georges. 1992. *The Story of Alphabets and Scripts*. Translated by Jenny Oates. London: Thames and Hudson.

Jockers, Matthew L. 2013. *Macroanalysis: Digital Methods and Literary History*. Urbana: University of Illinois Press.

Jockers, Matthew L. 2014. "Body Features." Wordcloud. http://www.matthew jockers.net/macroanalysisbook/macro-themes/?topic=BODY _FEATURES. Licensed under a Creative Commons Attribution- Share Alike 3.0 Unported License. October 27.

John, Juliet. 2010. *Dickens and Mass Culture*. Oxford: Oxford University Press.

Johnson, Mark. 1987. *The Body in the Mind: The Bodily Basis of Meaning, Imagination and Reason*. Chicago: University of Chicago Press.

Johnson, Patricia. 2001. *Hidden Hands: Working-Class Women and Social-Problem Fiction*. Athens: Ohio University Press.

Jones, Jason B. 2006. *Lost Causes: Historical Consciousness in Victorian Literature*. Columbus: Ohio State University Press.

Jordan, John O. 1989. "The Purloined Handkerchief." *Dickens Studies Annual* 18: 1–17.

Jordan, John O. 2011. *Supposing Bleak House*. Charlottesville: University of Virginia Press.

Joshi, Priti. 2011. "A Hand from the Past: A Father's Letters to his Daughter." Presented at the Victorian Futures Conference, The Dickens Universe, University of California, Santa Cruz, July 29.

Kaufmann, David. 1878. *George Eliot and Judaism: An Attempt to Appreciate "Daniel Deronda."* Translated by J. W. Ferrier. Edinburgh: Blackwood.

Kearns, Katherine. 1996. *Nineteenth-Century Literary Realism: Through the Looking-Glass*. Cambridge: Cambridge University Press.

Kermode, Frank. 1967. *The Sense of an Ending*. New York: Oxford University Press.

Ketabgian, Tamara. 2011. *The Lives of Machines: The Industrial Imaginary in Victorian Literature and Culture*. Ann Arbor: University of Michigan Press.

Kettle, Arnold. 1954. *An Introduction to the English Novel*. London: Hutchinson.

Kiernan, V. G. 1998. *The Duel in European History*. Oxford: Oxford University Press.

Kingsley, Charles. 1877. *Charles Kingsley: His Letters and Memories of His Life*. London: Henry S. King.

Knoepflmacher, U. C. 1965. *Religious Humanism and the Victorian Novel.* Princeton: Princeton University Press.

Knox, Robert. 1862. *The Races of Men.* London: Henry Renshaw.

Konner, Melvin. 2009. *The Jewish Body.* New York: Schocken.

Kovačević, Ivanka, and S. Barbara Kanner. 1970. "Blue Book Into Novel: The Forgotten Industrial Fiction of Charlotte Elizabeth Tonna." *Nineteenth-Century Fiction* 25, no. 2 (September): 152–73.

Kreilkamp, Ivan. 2007. "Dying Like a Dog in *Great Expectations.*" In *Victorian Animal Dreams: Representations of Animals in Victorian Literature and Culture,* edited by Deborah Morse and Martin Danahay, 81–94. Burlington: Ashgate.

Kucich, John. 2011. "The Unfinished Historicist Project: In Praise of Suspicion." *Victoriographies* 1:1: 58–78.

Kurnick, David. 2012. *Empty Houses : Theatrical Failure and the Novel.* Princeton: Princeton University Press.

Lacqueur, Thomas. 1989. "Bodies, Details and the Humanitarian Narrative." In *The New Cultural History,* edited by Lynn Hunt, 176–204. Berkeley: University of California Press.

The Ladies' Work-Table Book. 1843. London: Clarke.

Lakoff, George, and Mark Johnson. 1980. *Metaphors We Live By.* Chicago: University Chicago Press.

La Mettrie, Julien Offray de. 1960 [1748]. *L'homme-machine.* Edited by Aram Vartanian. Princeton: Princeton University Press.

Langbauer, Laurie. 1990. *Women and Romance: The Consolations of Gender in the English Novel.* Ithaca: Cornell University Press.

Langland, Elizabeth. 1984. *Society in the Novel.* Chapel Hill: University of North Carolina Press.

Langland, Elizabeth. 1995. *Nobody's Angels: Middle-Class Women and Domestic Ideology in Victorian Culture.* Ithaca: Cornell University Press.

Langland, Elizabeth. 2001. "Women's Writing and the Domestic Sphere." In *Women and Literature in Britain, 1800–1900,* edited by Joanne Shattock, 119–41. Cambridge: Cambridge University Press.

Langland, Elizabeth. 2002. "Dialogue, Discourse, Theft, and Mimicry: Charlotte Brontë Rereads William Makepeace Thackeray." In *Telling Tales: Gender and Narrative Form in Victorian Literature and Culture.* Columbus: Ohio State University Press.

Lavater, Johann Kaspar. 1840 [1775–78]. *Essays on Physiognomy.* Translated by Thomas Holcroft. 3rd ed. London: Blake.

Law, Jules. 2010. *The Social Life of Fluids: Blood, Milk, and Water in the Victorian Novel*. Ithaca: Cornell University Press.

Leavis, Q. D. 1970. *Dickens and the Novelist*. London: Chatto & Windus.

Ledbetter, Kathryn. 2010. "Victorian Needlework: An Ancient, Honorable Abomination." Paper delivered at the Interdisciplinary Nineteenth-Century Studies meeting. University of Texas, Austin. March 27.

Ledbetter, Kathryn. 2012. *Victorian Needlework*. Santa Barbara: Praeger.

Ledger, Sally. 2010. *Dickens and the Popular Radical Imagination*. Cambridge: Cambridge University Press.

Lee, Louise. 2011. "Lady Audley's Secret: How *Does* She Do It? Sensation Fiction's Technologically Minded Villainesses." In *A Companion to Sensation Fiction*, edited by Pamela K. Gilbert, 134–46. Blackwell: Malden.

Lee, W. R. 1964. "Robert Baker: The First Doctor in the Factory Department. Part 1. 1803–1858." *British Journal of Industrial Medicine* 21. no. 2 (April): 85–93.

Lesjak, Carolyn. 2006. *Working Fictions*. Durham: Duke University Press.

Levine, George. 1979. "The Ambiguous Heritage of *Frankenstein*." In *The Endurance of Frankenstein: Essays on Mary Shelley's Novel*, edited by George Levine and U. C. Knoepflmacher, 3–30. Berkeley: University of California Press.

Levine, George. 1988. *Darwin and the Novelists*. Cambridge, MA: Harvard University Press.

Levine, George. 2001. "*Daniel Deronda*: A New Epistemology." In *Knowing the Past*, edited by Suzy Anger, 52–71. Ithaca: Cornell University Press.

Levine, George. 2008a. *How to Read the Victorian Novel*. Malden: Blackwell.

Levine, George. 2008b. *Realism, Ethics and Secularism: Essays on Victorian Science*. Cambridge: Cambridge University Press.

Lewes, George Henry. 1860. *The Physiology of Common Life*. New York: Appleton.

Lewes, George Henry. 1866. 'Farewell Causerie.' *Fortnightly Review* 6 (December 1): 890–96.

Lewes, George Henry. 1875. *On Actors and Acting*. London: Smith, Elder, & Co.

Lewes, George Henry. 1879. *Problems: A Cultural Study of Life and Mind*. Boston: Houghton.

LG G$_2$ Phone. 2013. *The New Yorker*. December 16. Advertisement.

LG G$_2$ Phone. 2014. iSpot.tv, March 2. Web. Commercial.

Lightman, Bernard. 1997. "'The Voices of Nature': Popularizing Victorian Science." In *Victorian Science in Context*, edited by Bernard Lightman, 187–211. Chicago: University of Chicago Press.

Litvak, Joseph. 1992. *Caught in the Act*. Berkeley: University of California Press.

Loesberg, Jonathan. 1986. "The Ideology of Narrative Form in Sensation Fiction." *Representations* 13, no. 2 (Winter): 115–38.

Loesberg, Jonathan. 2001. "Aesthetics, Ethics, and Unreadable Acts in George Eliot." In *Knowing the Past: Victorian Literature and Culture*, edited by Suzy Anger. Ithaca: Cornell University Press.

Logan, Thad. 2006. *The Victorian Parlour: A Cultural Study*. Cambridge: Cambridge University Press.

Loofbourow, John. 1964. *Thackeray and the Form of Fiction*. Princeton: Princeton University Press.

Lougy, Robert. 1975. "Vision and Satire: The Warped Looking Glass in *Vanity Fair*." *PMLA* 90, no. 2 (March): 256–69.

Lukács, Georg. 1964. *Studies in European Realism*. New York: Grosset & Dunlap.

Lutener, William. 1832. Testimony from Select Committee on the "Bill to Regulate the Labour of Children in the Mills and Factories of the United Kingdom." August 7. *Parliamentary Papers* (1831–32 XV), Report.

Lynch, Deidre. 1998. *The Economy of Character*. Chicago: University of Chicago Press.

MacKay, Carol. 2011. "Colossal Forces: *Vanity Fair* Meets *Jane Eyre*." In *Critical Insights*: Vanity Fair by William Makepeace Thackeray, edited by Sheldon Goldfarb, 16–21. Hackensack: Salem Press/ EBSCO.

Macleod, Norman. 2002. "Which Hand? Reading *Great Expectations* as a Guessing Game." *Dickens Studies Annual* 31: 127–57.

Malthus, Thomas. 1959 [1798]. *Essay on the Principle of Population*. Ann Arbor: University of Michigan Press.

Mansel, H. L. 1863. "Sensation Novels." *Quarterly Review* 113, no. 226 (April): 482–514.

"March of Machines." 2013. *60 Minutes*. CBS. January 13. Television.

Marcus, Sharon. 2007. *Between Women: Friendship, Desire, and Marriage in Victorian England*. Princeton: Princeton University Press.

Marcus, Sharon, and Stephen Best, eds. 2009. *The Way We Read Now*. Special issue of *Representations* 108, no. 1 (Fall).

Markoff, John. 2013. "Making Robots Mimic the Human Hand." *New York Times*, March 29.

Markoff, John. 2014. "Brainy, Yes, but Far From Handy." *New York Times*, September 1.

Marx, Karl. 1990. *Capital*. Vol. 1. Edited by Ernest Mandel, translated by Ben Fowkes. London: Penguin.

Matt, Daniel Chanan. 1995. *The Essential Kabbalah*. New York: Harper-Collins.

Matt, Daniel Chanan, ed. and trans. 2007. *The Zohar*. Stanford: Stanford University Press.

Matz, Aaron. 2010. *Satire in the Age of Realism*. Cambridge: Cambridge University Press.

Mauss, Marcel. 1973. "Techniques of the Body." *Economy and Society* 2(1): 70–88.

McClintock, Anne. 1995. *Imperial Leather*. New York: Routledge.

McCormick, John. 2004. *The Victorian Marionette Theatre*. Iowa City: University of Iowa Press.

McCullough, Malcolm. 1996. *Abstracting Craft*. Cambridge, MA: MIT Press.

McIntyre, Matthew H. and Peter T. Ellison, Daniel E. Lieberman, Ellen Demerath, Bradford Towne. 2005. "The Development of Sex Differences in Digital Formula from Infancy in the Fels Longitudinal Study." *Proceedings of the Royal Society B* 272(1571): 1473–79.

McLaughlin, Kevin. 2005. *Paperwork: Fiction and Mass Mediacy in the Paper Age*. Philadelphia: University of Pennsylvania Press.

McLaughlin, Rebecca A. 2004. "'I Prefer a *Master*': Female Power in Charlotte Brontë's *Shirley*." *Brontë Studies* 29 (November): 217–22.

McMaster, Juliet. 2004. *Reading the Body in the Eighteenth-Century Novel*. New York: Palgrave Macmillan.

Meisel, Martin. 1983. *Realizations: Narrative, Pictorial, and Theatrical Arts in Nineteenth-Century England*. Princeton: Princeton University Press.

Mellor, Anne K. 1988. *Mary Shelley: Her Life, Her Fiction, Her Monsters*. London: Methuen.

Mellor, Anne K. 1998. "A Feminine Critique of Science." In *Critical Essays on Mary Wollstonecraft Shelley*, edited by Mary Lowe-Evans. New York: G.K. Hall.

A Memoir of Robert Blincoe. 1977. Edited by John Brown. Sussex: Caliban Books.

Merleau-Ponty, Maurice. 1962. *The Phenomenology of Perception*. London: Routledge.

Merleau-Ponty, Maurice. 1969. *The Visible and the Invisible*. Translated by Alphonso Lingus. Evanston: Northwestern University Press.

Michie, Helena. 1987. *The Flesh Made Word: Female Figures and Women's Bodies*. Oxford: Oxford University Press.

Miller, J. Hillis. 1958. *Charles Dickens: The World of His Novels*. Cambridge, MA: Harvard.

Miller, J. Hillis. 1991. *Victorian Subjects*. Durham: Duke University Press.

Miller, J. Hillis. 1992. *Illustration*. Cambridge, MA: Harvard University Press.

Miller, J. Hillis. 2001. "Moments of Decision in *Bleak House*." In *The Cambridge Companion to Charles Dickens*, edited by John O. Jordan, 49–65. Cambridge: Cambridge University Press.

Milne-Tyne, Ashley. 2013. "Etsy's New Policy Means Some Items Are 'Handmade in Spirit.'" *NPR*. National Public Radio, October 29. Web.

Milton, John. 2007 [1667]. *Paradise Lost*. Edited by Barbar K. Lewalski. Malden: Blackwell.

Minutes of the Committee of Council on Education. 1841. London: William Clowes.

"The Missing Link." 1862. *Punch*. Oct 18, 165.

Mitchell, Robert. 2013. *Experimental Life: Vitalism in Romantic Science and Literature*. Baltimore: Johns Hopkins University Press.

Mitchell, W. J. T. 1987. *Iconology*. Chicago: University of Chicago Press.

Monboddo, James Burnet, Lord. 1782. *Ancient Metaphysics*. Edinburgh: Cadell and Balfour.

Monboddo, James Burnet, Lord. 2001. *De Partibus Animalium*. Translated by James G. Lennox. Oxford: Oxford UP.

Monsarrat, Ann. 1980. *An Uneasy Victorian: Thackeray the Man, 1811–1863*. London: Cassell.

Moore, Jack B. 1965. "Hearts and Hands in *Great Expectations*." *Dickensian* 61: 52–56.

Morely, Henry. 1854. "Ground in the Mill." *Household Words*, no. 213 (April 22): 224–27.

Moretti, Franco. 1982. "The Dialectic of Fear." *New Left Review* 136 (Nov.–Dec.): 67–85.

Morgentaler, Goldie. 1998. "Mediating on the Low: A Darwinian Reading of *Great Expectations*." *SEL* 38(4): 707–21.

Morton, Timothy. 1994. *Shelley and the Revolution in Taste: The Body and the Natural World*. Cambridge: Cambridge University Press.

"Mr. Van Ploos on Penmanship." 1850. *Household Words*. October 5, 38–40.

Mulhauser, Marc Antoine. 1849. *A Manual of Writing: Formed on Mulhauser's Method*. London: Parker.

Murray, John. 1981 [1829]. *Practical Remarks on Modern Paper*. North Hills, PA: Bird and Bull Press.

Nayder, Lillian. 2000. "Rebellious Sepoys and Bigamous Wives: The Indian Mutiny and Marriage Law Reform in *Lady Audley's Secret*." In *Beyond Sensation: Mary Elizabeth Braddon in Context*, edited by Pamela K. Gilbert, Marlene Tromp, and Aeron Haynie, 31–42. Albany: State University of New York Press.

Neef, Sonja. 2011. *Imprint and Trace: Handwriting in the Age of Technology*. Translated by Anthony Matthews. London: Reaktion.

The New Oxford Annotated Bible. 2001. Edited by Michael D. Coogan. Oxford: Oxford University Press.

The New Standard Jewish Encyclopedia. 1992. Edited by Geoffrey Wigoder. Oxford: Roundhouse.

"News In Brief." Times [London]. 24 Apr. 1838: 2. *The Times Digital Archive*. Web. 24 Oct. 2014.

Newton, K. M. 1999. *George Eliot*. New York: Longman.

Noland, Carrie. 2009. *Agency and Embodiment: Performing Gestures/Producing Culture*. Cambridge, MA: Harvard University Press.

Nord, Deborah Epstein. 2006. *Gypsies & the British Imagination, 1807–1930*. New York: Columbia University Press.

Novak, Daniel A. 2004. "A Model Jew: 'Literary Photographs' and the Jewish Body in *Daniel Deronda*." *Representations* 85: 58–97.

Novak, Daniel A. 2008. *Realism, Photography, and Nineteenth-Century Fiction*. Cambridge: Cambridge University Press.

Nunokawa, Jeff. 1994. *The Afterlife of Property*. Princeton: Princeton University Press.

O'Farrell, Mary Ann. 1997. *Telling Complexions*. Durham: Duke University Press.

Official Descriptive and Illustrative Catalogue of the Great Exhibition of the Works of Industry of All Nations. 1851. London: Spicer.

Ong, Walter J. 1982. *Orality and Literacy*. London: Methuen.

Ortiz-Robles, Mario. 2010. *The Novel as Event*. Ann Arbor: University of Michigan Press.

Orwell, George. 1965 [1946]. *The Decline of the English Murder*. Harmondsworth: Penguin.

Otter, Chris. 2008. *The Victorian Eye*. Chicago: University Chicago Press.

Paley, William. 1840 [1802]. *Natural Theology*. New York: Harper and Brothers.

Palmer, Beth. 2011. *Women's Authorship and Editorship in Victorian Culture: Sensational Strategies*. Oxford: Oxford University Press.

Paris, Bernard. 1974. *A Psychological Approach to Fiction*. Bloomington: Indiana University Press.

Paroissien, David. 2010. Message to the author. July 7. Email.

Parsons, James. 1747. *Human Physiognomy Explain'd*. London: Davis.

Pasanek, Brad. n.d. *Hands on Literature*. Tumblr. Web.

Peacock, Thomas Love. 1891 [1817]. *Melincourt*. Edited by Richard Garnett. New York: J. M. Dent.

Peake, Richard. 1992 [1822]. *Presumption: Or, the Fate of Frankenstein*. In *Seven Gothic Dramas: 1789-1825*. Edited by Jeffrey N. Cox. Athens: Ohio UP.

Pearl, Sharrona. 2010. *About Faces*. Cambridge, MA: Harvard University Press.

Perloff, Marjorie. 2004. *Differentials: Poetry, Poetics, Pedagogy*. Tuscaloosa: University of Alabama Press.

Perry, L. Curtis, Jr. 1971. *Apes and Angels: The Irishman in Victorian Caricature*. Washington, DC: Smithsonian Press.

Peters, Catherine. 1987. *Thackeray's Universe*. London: Faber and Faber.

Peters, Laura. 2013. *Dickens and Race*. Manchester: Manchester University Press.

Peterson, Linda H. 2009. *Becoming a Woman of Letters : Myths of Authorship and Facts of the Victorian Market*. Princeton: Princeton University Press.

Pettitt, Clare. 2004. *Patent Inventions*. Oxford: Oxford University Press.

Phelan, James. 1989. *Reading People, Reading Plots*. Chicago: University of Chicago Press.

Phelan, James. 1990. "*Vanity Fair*: Listening as a Rhetorician—and a Feminist." In *Out of Bounds: Male Writers and Gender(ed) Criticism*, edited by Laura Claridge and Elizabeth Langland, 132–47. Amherst: University of Massachusetts Press.

Piper, Andrew. 2012. *Book Was There: Reading in Electronic Times*. Chicago: University Chicago Press.

Place, Francis. 2003. "Hand Loom Weavers and Factory Workers: A Letter to James Turner, Cotton Spinner." In *Factory Production in Nineteenth-Century Britain*, edited by Elaine Freedgood, 165–77. Oxford: Oxford University Press.

Plotz, John. 2000. *The Crowd: British Literature and Public Politics*. Berkeley: University of California Press.

Plotz, John. 2008. *Portable Property: Victorian Culture on the Move*. Princeton: Princeton University Press.

Poe, Edgar Allan. 1985 [1841]. "The Murders in the Rue Morgue." In the *Works of Edgar Allan Poe*, 246–68. New York: Random House.

Pollock, G. 1993–94. "The Dangers of Proximity: The Spaces of Sexuality and Surveillance in Word and Image." *Discourse* 16: 3–50.

Poovey, Mary. 1984. *The Proper Lady and the Woman Writer: Ideology as Style in the Works of Mary Wollstonecraft, Mary Shelley, and Jane Austen*. Chicago: University of Chicago Press.

Poovey, Mary. 1988. *Uneven Developments: The Ideological Work of Gender in Mid-Victorian England*. Chicago: University Chicago Press.

Poovey, Mary. 1995. *Making a Social Body: British Cultural Formation 1830–1864*. Chicago: University of Chicago Press, 1995.

Poovey, Mary. 2004. "The Limits of the Universal Knowledge Project: British India and the East Indiamen," *Critical Inquiry* 31(1): 183–202.

Posthumanities Series logo. n.d. Cary Wolfe, Series Editor. University of Minnesota Press.

Press, Jacob. 1997. "Same-Sex Unions in Modern Europe: *Daniel Deronda*, *Altneuland*, and the Homoerotics of Jewish Nationalism." In *Novel Gazing: Queer Readings in Fiction*, edited by Eve Kosofsky Sedgwick, 299–329. Durham: Duke University Press.

Preyer, Robert F. 1960. "Beyond the Liberal Imagination: Vision and Unreality in *Daniel Deronda*." *Victorian Studies* 4, no. 1 (September): 33–54.

Price, Leah. 2012. *How to Do Things with Books in Victorian Britain*. Princeton: Princeton University Press.

Pykett, Lyn. 1992. *The 'Improper' Feminine: The Women's Sensation Novel and the New Woman Writing*. New York: Routledge.

Qualls, Barry. 2001. "George Eliot and Religion." In *The Cambridge Companion to George Eliot*, edited by George Levine, 119–37. Cambridge: Cambridge University Press.

Raby, Peter. 1997. *Bright Paradise: Victorian Scientific Travellers*. Princeton: Princeton University Press.

Radford, Andrew. 2009. *Victorian Sensation Fiction*. New York: Palgrave Macmillan.

Ragussis, Michael. 1995. *Figures of Conversion: "The Jewish Question" & English National Identity*. Durham: Duke University Press.

Rampell, Catherine. 2013. "Raging (Again) Against the Robots." *New York Times*, February 2. Web.

Rauch, Alan. 2001. *Useful Knowledge: The Victorians, Morality, and the March of the Intellect*. Durham: Duke University Press.

Rawlins, Jack. 1974. *Thackeray's Novels*. Berkeley: University of California Press.

Ray, John. 1827 [1691]. *The Wisdom of God as Manifested in the Works of Creation*. London: J. F. Dove.

Reay, Barry. 2002. *Watching Hannah: Sexuality, Horror and Bodily Deformation in Victorian England*. London: Reaktion.

Redgrave, Richard. 1846. *The Sempstress*. Oil on canvas. Forbes Collection, New York.

Reed, Walter L. 1981. *An Exemplary History of the Novel*. Chicago: University Chicago Press.

Reese, Diana. 2006. "A Troubled Legacy: Mary Shelley's *Frankenstein* and the Inheritance of Human Rights." *Representations* 96, no. 4 (Fall): 48–72.

Richards, Thomas. 1990. *The Commodity Culture of Victorian England*. Stanford: Stanford University Press.

Richardson, Samuel. 1985 [1747–48]. *Clarissa*. Edited by Angus Ross. New York: Viking Penguin.

Richardson, Samuel. 2001 [1741]. *Pamela*. Edited by Thomas Keymer and Alice Wakely. Oxford: Oxford University Press.

Rilke, Ranier Maria. 2004 [1902, 1907]. *Auguste Rodin*. Translated by Daniel Slager. New York: Archipelago Books.

Robbins, Bruce. 1993 [1986]. *The Servant's Hand: English Fiction from Below*. Durham: Duke University Press.

Robinson, Charles E. 1996. *The Frankenstein Notebooks*. Part Two: *Draft Notebook B* and *Fair-Copy Notebooks C1 and C2*. New York: Garland Publishing.

Robinson, Charles E. 2008. *The Original Frankenstein*. Edited by Charles E. Robinson. Oxford: Bodleian Library.

Robinson, Charles E. Email message, January 18.

Roesch, Etienne B. 2013. "A Critical View of Classical Computational Approaches to Cognitive Robotics: Case Study for Theories of Cognition." In *The Hand, An Organ of the Mind*, 401–19. Cambridge, MA: Massachusetts Institute of Technology Press.

Rousseau, Jean-Jacques. 1968 [1761]. *Julie, or The New Eloise*. State College: Penn State University Press.

Rousseau, Jean-Jaques. 2009 [1775]. *Discourse on the Origin of Inequality*. Translated by Franklin Philip. Oxford: Oxford UP.

Rowe, Katherine. 1999. *Dead Hands: Fictions of Agency, Renaissance to Modern*. Stanford: Stanford University Press.

Ruskin, John. 1903. *The Collected Works of John Ruskin*. 39 vols. Edited by E. T. Cook and Alexander Wedderburn. London: George Allen.

Ruston, Sharon. 2005. *Shelley and Vitality*. New York: Palgrave Macmillan.

Ruth, Jennifer. 2006. *Novel Professions: Interest and Disinterest and the Making of the Professional in the Victorian Novel*. Columbus: Ohio State University Press.

Salmon, Richard. 2013. *The Formation of the Victorian Literary Profession*. New York: Cambridge University Press.

Samuel, Raphael. 1977. "Workshop of the World: Steam Power and Hand Technology in Mid- Victorian Britain." *History Workshop*. no. 3 (Spring): 6–72.

Sartre, Jean-Paul. 1979 [1938]. *Nausea*. Translated by Lloyd Alexander. Cambridge: R. Bentley.

Sassoon, Rosemary. 2007. *Handwriting of the Twentieth Century*. Bristol: Intellect.

Scarry, Elaine. 1994. *Resisting Representation*. Oxford: Oxford University Press.

Schaffer, Talia. 2011. *Novel Craft: Victorian Domestic Handicraft and Nineteenth-Century Fiction*. Oxford: Oxford University Press.

Scheinberg, Cynthia. 2010. "'The Beloved Ideas Made Flesh': *Daniel Deronda* and Jewish Poetics." *ELH* 77, no. 3 (Fall): 813–39.

Scholem, Gershom. 1990. *Origins of the Kabbalah*. Edited by R. J. Zwi Werblowsky. Translated by Allan Arkush. Princeton: Princeton University Press.

Scott, Walter. 1827. *Chronicles of Canongate*. Edinburgh: Cadell.

Scott, Walter. 1853 [1822]. *The Fortunes of Nigel*. Edinburgh: Adam and Charles Black.

Scott, Walter. 1978. *The Prefaces to the Waverly Novels*. Edited by Mark A. Weinstein. Lincoln: University of Nebraska Press.

Secord, James A. 2000. *Victorian Sensation: The Extraordinary Publication, Reception, and Secret Authorship of* Vestiges of the Natural History of Creation. Chicago: University of Chicago Press.

Shattock, Joanne. 2001. *Women and Literature in Britain 1800–1900.* Cambridge: Cambridge University Press.

Shaw, Harry E. 1999. *Narrating Reality.* Ithaca: Cornell University Press.

Shaykin, Benjamin. 2009. *GOOGLE HANDS.* Paperback book.

Shelley, Mary. 1818. *Frankenstein.* Edited by J. Paul Hunter. New York: Norton, 1996.

Shelley, Mary. 1831. *Frankenstein.* Edited by Maurice Hindle. New York, Penguin, 2003.

Shelley, Mary. 1996. *Frankenstein.* Edited by J. Paul Hunter. New York: Norton.

Shelley, Mary. 2003. *Frankenstein.* New York: Penguin Classics.

Shelley, Mary. 2007. *Frankenstein.* Edited by Susan J. Wolfson. New York: Longman.

Shelley, Mary. 2012a. *Frankenstein.* Edited by J. Paul Hunter. New York: Norton.

Shelley, Mary. 2012b. *Frankenstein.* Edited by D. L. Macdonald and Kathleen Scherf. New York: Broadview.

Shelley, Percy Bysshe. 1964. *The Letters of Percy Bysshe Shelley.* Edited by Frederick L. Jones. Oxford: Clarendon Press.

Shelley, Percy Bysshe. 2002. "On Life." *Shelley's Poetry and Prose.* Edited by Neil Fraistat and Donald H. Reiman. 2nd ed. New York: Norton.

Shillingsburg, Peter. 2001. *William Makepeace Thackeray: A Literary Life.* London: Palgrave.

"Shiviti." 1800? Hands over menorah. Mizrach Plate. Benguiat Collection. Jewish Theological Seminary of America.

Shklovskii, Viktor. 2012 [1917]. "Art As Technique." *Russian Formalist Criticism: Four Essays.* Translated and with an Introduction by Lee T. Lemon and Marion J. Reis. New Introduction by Gary Saul Morson. Lincoln: University of Nebraska Press.

Showalter, Elaine. 1985. *The New Feminist Criticism: Essays on Women, Literature, Theory.* New York: Pantheon.

Shuttleworth, Sally. 1984. *George Eliot and Nineteenth-Century Science: The Make-Believe of a Beginning.* Cambridge: Cambridge University Press.

Shuttleworth, Sally. 1996. *Charlotte Brontë and Victorian Psychology.* Cambridge: Cambridge University Press.

Silver, Anna. 2002. *Victorian Literature and the Anorexic Body*. Cambridge: Cambridge University Press.

Silverman, Kaja. 1992. *Male Subjectivity at the Margins*. New York: Routledge.

Simms, Joseph. 1872. *Physiognomy Illustrated*. New York: Murray Hill.

Siskin, Clifford. 1998. *The Work of Writing*. Baltimore: Johns Hopkins.

Skelton, John Henry. 1837. *My Book; or, The Anatomy of Conduct*. London: Simpkin and Marshall.

Smith, Adam. 1981 [1776]. *An Inquiry into the Nature and Causes of the Wealth of Nations*. Edited by R.H. Campbell and A.S. Skinner. Indianapolis: Liberty.

Smith, Albert. 1842. "The Physiology of London Evening Parties." *Punch*, January 1–December 1.

Smith, Samuel. 1831–32. Testimony from Select Committee on the "Bill to Regulate the Labour of Children in the Mills and Factories of the United Kingdom." August 7, 1832. *Parliamentary Papers* (XV), Report.

Smollett, Tobias. 1929 [1771]. *The Expedition of Humphry Clinker*. New York: Modern Library.

Speaight, George. 1990. *The History of the English Puppet Theatre*. Carbondale: Southern Illinois University Press.

Spencer, Herbert. 1872. *The Principles of Psychology*. New York: Appleton.

St. Clair, William. 2004. *Reading the Nation in the Romantic Period*. Cambridge, Cambridge University Press.

Stallybrass, Peter, and Ann Rosiland Jones. 2001. "Fetishizing the Glove in Renaissance Europe." *Critical Inquiry* 28, no. 1 (Autumn): 114–32.

Stallybrass, Peter, and Allon White. 1986. *The Politics and Poetics of Transgression*. Ithaca: Cornell University Press.

Stanley, L. 1986. "Biography as Microscope or Kaleidoscope? The Case of Hannah Cullwick's Relationship with Arthur Munby." *Studies in Sexual Politics* 13/14: 28–46.

Steinlight, Emily. 2012. "Why Novels Are Redundant: Sensation Fiction and the Over- Population of Literature." *ELH* 79, no. 2 (Summer): 501–35.

Stevens, Joan. 1968. "A Note on Thackeray's 'Manager of the Performance.'" *Nineteenth-Century Fiction* 22 (March): 391–97.

Stevenson, Robert Louis. 1981. *Robert Louis Stevenson: The Critical Heritage*. Edited by Paul Maixner. London: Routledge & Kegan Paul.

Stevenson, Robert Louis. 2002 [1886]. *The Strange Case of Dr Jekyll and Mr Hyde*. New York: Penguin.

Stewart, Garrett. 1996. *Dear Reader: The Conscripted Audience in Nineteenth-Century British Fiction*. Baltimore: Johns Hopkins University Press.

Stoker, Bram. 2003 [1897]. *Dracula*. New York: Penguin.

Stoler, Ann. 2010. *Along the Archival Grain: Epistemic Anxieties and Colonial Common Sense*. Princeton: Princeton University Press.

Stone, Elizabeth [The Countess of Wilton]. 1841. *The Art of Needle-work*. London: Colburn.

Stone, Harry. 1979. *Dickens and the Invisible World*. Bloomington: Indiana University Press.

Sussman, Herbert. 1968. *Victorians and the Machine: The Literary Response to Technology*. Cambridge, MA: Harvard University Press.

Sussman, Herbert. 1995. *Victorian Masculinities*. Cambridge: Cambridge University Press.

Sussman, Herbert. 2009. *Victorian Technology: Invention, Innovation, and the Rise of the Machine*. Santa Barbara: Praeger.

Sutherland, John A. 1976. *Victorian Novelists and Publishers*. London: Athlone.

Sutherland, Kathryn. 1987. "Fictional Economies: Adam Smith, Walter Scott and the Nineteeth-Century Novel." *ELH* 54, no. 1 (Spring): 97–127.

Tallis, Raymond. 2010. *Michelangelo's Finger*. New Haven: Yale University Press.

Taylor, Harriet. 1851. "Enfranchisement of Women." *The Westminster Review* 55, no. 109 (July): 149–61.

Taylor, Jenny Bourne. 1988. *In the Secret Theatre of Home: Wilkie Collins, Sensation Narrative and Nineteenth-Century Psychology*. London: Routledge.

Taylor, Jenny Bourne. 1998. Introduction (with Russell Crofts) to *Lady Audley's Secret*. New York: Penguin.

Thackeray, William. 1837. "Fashnable Fax and Polite Annygoats." *Fraser's Magazine* (November): 434–43.

Thackeray, William. 1846–47. "The Snobs of England." *Punch*, February 28–February 27.

Thackeray, William. 1991 [1848–50]. *The History of Pendennis*. New York: Garland.

Thackeray, William. 2001 [1848]. *Vanity Fair*. Ed. Peter Shillingsburg. New York: Norton.

Thomas, Deborah. 1993. *Thackeray and Slavery*. Athens: Ohio University Press.

Thomas, Ronald. 2003. *Detective Fiction and the Rise of Forensic Science.* Cambridge: Cambridge University Press.

Thompson, E. P. 1963. *The Making of the English Working Class.* New York: Vintage.

Thompson, E. P. 1990. "Time, Work-Discipline, and Industrial Capitalism." In *Customs in Common*, 352–403. New York: New Press.

Thornton, Tamara Plakins. 1996. *Handwriting in America.* New Haven: Yale University Press.

Tillotson, Kathleen. 1954. *The Novels of the Eighteen-Forties.* Oxford: Oxford University Press.

Titian. *Man with a Glove.* 1519–1523? Oil on canvas. Louvre, Paris.

Tonna, Charlotte Elizabeth. 1841 [1839–40]. *Helen Fleetwood.* New York: Taylor.

Topham, Jonathan R. 1993. "'An Infinite Variety of Arguments': The *Bridgewater Treatises* and British Natural Theology in the 1830s." Diss. University of Lancaster. British Library EThOS. Web. January 4, 2012.

Topham, Jonathan R. 1998. "Beyond the 'Common Context': The Production and Reading of the Bridgewater Treatises." *Isis: The History of Science Society* 89: 233–62.

Torgerson, Beth. 2005. *Reading the Brontë Body.* New York: Palgrave Macmillan.

Tritter, Daniel. 1997. "Mr. Jaggers at the Bar." *Dickens Quarterly* 14, no. 2: 92–107.

Trollope, Frances. 1840. *Michael Armstrong, Factory Boy.* London: Colburn.

Tucker, Irene. 2000. *A Probable State: The Novel, The Contract, and the Jews.* Chicago: University Chicago Press.

Tucker, Irene. 2012. *The Moment of Racial Sight.* Chicago: University Chicago Press.

Turner, F. M. 1981. *The Greek Heritage in Victorian Britain.* New Haven: Yale University Press.

Tyler, Tom. 2012. *Ciferae: A Bestiary in Five Fingers.* Minneapolis: University of Minnesota Press.

Tyndall, John. 1984 [1874]. "The Belfast Address." In *Science and Religion in the Nineteenth Century*, edited by Tess Coslett. Cambridge: Cambridge University Press.

Tyson, Edward. 1751 [1698]. *The Anatomy of a Pygmy.* 2d ed. London: T. Osborne.

Ure, Andre. 1861 [1835]. *The Philosophy of Manufactures*. London: H. G. Bohn.

Vicinus, Martha. 1974. *The Industrial Muse: A Study of Nineteenth Century British Working-Class Literature*. New York: Harper and Row.

Vicinus, Martha. 1977. *A Widening Sphere: Changing Roles of Victorian Women*. Bloomington: Indiana University Press.

Victorian Literature and the Victorian Visual Imagination. Edited by Carol T. Christ and John O. Jordan. Berkeley: University of California Press, 1995.

Vieth, Karissa. n.d. *Nebraskans Against the Death Penalty*. Lincoln, NE: NADP.

Voskuil, Lynn. 2001. "Acts of Madness: Lady Audley and the Meanings of Femininity." *Feminist Studies* 27, no. 3 (September): 611–63.

Vrettos, Athena. 2000. "Defining Habits: Dickens and the Psychology of Repetition." *Victorian Studies* 42, no. 3 (Spring): 399–426.

Wagner, Peter. 1996. *Icons, Texts, Iconotext*. New York: de Gruyter.

Walker, Alexander. 1987 [1839]. *Woman Physiologically Considered as to Mind, Morals, Marriage, Matrimonial Slavery, Infidelity and Divorce*. New Delhi: Mittal.

Warhol, Robyn. 1989. *Gendered Inventions: Narrative Discourse in the Victorian Novel*. New Brunswick: Rutgers University Press.

Webb, Igor. 1981. *From Custom to Capital*. Ithaca: Cornell University Press.

Welsh, Alexander. 1971. *The City of Dickens*. Oxford: Clarendon.

Wicke, Jennifer. 1988. *Advertising Fictions: Literature, Advertisement, and Social Reading*. New York: Columbia University Press.

Wilburn, Sarah A. 2006. *Possessed Victorians: Extra Spheres in Nineteenth-Century Mystical Writings*. Aldershot: Ashgate.

Wilkenfeld, Roger. 1971. "'Before the Curtain' and *Vanity Fair*." *Nineteenth-Century Fiction* (December): 307–18.

Williams, John. 2000. *Mary Shelley: A Literary Life*. London: Palgrave.

Williams, Raymond. 1973. *The Country and the City*. New York: Oxford University Press.

Wilson, John. 1833. "The Factory System." *Blackwood's Edinburgh Magazine* 33, no. 206 (April): 419–50.

Winner, Anthony. 1974. "Character and Knowledge in Dickens: The Enigma of Jaggers." *Dickens Studies Annual* 3: 100–121.

Winter, Sarah. 2009. "Darwin's Saussure: Biosemiotics and Race in Expression." *Representations* 107, no. 1 (Summer): 128–61.

Witemeyer, Hugh. 1979. *George Eliot and the Visual Arts*. New Haven: Yale University Press.

Wolff, Robert Lee. 1979. *Sensational Victorian: The Life and Fiction of Mary Elizabeth Braddon*. New York: Garland.

Wolfson, Eliot. 2005. *Language, Eros, Being: Kabbalistic Hermeneutics and Poetic Imagination*. New York: Fordham University Press.

Woloch, Alex. 2003. *The One Vs. the Many: Minor Characters and the Space of the Protagonist in the Novel*. Princeton: Princeton University Press.

"The Work Basket." 1849. *Ladies' Companion*. December 4–5. Rpt. In Logan 2001, 168.

Wynne, Deborah. 2006. "'Scenes of 'Incredible Outrage': Dickens, Ireland, and *A Tale of Two Cities*." *Dickens Studies Annual* 37: 51–64.

Young, Iris Marion. 2004 [1990]. *On Female Body Experience: "Throwing Like a Girl" and Other Essays*. Oxford: Oxford University Press.

Young, Jeffrey R. 2013. "The New Industrial Revolution." *The Chronicle Review* 29 (March): B6+.

Zlotnick, Susan. 1998. *Women, Writing, and the Industrial Revolution*. Baltimore: Johns Hopkins University Press.

Index

Made in the USA
Columbia, SC
21 June 2020